Table of Contents

W9-CTU-325

CULTIVATING **CANADA**

RECONCILIATION THROUGH THE LENS OF CULTURAL DIVERSITY

Edited by
Ashok Mathur
Jonathan Dewar
Mike DeGagné

Aboriginal Healing Foundation Research Series | 2011

© 2011 Aboriginal Healing Foundation

Published by:
Aboriginal Healing Foundation
75 Albert Street, Suite 801, Ottawa, Ontario K1P 5E7
Phone: (613) 237-4441
Toll-free: (888) 725-8886
Fax: (613) 237-4442
Email: research@ahf.ca
Website: www.ahf.ca

Design & Production:
Glen Lowry

Printed by:
Dollco Printing
Ottawa, Ontario

Reprinted by:
Hemlock Printers
Burnaby, British Columbia

Printed version:
ISBN 978-1-897285-98-5
Electronic version:
ISBN 978-1-897285-99-2

Non-commercial reproduction of this document is, however, encouraged. This project was funded by the Aboriginal Healing Foundation (AHF), but the views expressed in this report are the personal views of the author(s).

Ce document est aussi disponible en français.

Rinaldo Walcott

Rinaldo Walcott is Associate Professor and Chair of the Department of Sociology and Equity Studies in Education at the Ontario Institute for Studies in Education and the Women's and Gender Studies Institute, both of the University of Toronto. His teaching and research is in the area of black diaspora cultural studies and post-colonial studies with an emphasis on questions of sexuality, gender, nation, citizenship, and multiculturalism. From 2002 to 2007 Rinaldo held the Canada Research Chair of Social Justice and Cultural Studies where his research was funded by the Social Sciences and Humanities Research Council of Canada, the Canadian Foundation for Innovation, and the Ontario Innovation Trust. Rinaldo is the author of *Black Like Who?: Writing Black Canada* (Insomniac Press, 1997, with a second revised edition in 2003); he is also the editor of *Rude: Contemporary Black Canadian Cultural Criticism* (Insomniac Press, 2000). These two editions are credited with opening up the question of black Canadian studies beyond the field of history. As well, he is the co-editor with Roy Moodley of *Counselling Across and Beyond Cultures: Exploring the Work of Clemment Vontress in Clinical Practice* (University of Toronto Press, 2010). Currently, Rinaldo is completing *Black Diaspora Faggotry: Readings Frames Limits,* which is under contract to Duke University Press. Additionally, he is co-editing with Dina Georgis and Katherine McKittrick *No Language Is Neutral: Essays on Dionne Brand* forthcoming from Wilfrid Laurier University Press. As an interdisciplinary black studies scholar, Rinaldo has published in a wide range of venues. His articles have appeared in journals and books, as well as popular venues like newspapers and magazines. As well, he has appeared on television and radio to discuss issues of relevance to black Canadian and queer life.

Introduction

This third and final volume in a series of publications dedicated to reconciliation comes as the Aboriginal Healing Foundation prepares to close its doors after nearly one-and-a-half decades of work. Its publication constitutes the literal final word in the AHF's research agenda, but not the metaphorical final word on the subject of reconciliation. The Aboriginal Healing Foundation has for years underscored the message that addressing the historical trauma resulting from Canada's policy of forced assimilation will require a long-term commitment. This work began before there was an Aboriginal Healing Foundation, and one may reasonably expect the journey of healing and reconciliation to continue when the AHF is no more.

This third volume is populated by the perspectives of new Canadians and those outside the traditional settler communities of British and French. Because Canada is a nation of diverse cultures, its people drawn from every region of the world, any discussion of reconciliation must include the perspectives of those who have arrived in more recent days and those who trace their family histories beyond western European colonial states. The reason for this is simple. Aboriginal people have a unique historical relationship with the Crown, and the Crown represents all Canadians. From this it follows that all Canadians are treaty people, bearing the responsibilities of Crown commitments and enjoying the rights and benefits of being Canadian.

From this simple principle we proceed to much complexity. The subjects of historical wrongdoings and redress, healing, and reconciliation have many localized variants, among them the internment of Japanese Canadians during the Second World War and the demolition of Africville in the 1960s, for examples. Those who have arrived in Canada from places of colonization, war, genocide, and devastation will very likely have valuable insights into historical trauma; their perspectives should be considered also.

We hope this approach will draw Canadians of all backgrounds into the reconciliation discussion, on the understanding that they indeed have a unique and necessary place in the circle. Much of the dialogue to date has taken place within Aboriginal communities, among survivors of abuse and their families, both issuing from and bolstering the Main Street idea that the Indian Residential School System is an "Aboriginal issue," a side discussion on, if not beyond, the margins of Canadian society. Further, this notion is compounded by the reserve system, rooted in Canada's nineteenth-century conception of "the Indian problem." In both cases there exists the misassumption that a brief period of reconciliation will allow for a return to business as usual.

It does not have to be that way. However, genuine dialogue requires that Aboriginal people too fulfill their responsibilities. We must listen as well as speak, and actively reach out to others, crossing both the material and notional boundaries that assign Aboriginal people to the margins. This volume takes up that responsibility.

Introducing the larger context is a piece by lead editor Ashok Mathur, who foregrounds the many themes found within the volume as he weaves a personal narrative that traces his own history, immigration, and reflections. The volume itself is divided into three sections: *Land, Across,* and *Transformations.* In *Land*, we begin with Shirley Bear, an artist and activist whose work has been dedicated to improving the quality of life within and across cultures. This poetic back and forth leads the collection from a place of strength, wisdom, and tireless dedication. Following is Henry Tsang's visual work, an extension of the volume's cover image (described within), contextualizing the larger sense of land, people, and development in all senses of the word. This takes us to a three-way dialogue between Cheryl L'Hirondelle, Joseph Naytowhow, and b.h. Yael, a compelling articulation of rights and land from Canada through to Israel/Palestine. Another dialogue follows, between Elwood Jimmy and Sandra Semchuk, who address the complex histories of Saskatchewan, complemented by photographic works from Semchuk with her late husband James Nicholas. And staying within the context of land and reconciliation, Dorothy Christian's article questions how people might come to terms with these complex ideas and ideologies. Picking up on this theme is Rita Wong, whose treatise on water asks us to rethink radically how we have been considering our natural resources. Sylvia Hamilton presents us with a different sense of place, specifically the history and position of Black education in Canada, which she articulates by describing the short film she made to address these hidden histories. And Meera Margaret Singh closes out this section with a visual project that presents contemporary migrants who work the farmland of the Canadian greenbelt.

In *Across*, we begin with a timeline (somewhat akin to those we published in our earlier two volumes) constructed by Jamelie Hassan and Miriam Jordan to address some of the personal and cultural histories engaging Canada and the Middle East. Renisa Mawani's article, a reprint from the academic journal, *BC Studies,* takes a theoretical and historical approach to the context of race and contact on the west coast. Rhose Harris-Galia gives us a personal reflection from a Filipina perspective from Iqaluit. Sid Chow Tan takes a creative approach to personal history, presenting two pieces that tell the same story of early interactions between Aboriginal and Chinese people in British Columbia and how such hidden histories are possible to re-imagine. Ronald Lee lays out a detailed history of the Roma people whose persecutions bear remarkable resemblance to stories we hear about residential schools. An important reprint follows by Bonita Lawrence and Enakshi Dua, whose article on decolonizing the practices of anti-racism interrogates the foundations of progressive movements and how they must be complicated by a serious understanding of Indigenous issues. Robinder Kaur Sehdev revisions how we see the notions of treaty, suggesting that people of colour need to be aware of how they are affected through its discourses. Srimoyee Mitra demonstrates how Aboriginal and South Asian artists have been working and showing together recently to disrupt the notion of "Indian" as well as producing collaborative work that has resonance for contemporary art. Malissa Phung disrupts the assumption that the term "settler" is eschewed by people of colour and asks us to revisit this in all its attendant complications. And Henry Yu describes the recent collective work that has nurtured dialogues among First Nations, urban Aboriginal, and immigrant communities in Vancouver.

The third section, *Transformation*, begins with Roy Miki, who uses creative practice and poetic moments to reflect upon the Japanese Canadian redress movement. Ravi de Costa and Tom Clark share their interview data about non-Aboriginal attitudes toward reconciliation in Canada. Rinaldo Walcott challenges the very premise of reconciliation and suggests a radical, alternative way of seeing this collective practice as but a beginning in a much more deeply inflected process. Mitch Miyagawa, in a reprint from *The Walrus*, shows through a personal narrative how we have become caught in a web of apology that often amounts to an empty gesture. Jen Budney writes about the art practice of Jayce Salloum, whose work with Aboriginal youth explores activism across local and global arenas. Rita Deverell looks at the more recent media history of race in Canada, following her own trajectory in terms of connections between people of colour and Indigenous people. George Elliott Clarke makes a case for the under-investigated notion of shared histories and ancestries between Blacks and Aboriginal peoples in Nova Scotia. In a visual response, Diyan Achjadi shows how her creative practice accentuates the excessive and challenges the precepts of nationalism and militarism in how they construct our identities. And finally, Kirsten Emiko McAllister thinks through the ways we recognize, and are mis-recognized, as she explores a memoryscape of postwar British Columbia.

Ashok Mathur

Ashok Mathur is a writer, educator, and cultural organizer interested in new models of artistic research and interdisciplinary collaboration. He is Canada Research Chair in Cultural and Artistic Inquiry at Thompson Rivers University (Kamloops, British Columbia) where he directs the Centre for innovation in Culture and the Arts in Canada (CiCAC), a creative think-tank looking at progressive models of research. He is also Associate Professor, cross-posted to the departments of Visual and Performing Arts and Journalism, Communications, and New Media at TRU. His research interests are in critical/creative practices that pursue a social justice agenda. He has published four books that address, through creative writing, the underpinnings of race, reconciliation, and the politics of gender and sexuality, and he also addresses these issues through artistic practices blending text with installation. His publications include a poetic novella, *Loveruage: a dance in three parts* (Wolsak and Wynn Publishers Ltd., 1994), and three novels: *Once Upon an Elephant* (Arsenal Pulp Press, 1998), *The Short, Happy Life of Harry Kumar* (Arsenal Pulp Press, 2001), and *A Little Distillery in Nowgong* (Arsenal Pulp Press, 2009). This last novel was simultaneously developed into a collaborative, cross-disciplinary installation project that exhibited across the country and was part of the year-long *DIASPORArt* show at Rideau Hall, official residence of the Governor General of Canada, featuring culturally diverse artistic practices. Ashok was born in Bhopal, India, to a Hindu (*Kyasth*) father and a Parsi mother, and was raised in Nova Scotia and Alberta. These factors of family, migration, and hybrid cosmology figure prominently in his creative and critical practices. Since the early 1990s, he has worked within diverse cultural sectors in Canada and abroad, including Aboriginal, immigrant, and other racialized communities. His current work investigates the historical undercurrents of race and reconciliation, locally and internationally.

Cultivations, Land, and a Politics of Becoming

When my parents immigrated to Canada with two young children in tow, it was with the bright promise of arriving in a new land, finding a place to call home, and putting down roots in a country far from familial histories and ancestral birthrights. If this isn't the dream shared by all immigrants, it does approximate the sensations and parallels the trajectories taken by those who come, through will or circumstance, leaving behind history and walking into what we believe, for all intents, to be a tabula rasa. It is not without a hint of irony that I acknowledge the language of 'newness' and the notion of settling on a pristine landscape as part of this immigrant dreamscape. Of course, a more appropriate metaphor than a blank slate would be a geographic palimpsest, a land whose history is always alluded to by the tracings and markings that, however obscured or willfully ignored, can never be erased. This is the land we came to, not a terra nullius but a land weighted with official and unofficial histories, some of which new immigrants were made to understand quite well, and others which remained and remain un-interrogated. Compounding the complexity, after the initial wave of colonizing settlers from western Europe, increasing numbers were arriving from Asia and Africa, constituting an ever-larger group of non-white immigrants. When we enter into the political jurisdiction of Canada, we acknowledge the Crown, and through it, an explicit history of empire, colonial enterprise, and global interconnections. But we all too often remain blithely unaware of histories inscribed into the land that far predate Confederation and both British and French incursions onto this terrain. And if there is any awareness of First Peoples and their inhabitation and proprietorship of this land, it is most frequently mediated through colonial narratives of contact (and concomitant anthropological assumptions of pre-contact histories), such that the racialized immigrant's awareness of Aboriginality is almost always pre-configured through a colonial gaze. Layered upon this is the familiarity with contexts of oppressive histories frequently experienced by immigrants and their descendants, either acts of aggression committed by dominant communities or governments in former homelands, or those perpetrated post-arrival to these shores—persecution of African diasporic peoples, internment of Japanese Canadians, repressive laws that targeted racialized communities, to name but a few instances addressed far more thoroughly in the articles that are contained in this volume.

But I want here to return to the very idea of the land. Unaware of the aforementioned palimpsestic nature of the place we ended up inhabiting, my family settled in the suburbs on the southern edge of Calgary. The sole bus route to the downtown core terminated several blocks north of our home in a gravel turnaround; and while our neighbourhood was not exactly being built up around us, immediately adjacent communities were still rife with non-landscaped lots and newly planted poplars. Sod was laid down to cover mounds of freshly turned earth, the lines between the squares gradually fading over those first springs and warm summers, creating that peculiar uniformity so desired in middle-class suburban landscapes. Even the schools sprung up around us just in time to educate growing families— my older sister had the unique high school perspective of always being in the senior class, since the school opened at first only to house an initial intake of grade ten and laddering over the next two years to eventually graduate its first cohort of grade twelve students. Despite its beginnings as an almost all-white suburb, the growth of the city brought immigrants (and transplanted Canadians) that gradually shifted the racial mix. But through the fissures of suburban experiences and cultural shifts, the land still seeped through. Just a couple of miles to the west of this high school, the wide Albertan road turned narrow and winding, crossing over a small brook into a treed region where a small wooden sign indicated to travellers they were now on (what was then called) the Sarcee Reserve. On weekend outings we would take the TransCanada to Banff, the jewel of the provincial tourism crown, barely noticing the black-lettered sign halfway to the foothills noting that we were passing through Stoney land. And if the car were to turn a hundred and eighty degrees and travel eastward instead, as soon as the mountains became indistinct in the rearview mirror, looming on the horizon was an ominous brick building on the prairie that I would find out many years later was Old Sun, the residential school on Blackfoot territory. So this was our knowledge of Calgary, a suburb where everyone seemed transported from somewhere else—but a short distance away was clearly not the city at all, not a Canada we knew, and certainly not one we had the tools to recognize. Language and nomenclature changed as the years passed—the Sarcee sign was replaced with one announcing the Tsuu T'ina Nation, and while Old Sun remained standing, it became a university outreach site on the Siksika Nation—but the land persisted.

Growing up in Calgary, amidst urban landscaping embedded in the prairie landscape all situated within the context of three First Nations, the complexity of these multiple layers eluded me, but the contradictions of misidentification did not. This was some years before it became an accepted practice, for reasons of clarity and geographic rather than nationalistic identity, to call oneself "South Asian," a reference to a point of origin of a subcontinent rather than a geopolitical state. Yet back on that prairie landscape, within a tight and growing expatriate population from India, everything from food to dress to custom was all too readily *adjectivized* with "Indian," which was simple enough to understand within that first-generation homogeneous community. But in that all-too-altered second generation, where differentiations of manner, language, and accent were ameliorated through a peer-informed culture, this same modifier rendered quite surprisingly. Here, the brown child who walked and talked and dressed like his classmates, yet called himself "Indian," was a unique creature indeed. Slippage of history and identity, a mismatched nomenclature that, truth be told, was inaccurate for both the South Asian and Aboriginal body, a name that stuck through misunderstandings and misappropriations. Nonetheless, there I was, an Indian in Calgary, in a place and time where such an identity stood in binary opposition to "Cowboy" and where the only way a young child could try to correct his misinformants was, curiously enough, by using the very same adjective to modify the noun: "No, not *that* kind of Indian; I'm an *Indian* Indian." That was, perhaps, the first point of coming into being by identifying both by who or what I was and was not. In such negative cogitation, I was left with the burning question of who this Indian might be, imagined and projected upon my body, and yet otherwise (in my neighbourhood, community, consciousness) so completely absent.

The same mis-identity became even more apparent when, as a fresh graduate from photojournalism school, I toured southern Alberta rodeos, a different but no less absurd version of the cowboy/Indian dichotomy. However, here is where I found out something quite real about the notion of place and land, of who went where, and why. I found out about reserves as I talked to people at powwows and band offices that seemed a distant remove from those I had learned about in high school history classes where voyageurs opened up the fur trade with their 'contacts,' and various textbook alliances resulted in conflicts small and large between French and British. This was something else, something in and of the land. But this reality did not truly come to mind until I was all but finished my Master's degree in English and, in the weeks before my defense, I was offered the chance to teach a course (a full course of my own, for the first time), not at the university, but a first-year transfer English course to be offered out at Old Sun on the Siksika Nation. Situated exactly 100 kilometres east of the university carpool where I received a vehicle each week, Old Sun was where I first set foot into what was once a residential school. It was an odd experience; the English teacher who came in from the city campus (where, ironically enough, students from Siksika had to venture out once per week to learn Blackfoot as it was only taught as a university credit in Calgary) to talk about how to study literature by looking at a handful of novels and short stories written over the past two centuries. I vividly remember trying to get into the shared faculty office one day to retrieve my textbooks, only to find it locked, and being suddenly and severely chastised by another teacher, a middle-aged white guy, for trying to get into 'his' office. I apologized, thinking that perhaps this was not shared faculty space after all, but still he glared at me for trying to gain access. It was only later in the day that he passed by my classroom, saw me leading discussions, and came to me after, offering his own profuse apologies: "I'm so sorry: I thought you were a student." These words resonated with me for some time after—as a student, I was deserving of rebuke, but as a 'fellow' faculty member, I was deserving of apology. Strange misidentifications again, as more than once students and faculty mistook me for a different kind of Indian, again igniting in me the curiosity of what it meant to be *in* a place, but not *of* a place, and the rights and privileges thus afforded.

Years later, in a different incarnation yet again, I found myself working in visual and literary arts both in educational and organizational capacities, wondering about the connections forged (and not) and the relationships conceived of (or not) between official multiculturalism and Aboriginal policies as perceived by a government and general populace. In those heady days of identity politics, particularly in the arts, where the struggle was both one of expression and visibility, it seemed like there were such barriers. I remember even resurrecting the misnomers of my childhood, teaching an international literature course at the Alberta College of Art and Design and exploring the contents of South Asian and First Nations novels in this *Indian* Indian course. Or the troubles that ensued when the Minquon Panchayat came together in 1992 to challenge the white autocracy of the artist-run centre scene in Canada, its very name and membership comprised of a blend of Aboriginal and immigrant, racialized and radicalized *in extremis*, an exercise in both alliance and inner contestations. All of this, a fertile (yet sometimes feeling futile) landscape that invited further, deeper, and evermore complex matrices of coming to terms, coming of age, in a place where histories are elided, ignored, or overly emphasized, all depending on the desire of the day, the whims of those who hold sway.

When the Aboriginal Healing Foundation first approached me to edit this, the third of three volumes addressing the complexities of reconciliation in Canada, I was asked to develop an anthology that could bring in non-Indigenous voices to somehow widen the breadth of the current discourses on the issue that, to date, have largely centred on the difficult binary of colonizer and colonized, of White settlers and Aboriginal peoples. The central desire, it seemed, was to solicit the words from different centres of investment—immigrant, racialized, 'new' Canadians, and other minoritized communities—whose stories thus far had gone, if not untold, then largely unnoticed. How do such communities relate to the intricacies of reconciliation as a concept, not just of Aboriginal histories, but of different trajectories that have led to the current configuration and conglomeration of peoples on this land? Pronouncements of official bilingualism, multicultural mosaics, and typically national attributes of politeness and compassion often overdetermine what it means to be a Canadian citizen. But our bodies and our lives are as marked by the invisible (or invisibilized) testimonies that circulate around and through, naming us through an absence that charges us with a moral obligation to resist the quietude that is otherwise encouraged by the parliamentarians of passive democracies, and to react and respond as critical and creative agents. This is no easy task within an economy that thrives on paths of least resistance in favour of troubling, unsettling analyses that disrupt if not uproot histories. Simply put, our current codes of success suggest we put the past behind us, blinker ourselves as we negotiate transit to the future, unencumbered by the unseemly realities that, were they given attention, might discomfit and derail us from our chosen destiny. The question to be asked, then, is how can we possibly come into being if we refuse the hauntings of the past, favouring official retellings of history that inscribe a singularity, a unity that belies the fragmented and disharmonious realities that are at once far more honest as much as they are contradictory and fractious? Perhaps this is both a rhetorical and unanswerable question, but it seems that investigating this process, at the very least, is the only way to begin to understand the vectoring of the past.

Cultivating Canada: Reconciliation through the Lens of Cultural Diversity is an attempt at such a beginning. From its conception, this book defied a linear description. Indeed, constructing the very title was an ongoing exercise as we struggled to find the words that encapsulated without restraining the ideas this book would contain. Acknowledging the centrality of the *idea* of land meant that the title should reflect this without re-inscribing simplified tropes of belonging and proprietorship, and yet we also wanted—needed—to address the vast historical and migrational complexities of working on, with, and in this geographic space. As with other elements of this anthology, it was artistic practice that lit the way. Upon studying the potential cover images from Henry Tsang's *Napa North* project—through gritty images juxtaposing scenic landscapes, urban development, and agriculture that addresses the complexities of Indigenous histories and post-contact culture—it became clear that what was at the heart of the matter here was a viewing and reviewing of the physical landscape around us as both a metaphor and a reality. While the cold light falling across the orchards in the cover image might present a literal cultivation (with all its attendant pros and cons), looking deeper we can see the possibilities afforded by a nurturing hand. A metaphorical and collaborative turning of the soil allows us, through and from a variety of diverse lenses, to perceive with new eyes, perhaps to recreate a vision that will bring us closer to understanding both our collective and disparate pasts and our possible and potential futures. Riel is often credited with insisting that creative visionaries among his people will lead the way out of troubling times. He spoke particularly to and about the Métis of the land, and while this anthology stands as testament that our complex realities may only benefit from the participation of artists who can see past the clinical and analytical approaches,it is incredibly useful, but may only be a partial solution to the circumstance of reconciliation.

Like many multi-authored anthologies, this one does, of course, exceed the sum of its parts; yet these parts—the individual contributions from academics, writers, artists—are often in and of themselves beyond a singular thesis. While all of them take on the notion of reconciliation in at least a tacit manner, their methods and modalities range remarkably. Where the first two volumes in the series directly addressed the history, legacy, and consequences of Indian residential schools and the Truth and Reconciliation Commission, this third and final volume is much more amorphous in its central question and resultant content. Although the contributors were provided with a contextual statement addressing the nation's history around residential schools, apology, and reconciliation, the solicitation was for work that would take such histories into account without necessarily addressing them in direct or even indirect fashion. Rather, the call was for a larger consideration of what it meant to be on this land, to be part of this nation-state, what cultural particularities and peculiarities were brought to bear on this issue. This was the statement sent to contributors for them to ponder:

> The question of reconciliation in a Canadian landscape is mediated by multiple histories that cross and overlap borders of race, identity, and culture. When the Canadian government officially recognized the Japanese Canadian redress movement in 1988, it was the first in a litany of claims and efforts from communities to address past injustices. The notion of apology, reconciliation, and redress has taken many forms, contingent on affected communities, but the overarching bridge is the connection to land. This volume on reconciliation will focus on migrant/new Canadian perspectives, but with an understanding that such viewpoints need to be aware of what has come before them—specifically, Aboriginal populations and the history of the land that is determined not by colonizing definitions, but by pre-Contact awareness. Although the expectation is not that each solicited article will make direct referential crossovers between immigrant and Aboriginal communities, the volume as a unit will promote an awareness of these social and political matrices.

For some, this meant a type of subjective spectatorship, looking at a specific issue through a distinctive cultural lens; for others, it meant a recapitulation of different histories of race, migration, inhabitation to come to terms with the present; and for still others, what was implied was a necessary engagement on practical, theoretical, and aesthetic levels. If there was an overarching commonality, I would have to say it was the acknowledgement that we must be creative in our approach if we are not to be overwritten by our pasts. In other words, models of artistic inquiry allow for a new point of entry. This is not to say that art practice per se is the central or identifying moment of this collection; there is powerful imagery in these pages from Henry Tsang, Roy Miki, Jamelie Hassan and Miriam Jordan, Meera Margaret Singh, Sandra Semchuk with James Nicholas, Jayce Salloum, Shirley Bear, Sylvia Hamilton, Diyan Achjadi, and others—but that creative thinking ultimately opens the most productive avenues through whatever form it takes.

To facilitate this process, this collection is separated into three highly interlinked sections that themselves function as aesthetic openings rather than critical enunciations: first, *Land*; second, *Across*; and third, *Transformation*. The initial section, *Land*, is intended as a ground-setter, so to speak, where the articles situate us and give us a solid place to understand our potential movements. While the initial focus of this volume was and is to be on non-Aboriginal voices, it became apparent that such arbitrary delineation would not serve our purpose well. Although simply placing voices in dialogue is not always as productive as some might argue, as there can be a deep value to the context of such conversations, and this opening section is evidence of that. The articles here are often multi-authored, and this section also contains a number of Aboriginal voices, setting an initial tonal quality that carries forward through the book. The middle section, *Across*, develops this sense of critical engagement through a series of dialogues between communities and between historical moments, giving us a space to comprehend how collaborative principles might support this venture. Eschewing the practice of a clear, noun-based section title, the very prepositional nature of this section is flagged through its header. Here, the contributors pose various notions on how to situate themselves, ourselves, as we move through history and identity. And the final section, *Transformation*, is a collection of creative possibilities, still rife with dialogue and history, but encased in the language of change. Although a daunting task, the construction of a future that is able to encompass reconciliation in its myriad forms retains a glow of possibility. This is not an inevitability and the path ahead is replete with difficulties, but the opportunity of change becomes something within our grasp should we choose to accept this responsibility.

In its sum, *Cultivating Canada* is both a burst of creative energy and a reconsideration of our pasts. This volume is and is not about reconciliation; although it might refute easy categorization, the central tenet found in the pages that follow is the importance of eliding comfort levels and insisting on a new way of seeing. This vision is neither myopic nor utopic, and any change will not come without intense forms of work from cultural workers, policy makers, and citizens of all walks. But, perhaps, using the various lenses at our disposal, this is how we may cultivate a new future.

Note

As lead editor, I am indebted to the tireless work that went into the production of this book. The research team members at the Aboriginal Healing Foundation were both meticulous and generous with their time and skill, so deep appreciation to Jonathan Dewar, Mike DeGagné, Flora Kallies, Jane Hubbard, and Pamela Verch; also, to Ayumi Goto for her dedicated copy edits as we fast approached deadline; to Glen Lowry for designing the entire volume to showcase the work within; and, of course, to the contributors with whom I have had numerous, informed, and detailed communications over the course of developing this book.

Section 1: Land

Shirley Bear

Shirley Bear is a multimedia artist, writer, and traditional First Nation herbalist and Elder. Born on the Tobique First Nation, she is an original member of the Wabnaki language group of New Brunswick. Shirley studied art in New Brunswick, New Hampshire, Boston, and Vancouver. As an artist, poet, and activist she has played a crucial role in First Nation women's creative and cultural communities. In 1989, she curated *Changers: A Spiritual Renaissance*, a national show of work by Aboriginal women artists that toured all major galleries across Canada. She has worked extensively as a lecturer, performer, activist, and curator including serving as Cultural Advisor to the British Columbia Institute of Technology, First Nations Education Advisor at Emily Carr Institute of Art & Design, and Resident Elder for First Nations House of Learning at University of British Columbia. Shirley has exhibited internationally, and her work has been purchased by collections across Canada, including the Canadian Museum of Civilization, the National Arts Centre, the New Brunswick Art Bank, First Nations House of Learning at UBC, and the Beaverbrook Art Gallery. Shirley was the 2002 recipient of the New Brunswick Arts Board's Excellence in the Arts Award. Her writing has been included in several anthologies including *Kelusultiek* (Mount St. Vincent University, 1994) and *The Colour of Resistance* (Sister Vision Press, 1993), as well as the catalogues for the exhibits *Kospenay* (1991) and *Changers: A Spiritual Renaissance* (1989). She has been profiled for film and television, by CBC, the National Film Board, and independent producers in such films as *Minquon, Minquon: Wosqotmn Elsonwagon/Shirley Bear: Reclaiming the Balance of Power* (1990) and *Kwa'Nu'Te* (1991) by Cathy Martin, *Keepers of the Fire* (1994) by Christine Welsh, and *The Sacred Feminine* (1995). She has published a book of poetry, *Virgin Bones* (McGilligan Books, 2006).

Ramblings and Resistances

What follows are the words, reflections, and artworks of Shirley Bear who, as a creator and a cultural activist, has inspired so many through her care, her compassion, and her ability to see beyond the immediate. Through her career, her life, Shirley has had a passion for creative practice that is equalled only by her passion for justice. With these dual energies as her guide, she has treaded into difficult territories, never fearful, but often fearsome, refusing to abide by wrong-headed values or to be swayed by unjust causes. Rather, she has walked her own walk, and those fortunate on occasion to walk alongside have learned together, laughed together, and grown to see the world as a place that might pose immense challenges, but also one where anything is possible.

Shirley:
"I learned today the world is round, like a big rubber ball—"

A child's memory, but why did that stay in my memory?

Other things are just as memorable.

Like what did my brother look like?

What did he like to talk about, to eat, to drink, to wear?

He liked keeping my mother's house clean.

He liked to cook. He loved his little sister, called her "B"—

"Queen Bee," he'd say.

I grew up with five brothers and one sister. I got married and my mother had another boy.

A year later I had my first child, Lance, followed by my daughter, Stephanie.

We moved around a lot, travelled down south to the US because the man I had married never had a well-paid job. I had to work to compensate for what he couldn't earn.

Those early years were difficult, but I was young and had a lot of energy. I knew how to draw and made extra money doing portraits. I was also very social, so my friends were people who enjoyed art, and soon I worked my way to a better job and a higher pay scale. Most of the friends that I had were socially conscious, and we used to spend hours discoursing about issues not always discussed by my husband or his family, who chastised me for my *loftiness*. Following many major marital differences and racism from my first husband's family, I found my way back north, to Canada.

Ashok:
When talking to Shirley, it becomes apparent that family is of incredible value to her. But before long, it becomes further evident that Shirley's concept of family is expansive and inclusive, certainly not contained by bloodlines, and not by community or nation. Rather, she surrounds herself—is surrounded by—a vast network of people, some of whom could not be more different than her. What binds them together, however, is the common trust in fairness, in making things right, and in exploring creativity as far as it will go. When I first met Shirley, she was part of an incisive and culturally diverse group of artists who came together to challenge the racially homogeneous and exclusionary practices of artist-run centres in the early 1990s.[1] This group was called the *Minquon Panchayat*, itself a blend of unlikely cultures. Traditionally, in South Asia, a *panchayat* is a village council of elders that makes decisions for the benefit of its community. The name "Minqwôn Minqwôn" is actually Shirley's spirit name in Wabnaki, translated as, "Double Rainbow,"[2] and she loaned this special name to the coalition. Thus, the Minquon Panchayat was a type of rainbow coalition, charged in 1992 with changing the face and direction of a network then known as the Association of National Non-Profit Artists Centres/*Regroupement d'artistes des centres alternatifs* (ANNPAC/RACA), whose membership attempted to recognize that for historical, colonial, and political reasons, the organization was unable to exercise the inclusivity that so many within its ranks desired. Shirley bestowed this name upon the group of First Nations artists and artists of colour who began the long road of making radical shifts to provide this necessary shift.

Shirley:
I learned today the world is round, like a big rubber ball, with China on the other side down there below us all, and so I went and dug a hole, beside the garden gate, and dug and dug and dug and dug and thought, "what fun it will be to get a ladder tall, and climb down to China, to that land below us all."

Life isn't always as we imagine it to be, not so precise, easy, or magical. Somewhere in the journey of "finding out," something resembling magic does happen, and it was on this journey that I found a soulmate, Peter, got married,

Shirley Bear, *Wigisi Eb'eskum'ok'nsiss, (Let's play golf)* (1991)
This was a tribute to the women warriors at K'nesatkii
Serigraph on paper, 54 x 72 cm

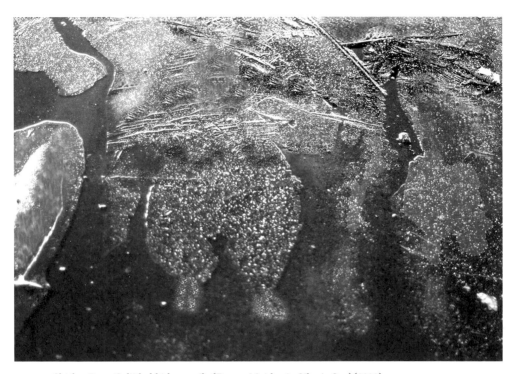

Shirley Bear, *Geljid ahbid pqomik, (Frozen Maiden in Siberia Sea)* (2000)
Oil painting on dry inks, 14 x 16 cm

had another girl, and named her Ramona. Peter and I decided to home-school her. When Ramona was seven years old we settled in Negootkook, New Brunswick.

It was then that I started to realize that I had a keen understanding of injustice and that I was basically fearless, which helped in making decisions and addressing the government of Canada on their treatment of the First Nations' women in my community.

Sandra Lovelace-Nicholas was testing the government of Canada for the sexist clause 12(1)b within the *Indian Act*, a law that governed the daily lives of First Nations who lived on reserve land.

In 1985, the women from Negootkook (Tobique) celebrated the elimination of 12(1)b from the *Indian Act of Canada*. The publication of a book titled *Enough is Enough: Aboriginal Women Speak Out*, which chronicles the adult lives of thirteen women from Negootkook, told our stories.[3]

Ashok:

I was not privy to Shirley's years prior to *Enough is Enough*, but her rallying cry behind the Minquon Panchayat made it clear she had come to such cultural activism with the depth and wisdom of experience. The Minquon Panchayat worked with ANNPAC for that first year, bringing its energy and dedication to an incredible showcase of talent and potential to the It's a Cultural Thing gathering in Calgary in 1993. But it was here many of us realized that progressive action does not win over conservative histories easily. During a formational meeting at the Native Friendship Centre where ANNPAC was discussing the Minquon Panchayat's provisional plan for realignment, some felt the prescribed action of moving quickly to bring in new member organizations was far too swift, an affront to those, I suggest, who wanted change to be more cosmetic than radical. At one point, a frustrated ANNPAC executive member voiced dissent at the proposed changes, saying that the organization was already making progressive moves as it had *allowed* the Minquon Panchayat to present this prospectus. I can still hear Shirley's voice as she raised first her eyebrows, and then her entire body from the seated circle. "Allow?" she asked. "You *allowed* us?" And without another word, Shirley slowly walked along the outside of the circle, with no more than a glance to her colleagues, enough to have us all rise as one and follow her upstairs. There, she led us in a healing circle, and when some of our number wondered whether we could still reconcile and salvage something from this situation, Shirley, so calmly smudging with sweetgrass, shook her head. No, she told us, this was not the time. Only that. And that was all she needed to say for the rest to understand.

When Annie Mae Pictou-Aquash was killed at Pine Ridge, it was an assault to all the women of the world. She had always been very outspoken for the rights of women; and to have this happen to her in Pine Ridge, the home (temple) of the some of the most male-dominated spiritualists in the First Nations community, was an outright insult to womanhood.

In the years of the Native Women's Rights battle, many changes developed in me through art. It was reconfirmed by past teachings that women, as life-givers, had a special place in the community, and, in my case, as decision-makers within the family, community, and country.

In my forties, I went on a spiritual quest and found more insidious rules and sexist activities against women. All supposedly because of the laws of *Kisiulinaqô* (in the name of god), and because my language is not written, I had never read or heard of such rules. I fasted for several years and prayed to be given the truth, but as each year went by I was more convinced that there were no such rules and that they were pretty much a warped creation of men who did not want women to attain a spiritual understanding. These men were brainwashed by the Catholic Church.

My art speaks the truth of its creator.

Ashok:

Years later, I saw Shirley Bear on stage engaged in dialogue with writer Susan Crean. They were playing out a biography of Emily Carr (ironically enough, in the lecture theatre of the Vancouver art school named for that artist) that Crean had written. It explored various lesser documented elements, most notably Carr's friendship with Aboriginal artist Sophie Frank from whom, Crean argued, Carr had learned a great deal about Aboriginal people of the West Coast. Here, Susan Crean played Emily Carr, Shirley Bear played Sophie Frank, and the retelling spoke volumes about the relationships among women, art, and culture, across land and across time. I remember Shirley telling me soon after that she thoroughly enjoyed reading the creative works of younger women of colour in Canada, for they spoke of what was possible. It brought to mind the healing circle of all those years before when Shirley rightly reminded us that change can and must happen, but we had to listen to our hearts as much as to our heads.

Shirley Bear, *Nil ewik'husi, (Self-portrait)* (2006)
Ink wash on hand pulled paper, 24 x 18.5 cm

Shirley:

Circle around,

beautiful   brown women

Beautiful brown   women

Drum singing for the women

Owl eyes hey ye   hey ya

Red tablecloth

yellow lamp burning.

Red mind singing,

yellow love burning

        beautiful

            brown women[4]

Notes
1   See Gagnon, Monika Kin (2000:63). *Other Conundrums: Race, Culture, and Canadian Art*. Vancouver and Kamloops, BC: Arsenal Pulp Press, Artspeak Gallery, and the Kamloops Art Gallery.
2   Crean, Susan (2009: 37). N'tow'wik'hegat (She Who Knows How to Make Pictures). In T. Graff (curator), *Nekt wikuhpon ehpit (Once there lived a woman): The Painting, Poetry, and Politics of Shirley Bear*. Fredericton, NB: Beaverbrook Art Gallery.
3   Silman, Janet (ed.) (1987). *Enough is Enough: Aboriginal Women Speak Out*. Toronto, ON: The Women's Press.
4   Excerpted from the poem, "Dawn." In Shirley Bear (2006:20-21). *Virgin Bones: Belayak Kcikug'nas'ikn'ug*. Toronto, ON: McGilligan Books.

Henry Tsang and Glen Lowry

Henry Tsang is a visual and media artist and occasional curator whose work incorporates digital media, video, photography, language, and sculptural elements in the exploration of the relationship between the public, community, and identity in the new global order. Projects in the public sphere range from community-based curatorial and engagement practices to permanent commissioned artworks. Video installations such as *Orange County* (2004) and *Olympus* (2006) shot in California, Beijing, Torino, and Vancouver examine overlapping urban and socio-political spaces. *Napa North* (2008) looks at the relationship between wine, real estate, and cultural translation in British Columbia's Okanagan Valley. His *Welcome to the Land of Light* is a 100 metre-long installation located on the seawall handrail along Vancouver's False Creek. Comprised of fibre optic cable lighting and marine-grade aluminum lettering, it literally underscores Chinook Jargon, a nineteenth century local trade language, and the English that replaced it, to speak about the promise of technology and how different cultures have come to live together in that part of the world. Henry received the VIVA Award in 1993 and is an Associate Professor at Emily Carr University of Art & Design in Vancouver.

Glen Lowry is Vancouver-based writer, educator, and editor, who teaches Critical and Cultural Studies at Emily Carr Institute for Art + Design. Glen edits *West Coast Line* and is also a founding editor of LINEbooks: Burnaby, a micropress specializing in experimental poetry and poetics. With Henry Tsang and M. Simon Levin, Glen is collaborating on the Maraya project, an art-/media-based initiative attempting to connect urban waterfront developments in Vancouver, Canada, and Dubai, United Arab Emirates.

Napa North

[Napa North *consists of a series of colour photographs, a 3-Channel video installation, and wine tastings at a custom-designed wine tasting bar, complemented by native Okanagan language and cultural workshops at the Kelowna Art Gallery, Alternator Gallery, and Penticton Art Gallery. Over the course of a year and a half, Henry Tsang worked with local farmers, winemakers, land developers and cultural communities in British Columbia's Okanagan Valley to explore their hopes and concerns. Once known as the province's agricultural breadbasket, this region has experienced rapid urban development while rebranding itself as a site for luxury lifestyle living. Central to the project is Osoyoos Indian Band elder Modesta Betterton, whose stories about her community's history and economic development is interwoven with active translations of language employed by the local wine, real estate and tourism industries.*]

Terroir / as in Translation[1]

Ic maý stm ankʷ ulməntət tl'a sapi t‿apna? k̓al skəcəctət k̓al sənsiu̓łkʷtn. łac kʷulstm I‿sɨ́mʕalt łac naixʷisum iʔ təmtmutn. nʔaip ic kʷulstm I‿cic.[2]

A focal point of Henry Tsang's *Napa North* is a video of Modesta Stelkia Betterton, Osoyoos Indian Band (OIB) elder and N'syilxcen (Okanagan) language teacher. Moving between N'syilxcen translations of statements prepared by Tsang from local promotional materials and conversations with the artist (in English) about OIB involvement in contemporary viticulture, Betterton reflects on the transformation of British Columbia's Okanagan valley into a destination for wine tourism and luxury living, her impromptu narrative framing the rapid emergence of Napa North. Recalling an initial partnership with Andres Wines and the band's subsequent decision to develop Nk'Mip Cellars, Betterton tells us, "The grapes [were] started because we wanted our people to come to work here at home instead of going to the States." Betterton's story strikes a balance between the ambitious scope of regional development and basic needs. Her anecdotes place the proliferating luxury real-estate developments on a decidedly human scale. In a context that includes The Rise (near Vernon) and Greata Ranch (between Kelowna and Penticton), a partnership between Cedar Creek Winery and real-estate developer Concord Pacific, the OIB Development Corporation's $25 million real-estate development project— which includes two restaurants, luxury spa and conference facilities, a

Henry Tsang, *Napa North (The Rise)* (2008)
colour photograph

year-round campground and RV park, nine-hole golf course, and cultural centre—is a fascinating foil with which to view the effects of neoliberal government policy on a relatively small group of people. The collective success of the 370-member OIB is an example of the intricate, contradictory histories at play in the regeneration of regional economies, and of the translation—re-packaging and branding—of these histories for global consumption.

Historically, the concept of terroir is linked with a system for classifying the production and distributions of comestibles—coffee, tea, and wine; perhaps the best known example of which is France's *Appellation d'origine contrôlée* (AOC). Recently, however, terroir has undergone a process of translation. Appropriated by copywriters to sell New World wines and by wine aficionados to categorize (or brand) differences among varietals, terroir has come to be used to generalize geo-climatic traits in order to position emerging producers among global leaders. Thus, the notion of terroir explored through the various facets of *Napa North* hinges on the play between historical references and looser abstract or metaphorical meanings.

Staging a dialogue between local wine production and advanced capitalism, historical specificity and the homogenizing drives of global taste, *Napa North* draws on the potent symbolism that surrounds wine—its association with land ownership, trade, consumption, and culture; its role in developing material practices and spiritual beliefs, as well as in defining social values of refinement and decadence. Characteristic of Tsang's commitment to cross-cultural collaboration, this work continues an installation and public art practice spanning two decades of negotiation with racialized subjectivity in Canada. Tsang's engagement with the Osoyoos people and their transformation of one of Canada's largest remaining tracts of desert land raises crucial questions about the fluidity of wealth, the politics of entitlement, and the limits of enfranchisement that continue to trouble nationalist discourses.

Something of the work's humour and sly intentions are available in Tsang's reworking of Edouard Manet's *Bar at the Folies Bergères* (1882). Tsang's photographic take on this touchstone of Western art history is suggestive of a critical engagement with the history of European modernism and its particular re-configuration of the artist figure. In Tsang's version (p. 33), unlike Manet's, the female subject smiles back, returning our gaze and defying the solemnity of the canonical work. An image of celebration, she flouts critical commentary—*remind me again who is being left out of the party*—and common sense—*this real-estate boom can last forever.*

This photograph and the Betterton video are but elements of *Napa North*'s variegated form, which includes videotaped interviews and scenic footage,

Henry Tsang, from *Napa North* (2008)
Video Stills with Modesta Stelkia Betterton and Lane Stelkia,
3-Channel Video Installation, 30 minutes

Henry Tsang, *Napa North (The Rise)* (2008)
colour photograph

Henry Tsang, *Napa North (Spirit Ridge)* (2008)
colour photograph

photographs of regional landscapes, production facilities, and real-estate developments, food and wine tastings (presented in conjunction with the project's Napa North Wine Club, napanorth.org), public talks, and cultural workshops (supported by the OIB's Desert Cultural Centre). The events, rather than being addenda to the main body of work in the galleries, are integral to Tsang's relational art practice. The expansive nature of Napa North remains grounded in the complex ethical engagements proposed through the work.

Returning to the fertile terrain of his earlier artworks, Tsang continues to work themes of linguistic specificity, geographic mobility, cultural memory, and translation. *Napa North* is reminiscent of Tsang's work with Chinook Jargon, most notably *Welcome to the Land of Light* (1997), a public art installation based on translations of real-estate propaganda and subsequent banner series for the World Urban Forum (2006). It also conjures up the artist's engagement with bifurcating 21st century geographies—e.g., *Orange County* (2004), which looks at Orange County, California, and Orange County, Beijing, and *Olympus* (2005), shot on sites for the Torino 2006 and Vancouver 2010 Winter Olympics. These works remind us that, increasingly, "[w]e are in the epoch of simultaneity: we are in the epoch of juxtaposition, the epoch of the near and far, of the side-by-side, of the dispersed" and that "our experience of the world is less that of a long life developing through time than that of a network that connects points and intersects with its *own* skein."[3]

In the spirit of this unfolding network, *Napa North* invites us to look at a world in which market forces and land reserves intersect to produce barely imaginable futures, utopian dreams of shared prosperity and luxury. Engaging with the work of the Osoyoos people and their negotiations with advanced capitalism, seeking the exception rather than the norm, Tsang's work provides space for reflection on our respective participation in a process of urbanization that is re-engineering country and city alike. As we gather, sampling the seasonal blends of disparate investments and labours, tasting the fruits of this year's socio-economic climate, we might do well to think ahead to the next millennium and to ask which or whose terroir is most likely to produce the best returns next year, or the season after that.

Notes

1 This is a reprint from: Lowry, Glen (2008). Terroir / as in translation. In *Edges of Diversity* [catalogue]. Kelowna, BC: Alternator Gallery for Contemporary Art.

2 N'syilxcen translation of the following: "We share our history and traditions with those who visit the winery. From the early years of ranching, trading and small farms, we have continued to change with the times."

3 Michel Foucault. Of Other Spaces (1967), Heterotopias. Retrieved 9 February 2011 from: http://www.foucault.info/documents/heteroTopia/foucault.heteroTopia. en.html

Henry Tsang, *Napa North (Summerhill Winery Tasting Room)* (2008)
colour photograph

Napa North (Spirit Ridge) (2008)
colour photograph

Cheryl L'Hirondelle

Joseph Naytowhow

b.h. Yael

Cheryl L'Hirondelle is a much sought-after multi- and interdisciplinary artist, singer/songwriter and curator. A nomadic mixed-blood (Métis/Cree-non-status/treaty, French, German, Polish) originally from Alberta, her creative practice investigates the junction of a Cree world view in contemporary time and space. Since the early 1980s, Cheryl has created, performed, and presented work in a variety of artistic disciplines, including: music, performance art, theatre, spoken word, storytelling, installation, and media art. In the early 1990s, she began a parallel career as an arts consultant and programmer/curator, cultural strategist/activist, and director/producer of both independent works and projects within national artist-run networks. Cheryl's activities have found her working in the Canadian independent music industry, educational institutions, community organizations, the prison system, First Nations bands, tribal councils, and various Canadian governmental funding agencies, provincially and federally. Cheryl's practice as a musician and artist has also garnered several awards and honours. In 2004, Cheryl was the first Aboriginal artist invited to present her new media work at DAK'ART Lab, as part of the sixth edition of the Dakar Biennale for Contemporary African Art, Dakar, Senegal. In both 2005 and 2006, L'Hirondelle was the recipient of the imagineNATIVE New Media Award for her net.art projects: *treatycard*, *17:TELL* and *wêpinâsowina*. In 2006 she won Best Female Traditional Cultural Roots Album, and in 2007 won Best Group Award from the Canadian Aboriginal Music Awards for her work with *M'Girl*. Her 2008 interdisciplinary project *nikamon ohci askiy (songs because of the land)*, was recognized as an honouree in the NetArt category of the 13th Annual Webby Awards.

Joseph Naytowhow is a gifted Plains/Woodland Cree (nêhiyaw) singer/songwriter, storyteller, and voice, stage, and film actor from the Sturgeon Lake First Nation Band in Saskatchewan. He is renowned for his own unique style of Cree/English storytelling, combined with original hybrid and traditional First Nations drum and rattle songs. Joseph is the recipient of the 2006 Canadian Aboriginal Music Award's Keeper of the Tradition Award and the 2005 Commemorative Medal for the Saskatchewan Centennial. In 2009 Joseph also received a Gemini Award for Best Individual or Ensemble Performance in an Animated Program or Series for his role in *Wapos Bay: The Series*. That same year he was also awarded Best Emerging Male Actor at the Winnipeg Aboriginal Film Festival for his role in *Run* and won Best Traditional Male Dancer at the John Arcand Fiddlefest in Saskatchewan. Joseph's generosity and compassion for sharing cultural knowledge makes him a much sought-after speaker, performer, and teacher for children and adults alike. He has performed for the Prince of Wales, the lieutenant-governor of Saskatchewan, former United States President Jimmy Carter, and many other notables. His demanding schedule continues to take him to conferences, symposia, forums, festivals, and film sets across Canada, North America, and around the world. From 1995 to 2000 he served as the Storyteller-In-Residence for Meadow Lake Tribal Council; as a child, he was influenced by his grandfather's traditional and ceremonial chants as well as the sounds of the fiddle and guitar. He holds a Bachelor of Education degree from the University of Saskatchewan.

b.h. Yael is a Toronto-based filmmaker and video and installation artist. She is Professor of Integrated Media at Ontario College of Art and Design University. Yael has received many arts awards including a Chalmers Fellowship. Her most recent work, Trading the Future (2008), recently won the Audience Award at the Ecofilms 2009 festival in Rhodes, Greece. Yael's work has exhibited nationally and internationally and has been shown in various settings, from festivals to galleries to various educational venues. Her work has been purchased by several universities. Her past film and video work has dealt with issues of identity, authority, and family structures at the same time addressing the fragmentary nature of memory and belonging. More recent work focuses on activist initiatives, political fear, apocalypse, and gender. *Fresh Blood, A Consideration of Belonging* (1996) dealt specifically with the many intersections of identity, including its racialized aspects within Jewish culture. *Palestine Trilogy* (2006) includes three videos that focus on activist initiatives and address the politics of Palestine and Israel. Yael has produced work as part of various artist projects: *(of)fences* (2001) is part of *blah blah blah (re)Viewing Quebec* (2002); installation works such as *Home Rule* (1989) and *Bomb Shelters* (1993) have exhibited with the Spontaneous Combustion Collective; and *pacts* (2003), produced for *The Olive Project* (2004) by the Hard Pressed Collective. An ongoing project, *the fear series*, involved separate video projections at the Koffler Gallery as part of *DIG/DUG* and as part of *Images Festival's Contained Mobility* show at Harbourfront's York Quay Gallery. In collaboration with Johanna Householder, Yael has produced *Approximations* and *Verbatim* (2007), a series of short works examining filmic representations of gendered redemption.

Land Project: A Conversation between Canada and Israel/Palestine

Cheryl: *(to Yael)—tânisi—awîna kîya?*—tell us who you are.

Yael: It's a big story but in a nutshell, my mother's from Iraq and my father's from Poland. I was born in Israel. Both of them were Jewish with very different histories.

Because I was brought up by my Mum, I felt much closer to that history, to the Iraqi Jewish narrative and the consideration of how Mizrahi or Arab Jews experienced racism in Israel. I have been thinking a lot about the politics of Israel, vis-à-vis Palestine, in the last number of years: about Indigenous issues in relation to Palestinians, about what happened to Jews in Europe, and the subsequent impact on Arab Jews in predominantly Muslim countries, and about the export of European racism by Ashkenazi (European) Jews as instituted in the state of Israel and in the Territories they occupy.

Joseph: I'm from Treaty 6 on a reserve called Sturgeon Lake. I live in Saskatoon now, but I travel about to other areas, respectfully and honorably.

Cheryl: I'm a non-status Treaty Indian and Métis, something a lot of people think is an anomaly. There's all kinds of politics around identity and jurisdiction about who owns my hide. What happens is if you say you're 'Métis' you have to sign away your status, but I don't like to give the Canadian government that much authority over me. Not much has changed since the days of the scrip. I prefer to think of identity as an historical chronology and am interested in the layers as opposed to the way things are at any one time. I'm also from Treaty 6 and Joseph is my Indian-adopted brother.

Land

Yael: Can you explain Treaty 6, that connection?

Cheryl: Treaty 6 is a land-based treaty on this land now known as Canada. There are provisions into infinity, one that was called the medicine chest, for health, and others were for education and mineral rights, etc. I've heard that settlers who came couldn't own mineral rights, but they could have a plough share of the land—literally as deep as the plough could go is how much land they could claim to own. Yael, can you re-cap the focus of this discussion?

Yael: This project is partly an account of the histories of trauma coming out of the residential schools, and a consideration of the repercussions on subsequent generations. As I understand, this third volume emerges from a desire to expand the discussion beyond the Aboriginal context in Canada, to consider the politics of other people and places and the connections to the kind of logic or rationale in which governments have operated and how people have been determined by these policies.

Cheryl: So it's around issues of land?

Yael: Land is a big issue as to how it plays out in Palestine and Israel. These issues and the residential school experiences reveal a Euro-colonial lens. The personal resonance for me is in the example of what Iraqi Jews, including my family, experienced in the newly formed Israel. They were seen as inferior. My Mum and her older brother were taken to the kibbutz, away from their family; they were not allowed to speak their first language which was Arabic; they were re-named. My mother's name was Nadra; she became Noga, which was a Hebrew name. In the Yemenite community children were taken away from their families and adopted out; the families never knew what happened to those children. They were adopted into European families.

Cheryl: Wow, and what would be the rationale to do that?

Yael: The Arabs, including Arab Jews, were seen as uncivilized, not educated, not sufficiently advanced or developed, which was significantly untrue for many, especially those who came from the urban centres. This was part of the strategy to foster and accelerate assimilation, to *Judaize* the land.

Cheryl: Are you suggesting that when modern day Israel was starting that there was a European order that dominated the construct?

Yael: Absolutely. That's exactly why there is a connection between what happened in Canada and many places around the world, determined by a Euro-colonial mindset. In Israel it had more of a Euro–Zionist rationale, an exclusively Jewish state, but again, with its politics dominated by a European elite.

Cheryl: I think we have to stay clear on the distinction, because we can't say that the reserve systems are the same as the Palestinian islands we saw in your video, *Palestine Trilogy*. But what we could say is that the repercussions of the Indian Act on native peoples, and how native peoples on the same land base treat each other, is similar. One of the things I noted in your work is that it's about a land base where people, whether they were Jewish or Arab or Palestinian, there is a history or lineage that they originated from there.

Yael: There are of course a lot of differences between the occupation of Palestine and the reserve system in North America, but there are similarities emerging from colonialism, the attempt to dominate the land and resources, as well as people. Whether Jews have a claim to that land is contested. I think what's clear is that Palestinians are the indigenous people to that land; that narrative has been erased by Israel, as has the claim. The creation of the state of Israel is a colonial project.

Cheryl: Neal McLeod briefly speaks about how we all have been colonizers at one time or another in his book *Cree Narrative Memory*.[1] Even for Native people on this large continent, we've all entered "enemy territory"—or someplace not of our origin. Historically, when successful, or a skirmish was won, the right was gained to some resources. If you lost, you would either leave the land or live under somebody else's terms.

Joseph: In some areas they're allies like the Cree and the Métis in Treaty 6 where I come from. There are stories where people come to some agreement and the land becomes more or less home or shared by the two territorial groups. The Blackfoot and Cree from Treaty 4 created a peace treaty initiated by this one chief Maskipiton and there's never really been fighting after that, so it remains Cree territory. The Crees pushed the Dene further north and the Blackfoot further west towards Alberta, so we were colonizers in that sense.

Cheryl: I was always told the Crees stole Blackfoot women and the Blackfoot stole Cree horses (*laughs*) though the Cree where I'm from—*amiskwaciya* or "the beaver hills"—taught their horses to return home. There's another story I acquired from Sherry Farrell Racette about the Métis and the Dakota called *The Battle of Bear Butte* or *The Bare Naked Lady Battle*. It's a long story, so I won't tell it here, but in short, it had to do with the Metis from around what was Fort Garry and the buffalo hunt. They would always have to go into someone else's territory and have to win the right to be there to hunt buffalo for that season. We don't live that way anymore, now we have the Canadian government and things like the *Indian Act* that homogenizes identity and instead pits people against each other. Now we see polarities and agreements/treaties forgotten so it becomes about being status, or non-status or Métis. In the old way, as Joseph is suggesting, there would be skirmishes and then they would come to an agreement.

Yael: I think from the stories you're talking about, there's a difference between tribal conflicts, the ways that those were worked through in very specific and located agreements, and colonialism. Tribal skirmishes have gone on in many places around the world; people inter-marry, the idea of purity is suspect, whether by action or blood or whatever. I think it's worth contesting these notions. However, what's been going on in Canada over the past few centuries is domination, both by settlers and the complicity of immigrant cultures, and this has made a huge impact on First Nations people. It's brought in a whole different system.

Territoriality

Joseph: One of the experiences from the residential schools was that it brought people together where at one time they would have been enemies. That's what I've noticed throughout my life. There's still territoriality, but you may not know that unless you've gone to university. You're educating yourself and if you're lucky to have also kept your language you can access the knowledge through the elders who are still alive, the ones who have the stories. All the tribal people in this area, the Cree, Blackfoot and Dene, have been suppressed and oppressed so much that we get along somewhat but also still fight among ourselves. So if the white people aren't keeping us down through policies and laws, we're keeping each other down.

Cheryl: It's what they say as the gift that keeps on giving—what colonization has done for Native people in this land. It set in motion notions of a new order, hierarchies where status equals wealth and fostered a chasm between the haves and have-nots. There's a word in Cree for people who are to be pitied—

Joseph: *kitimâkisiw*

Cheryl: Yes, *kitimâkisiw*. Within a Cree worldview we know that when somebody doesn't have something you have to share your resources.

Native people all across this land showed wealth by *sharing* wealth. We've changed, and that was a part of the colonial gift. Now we're saying that treaty with the government is more important than the way we treat each other. Compassion seems to be replaced with a new territorialism. Identity is now based on things like blood quantum and government pedigree without a sense of the natural law of balance.

Joseph: Cheryl is right about sometimes when people become settled in a certain area they will protect it, because it's all connected with their ceremonies, medicine and sacred places—and people will fight for that. Back at the time of the signing of the treaties, things went immediately wrong. Now I think we are dealing with these wrongs on a spiritual level.

Yael: In Israel/Palestine land conflicts are still very basic. Though people make the claim that the conflict in Israel and Palestine is between Jews and Muslims, that it is a religious struggle, this does not represent the complexity; it is much more so a political conflict. One of the quotes in that first volume of this Aboriginal Healing Foundation series, about the history of Aboriginal occupancy and traditional lands and territories, mentioned the "doctrine of *terra nullius*, the claim that North America on discovery by Europeans was empty land, open to occupation and cultivation by civilized peoples."[2] Christianity was used to dominate; however, Europeans saw North America as this place they could take. There were some troublesome Aboriginal people here, but they weren't seen as being rightful owners or rightful heirs to the land. Likewise the Zionist narrative was that Palestine was empty and waiting for its Jewish identity or destiny. "Land for a people, for a people without Land." Potential settlers were told that, and the narrative was perpetuated in Israeli culture. These are colonial and political parallels.

From One Nation to Another

Cheryl: I get what you're saying: the similarity is that Arabic people, whether they be Palestinian or Arab Jews, are seen as sub-human. This is part of the imperialist mentality—if you're not living our worldview, you are not equal.

Yael: It was very much an idea around racial supremacy, which also had a hierarchy. Of course Arab Jews, as they were needed in terms of demographics, were still better than Palestinians.

Cheryl: Yes, that's very much what happened here. I don't think that among Native people from one nation to another we ever saw ourselves as superior unless we earned it. I don't think there was a supposition of racial superiority. We just knew via our stories and accounts, we were superior in knowledge, number, in certain skills, and in battle.

Yael: Some of the contemporary indicators of such discriminations in Israel/Palestine, much as it is here, are the high levels of incarceration, or poverty, or impediments to education, or access to senior postings, academic or whatever. In Israel the higher percentage of Arab Jews who are incarcerated, less educated or generally have a much harder time, is an indication of systemic racism. For Palestinians, it is even more marked, because they have experienced expropriations of land, unlawful incarcerations without due process, occupation, and exclusion from any access to the terms of power.

Cheryl: What I discerned from your documentaries was the idea that the Palestinians who were being displaced were very much *of* the land they lived on. They weren't looking at a hill as a vantage point or a place of domination but as a place for sheep to graze. Joseph, could you speak about some of the men's societies, how the English word for warrior doesn't adequately describe roles? What was that term again?

Joseph: *Okihcitâw*—it means, worthy young man. These men didn't go out and fight, but stayed within the community to work and provide for and protect the camp from within. The others that went out, were called *nâpêhkâsow—iyiniwak* which translates to "acting like a man." The *okihcitâw* perhaps had a special role also, requiring preparation in sacred rituals. Their preparation in that society was a lot more unique in terms of being called the protectors.

Cheryl: Joseph, you explained to me once that those men were providers, that they always made sure everyone in the camp was fed and that they used their prowess to track a deer. Whether they were protectors or warriors, the stories I've read and heard have imparted that how from an early age one had to learn to be both strong and pliable. It had more to do with being able to survive the elements, be resourceful, and know the land. Yael, this is what I witnessed in your films as well—Palestinians being displaced from their land, and yet there was something enduring I sensed. I think it was that element of humour, how you can always laugh and be happy. That's very similar to Native people, hard times can be happening, but you still have to find the humour to keep on.

Passive Assertion

Joseph: What I appreciated about the documentary was its passive assertion in using the law, finding ways to keep their land intact. We've had to do that here because some of our land has been appropriated for hay or trees, taken illegally. The government or some business-minded Europeans removed treaty-marking posts that our reserve lands were defined by. Some situations around compensation, where Canadian settlers/farmers have used First Nations land for timber or haying, can take years to settle. There are many cases throughout Treaty 6 that have yet to be settled.

Yael: In Israel and Palestine recourse to the legal system has a mixed history, mostly problematic. It still seems unjust that people who are oppressed or whose land has been taken away are the ones who have to take on the cost of bringing these cases to the courts. In the few cases where the courts in Israel have found favour for these Palestinian communities, there is no follow-up on the legal decision. There are lots of places in Israel proper, in the Negev or up in the Galilee area for example; though the court found in favour of the village, they were never allowed back. Or in the West Bank, many villages, such as Bil'in where the wall has divided the village, Israel has taken 60 per cent of the village's land; they can't access their olive groves and farmlands.[3]

Cheryl: This is why I'm a non-status treaty Indian. If the government wanted a piece of land, another method was to deem it to be "surrendered." The reserve—in Cree the term is *iskonikan askiy* — means leftover land, so it refers to a strip of land that perhaps had the least value that would have been part of a larger territory that a band originally existed on throughout the cycle of the seasons. How the surrender worked is that government representatives went to that reserve during a time of year when people were away hunting and/or gathering. Since all they would find were a few people left in the enclave, they would say, "no one's living on this land anymore so we're going to take it back," and this is what they called "surrendered." There are still a lot of cases in the courts and still more cropping up, as this practice was common from the signing of the treaties and into the 1900s. Many displaced by this system would move onto other reserves or go take scrip and become Métis.

Yael: That's interesting. There must have been some similar strategies. But also some were very violent offences. In 1947 when the United Nations mandate gave the new Jewish state 56 per cent of historic Palestine,[4] Jews who wanted to expand that land base used military force. Some Jewish groups, such as the Irgun and the Stern gang, were considered to be terrorist groups at the time. The *Deir Yassin Remembered* video, you might have seen in *Palestine Trilogy*,[5] documents one such example, but there were a number of massacres in other Palestinian villages. Because of the violence, many Palestinians left their homes. When I would talk to my mother about what happened she would say the Arab leadership told everyone to leave. In effect she is saying it was not Israel's fault that there are refugees. The Arab leadership created this vacuum and emptied the land. It's a kind of divestment of responsibility for Palestinian dispossession and the homes and lands that Jews took over. In the end Israel ended up with 78 per cent of historic Palestine, and the West Bank and Gaza were just 22 per cent of it. There was a race, just as there is now within the remaining 22 per cent, as to how much land could be procured before borders were declared.

Cheryl: The Canadian government starved Indian people during the signing of the treaties—one of many divide-and-conquer methods. It split apart bands and made it extremely difficult for some of the great chiefs like Big Bear to negotiate a better deal for everyone in the Treaty 6 area. But there were other strategies employed as time went by. While we were storytellers-in-residence at Meadow Lake Tribal Council in northern Saskatchewan, we heard a story from Mr. Alfred Bekkattla who told us how the government finally infiltrated the Dene communities in the north, in Treaty 10.[6] The Dene were different than the Cree, in that they lived in small family enclaves on lands that were not suitable for agriculture, hence not as desirable for repopulating with settlers. Their treaty wasn't signed until the beginning of the 1900s, and it took the government a while to figure out how to make them subservient. They went into their communities in the wintertime, again when the men were out hunting, to the home of a woman, with many children, usually very low on food because she was waiting for the husband to return. They'd say, "your husband has left you here starving when he should be providing for you," and then promised the woman that the government would take care of her and ensure there was always food in the house, but she would have to be obedient to the government, like it was her new husband. That was how welfare entered these communities and started to erode their family structures. Maria Campbell also told us the Cree had these rings of protection within a band that at the core was their children. The government came in and slowly eroded all of these protective rings with starvation, disease, imprisonment, alcohol, et cetera and eventually got to the children. That was the beginning of the residential school scoop—re-educate the children and strip the language.[7] Once accomplished, be rid of the worldview. Isn't that what Trudeau's *White Paper* was all about?[8]

Yael: Well it seems that divide and conquer has always been very much part of the colonial strategy: in India between Hindus and Muslims, and certainly in Palestine. But it's weird to hear about it in First Nations communities, how it happened at the levels of family, not just tribes or ethnic groups, and that's really amazing.

Cheryl: Joseph, what is that term I've heard you use for when things went wrong?

Joseph: *Mâyipayiwin.*

Cheryl: Cree people will use that term when discussing what happened around the time of the signing of Treaty 6—like when we watched your film about—

Yael: Deir Yassin.

Cheryl: There was mention of something similar—it was called—

Yael: The *Nakba*.

Cheryl: I think it's the same concept. There was a promise made and then things went terribly wrong.

Yael: Yes, the Nakba for Palestinians was significant. It means "the disaster"; it's the moment in which they lost their lands and many became refugees, exiled from their lands. At the same time Israelis celebrate independence, of getting the land. Israel does not want to acknowledge the previous inhabitants. What's happened in the last number of years is that the state has created laws that Palestinians are not allowed to commemorate the Nakba within Israel; it's an attempt to criminalize memory and commemoration. It has been legally entrenched: flying the Palestinian flag or talking about the trauma and rupture that Palestinians experience is now illegal. Of course people break that law, including Israelis. The Israeli organization *Zochrot* (it's a feminine word for remembering) deliberately speaks about the Nakba to Israelis. It's important for Israelis to acknowledge that this happened—that this Disaster is part of our narrative, and to try and educate Israelis about the many villages that were destroyed and disappeared and about those who were on the land previously.

Joseph: It still happens here, there's still silence among people who can't really do any protesting in a real way. It takes infrastructure and planning to try and get the rights settled and we don't have that. The perception is that Indian governments are either displaced or are pawns of the Canadian government.

Cheryl: There are small pockets of Indians who practice international law, trying to honour earlier ways. They get rid of their status cards and squat on Crown lands and follow teachings from people like Peter O'Chiese (hereditary Chief from Alberta). We've heard stories how their modest homes are mysteriously set on fire, forcing them to relocate. But these people are extreme cases and not everyone is willing or able to take such risks for their rights.

Joseph: A lot of our Chiefs and leaders try to heed Canadian legislation; they need it to function and provide for their bands.

Yael: The system favours the Canadian government and determines that First Nations are limited in their sovereignty. In Palestine there was an attempt at an agreement, and more recently the *Oslo Agreement* in '93,[9] which created the Palestinian Authority, to ostensibly allow Palestinians some level of governance, some control over their own properties and lands. But in fact these agreements and the Authority have been hugely compromised. Palestinians have really lost faith in the possibility that the Palestinian Authority could have any kind of independence because Israel controls everything. Israel always has the upper hand whether it's about people getting permits to go into Jerusalem, or whether it's about building permits, or whether one can leave the country, let alone controlling resources such as water rights, farming, or access to ports.

Joseph: Same narrative as it is here, similar because it will happen outside of our knowing. While we're negotiating with bureaucracy the corporations are going in and mining and cutting down trees, polluting and patenting medicines.

Yael: A few years ago I read this analogy of the sandwich addressing the negotiation over land[10] and specifically the Oslo agreements by Palestinian intellectual and author Edward Said—you and I are sitting across the table from each other and we're discussing how we're going to share this sandwich and I'm eating the sandwich while we're talking about it.

Joseph: Yeah, that's a good analogy. A very prominent leader from way up north knew and spoke his language so his leadership fostered a solid identity among his people. He was working within the basis of the natural laws, not anything man-made.

Cheryl: We have visited hereditary chiefs in some of the communities we've spent time in who were well respected by the people because more than just having knowledge of history they also understood what was happening on a spiritual and ecological level too. Though not all are currently elected chiefs, they embody their sense of responsibility on an intrinsic level that spans across space and time.

Joseph: Yes, exactly. Cheryl already mentioned hereditary Chief Peter O'Chiese, but we know another from northwest of Saskatoon in Saskatchewan who still lives by traditional Cree principles that are built on natural laws.

Reservations to Apartheid

Yael: There was one other connection that I wanted to make because I've read in a number of places that the whole reservation system that was implemented in North America actually influenced the way that apartheid was developed in South Africa.

Cheryl: I've heard that too that the South Africans were looking for and saw the Canadian system and went back and developed the townships on what they witnessed.

Yael: By extension—in Israel and Palestine—that system in South Africa has influenced *Hafradah* (meaning "separation" in Hebrew), which is official Israeli policy. There are people who object to the use of the term "apartheid" being applied to Israel's occupation of the West Bank and of Gaza saying, "well it's not the same," and of course none of these separations, cultural genocides, whatever, none of them are ever exactly the same. But that does not mean that the term is not applicable, and certainly it fits the United Nations' definition of apartheid. It's worthwhile to think about this genealogy: what happened to First Nations people in Canada then migrates to South Africa then to Israel/Palestine and that these political systems are connected.

Cheryl: It's like we've been forced to live in a petri dish under constant scrutiny and in a fixed environment so our characteristics could be monitored and understood. Then factors and elements were added to gauge a response. The findings from this experiment were sold to the rest of the world.

Histories

Joseph: There was a time here in the fifties when we couldn't gather or they'd separate us.

Cheryl: And ceremonies were outlawed.

Joseph: At one point the government tried to retrieve all the treaty medals that had originally been given out to try to stop or deny what they represented:[11] the Canadian agreement according to international law. There were times when they just shamed the people—a practice where they'd line up all the Elders and confiscate their sacred pipes and destroy them by throwing them into a fire. Something akin to desecrating the Holy Grail.

Cheryl: Joseph was involved with The Office of the Treaty Commission in Saskatchewan and they produced a great book entitled *Treaty Elders of Saskatchewan*.[12] The thing about the book I think is so important is it presents the treaties from an Aboriginal perspective that is still rooted in the old ways and explains how kind, generous, and caring the people are. I think in the same way that you, Yael, are a Jewish woman who is very responsible about this whole issue around land and identity in an honourable way—it's something inclusive. So there's a concept the old people talk about that is essentially pre-treaty.

Joseph: It's *wêtaskêwin* and means "living in harmony with one another." For example, I come from Sturgeon Lake and the land is not really owned by individual people, it's a communal piece of land owned by everyone. There's no such thing as ownership on reservations, but there are roles, responsibilities, and agreements. We share the resources of the land.

Yael: It was amazing to me to find out that over nine hundred treaties have not been settled in Canada.

Joseph: There's still a lot of shame Canadians feel today. In high school they know nothing about First Nations, Inuit, or Métis people. They get to university and study us and suddenly they are aware of their history—it's a shame to be a citizen of this country, Canada. Treaties are now being taught in elementary school to a degree as well as high school, yet it's still not compulsory learning for university.

Yael: The rationale and politics that prevail in both locations are: you lost, so go away and shut up. Histories are erased. It's counterproductive to what people really need—to know their own histories and to act out of that knowledge.

Joseph: It's difficult to watch your documentary work. It pushes buttons and reminds me how I was treated in residential school. On an emotional and psychological level what you portray is now that we're safe at the moment, and having signed treaty we are now trying to be more equal in our efforts to bring fair treatment at all stages of the Treaty Rights fulfillment owing to First Nations from here on in.

Cheryl: It really does connect the greater peace with the world, what's happening in the lands that your documentary films are about. When we start to drive off the people who have a deep connection to the land, the ceremony of communing with the land is disrupted and these are some of the very rituals that help keep the world on its axis.

Yael: Being close to the land and working the land, having that connection, is an incredibly powerful place to be. That has been lost, certainly for me. I can bring some analysis about the disruption and displacement, but I don't have a connection that comes out of place. I think it is necessary to have a different kind of system, to be able to hear and understand and interact with First Nations communities and Elders, and to likewise think about and access the histories that are here.

Joseph: To remain calm and peaceful and follow the essentials of kindness, love, respect, and sharing and to continue practising our rituals and prayers is for me the only way. It's all about balance.

Notes

1   McLeod, N. (2007). *Cree Narrative Memory: From Treaties to Contemporary Times*. Saskatoon, SK: Purich Publishing.

2   See: Castellano, Marlene Brant, Linda Archibald, and Mike DeGagné (2008:1). Introduction: Aboriginal Truths in the Narrative of Canada. In Marlene Brant Castellano, Linda Archibald, and Mike DeGagné (eds.), *From Truth To Reconciliation, Transforming the Legacy of Residential Schools*. Ottawa, ON: Aboriginal Healing Foundation.

3   FTP/HGL (2010, October 30). Israel attacks anti-apartheid wall demo. PressTV [online]. Retrieved 4 November 2010 from: http://www.presstv.ir/detail/148838.html

4   Parrott, R. (1995). Opinion: Dividing Palestine [letter to the editor]. *The New York Times*, 23 July 1995. Retrieved 10 February 2011 from: http://www.nytimes.com/1995/07/23/opinion/l-dividing-palestine-184795.html?src=pm A

5   Yael, b.h. (Director/Filmmaker) (2006). *The Palestine Trilogy: Documentations in History, Land and Hope* [Film]. Canada: b.h. Yael. Available at: http://www.vtape.org

6   When Joseph and I were the Storytellers-in-Residence for Meadow Lake Tribal Council (Joseph by himself from 1995–1997 and the both of us from 1997–2001), we hosted many events. This information came from a 1995/6 event called, Pê-Âcimow/Ho-ne: Come and tell a Story, which brought Elders from the nine MLTC First Nations to the Flying Dust Gymnasium for an evening of sharing stories. This story and information from Mr. Bekkattla came from this event.

7   In 1998, Maria Campbell hosted 4th Line Theatre and several theatre artists, storytellers and performance artists on her land at Gabriel's Crossing, to workshop a script by Bruce Sinclair (replaced by Greg Daniels in 2000) and Robert Winslow called, The Bell of Batoche. During the evening Maria would come out and sit with us by the fire and tell us stories. This information was from one such evening storytelling session.

8   Government of Canada (1969). Statement of the Government of Canada on Indian Policy, 1969, 28th Parliament, 1st Session by the Honourable Jean Chrétien, Minister of Indian Affairs and Northern Development. Ottawa, ON: Indian Affairs and Northern Development.

9   United Nations Relief and Works Agency for Palestine (1993, September 13). Declaration of Principles on Interim Self-Government Arrangements ("Oslo Agreement"), A/RES/50/28. Retrieved 4 November 2010 from: http://www.unhcr.org/refworld/docid/3de5e96e4.html

10 This metaphor has morphed from sandwich to pizza, retaining the same idea of a refusal to negotiate in good faith. See Avi Schlaim's blog entry, The Dishonest Broker. Available at: http://newsgroups.derkeiler.com/Archive/Soc/soc.retirement/2010-10/msg01999.html

11 See: Federation of Saskatchewan Indian Nations. Available at: http://www.fsin.com/index.php/component/content/article/1-latest-news/489-fsin-communique-september-24-2010.html

12 Cardinal, Harold and Walter Hildebrandt (2000). *Treaty Elders of Saskatchewan: Our Dream Is That Our Peoples Will One Day Be Clearly Recognized As Nations*. Calgary, AB: University of Calgary Press.

Sandra Semchuk (with James Nicholas) and

Elwood Jimmy

relocation dislocates

Seeds of Lubestrok and *Stolen Strength* are two works from a substantial body of work that Sandra and James used to trace and deepen the dialogue between the indigenous and the non-indigenous in Canada. James and Sandra recognized that their intercultural marriage was, in day-to-day life, an opportunity to make political, social, and psychological structures created by histories of colonialism, occupation of the land, and racism visible to themselves and others through their art practices. The late **James Nicholas** was Rock Cree from Nelson House, Manitoba. His great-grandfather was medicine man Pierre Moose. His parents, Lionel and Sarah, used traditional medicines to help their community. James grew up traditionally on the trapline. At the age of eight he was sent to residential school. In the 1970s he studied in British Columbia working with Bob Manuel, son of native strategist George Manuel, while continuing his dialogues with political activists Rodney Spence and Phil Fontaine from Manitoba. He provided leadership to his community in education, economic development, and government-to-government liaison. In the 1990s James relocated to Vancouver where he engaged the arts of acting, writing, and art. He made many collaborative works with his wife, **Sandra Semchuk**, and these challenge the known history of relations between First Nations and settler cultures. James was killed in 2007 when he fell from a cliff at a fishing camp on the Fraser River. Sandra is Ukrainian Canadian, a photographer and videographer. Sandra grew up in a grocery store in Meadow Lake, Saskatchewan. Martin Semchuk was a socialist who helped bring in medicare to Saskatchewan. Her mother ran the grocery store. Sandra's photographic collaborations and video works use autobiography and dialogue as the basis for recognition and identity. She collaborated with her father through four near-death experiences. As a partner in Treaties (where there are Treaties in Canada), member of the settler culture and widow of James Nicholas, Sandra tries to disrupt myths that historically have shaped settler relations to First Nations, using personal experience as a basis for storytelling. A number of collaborations with James are still in production after his death. Sandra teaches at Emily Carr University of Art and Design in Vancouver and has recently completed a residency in Prince Albert, Saskatchewan, sponsored by the Indigenous Peoples Artists Collective and Common Weal Community Arts. Her collaborations are exhibited nationally and internationally.

Elwood Jimmy is originally from the Thunderchild First Nation in west central Saskatchewan. Currently based in the city of Regina, he is the director of Sâkêwêwak Artists' Collective, southeastern Saskatchewan's centre for contemporary Aboriginal art production, presentation, and education. Apart from his work with Sâkêwêwak, Elwood works independently as an artist, curator, and writer. His work has been presented across Canada in several communities from British Columbia to Quebec and the Northwest Territories.

'On Loan': Thoughts on stolen strength, seeds of lubestrok, seeds of truth, seeds of reconciliation

A conversation on the collaborative work of Sandra Semchuk and James Nicholas[1]

Long before the arrival of the Europeans, *papâmihâw asiniy* falls to the earth; it is revered as a gift, a sign, a protector, as medicine from the Creator to the First Peoples of the plains.

In 1821, George Millward McDougall is born. In 1860, as the newly appointed Chairman of the Western Methodist Missionary District, McDougall establishes and oversees missions all over the region that we now know as Manitoba, Saskatchewan, and Alberta, including the Victoria Mission on the north bank of the North Saskatchewan River.

In 1866, McDougall encounters *papâmihâw asiniy.*

McDougall promptly and boldly steals *papâmihâw asiniy* from its original site in efforts to strip all vestiges of Aboriginal culture and world view. It is moved to the farmyard of the Victoria Mission. McDougall believes by stealing *papâmihâw asiniy*, the First Peoples will embrace the church. It has the opposite effect. Fearing more conflict, McDougall has *papâmihâw asiniy* taken to Winnipeg, where it is taken to Victoria College in Toronto, where it is taken to the Royal Ontario Museum vault.

I do not know the truth of this iron rock, this fallen meteor, as did my late husband, Pau was stik, James Nicholas, or as you, Elwood, do, or as your mother does. I witnessed that James's prayers were humble. Through them he understood Big Bear's realization that when papâmihâw asiniy *was stolen the newcomers' intentions were not good. This was a turning point in the relations between those that had inherent rights to the land, your people Elwood, and those that wanted them.*

My understanding of how the past is the present, is and is not lived through my late husband's eyes, or from my awareness of you Elwood, your compassion, your history, and your struggle to help your people. I am not informed by speaking Cree but through dialogue with James, and with you I have learned something of the depth of the language and the laws and wisdom embedded in language that are in resistance to colonization.

floor

leaving Ukraine
Baba wore three skirts
in the middle one
she sewed, pocketed, enveloped
invisible to the new world
seed of lubestrok
from her Hnatechki
for the new land
thinking
Kakissiskachewhac

floor

stolen strength
(don't call it theft to take it back)

my

relocation dislocates

you

I have witnessed icons of cultures and civilizations destroyed in New York and in Baghdad as attempts to break people, but this theft you speak of is different. Papâmihâw asiniy is not an icon… not a symbol. "It has pim ma tis i win, life itself," as James would tell me, "It is at once animate and inanimate." How can I, a granddaughter of Ukrainian and Polish immigrants know this as you do? How do I hear the prophesies without my mind being clouded by guilt? Or denial and skepticism? How do I protect myself from the truth of how white history betrayed me, made me complicit in terrible historical wrongs?

Medicine men and Elders foretell visions of plague, the loss of the buffalo herds, famine, and war with the removal of *papâmihâw asiniy.*

All the visions of the medicine men and Elders come to fruition within a decade.

Much of the work that James and I did together in dialogue was done here at Murray Lake in Saskatchewan. When the drought came, buffalo bones and teeth revealed a buffalo jump here. James carefully returned the bones to the lake. A dream told him to. This home is across the road from where Big Bear was born on Jackfish Lake. We canoed there to honour him. A great feather rose vertically in the sky. James told me that day that Big Bear, a visionary and an orator and one of the leading chiefs among the buffalo-hunting northern Plains Cree, knew from the prophesies that the buffalo would disappear when papâmihâw asiniy *was taken. Big Bear, James said, knew what his people would face. Although the chains were not yet around his feet, around his wrists—although he had not yet been charged with treason against a nation not his own—Big Bear knew that the white man would force his Cree nation off their land. To this day his people have not received even a reserve.*

Elwood, I know this has been no peaceful settlement. Prince Rupert's evocation of "terra nullius" was a sham. Your people were here. Treaties were signed under duress of possible extinction.

Throughout the twentieth century, aggressive Western expansion continues to relocate and dislocate intact collective-based communities of First People and their connection to their land, their spirit, their culture, their power.

The accompanying migration and agricultural practices of non-Indigenous people transform the land and its use.

My Dad, Martin Semchuk, asked me, "Can you imagine what this land would be like if we had not arrived?" He gave a damn and did what he could to subvert colonization even while participating in it. As Ukrainians we came as pawns of the British to occupy the land, to lay the foundation of a nation by breaking the land. We made the land ours, like the old country, rich with agriculture by breaking the prairie wool and clearing the land. We brought our animals, our plants, our beliefs, our fears, and our hopes for a new beginning, a chance to survive, to exist. Ukraine's existence was denied. We did not see what was here so much as we saw what we had lost and what we had been continually losing for centuries. We attempted to recreate our homeland because that was what we knew, what we desired, and what sustained us, nourished us. It was what we had fought for, lost our lives for, suffered for ... experienced rape, torture, and death. In 1885, when Poundmaker averted the massacre of his people, routed Otters' militia and forced them to flee, serfdom for Ukrainians was abolished by the Austro–Hungarian Empire. We were yet indentured to the land, pawns of other nations who took the grain we produced as payments for the small bits of land that could not easily sustain our children, our grandchildren, and their grandchildren into the futures. We were still slaves. We had to buy our own land back from the conquerors.

Here we expanded. I was told that your people were forced to contract onto reserves and use passes to go off reserve. On your reserve, given by Treaty 6, Thunderchild Reserve, the land was taken yet again and sold to foreign buyers while your people were yet again forced off, dislocated onto poorer land. How did this affect your mother's life, your life, Elwood?

There are few ecologies on earth as utterly transformed as Saskatchewan— this time by the plough. We wrote our names on the land with the seeds we brought. Wheat created a monopoly, expanded at the expense of local flora, fauna, and knowledge.

We did not know that like the Scottish who experienced the Clearances in Scotland and came for a new life in Canada, we were complicit in creating the echoes of the old violences here in the new country. We were after all invited, lured to come with promises of free land.

Whose land?

In 1972, *papâmihâw asiniy*—a connection between earth and sky, between Creator and Creations—makes a return engagement to the Plains region, this time *on loan* to the Royal Alberta Museum from the United Church of Canada.

I know you liked James, Elwood. You were one of the last people to speak with him while he was alive. He respected you and was grateful for how you treated our work.

James and I witnessed papâmihâw asiniy *in forced confinement at the Royal Alberta Museum. Offerings are made there—tobacco and sweetgrass, sage and cloths. First Nations people don't have to pay. I do. James put his hands on* papâmihâw asiniy *and held them there for a long time. Did he give or receive? We learned what we could about where* papâmihâw asiniy *fell. Could we find this sacred place? James was tired, weary from the battle and non-recognition. He collapsed in exhaustion at Rib Rocks. I rested. We found what we think is the site of* papâmihâw asiniy'*s landing, high on a hill. Prairie sage grows there.*

We will not show it in photographs.

James prayed and made offerings. I joined him. We returned to the land at Murray Lake. The plants he has watered, lubestrok, came in small seeds in my great-grandmother's pocket from Ukraine. It has grown large and strong. We ate from this plant and in the fall seeds are gathered so that it can be planted again. Each seed a choice, an action, a gesture of planting, a bending down to the land. James wrote my great-grandmother's story. He put the word Ka kiss is kach e whak,[2] *Saskatchewan, in her mouth, a meal of river moving swiftly around a bend, a meal of land, a province.*

I acknowledge to you, Elwood, that my family's relocation dislocates First Nations just as we had been dislocated from our homes over all of those centuries. I acknowledge that with this awareness comes responsibility. Without taking responsibility for my privilege and for the acts of my grandparents I too become complicit in the ongoing systemic effects of colonization, racism, and non-recognition of the inherent rights and the extraordinary knowledges of First Nations, the laws of being specific to their nations and to the diversity of individuals.

By many accounts spread over centuries, *papâmihâw asiniy* grows heavier with time—heavier in McDougall's farmyard, heavier in Winnipeg, heavier in Toronto.

Heavier with the burden of theft by the people who claim to own it and presume they can 'loan' it?

Heavier with the power and strength of a people, a power and strength—like *papâmihâw asiniy*—temporarily *on loan* and one day restored?

Coming to Canada gave my family possibilities to thrive, to diversify, and become more complex and innovative in the choices each member could make to create their own lives. These possibilities came at a great cost to you from a First Nation as immigration overcame the Indigenous, as plants and animals were destroyed or pushed aside. The choices for First Nations became truncated and limited within paradigms that were not their own.

This stole strength. This stole identity. Marshall Forchuk is a descendent of a Ukrainian internee during WWI in Canada. Ukrainians, Serbians, Croatians, and others with Austro-Hungarian or German passports were imprisoned behind barbed wired like animals, called enemy aliens, and forced to labour for no reason other than where they were born. Forchuk said he learned from his father who escaped the camps, "You can steal my house, you can steal my car and you have taken nothing. But if you steal my identity like we did when we put First Nations kids into residential schools then you have really stolen something." Ukrainians have only recently become white through assimilation, another loss of culture. All those centuries under duress we held our culture sacred. With wealth and security we too are losing culture and language—and, as James would say, our medicine bundles.

Privilege has come at too high a cost. Ukrainians in Canada became respected political leaders and professional in every field. Yet our silence about the injustices done to us re-forms too often in our silence in speaking out against the ongoing effects of colonization against First Nations and Métis. Do we have many of the old terrors of speaking out against authority and abuse? Are we unconsciously afraid of reprisals, being hurt in a less obvious way? Has it become normalized to become perpetrators by denying the truth, creating ongoing suffering? This is not how we think of ourselves. We think of ourselves as good people. Now we think of ourselves as people who have education, power, and authority—not as people who have been made crazy by the violence and abuse of others. Yet we are still in the cycle of violence … polite and legal violence.

Within a contemporary context, *papâmihâw asiniy* synthesizes a number of very basic and universal concepts and laws of being. It also magnifies the challenges regarding the navigation and negotiation of the relationship between the Indigenous and the non-Indigenous—the world views, the people, the animals, the minerals, the plants—that define and mark the story of this place.

Elwood, I watch over and over in nature the violence and community building of plant and animal colonization, the unthinking ways in which plants and animals both dominate and cooperate in order to survive, create communities, and create endless adaptations. Can we think, I wonder, about what we are doing and make choices that embrace the richness of the diversity of nations, the deep wealth that creates possibilities for the planet as it has for us?

Can we acknowledge that we are a part of nature, all my relations' points of views, the knowledges that First Nations have always shared freely with those who were attentive? We are not, as we would believe, the generous ones, although generosity is the basis of many immigrant cultures as much as First Nations cultures.

"You don't understand," James said, "Sharing is the law. The Land owns itself."

Who loans the land? Who will restore the land? The waters?

By working with the land, with our communities, we can work towards spaces of

Decolonization

Transformation

Truth

Reconciliation

Are we there yet? No.

James's best friend, Walter Wastesicoot, visiting now at this home on Murray Lake, was compelled to write the following in response to this text by Elwood and me: As a residential school Survivor, I have learned much of the colonizer's malice. He offers me reconciliation while I have an outstanding case against him for sexual and physical abuse suffered while resident at one of his institutions of assimilation. He offers my people reconciliation while he holds our lands and resources in abeyance, ensuring our continued survival by his hand only. Reconciliation is said to be a personal privilege, offered to one who has made amends for past wrongs. Something is skewed in the colonizer's offer of reconciliation. He carries with him centuries of shame, for which I and my people will continue to suffer in a marginalized existence in his hope for reconciliation.

Does taking responsibility for the effects of colonization diminish the shame?

But the seeds are there.

Notes

1   Elwood Jimmy acknowledges the following resources that were helpful in composing this interaction with Sandra's and James's artwork: *The Alberta Encyclopedia* and the Royal Alberta Museum; Cuthand, Doug (2007). *Askiwina—A Cree World*. Regina, SK: Coteau Books; the Blue Quills First Nations College website (available at: http://www.bluequills.ca/); and the words and thoughts of others, including my mom, who knew about the stone.

2   *Ka kiss is kach e whak* is the spelling of the Rock Cree word used by the late James Nicholas as he understood to be the basis for the word, Saskatchewan. It is this version of the word that appears in the photographic installation.

stolen strength
(don't call it theft to take it back)

Dorothy Christian

Dorothy Christian's Secwepemc (Splatsin) name is Cucw'la7 meaning Meadowlark. In 2007, the old ladies from her community named her this because "she is not afraid to talk….she won't hide anything that has to be revealed, like the meadowlark she travels to see all and [to come home to] talk about it." Dorothy is the eldest of ten, has one daughter and over fifty-five nieces and nephews and great-nieces and -nephews. She has never been to residential school, but was affected intergenerationally because her mother, her aunt, her uncles, and her cousins are residential school Survivors. Dorothy and her siblings are survivors of the next generation of assimilation policies that put them into white foster homes during what is known as the Sixties Scoop. In her life path she seeks truth and reconciliation on all levels: personally, politically, professionally, and spiritually. Dorothy's reclamation of her Indigenous spiritual ways led her to the Black Hills of South Dakota to find her personal truth where she fasted under the guidance of a Sioux Medicine man in 1990. A watershed year that opened up an exploration of what an authentic political truth and reconciliation with the settler peoples in Canada means. Dorothy is currently in Ph.D. studies at the University of British Columbia where she is seeking to reconcile Indigenous and Western systems of knowledge.

Reconciling with The People and the Land?

What is truth and reconciliation to this Secwepemc–Syilx (Shuswap–Okanagan) woman whose homelands lie within a geo-political state where the Prime Minister claims, "*We also have no history of colonialism*"?[1] How does that lack of political will trickle down to the day-to-day activities of my life? I did not attend residential school but my Mother, Aunt, and Uncles did. However, I am a survivor of the "60s Scoop," which was the next wave of assimilation policies that separated me from my Indigenous family and put me in five foster homes in five years time. I ran away every time to go home to see my Granny. She told me, "Go to school, we need to know how those people think."

Luckily, I have a mind for school, but before I could pursue my academic studies, I had to deal with some harsh life lessons that had me "wast[ing] a lot of time spinning my wheels in a destructive anger."[2] In the late 1980s, I started consciously to seek healing from the horrific life experiences that colonialism wrought upon me, my family, and my community. In order to do that, I put Indigenous and settler relationships under scrutiny. Like most people, I only thought of white people as settlers; however, as my healing journey evolved and my experience expanded I turned my attention to non-white settlers too. My examination of Indigenous intersections with non-white settlers from other races, identities, and cultural groups consciously[3] started when I began working on a diverse team of producers with Rita Shelton Deverell at Vision TV where I met Muslims, Hindus, Sikhs, Zoroastrians, Buddhists, Jews, and Christians who came from many different races and cultures. This article is a reflection on some of my healing journey; part of that is seeking a peaceful co-existence with settler folks.

The slide plate under my microscope focused in a very up-close and personal way during the so-called 1990 Oka Crisis in Mohawk territory and then the 1995 Gustafsen Lake standoff in Secwepemc territory. I worked behind the scenes in communications at these two armed land rights conflicts to elevate consciousness to the international media. During the Gustafsen Lake standoff, Ipperwash was happening in Ontario at the same time. I experienced first-hand the psychological warfare of the Canadian military.[4] My healing journey towards my truth and reconciliation with the settler peoples was catapulted forward by these two life-changing events. Since these modern-day Indian wars where two lives were lost[5] I have been asking, "Is it possible to have peaceful co-existence within a state that denies its colonial history and will mobilize their military against the Original Peoples?"

During the 1990s, a highly volatile time in Canada, Indigenous communications were largely ignored by the national media while most sensationalized the violence and promoted coverage that "racialized and criminalized" images of the people defending the land rights. In the 1990 78-day siege, only one media outlet, the multi-faith and multicultural broadcaster, Vision TV, picked up on my press releases about a peaceful, spiritual cross-country run initiated by the Syilx (Okanagan) and the Secwepemc (Shuswap). In 1995, during the Gustafsen Lake standoff, my cell phone was scrambled and the RCMP media liaison tried to exclude me from the press scrums. I refused to be intimidated and declared that I was accredited media and worked for a national broadcaster, but I and my questions were ignored in the subsequent press scrums where I was the only person of colour.

After 1990 I wanted to leave this country, which had demonstrated such hateful behaviour towards us, but then I thought, "Where would I go, this is my homeland. This is where my people have been for generations and generations!" Since then I have often wondered what immigrants think when they come to this country. I wonder what it feels like to leave their homelands, especially the more recent immigrant groups who are largely non-white and are forced to leave their traditional lands because of war, political instability, or other untenable circumstances.

Many other questions arose in the following decade while I uncovered what truth and reconciliation mean to me. My interrogation centred on how Indigenous peoples relate to the settler peoples who have chosen our homelands as their place of residency. This line of questioning motivated my engagement in many activities. When I examine my personal and political involvements since the 1990s, I see that my work has focused on many facets of Indigenous and non-Indigenous relationships in Canada.

Following Oka, I developed a relationship with Rita Shelton Deverell who was then Vice-President of Production and Presentation at Vision TV and one of the founders of the specialty station, which is the only multi-faith broadcaster in the world. She mentored and trained me to produce for television and contracted me as part of a team of multi-faith and multicultural producers from across Canada for eight television seasons. Rita's leadership had a critical impact in my quest of examining whether or not a peaceful coexistence was possible with settler cultures in Canada.

One significant memory I have is at an annual party at Rita's home in Toronto. I remember standing at the edge of the room with my camera eye on and watching my fellow producers from all cultures and faith groups, some of them dressed in their traditional garb, dancing, and some people laughing as they engaged in lively conversations. I thought how incredible this scene was, and I wished Canadians could see this. Here we were individuals from the spectrum of the multicultural mosaic of Canada, all working towards upholding the mandate of the program, which included peace. This does not mean we all agreed on political, social, or spiritual issues; however, we were able to go beyond the parameters of the "tolerance" policies of diversity and actually extend respect to each other's point of view. I have come to recognize my time at Vision TV as a very blessed experience because racism, sexism, and homophobia were given assumptions when producing our stories. I may have an idealistic memory of my experience because I was not located in Toronto where, no doubt, there were the usual office politics that I was thankfully not a part of. However, I do know from this experience that it is possible to work in a peaceful way while coexisting with other cultural groups in the cultural interface.

Throughout the evolution of my multi-dimensional identity—that is, my personal, political, social, spiritual, and academic development—I have looked closely at the intersections of race, identity, and culture, including the multiple histories of the settler peoples in coexistence with Indigenous peoples. My quest started by examining the "white people" settlers, which I discuss extensively in *The History of a Friendship or Some Thoughts on Becoming Allies.*[6]

In my history with Victoria Freeman, a thirteenth-generation North American settler,[7] we have decolonized ourselves and looked at what institutional decolonization might look like. Decolonization is one of those big conceptual words that encompass many things and no doubt means different things to different people. For me it meant dealing with the deeply embedded racism we felt towards each other and deconstructing the many preconceived notions we had about each other to finally reach a place where we can honour each other's dignity and achieve a true reconciliation as human beings. Luckily, both Victoria and I had the tenacity and desire to develop our *decolonized* relationship. It is a difficult and sometimes heartbreaking process that requires a level of commitment to a relationship that is rarely found in friendships.

In 2003, Victoria and I were invited to a conference in Switzerland where we addressed an audience of 700 people from diverse cultures from around the world. We co-presented about our colonizer-colonized relationship in Canada. In my talk, I suggested the colonization process was brutal and that both sides of the colonial divide needed to engage in a healing process. However, before healing could begin, the reality of the situation had to be acknowledged.

> When referring to my relationship with the colonizers of my land, many times I apply the metaphor of an abusive relationship; that is, as a 'colonized' person I am the assumed victim, and the colonial state, including the settlers, is the offender. In an abusive relationship, the offender controls the situation with a constant threat of violence that creates a situation where both parties 'walk on eggshells' around each other because at any given moment violence may erupt. In the dysfunctional relationship between Indigenous peoples and the settler peoples of North America, there is an undefined 'walking on eggshells' that sits between us as a 'pregnant pause' or as a very LOUD silence.[8]

I see the three armed conflicts in Canada during the 1990s as Indigenous peoples "breaking the silence" about the abusive behaviour of the colonizing settler governments in Canada. When a victim breaks the silence in an abusive relationship, this is a clear call for change because the status quo of the old relationship is no longer acceptable. If both parties take responsibility for their actions and/or non-actions, then the healing can begin.

In our old relationship with the settlers, there is a normalized notion of white European settler peoples; however, in this time of globalization, the settler face has changed to include the faces of the many, many other peoples from diverse cultures who immigrate to our homelands, seeking a new home. Now the settler face includes people from all the countries of the African continent, people from China, Taiwan, Hong Kong, Japan, India, Pakistan, Eastern Europe, countries of the Middle East, the South East Asian countries, such as Malaysia, Indonesia, and Thailand, and people from the UK, Australia, and New Zealand continue to immigrate to these lands.

In 2002, when writer Lee Maracle was scholar-in-residence at the University of Western Washington in Bellingham, she hosted a conference to discuss Native–Chinese relations that set off a chain of involvements for me. In 2004, I started researching a film on Native–Chinese relations in my territories, which started an exploration of the relationship with one of the longest standing, non-white settler communities in Canada. I found stories in our shared oral histories that revealed how Indigenous peoples have familial relationships with the Chinese that started in the late 1800s.[9] I discovered that economic partnerships were developed in the mid-1950s in the interior of BC where Chinese farmers leased lands on reserve and hired Indigenous people. In August 2004, I was invited to speak at a "Walk with Women Warriors" workshop in Chinatown[10] where I acknowledged our shared oppressions and discussed some of the shared history I had uncovered.[11] At the end of my talk, I asked the Chinese community who would be standing next to me the next time an army tank is coming at me? Since then my conversation with the settler peoples of Canada has expanded and evolved.

In September 2007, I was invited to participate on a conference panel, "Women, Resistance, and Cultural/Community Activism—Catalyzing Agents: The Ethics of Doing 'Asian Canadian',"[12] where I took the opportunity to expand the conversation, beyond the Chinese-Canadian communities, to include the Japanese-Canadian and Indo-Canadian participants. I explained that this was not a comfortable conversation for me as the only Indigenous person in the room; however, growth and change can only happen when we deal with the hard issues. At the end of my presentation, I asked them *when* they were going to start giving back to the lands they had chosen as their new home and, also, *what* they would give back.

In February 2009, I was invited to do a keynote address at the University of Victoria's Diversity Conference, "Critical Conversation Continue," where the spectrum of settler communities was represented in the community-engaged researchers, students, faculty, and community members. My talk was an hour long so I was able to link a number of issues; however, the primary focus was media (mis)representation of Indigenous peoples in Canadian programming. I started with *wartime images*, *peacetime images*, and then discussed *alliance building*. In looking at how the Canadian screen culture manages the visual narratives about Indigenous peoples, I gave a critical analysis of some of the television programming in Canada. In my keynote address, I included:

> How many of you watch Canadian TV? Have any of you seen *The Border?* It's quite an exciting and very dynamic series produced by Peter Raymont at the CBC. It's been receiving lots of attention. I make a point of watching it, not only because I like the stories but because from time to time, they include Indigenous people in their scripts. The writers of that series have not erased us. They are dealing with contemporary race issues in Canada at the fictional immigration agency.

> On the other hand, another CBC series, *Little Mosque on the Prairie* totally exists in a bubble. Apparently, this Muslim community in Saskatchewan has no Cree, Métis or Sioux people in that little town. I stopped watching the series when I saw that we weren't included in the scripts. I sent a question via their blog; I asked the writers of the series why their scripts do not include the Indigenous peoples of Saskatchewan. And of course I have not had a response. Ironically, this series has been syndicated in the Middle East where the land issue between the Palestinians and the Israelis is the cause of a major war (that has huge global implications); yet, here in Canada they do not deal with the original peoples who also contest the presence of the settlers on the land.[13]

While I understand the necessity of creative freedom in writing scripts, is it not the ethical responsibility of the writers of Canadian series television to also address the complexities of living on the lands of the Original Peoples? How many Canadian producers hire Indigenous writers for their writing teams? When will Canadian producers stop bringing us in as mere "cultural consultants" for our opinions/suggestions, which are rarely incorporated and hardly ever includes the opportunity to submit an invoice for our time? When will they start hiring us for the substantive key creative positions as directors, directors of photography, or as supervising editors? There are enough of us with experience and training now.

It's complicated, but it is all interrelated. At the University of Victoria, I also linked Indigenous–settler relations in terms of the environment; the lands that people have chosen to make their home. At the Victoria conference I explained how, in many Indigenous cultures, there is a concept of *giving back*—it is complicated yet very simple. For instance, when we go out on the land, we don't take more than what is to be used for that season. If a person is being responsible, they will give back to the land by taking care of their picking grounds, they will do what is needed to take care of those lands that provide food. Another simpler example is when we go and harvest trees and branches to build a sweat lodge, we offer tobacco and ask the tree for its blessing as we explain what the branches are to be used for. Of course, I acknowledge it is much more complicated in human relations. My point is, we can't just keep taking and taking and taking and not give something back.

Settler peoples come from all over the world to these lands to reap the benefits of this land of milk and honey, and they send their financial and other resources to their homelands. What do they give back to the Original Peoples of these lands? Do they ever take the time to learn about the Indigenous people whose lands they occupy?

In the healing process, once the silence is broken and each party is taking responsibility for their part of the relationship and relating to each other as dignified, autonomous human beings, then a new relationship can begin. I see that a new way of being in the cultural interface of Indigenous peoples and all settler communities has to begin with a shared active engagement in the decolonizing process while simultaneously participating in a cultural healing of both communities, which I believe is necessary for both Indigenous peoples and non-Indigenous settler peoples of Canada.

One of the major things I have learned from my intercultural relationships with both white and non-white settlers is that it is critical to relate outside of the usual colonial binary of the colonizer and the colonized. In this approach, Indigenous peoples are consistently relegated to the "victim" role, which paralyzes our ability to assume responsibility for our actions and locks us in the perceptions of the common stereotypes; that is, the "noble savage," Hollywood's monosyllabic Tonto, the stoic cigar store Indian, the rebellious Billy Jack hero, the natural environmentalist, or the all-knowing spiritual Medicine Man or Woman. You know, the one with all that "woo-woo" spiritual energy who can do magical things!

In my intercultural work, the primary focus has been searching for and trying to understand what "peaceful coexistence" means in the cultural interface for Indigenous peoples who want to maintain their ancestral ties to their homelands, yet work together with the larger societies in seeking a sustainable environment where Indigenous peoples can finally realize some economic benefits. How can we work together? How do we stand together in alliances to fend off the globalization machine that perpetuates a neo-colonial approach? The land is integral to Indigenous cultures and, I argue, is the cause for the very "LOUD silence" that sits between us because "I believe this is founded in the fear that Indigenous peoples want the land back, that our suppressed rage compounded over centuries will explode at any given time on any given territory."[14]

> Settlers know that the original peoples of Canada have a birthright to our lands and any benefits from its resources. I truly believe the denial of this entitlement and the lack of integrity that the settler governments have in the colonial relationship is at the core of this fear. Settler governments know they have assumed a privilege and an entitlement to these lands; yet, at the same time they deny the privilege and entitlement of Indigenous peoples.[15]

Although many Canadians in the interfaith groups and cultural activists may theoretically understand the lack of integrity of the governments assuming this privilege on the land, it is difficult to exercise effective political actions that may change the status quo, because any real change is neutralized by diversity policies.

Over the years, I have witnessed how we come together oh-so-politely under the diversity policies that promote being tolerant of each other. I have sat in meetings where we are working together on a shared goal; however, when it comes to the human part of developing relationships, many people have to run to other meetings, answer phone calls/texts, or some other *more important* activities. Admittedly, most of the people who are engaged in intercultural/interfaith work are overtaxed as it is, and until we take the time to get to know each other as human beings, I see the activist community getting stuck in the policies of regulating aversion,[16] rather than engaging in a truly respectful, collaborative, and peaceful approach. In her book,

Regulating Aversion: Tolerance in an Age of Identity and Empire, Wendy Brown says, "It is noteworthy, too, that within this [tolerance] discourse the aim of learning tolerance is not to arrive at equality or solidarity with others but, rather, to learn how to put up with others."[17] If what Brown says is true that the tolerance discourse of Western liberalism regulates the presence of the Other both inside and outside the liberal democratic nation-state and that the notion of tolerance "affects all levels and domains of civil engagement"[18] while it acts as a "substitute for or as a supplement to formal liberal equality [that can] block the pursuit of substantive equality and freedom,"[19] then individuals and groups within the nation-state of Canada need to formulate new models of interrelating outside a tolerance discourse (including diversity or multicultural policies) that literally paralyzes a substantive reconciliation in this pluralistic society.

For me, part of reconciliation is taking the time to build respectful relationships and to create opportunities where we develop a new model of interrelating, a model that takes us beyond the usual multicultural sharing of food and dance and walks towards an authentic reconciliation. This will require a complex, multi-faceted approach; however, if the political will and desire of settler and Indigenous communities are there, I truly believe it is possible to build a peaceful coexistence with each other.

Some of this is happening all across the country;[20] however, there are still complications and contradictions to the Indigenous reality in Canada that cause incongruent perceptions. The spin doctors for the provincial and federal governments in Canada perpetuate many myths about our reality. The mainstream media manage mainstream Canada's perceptions of us by writing about how privileged we are to be receiving tax exemption, yet they do not write about the long overdue back rent that is owed to our communities. If we are so privileged, then why are our suicide rates in our communities so high? Why are our men and women overrepresented in prison populations? Why are our women being murdered and disappearing off the streets and highways of this country? Why are our kids still not graduating from high school? And, why is there still a need for our kids to be in foster homes?

Is it not time for Canada to take true responsibility for its violent history with the Indigenous populations of these lands? Oh, I know we had a Royal Commission on Aboriginal Peoples in 1991 (after the three Modern-Day Indian Wars), then we had an apology from the Prime Minister in 2008, and now we have the Truth and Reconciliation Commission. My questions are: Will this be another commission that the mainstream media will regularly report as one whose costs come out of the Canadian taxpayers' pockets? And, will this be yet another lovely report that will sit on the shelves of many bureaucrats' offices, and that Indigenous political leaders refer to in pursuing real actions to bring about social change?

In a dysfunctional violent relationship, the abuser often pays off their victim; that is, if the abuser is a man, he will buy dresses, jewellery, vacations, and new cars to maintain the silence, to maintain the status quo. I do not mean to diminish the experience of the residential school Survivors; however, I wonder if this is what happened in the apology and the compensations that some people received for the horrific experiences they had as children. Have we been bought off?

It is time to set the record straight—we are NOT one of the special interest groups that the so-called liberal democracy of Canada is managing. We, as the Original Peoples of this country, have a unique social, political, and legal position because our Aboriginal Rights and Title are constitutionally protected in Canada. The policy-makers of the so-called diversity or multicultural policies in this country need to acknowledge that difference, rather than pitting us against the Other communities of colour.

The time has come for both parties of the dysfunctional, violent relationship to change the status quo in Canada by enacting an authentic reconciliation[21] that requires hard work on both sides. Indigenous Peoples are doing our part, slowly but surely—healing ourselves, our families, our communities, our Nations. When is Canada going to step up to the plate and start writing policies that bring about real change and not just manage how they tolerate our presence? What is each immigrant group going to do about building relationships with the peoples whose lands they reside on?

Notes

1   Stephen Harper made this statement at a G20 meeting in Pittsburgh, Pennsylvania, in September 2009 after he made the apology to residential school Survivors in Canada's legislature in 2008. Retrieved 4 April 2010 from Harsha Walia Blog at: http://communities.canada.com/vancouversun/blogs/communityofinterest/archive/2009/09/28/really-harper-canada-has-no-history-of-colonialism.aspx

2   Christian, D. and V. Freeman (2010). The history of a friendship or some thoughts on becoming allies. In L. Davis (ed.). *Alliances: Re/Envisioning Indigenous-non-Indigenous Relationships*. Toronto, ON: University of Toronto Press.

3   I say consciously because when I was a child I read the book, *Black Like Me*, by John Howard Griffin. I distinctly remember hiding under the covers reading this book with a flashlight. I wonder if this is when I started questioning race? Griffin, John Howard (1961). *Black Like Me*. New York, NY: Houghton Mifflin.

4   Christian and Freeman (2010).

5   Corporal Lemay was killed at Oka in 1990. In 1995 while Gustafsen Lake was occurring in British Columbia, Dudley George was killed at Ipperwash Park in Ontario.

6   Christian and Freeman (2010).

7   Freeman is the author of: Freeman, V. (2000). *Distant Relations: How My Ancestors Colonized North America*. Toronto, ON: McClelland & Stewart Ltd.

8   Christian and Freeman (2010:381).

9   I wrote an article for the fall issue of *Rice Paper Magazine* in 2004 discussing some aspects of the historical relationship between Indigenous and Chinese peoples. I named the article "Is it Racism or is it Xenophobia?" and the editors changed the title to "Articulating the Silence." See: Christian, Dorothy (2004). Articulating the Silence. *Rice Paper Magazine* 9(3):22–31.

10 Christian, D. (2008:19). Remapping Activism (transcript of talk given on 28 August 2004). *West Coast Line* 42(1):15–20.

11 It is prudent to acknowledge that in my research of Native-Chinese relations in Canada, I have come to understand the complexities of the diverse Chinese diaspora and realize that the Chinese community is not one monolithic group. There are Chinese immigrants whose families came to these lands in the late 1800s, and the following waves of immigration include: Chinese from Singapore, Taiwan, Hong Kong, and China. The diversity of the Chinese diaspora brings unique cultural and historical experiences of why they chose to come to these lands.

12 The conference, The 1907 Race Riots and Beyond: A Century of TransPacific Canada, was co-sponsored by University of Victoria, University of British Columbia, and Simon Fraser University and held at SFU's downtown campus.

13 Information regarding syndication of *Little Mosque on the Prairie* was retrieved February 2009 from: http://www.theglobeandmail.com/servlet/story/ RTGAM.20070109.wlivezarqao110/BNStory/specialComment/home

14 Christian and Freeman (2010:381).

15 Christian and Freeman (2010:381).

16 Brown, W. (2006). *Regulating Aversion: Tolerance in the Age of Identity and Empire*. Princeton, NJ: Princeton University Press.

17 Brown (2006:184). Wendy Brown's critical analysis of the tolerance discourse and how it functions within contemporary liberal democracies deserves a whole chapter, if not a whole book, in terms of how its findings relate to Indigenous populations within the so-called liberal democracies of this globalized world.

18 Brown (2006:8).

19 Brown (2006:9).

20 At the 2006 Re-Envisioning Relationships Conference at Trent University, I witnessed many projects across this country where Indigenous and non-Indigenous peoples were working together towards a peaceful coexistence by building alliances outside the usual colonial relationship. These efforts are documented in: Davis, Lynne (ed.) (2010). *Alliances: Re/Envisioning Indigenous-non-Indigenous Relationships*. Toronto, ON: University of Toronto Press.

21 The theoretical framework for what I understand to be an "authentic reconciliation" comes from: Sutherland, Jessie (2005). *Worldview Skills: Transforming Conflict from the Inside Out*. Sooke, BC: Worldview Strategies Publications. See pages 19–40.

Rita Wong

Rita Wong was born where the traditional lands of the Tsuu T'ina (Sarcee), Siksika (Blackfoot) and Stoney First Nations intersect, otherwise known as Calgary. She lives and works on unceded Coast Salish territories, the lands of the Musqueam, Squamish, and Tsleil-Waututh Nations, also known as Vancouver. As a recipient of a fellowship from the Center for Contemplative Mind in Society, she has developed a humanities course that explores how cultural perspectives shape our interactions with water. Rita is the author of three books of poetry: *sybil unrest* (co-written with Larissa Lai, Line Books, 2008), *forage* (Nightwood, 2007), and *monkeypuzzle* (Press Gang, 1998). She received the Asian Canadian Writers Workshop Emerging Writer Award in 1997 and the Dorothy Livesay Poetry Prize in 2008. Her poems have appeared in anthologies such as *Prismatic Publics: Innovative Canadian Women's Poetry and Poetics*; *Regreen: New Canadian Ecological Poetry*; *A Verse Map of Vancouver*; *Rocksalt: an Anthology of Contemporary BC Poetry*; *Making a Difference: Canadian Multicultural Literature*; *Canadian Literature in English*; *The Harbrace Anthology of Poetry*; *Visions of BC*; *The Common Sky: Canadian Writers Against the War*; *Swallowing Clouds*; *Shift*; *Switch*; and more. Building from her doctoral dissertation that examined labour in Asian North American literature, her work investigates the relationships between contemporary poetics, social justice, ecology, and decolonization. Rita serves as Associate Professor in Critical and Cultural Studies at the Emily Carr University of Art and Design. She is currently researching the poetics of water with the support of a SSHRC Research/Creation grant in a project entitled Downstream.

What Would Restitution and Regeneration Look Like from the Point of View of Water?

Close to its headwaters, *stal'əw*,[1] otherwise known as the Fraser River, is clear translucent jade, liquid magic.

Fraser Crossing is the farthest point along the Fraser River that one can reach easily by car, without taking a day's hike into the Rocky Mountains. Recently, I went there as part of a trip to pay my respects to *stal'əw*, which, in its ceaseless flow for roughly 12 million years,[2] has created the landscape on which I live, otherwise known as Vancouver.

At Fraser Crossing, what I found in addition to the beautiful, burgeoning river, shocked me: a high pressure petroleum pipeline had been built underneath the river.

There in the so-called "protected wilderness" of Mount Robson Provincial Park, the Trans Mountain Pipeline has already been very busy.[3] In fact, the old 24-inch diameter pipeline has been joined by a new 30-inch to 36-inch diameter pipeline alongside it, accelerating the extraction of oil from the tar sands. The expanded pipeline runs from Hinton, Alberta, to Tete Jaune Cache, British Columbia.[4]

Currently, I am researching the meanings of water, and what the river taught me on this trip is that it is in danger from petroleum.

The day before I started writing this essay, a pipeline leak in Michigan released roughly 3 million litres of oil into the aptly named Battle Creek and Kalamazoo River.[5]

Months before I wrote this essay, we all heard about the horrific and enormous oil spill into the Gulf of Mexico.

Just imagine the pipelines and the rivers after an earthquake on the Pacific Rim, along the ring of fire.

You might wonder, what does this have to do with truth and reconciliation?

Everything, for me. And, I would propose, for you too.

Many authors in *Response, Responsibility, and Renewal*[6] have pointed out that an apology for the residential school system without appropriate action would be meaningless and could indeed damage the Canadian government's credibility. Thinkers ranging from Waziyatawin to Ian Mackenzie to Valerie Galley all assert the need for meaningful action. Roland Chrisjohn and Tanya Wasacase suggest that giving testimony at the Truth and Reconciliation Commission without concurrent substantive, structural changes is like giving a placebo to residential school Survivors.[7] As Alfred Taiaiake insightfully notes, reconciliation without restitution will only lead to a perpetuation of injustice. He writes, "When I speak of restitution, I am speaking of restoring ourselves as peoples, our spiritual power, dignity, and the economic bases for our autonomy."[8]

As anyone who studies even a little bit of ecology soon realizes, the economy depends on the environment, on the health of the land, the watershed. What systemic colonial violence tried to do was to remove the deep connections between Indigenous peoples and the watersheds to which they belong. It failed, but it has not given up, as the pipeline underneath the Fraser reminds us, for now Enbridge wants to build a petroleum pipeline to Kitimat on the Pacific coast, despite strong and concerted opposition from First Nations[9] across what could be called Aboriginal Columbia.

If the government that issued the apology for the residential schools was sincere, it would refuse to continue inflicting contemporary damage and violence onto Indigenous communities. For this to happen, the government needs to try to perceive and act from within an Indigenous world view, one that respects the land and watersheds as life-giving forces, not merely as resources to be exploited and controlled.

But today, Indigenous struggles to protect the land continue all over the continent. From the Chipewyan and Cree courageously speaking out against the Tar Sands in Northern Alberta[10] to the Secwepemc protests against Sun Peaks Ski Resort[11] to the Kitchenuhmaykoosib Inninuwug's (KI) stand against platinum mining[12] to the Innu struggle against Hydro-Quebec's attempts to dam the Romaine River,[13] Indigenous peoples and their allies are trying to protect the land and watersheds for future generations of Indigenous and non-Indigenous peoples.

This year, Tsilhqot'in Nation, Esketemc First Nation, Canoe Creek Band, and Northern Shuswap Tribal Council successfully fought to protect the life of Teztan Biny, or Fish Lake, up near Williams Lake.[14] Following a federal environmental assessment finding that Taseko Mines' proposed gold–

copper mine would "result in significant adverse environmental effects" on the water and the land that give life to these First Nations,[15] the mine was stopped in November 2010. However, it is important to remember that Teztan Biny was endangered because of a 2002 amendment to the *Fisheries Act*, a loophole known as Schedule 2, which allows for freshwater bodies to be reclassified as "tailings impoundment areas" for mining. Since fifteen other freshwater bodies across Canada continue to be threatened with becoming toxic wastewater dumps, Schedule 2 still urgently needs to be revoked.[16]

Violence to the people and to the land they belong to is not a thing of the past. It continues today, perhaps even in accelerated forms. An apology worth its salt would also entail a moratorium on the tar sands, on mining, on damming, on *fracking*,[17] when such so-called "developments" poison and destroy the watersheds of Indigenous, non-Indigenous, and non-human communities. Ducks, wolves, marbled murrelets, salmon, cedar, frogs, gophers, bears, and beavers have as much a right to clean water and land as humans.

John Ralston Saul argues in *Response, Responsibility, and Renewal* that most non-Aboriginal people want change and reconciliation with Indigenous peoples but do not know "how to go about it."[18] One of the barriers he identifies is the lack of a plan for change. I would like to respond that one way to move forward together, in peace and with respect, is to cooperatively focus on the health of the water that gives us all life.

Such a hydrological lens has the benefit of respecting Indigenous knowledges that have been documented and generously shared by Michael Blackstock, Ardith Walkem, Dorothy Christian, Jeannette Armstrong, Marlowe Sam, Cheryl Darlene Sanderson, and Josephine Mendamin, to name just a few Indigenous knowledge keepers.[19] And it also provides a very clear path for non-Aboriginal people, many of whom are increasingly concerned about the future and the environment in an era of global warming, widespread pollution, and rampant consumerism.

Attending to watersheds is a good way to move toward the paradigm shift that John Ralston Saul invites us to consider.

Within the *stal'əw* watershed, one can see Vancouver as an urban centre that has been modernized, industrialized, and gentrified by movements of global capital and labour. However, from another equally valid perspective, Vancouver is unceded Coast Salish land, still home to the Squamish, Musqueam, and Tsleil Watuth First Nations who hold cultural knowledges of the land and the water predating and exceeding that of settlers/invaders/immigrants.[20] As a non-Indigenous, uninvited guest, I am careful to proceed respectfully and humbly in the long process of building a peaceful society in the face of the immense violences that I, and anyone who lives on this land, have inherited.

One main strategy I have found inspiring is to approach life through a watershed mind. Where does the water come from? Where does it go? What has been done to it as it passes through the city? The water I swallow today might have previously hovered in rain clouds above the South China Sea, or might end up in the North Pacific Gyre, an ocean current that houses a collection of floating plastic garbage in the Pacific Ocean said to be twice the size of Texas. Half the oxygen I breathe was created by plankton in the ocean;[21] I am connected to flora and fauna, micro and macro, in all sorts of ways that Western science is only beginning to articulate, but which has often already been told in Indigenous stories. Water teaches me interdependency, something that many Indigenous world views understand very deeply.

I started going down this watershed route at the invitation of my sister–friend–comrade, Dorothy Christian, who organized an event with Denise Nadeau a few years ago called Protect Our Sacred Waters. I am humbled and honoured to learn from water with her.

From a watershed perspective, Canada can be seen as divided into five areas, draining into the Pacific Ocean, the Atlantic Ocean, the Arctic Ocean, Hudson's Bay, and (a little bit into) the Gulf of Mexico. From a watershed perspective, I understand that the water always circulates, connecting me to places I do not see, but nonetheless rely upon and affect. We would do well to keep in mind that human bodies are roughly 60 per cent water;[22] more awareness of water's dynamics could help to build a culture of peace and respectful interdependence. It has been said that "Rivers within yearn for rivers without."[23]

I've read that in the Musqueam language, verbs change form depending on where the speaker is standing in relation to the water.[24] The verbs you use will indicate if you're downstream or upstream, if the river is before you or behind you. The language automatically fosters an intimate attention to water as part of one's everyday consciousness. This brings me to the second important strategy I want to think about as a non-Indigenous person.

Valerie Galley wisely points out that meaningful action also entails granting Indigenous languages official status, as has been done in the Northwest Territories with Chipewyan, Cree, Dogrib, Gwich'in, Inuktitut, and Slavey.

She notes that back in 1988, the Assembly of First Nations was already recommending that this recognition be done at the federal level, and that "the federal government should place Indigenous languages on par with French where budget allocations were concerned."[25] Instead, what we witnessed in 2006 was the Conservative Minister of Canadian Heritage, Bev Oda, cutting $160 million from the $172.7 million budget that had been allocated by the Liberals for the revitalization of Indigenous languages over a period of 11 years.[26]

Because I know how precious my mother tongue, Cantonese, is to me, I want to support multilingual fluency in Canada. In order to live, languages need to be spoken in everyday life. I'd like to encourage those of us who love language to seriously consider learning an Indigenous language. If I had learned Siksikaitsipowahsin (the Blackfoot language),[27] or Tsuut'ina, or Cree as well as French as a child, I feel that my capacity for building the culture of peace that we want would be even stronger, gifted by the attunements and sensitivities that each language offers.

As a Chinese Canadian woman, I admit to feeling very ambivalent about Prime Minister Stephen Harper's apology in 2008. On the one hand, I truly wanted it to be a sign that the federal government was finally respecting the experiences and knowledges of Indigenous peoples. On the other hand, given how skeptical many people are about the political system, I was not convinced that this apology was genuine. I wanted to be convinced, but at my gut and heart levels, I was not so trusting. This reluctant skepticism was further reinforced when Prime Minister Harper announced that Canada had no history of colonialism at the G20 summit in Pittsburgh in 2009, just a year after the residential school apology.[28] This big disconnection between historical violence inflicted within Canada and contemporary capitalism-as-usual (mining, land exploitation, water destruction within our borders) is disturbing. It makes the apology seem like a political tactic to push Indigenous people's experiences into some irrecuperable past, closing the door on it so that business can speed up as people ignore the colonial violence that still exists today. It takes many generations for communities to heal from such violence, and it's important not to inflict more damage to the land while healing is happening. The healing of the land, of the watersheds, is the healing of the people.

Another symptom of the disconnection between the present and the past is the alarming rate at which Indigenous children continue to be apprehended by government agencies today. More than half of the children removed from their original homes and placed in foster care are Indigenous, and the recent case of Loni Edmonds suggests that there are cases where Indigenous children are being taken from their parents without due process or consent.[29] The Federation of Aboriginal Foster Parents points out that "Between 1995–2001 there was a 71.5% increase in the number of on-reserve children with status being placed in foster care."[30] Many observers have noted that some of the money spent on foster care would better be directed at assisting families to stay together when Indigenous parents want to keep and take care of their own children.

I mentioned earlier that human bodies are roughly 60 per cent water, and the ways in which Turtle Island's waterways have been dammed, diverted, and manipulated can be compared to how many Indigenous people continue to have their families broken apart, controlled, and reorganized by the colonial state apparatus. Whether it is watery human bodies, or larger water bodies themselves, imperial delirium imposes its own agenda and arrogantly assumes that its way is the best way, without making meaningful efforts to listen and learn from who and what are already there.

Today, I carefully watch what is happening to watersheds and Indigenous children across Turtle Island because, ultimately, this is what will determine whether the apology has real weight in terms of respecting Indigenous people's past, present, and future. It is also the test of how democratic and just Canada actually is—whether it is an imagined community that is actually based on healthy water and healthy children for everyone.

Notes

1 This is the downriver (Musqueam) spelling of the upriver *Stó:lō*, with thanks to Victor Guerin of the Musqueam.
2 Bocking, Richard (1997:3). *Mighty River: A Portrait of the Fraser.* Vancouver, BC: Douglas & McIntyre.
3 Kinder Morgan (2007). TMX – Anchor Loop Project Frequently Asked Questions. July 2007. Retrieved 28 December 2010 from: http://www.kindermorgan.com/business/canada/tmx_documentation/FAQ_v7.doc
4 Pipeline to the Pacific. *The Edmonton Journal* (2007, November 3). Retrieved 28 December 2010 from: http://www.canada.com/edmontonjournal/news/business/story.html?id=31c8d460-da17-4d52-af2b-a3b134b5c905&k=58903. While the old 24 in. pipeline is dormant for the time being, it may be reactivated in the future.
5 McCarthy, Shawn (2010, July 28). Enbridge spill yields fresh ammo for oil sands critics. *The Globe and Mail.* Retrieved 28 December 2010 from: http://www.theglobeandmail.com/globe-investor/enbridge-spill-yields-fresh-ammo-for-oil-sands-critics/article1654445/

6   See authors' works in Younging, Gregory, Jonathan Dewar, and Mike DeGagné (eds.) (2009). *Response, Responsibility, and Renewal: Canada's Truth and Reconciliation Journey*. Ottawa, ON: Aboriginal Healing Foundation.

7   Chrisjohn, Roland and Tanya Wasacase (2009:226). Half-truths and whole lies: Rhetoric in the "apology" and the Truth and Reconciliation Commission. In *Response, Responsibility, and Renewal*: 217–229.

8   Alfred, Taiaiake (2009:182–183). Restitution is the real pathway to justice for indigenous peoples. In *Response, Responsibility, and Renewal*: 179–187.

9   Forest Ethics (2010, April 1). First Nations in BC Declare Opposition Against Enbridge's Northern Gateway Pipeline. Retrieved 28 December 2010 from: http://www.forestethics.org/first-nations-in-bc-declare-opposition-against-enbridges-northern-gateway-pipeline

10 See for instance: Oil Sands and Truth (2008, April 29). Intervention at the United Nations by the Athabasca Chipewyan and Mikisew Cree First Nations. Retrieved 28 December 2010 from: http://oilsandstruth.org/intervention-united-nations-athabasca-chipewyan-and-mikisew-cree-first-nations

11 See for instance: Kennedy, Tehaliwaskenhas Bob (2007, March 30). Spotlight on Aboriginal Rights: Nicole Manuel and Beverly Manuel. *Turtle Island Native Network News*. Retrieved 28 December 2010 from: http://www.turtleisland.org/news/news-secwepemc.htm

12 See for instance: KI Wins Huge Victory over Ontario Mining Company (2006, July 31). *Ecojustice*. Retrieved 28 December 2010 from: http://www.ecojustice.ca/media-centre/press-releases/ki-wins-huge-victory-over-ontario-mining-company

13 See: Innu Seek to Block Romaine Hydro Project (2010, May 7). Retrieved 28 December 2010, from CBC News website: http://www.cbc.ca/canada/montreal/story/2010/05/07/mtl-romaine-injunction.html

14 See: Victory for Teztan Biny (Fish Lake)! (2010). Retrieved 28 December 2010, from RAVEN: Respecting Aboriginal Values and Environmental Needs website: http://www.raventrust.com/projects/fishlaketeztanbiny.html

15 Canadian Environmental Assessment Agency (2010, July 2). *Executive Summary: Report of the Federal Prosperity Review Panel*. Retrieved from: http://www.ceaa.gc.ca/050/documents/43937/43937E.pdf

16 See: Why is the Canadian Government Letting Mining Companies Turn Lakes into Toxic Dumps? Retrieved 28 December 2010 from The Council of Canadians website: http://www.canadians.org/water/issues/TIAs/index.html. See also: Milewski, Terry (2008, June 16). Lakes across Canada face Being Turned into Mine Dump Sites. Retrieved 28 December 2010, from CBC News website: http://www.cbc.ca/canada/story/2008/06/16/condemned-lakes.html

17 This term refers to the practice known as hydraulic fracturing, which has been known to emit human carcinogens such as benzene.

18 Saul, John Ralston (2009:311). Reconciliation: Four barriers to paradigm shifting. In *Response, Responsibility, and Renewal*: 309–320.

19 See the following: 1) Mother Earth Water Walk website (retrieved 28 December 2010 from: http://motherearthwaterwalk.com/); 2)Armstrong, Jeannette (2005). Siwlkw. In Sandra Laronde (ed.), *Sky Woman: Indigenous Women Who Have Shaped, Moved, or Inspired Us*. Penticton, BC: Theytus; 3) Blackstock, Michael (2001). Water: A First Nations' Spiritual and Ecological Perspective. *Perspectives: BC Journal of Ecosystems & Management* 1(1):1–14; 4) Christian, Dorothy and Denise Nadeau (2007, June). Protect Our Sacred Waters. *Common Ground* (retrieved from: http://commonground.ca/iss/0706191/cg191_waters.shtml); 5) Phere, Merrell-Ann (2009). *Denying the Source: The Crisis of First Nations Water Rights*. Calgary, AB: Rocky Mountain Books; 6) Sam, Marlowe (2008, March 15). Okanagan water systems: A historical retrospect of control, domination and change. Paper presented at the Ways of Being in the Academy: 6th

Annual Indigenous Graduate Students Symposium, University of British Columbia, Vancouver, BC; 7) Sanderson, Cheryl Darlene (2008). *Nipiy Wasekimew/Clear Water: the Meaning of Water, from the Words of the Elders.* Doctoral dissertation, Simon Fraser University, Vancouver, BC; (8) Walkem, Ardith (2007). The land is dry: Indigenous peoples, water, and environmental justice. In Karen Bakker (ed.). *Eau Canada.* Vancouver, BC: UBC Press.

20 Maracle, L. (2004). Goodbye, Snauq. In T. Cardinal, T. Highway, B. Johnston, T. King, B. Maracle, L. Maracle, J. Marchessault, R.A. Qitsualik, and D.H. Taylor, *Our Story: Aboriginal Voices on Canada's Past.* Toronto, ON: The Dominion Institute, Anchor Canada: 201–219.

21 Mitchell, Alanna (2009:27). *Sea Sick: The Global Ocean in Crisis.* Toronto, ON: McClelland and Stewart. Also see: TEDx Great Pacific Garbage Patch (2010, November 6) for more information about plastic pollution in the ocean. Retrieved from: http://www.tedxgreatpacificgarbagepatch.com/

22 Suzuki, D., with A. McConnell and A. Mason (2007:91). *The Sacred Balance: Rediscovering Our Place in Nature, Updated & Expanded.* (3rd ed.). Vancouver, BC: Greystone Books.

23 Sandford, Robert (2009:11). *Restoring the Flow: Confronting the World's Water Woes.* Calgary, AB: Rocky Mountain Books.

24 Zandberg, Bryan (2007, March 23). Reviving a native tongue. *The Tyee.* Retrieved 28 December 2010 from: http://thetyee.ca/News/2007/03/23/RevivingANativeTongue/

25 Galley, Valerie (2009:249). Reconciliation and the revitalization of indigenous Languages. In *Response, Renewal, and Responsibility*: 241–258.

26 Galley (2009:253).

27 Bastien, Betty (2004). *Blackfoot Ways of Knowing: The Worldview of the Siksikaitsitapi.* Calgary, AB: University of Calgary Press.

28 See: Prime Minister Harper Denies Colonialism in Canada at G20 (2009, September 29). *Canadian Business Online.* Retrieved 28 December 2010 from: http://www.canadianbusiness.com/markets/cnw/article.jsp?content=20090929_172501_0_cnw_cnw

29 Jones, Joseph (2010, July 27). BC Authorities Snatch Three-Day-Old Indigenous Baby. *Vancouver Media Co-op.* Retrieved 28 December 2010 from: http://vancouver.mediacoop.ca/story/bc-authorities-snatch-three-day-old-indigenous-baby/4303 (I hear that this case is currently being investigated by the BC Representative for Children and Youth.)

30 See: Federation of Aboriginal Foster Parents website. Retrieved 28 December 2010 from: http://www.fafp.ca/fosterparentinfo.shtml

Sylvia D. Hamilton

Sylvia D. Hamilton is a multi-award winning Nova Scotian filmmaker and writer who is known for her documentary films as well as her publications, public presentations, and extensive volunteer work with artistic, social, and cultural organizations at the local and national levels. She was born in the African Nova Scotian community of Beechville, founded by the Black Refugees from the War of 1812. She attended Beechville's segregated school from primary to grade three. Her mother, Dr. Marie Nita Waldron Hamilton, was a schoolteacher who taught in a number of segregated schools in Halifax County, Nova Scotia. *The Little Black School House*, inspired by her mother and other teachers who taught in Nova Scotia's segregated schools, was released in 2007 by her company, Maroon Films Inc. Her other films include, *Black Mother Black Daughter* (1989), *Speak It! From the Heart of Black Nova Scotia* (1992), and *Portia White: Think On Me* (2000). Her work has been recognized with a Gemini Award, The Portia White Prize for Excellence in the Arts, the Japan Broadcasting Corporation's Maeda Prize and CBC Television Pioneer Award, among others. She has received three honourary degrees and was appointed a 2008 Mentor with The Trudeau Foundation. She worked with the National Film Board's Studio D where she co-created New Initiatives in Film, a program for women of colour and First Nations' women, and was also Chair of the Women in Media Foundation. She held Nancy's Chair in Women's Studies at Mount Saint Vincent University and currently teaches part-time at the University of King's College in Halifax.

Stories From *The Little Black School House*

Introduction

This article explores the history and memory of Canada's all-Black segregated schools and the attendant struggle of African Canadians to ensure that their children have access to the full educational opportunities promised by Canadian society. Through advocacy, and a legacy of resistance, and by dint of committed work, teachers, community leaders, and parents fought for many generations to turn the 'promise' of freedom into reality.

Canadians can no longer engage in the dance of denial about the misery caused by the forced evacuation of Aboriginal and Inuit children when they were ripped from their families only to be placed in separate, segregated residential facilities, which, while called "schools," bore little resemblance to the caring, nurturing educational environment this word evokes. Rather, they were locations, *sites of memory*, where abuse and racism reigned. Why did this happen? In a word: *race,* the socially, not biologically constructed category that has stratified and negatively affected humans for generations, and what theorist W.E.B. Dubois spoke of when he said, "[t]he problem of the Twentieth Century is the problem of the color line."[1] What is not widely known or remembered is that in two Canadian provinces, because of their race, a large number of African Canadian children were also required by law to attend separate, segregated schools.

Legal scholar Constance Backhouse explains that from the middle of the nineteenth century, Black and white students could be separated by law. Legislation in both Nova Scotia and Ontario allowed this division.[2] Historian James W.St.G. Walker further points out that:

> By circumstance and public attitude, a colour line was drawn in Canada which affected the economic and social life of the blacks. The various attempts to give legal sanction to the line failed universally except in one important area: blacks were denied equal use of public schools in Nova Scotia and Ontario, and this division was recognized by the law. The most important manifestation of colour prejudice in Canadian history is in education.[3]

These all-Black schools were set up in rural areas of Nova Scotia and southern Ontario and, although not by law, there were a limited number of Black schools in New Brunswick, Alberta, and Saskatchewan where comparatively smaller populations of African-descended people lived.[4]

'Colour prejudice' directed against people of Asian and African descent was codified in government documents and by various actions taken to discourage their entry into Canada. The prevailing racial attitudes in the early part of the century were exemplified by Prime Minister MacKenzie King's declaration that Canada was a "white man's country."[5] By 1849 Ontario changed its *School Act* to permit separate schools to be set up for Black children. In Nova Scotia, legislation to allow officials to create separate schools was on the books by 1865.[6]

In spite of evidence, experiential and documented, to the contrary, we still face a prevailing assumption that, unlike the United States where *race* is a defining characteristic of American society, it plays a lesser role in Canada. If we in any measure accept this analysis, it becomes easier to be shocked and surprised when racial conflicts or racist events, such as a white teacher in *blackface* in a video, a cross burning, or the donning of KKK outfits, make the national news. They are characterized as "isolated incidents," or intended as a joke.[7] The logic works if we convince, or have convinced, ourselves that race is an insignificant indicator and that it has played a limited negative role in the Canadian nation. We can condemn the events without an understanding of the historical roots of racism.[8]

Racial segregation in education is deeply mired in concepts of white supremacy. The behaviours and actions that arose from these beliefs lead to the de-humanization of First Peoples, the segregation of African and Asian Canadians, and the immoral treatment of the most vulnerable members of any society: children.

While the way in which children of colour were treated cannot be collapsed or directly compared with the horrific experiences of Aboriginal and Inuit children, the core racist beliefs that yielded separation by race were the same, and this did not abate even after the adoption and proclamation of the *Universal Declaration of Human Rights* (UDHR) on 10 December 1948, of which Article 26 reads:

> Everyone has the right to education. Education shall be free, at least in the elementary and fundamental stages ... It shall promote understanding, tolerance and friendship among all nations, racial or religious groups, and shall further the activities of the United Nations for the maintenance of peace ... Parents have a prior right to choose the kind of education that shall be given to their children.[9]

For many Canadian students this right was denied solely because of their race. Racial prejudice, coupled with severe economic circumstances, meant that many Black people growing up in the first half of the twentieth century ended their formal schooling before finishing grade nine; some left before reaching grades five or six.

For these students, aspirations to higher learning and to various professions were quashed because the doors were usually closed. Educator and African Baptist minister Dr. W.P. Oliver put it bluntly when he said:

> Segregated schools are a barrier to good inter-group relations. They are a visible symbol of separation, and a denial of the right 'to belong.' Such schools became the stamp of approval of the mental apartheid that exists in many white minds.[10]

Within Black communities throughout Canada, education has always been constructed as society's passport to a better life and children viewed as our most precious resource, the jewels in our crowns. Education has been and continues to be held up as a fundamental right as articulated in Article 26 of the UDHR. How then does one explain why some children would have been allowed a level of resources that others were denied? Why was it deemed to be in the 'best interest' of Black children and white children that they be separated by race?

The desire for education on the part of African Canadians over time was matched by the equal desire of some Canadians to keep the races apart. For example, in 1843, even though Black parents in Hamilton, Ontario, had paid taxes, they were barred from sending their children to public schools. They petitioned Governor-General Lord Elgin after receiving little help from the local officials and eventually won their rights. Yet in the same region, Amherstburg parents were less successful. Hostility was so strong that local white school trustees threatened drastic action should Black students attend the school. They were quoted as saying that rather than send their children "to School with niggers they will cut their children's heads off and throw them into the road side ditch." Although African Canadian parents could hold no hope of consistent application of laws that would uphold their rights, they nonetheless continued over time to do all that they could to press government officials to do so.[11]

During the research and subsequent production of *The Little Black School House* documentary film, the links between segregation in education and the contours of segregation within the rest of society were starkly underlined. The historic practice of segregating groups of African Canadian students within the educational system reflected the broader segregation extant in Canadian society. In short, setting students apart in separate schools was no different from the denial of other public services. Retired University of Windsor professor and former member of Parliament, Dr. Howard McCurdy, states that during his childhood years, his family confronted direct racism in Amherstburg, Ontario. He lived in two towns in the same province, yet his experience had a marked difference:

> In London at St. George's school that I attended, my sister and I were the only Black students there. Where, I wasn't conscious of race in London, when I moved to Amherstburg, I became immediately conscious of it. Employment discrimination in Windsor and Amherstburg was widespread. In Amherstburg, Black people did not work in the town.[12]

Former museum curator Elise Harding–Davis' parents faced similar unsettling experiences. They were not permitted to buy a house in Windsor, Ontario, because of the restrictive covenants that prevented Black people and Jews from buying property.

Following World War II, Black soldiers in uniform who had just returned from fighting for democracy abroad were denied entry into some establishments in their hometown of Windsor.[13]

Overt and covert segregation in Canada continued into the 1960s. Research has documented the persistence of negative racial attitudes over time and across generations. Parents and educators continually express concerns about high dropout rates and the streaming of students into special programs.[14] At the same time as students were being segregated, general curriculum material either ignored African-descended people or presented them in a stereotypical fashion. The segregated system fostered such attitudes within the broader community. Advocates within African Canadian communities were not only concerned with the quality of education offered their students, but also with the representations of Black people in school texts that were available to all students in the public educational system.[15]

Generations of African people fought against racist content in the school curriculum, and the invisibility of African people in discussions about Canadian nation building.

Historical Background: Go Back and Fetch What You Forgot

In this ahistorical, highly disposable age, it is fundamental that we maintain our efforts to underline the importance of history and its relevance to our lives today; we need to stop, reflect, reconsider who we are, and how we arrived at this place at this in time. The Akan people of West Africa articulate a concept called Sankofa: *Se wo were fin a wo Sankofa a yenkyi*, which means, "it is not a taboo to return and fetch it when you forget."[16]

I am interested with two questions: first, what memories have we failed to represent, and second, what memories do we not want to represent and why? The enslavement of African-descended people in Canada sits at the cusp of these troubling questions.

Sylvia D. Hamilton, *The Little Black School House* (2007)
Production Still, Lincolnville, Nova Scotia

In a text titled, *History and Memory in African–American Culture,* editors Geneviève Fabre and Robert O'Meally use French historian Pierre Nora's *lieux de mèmoire,* or *sites of memory,* as the theoretical framework for an examination of the co-joined themes of history and memory. For them this idea pointed to a new set of potential historical sources such as paintings, buildings, dances, journals, novels, poems, orality—which, taken together, linked individual memories to create collective, communal memories of African American culture and life. This concept brings together the private, through oral storytelling and family histories, and the public, as found in archival documents.[17] This reading gave me a wider lens for viewing and understanding these elements within an African Canadian context.

Whether we wish to remember or not, the educational segregation of children of African descent in Canada and elsewhere is a direct by-product of the system of chattel slavery, an institution whose goal was to strip African people of their dignity and humanity in order to use them as vehicles of cheap labour for a profit-making system. In several of my film projects I have referenced slavery and, in post-screening discussions with predominantly white audiences, have been questioned about it. In many cases people are just astounded—how come they did not know this? I face silence when I explain that ministers, church leaders, and key political figures owned slaves and that there are wills on record bequeathing women, children, and men as part of household property to heirs and successors for ever and ever and ever; that the women and girls were looked upon for their capability to breed more property as it were. The first enslaved people in what we now know as Canada were people of the First Nations who were enslaved by French colonists who later replaced them with African people.

When I walk along the Halifax waterfront I think of the young children who were bought and sold there—of a young African girl child sold along with hogsheads (barrels) of rum. When I stand beside Halifax's St. Paul's Church, I think of the enslaved Africans who were baptized to 'save their souls' but their Black bodies were not their own. Their voices silenced, their memories haunt me still.

African people in early Canada acted on their thirst for education, in spite of the predominant societal attitude summed up by the common saying that if you educated a 'slave' you made him unfit for service.[18]

In my high school during the 1960s there were so-called *slave auctions*, where students could be bought for a few days, or a week, to be the *slave* for another student. The *slave* would carry the *owner's* books and do whatever was requested. Were they held as fund-raising events or part of winter carnival activities, I can't remember or, rather, my memory refuses to. As one of a handful of Black students in the high school, I, as well as they, kept our distance.

Talking about slavery in Canada has been taboo. The generalized narrative asserts that African-descended people arrived in Canada via the Underground Railroad. The *runaway slaves* followed the North Star to freedom with Harriet Tubman's words, "Live Free or Die," ringing in their ears. A Heritage Minute tells the Underground Railroad story[19] that is indeed true. Tens of thousands of African-descended people arrived in Upper Canada from the United States, especially after the passage of the *Fugitive Slave Act* of 1850. However, the promotion of the Underground Railroad story as *the* main narrative explaining how Black people came to Canada obscures vital parallel narratives: those that speak about the enslaved African people in the provinces, now known as Nova Scotia and Quebec, and, at the same time, those who speak about the runaways, the freedom seekers entering Canada. Historian Afua Cooper's *The Hanging of Angelique*, the story of the enslaved African woman Angelique and the Montreal fire she was accused of starting, has cracked open a space to begin a discussion of slavery in Canada. It is one that includes examination of the burial grounds of enslaved people in Nova Scotia, Ontario, and Quebec.[20] These *lieux de memoire* or *sites of memory*, by their very existence, challenge the dominant narrative and the resultant image that Canadians hold of themselves, especially in comparison to their neighbours in the United States. Slavery in Canada, when acknowledged, is often argued away on the basis of this comparison and on the question of numbers. Smaller numbers were supposed to have made the practice more palatable, less harsh. We are supposed to learn all that is important and significant as bodies of knowledge in our educational systems from the primary to post-secondary levels.

Yet, it is only in the last decade that we have seen glimmers of information about African peoples in Canada show up in public schools, and, all too often, relegated to events during Black History Month. Significantly, for many generations, we have learned nothing of Canada's history of all-Black schools, segregated by law and geography in Ontario and Nova Scotia, two provinces with long-standing, historic populations of African-descended people. I consider the locations and the extant former schoolhouses as *sites of memory*; there are generations of invisible stories embedded in these geographic sites and in the memories of the students, teachers, parents, and trustees who were the schools' communities. The segregated schools were a direct legacy of the enslavement of Black peoples and the conscious and unconscious racist societal attitudes that are intertwined with that heinous system. Traces linger in our language: *slave driver, working like a slave,* and *whip into shape* are common phrases uttered without much thought to their origins or how they might sound to a listener who may be of African descent.

The geography of Black settlements in Canada, and most particularly Ontario and Nova Scotia, can be traced to the residual political and racial attitude toward African people that began during slavery and colonization. Considered second- or lower-class citizens (the term *citizen* is used advisedly here as rarely were they accorded the benefits and rights assumed by other Canadians), they were allotted land accordingly. Nonetheless, from the earliest periods of settlement, African people created their own institutions, two primary ones being churches and schools. Denied access to common or public schools, they created their own at the same time as they fought for the right to send their children to public schools. Elise Harding–Davis can trace seven generations of her family history to 1798 when her ancestors crossed the Detroit River to Canada to start new lives. She explains that they came with nothing, "And so we often first built a church building. And we would use that as a school, a social center. Education was the most important facet of Black life."[21] Nova Scotia Judge Corrine Sparks, who attended a segregated school, points to the same primary connection for early Black settlers in Nova Scotia:

> Education and religion in an African Nova Scotian context are intricately related. Family life revolved around the church. Generally speaking the more educated people in the community would be the deacons and of course you'd have a minister who was really the leader of the community. So a lot of the educational grounding came from the organizational framework of the Black church.[22]

The link between church and school was not only philosophical, it was geographical; the schools shared the same land and were constructed beside the churches. In my home community of Beechville, located near Halifax, our two-room school was constructed on nearby property allocated by elders of the African Baptist church.

The desire of Black parents to educate their children was palpable as evidenced by the countless petitions they filed with governments to have their children attend common schools, and when denied access, for funds to build their own schools. In 1820, parents in the Black Refugee community of Preston, Nova Scotia, petitioned the authorities for financial help to pay for a teacher. Twenty-five years later, in 1845, eighteen families in Windsor, Nova Scotia, urged provincial authorities to assist them in establishing a school for their children.[23]

Site of Memory: *The Little Black School House*
When racial flare-ups at Nova Scotian schools topped the national news in the late 1980s, few watching were aware of the story's deeper background.

Among members of the media reporting the incidents, and even among the teaching and administrative staff of the schools involved, few knew the history and experience of some of the parents and grandparents of the Black students involved in the turmoil. Few knew of the long-standing struggle against racist practices in the educational system, nor of their origins. In September 1990, a group of retired teachers who had taught in Nova Scotia's segregated schools organized a weekend reunion during which they participated in a variety of activities, including a bus tour to the sites of several former schools in Halifax County. The footage I filmed during this memorable event was lost in a massive fire at the National Film Board in Halifax. The stories recalled, the places visited, and the commitment to not forget this history stayed with me.

After the fire I completed a short film titled *Speak It! From the Heart of Black Nova Scotia,* about Black youth, race, identity, and empowerment.[24] However, its important back story—one inspired by the reunion—still had to be told.

The Little Black School House is a one-hour documentary film[25] that tells the story of segregated schools in Canada, the teachers who taught there and the students they taught. It is also the story of the struggle of African Canadians to achieve dignity and equality through the pursuit of education. Segregation in education is associated with the United States and South Africa. In 1954, while the US Supreme Court was moving to prohibit racial segregation in schools by its landmark ruling in the *Brown v. The Topeka School Board* case,[26] schools segregated by race were in full operation in communities in Nova Scotia and Ontario. Structurally, the film is a multi-voiced narrative. Two categories of people appear: individuals who either taught in, had been students, or were the parents of children who attended segregated schools, and knowledgeable historians and educators who situate these schools within the broader socio-political context. They engaged in this public act of remembering, one where the individual stories taken together shape a collective memory.

This memory holds a complicated truth about segregation and what that meant: forced exclusion on the basis of race, lack of basic physical and educational resources, and limitations on access to further education. However, at the same time, for the most part, Black teachers who were fiercely devoted taught the students well, held them to the highest standards, inculcated a strong work ethic, and did all that they could to equip them to live in a society that might reject them because of their race. They displayed creativity, innovation, and resilience. Many of the teachers, after having attended Teacher's College, were limited in the teaching options open to them. Rarely would they be hired in schools other than those that were segregated. The oral testimonies of the film participants consistently maintained an emphasis on education, a legacy passed down from generation to generation, as demonstrated by the focus on education within the African United Baptist Association (AUBA) of Nova Scotia, whose Education Committee gave annual reports at Association meetings, such as one held in 1948 when Chair Rev. A.F. Skinner stated that:

> All Negro schools are staffed by Negro teachers almost all of whom have had special training for the work. They come to know intimately the needs of their pupils, and take pride in endeavoring them.[27]

The documentary was filmed in several locations in Nova Scotia and Ontario in the fall of 2006 and was first screened in September 2007.[28] Within the film, there are intergenerational scenes involving high school students in conversation with community Elders. In one, a surprised student listened intently as an Elder spoke about her early school days:

> From grade one to grade five. That's as high as the grades went. We just had the two teachers... Just one classroom. There's lots of times we didn't get to school on account of the snow storms or somebody would drive us with the horse and sled or something like that. No school buses. On foot.[29]

So engaged were they with each other, as they sat on a school bus touring sites of former schools in Guysborough County, Nova Scotia, they seemed unaware that this rare and fleeting moment, where memory was passed on, was being captured on film. The weekend we filmed in this district, our crew was welcomed by members of the Tracadie United Baptist Church as they celebrated its 184th anniversary, a milestone of survival and history that we recorded for the film.

Legislation, cited earlier, enabling segregated schools was routinely applied in areas with what were deemed significant Black populations, thus rural areas in Ontario and Nova Scotia where there was de facto segregation, were confirmed in their long-standing practices by law. In towns and cities where the population might be more numerous in particular areas, children would attend the nearest school, often located in a less affluent section of the city or town. There they faced streaming, isolation, and, in the case of the Willow Street school in Truro, Nova Scotia, separate bathrooms. Mercer Street School in Windsor, Ontario, attended by former teacher Lois Larkin when she was young, was a case in point. Remembering her experience when interviewed, she explained that she had one teacher at this inner-city school who was supportive but, for the most part, children of colour were not encouraged. Subsequently, "many of our children were streamed into what was called the

Sylvia D. Hamilton, *The Little Black School House* (2007)
Production Still, Tracadie, Nova Scotia

opportunity class and these children carried those labels and sadly as a result many of them did not go on to secondary school."[30] James Haines remembered his troubling experience at the Gagetown public school in New Brunswick:

> Gagetown school was terrible. The teacher was very prejudice. She punished us by putting soap in our mouth, strapping us. I do not want to remember those years and those things. I do not have good memories about those years. For example when Mrs. Alexander from the school board came to school she always said, "How are my little darky children." Even Santa Claus used the same word, 'darkies.'[31]

During my research and production process I was reminded of the compelling stories told in Isabelle Knockwood's *Out of the Depths: The Experiences of Mi'kmaw Children at the Indian Residential School at Shubenacadie, Nova Scotia*. She recounts the harrowing experiences of the children who were forced to eat spoiled potatoes and meat from tin plates while priests were served the best food. At five she was taken to the school along with her sisters where they were issued uniforms with numbers. She could only look forward to the weekly visit from her parents who walked five miles from the reserve each Sunday to see them. Knockwood's interviews showed that it was the children who did not have regular visits from parents who suffered the most abuse:

> Nearly always, when I taped interviews with former students, they would begin to cry as they recalled their experiences at the school. One man showed me physical scars that he still bore. I began to feel that I was carrying their pain, as well as my own, around with me ... For me too the ruined school began to take on its own individual personality. Even in its derelict state it seemed menacing. I spent a lot of time up on the hill, walking around the school grounds, looking at the decayed building. It was if I wanted it to talk to me.[32]

We learn about the intense amount of physical labour required of students in direct contrast to the minimal amount of academic work offered. There was little preparation for careers or work beyond the school. She, like other girls who reached grade five, regardless of age, were required to work in the school's kitchen. Some worked for a month, others remained there permanently.

Out of the Depths combines Knockwood's personal story with that of other Survivors of the school; by incorporating them into her memoir, she offers a collective history, much as I was attempting in constructing *The Little Black School House*.

The prickly challenge of *The Little Black School House* is in its counter-memory—it presents historical events, experiences, contained in the individual and collective memory of African Canadians, which runs counter to the stories in the popular imagination about Canada and its system of education and about segregated schools. Canada and segregated schools are words that rarely appeared in the same sentence: many assume they never existed in our country. Consider the power of the photographic images of Black children stalked by angry white parents and surrounded by United States' national guards as they are taken to school. These images, along with those from the white supremacist apartheid regime in South Africa, defined our Canadian understanding of segregation in education. The United States, being our closest neighbour geographically, and to some extent culturally, represented our yardstick, indeed our definition of segregated schools.

I chose not to use any archival footage from the US or South Africa in this film to ensure that the story would be clearly seen and defined as a *Canadian story*, a made-in-Canada experience, one hardly admitted and never before told in film. The sense of place, the geography, is of the utmost importance in *The Little Black School House* precisely because it is a Canadian story, and must be understood as such.

The question then is this: how can a memory be vivid, emotional, almost palpable, as if yesterday, in one sector of Canadian society, yet more broadly, in another, no apparent memory? I say *apparent* since it is hard to understand such absences in the memory of those who—given their proximity, geography, and time period—should have known.

This story has not been told in the foundational texts where such knowledge is codified, therefore "known" and taught. Throughout the various film production stages, from research to launch, people who were not of African descent asked how it was that they did not know this story and its many dimensions: a parallel (unequal) system of public education and the multi-generational resistance and struggle of parents and community leaders against segregation and exclusion. African Canadians simply said, "finally this story will be told."

The Little Black School House was released during the period when the Toronto District School Board was considering a proposal from Black parents to create a Black-focused school as one effort to stall the high dropout rate and the disengagement of their children from the city's public schools. While a discussion of this proposal and its aftermath is beyond the scope of this article, it bears mentioning that many opposed to the school cited segregation and turning the clock back as reasons for opposing it. The proposal called for a curriculum that focused on the history and contributions of people of African descent, and for teachers who understood and were knowledgeable of this ethic/approach; the school would be open to any student who wished to attend, a fact lost during the raging public debate. Few seemed to know the actual history of legalized segregation and, therefore, were not able to make a distinction in what the parents were advocating, nor able to draw the obvious connection to the long-standing existence of publicly funded Catholic or alternative schools in Toronto. While references to race were removed from the school legislation, religion was not. In Nova Scotia, Wade Smith, a school vice-principal and an engaged, thoughtful Black educator, while commenting on the high dropout rate of Black students in Halifax schools, was taken to task by media commentators and educational officials for suggesting that an alternative school rooted in a Black cultural experience might help to stem this tide. In both cases, Toronto and Halifax, the strongest voices decrying the suggestion of Black-focused schools, offered few alternatives, nor did they display an understanding or knowledge of the historical, tenacious roots of racism within the educational systems, as exemplified by forced, legal segregation, exclusion, and lack of parental choice.[33]

A Legacy of Resistance

The educational experiences of several racialized groups in the early years of the twentieth century—for example, Chinese, Japanese, and African Canadians—were characterized by racial isolation. These communities shared the negative racialized categorization of *other*, equated with inferiority. This racism, which also led to First Nations' children being placed in residential schools, was predicated on beliefs, conscious or not, of white superiority. Why else would these children be set apart?

Significantly, active resistance to racism and exclusion was common throughout the communities over several generations. Ontario writer Adrienne Shadd's research uncovered the case of parents in Chatham, Ontario, who in 1891 took direct action against their local school board rule that required all Black children to attend one school in Chatham, no matter where they lived in the city. After filing a petition in an organized action, parents proceeded to take their children to the school of their choice; the result was the de-segregation of Chatham's schools. In 1921, the Chinese community in Victoria, British Columbia, resisted efforts by the city's school board to segregate them into specific schools. Parents organized a student strike to force officials to allow their children to attend schools where they were registered. They kept their students out of school the entire year and set up their own school in defiance in order to maintain the strike and to provide an education for their children.[34]

Parents in Three Mile Plains, Nova Scotia, pulled their students from school in 1926, in protest over the poor conditions, and thereby closed the school. Their move forced the government and the local gypsum company, a main employer in the district, to produce funds to pay for repairs.[35] As late as 1964, parents and community leaders in South Essex County, Ontario, petitioned the local school board to allow their children to attend a new school that was under construction in the town of Harrow. Their school, SS 11 Colchester South, was in extremely poor condition and was the last segregated school in Ontario. They wrote:

> On behalf of parents and ratepayers, the residents have been patient for more than three decades. The fear and silence identified with the past has been supplanted with courage and determination to make certain that their children are going to receive the best possible education on an integrated basis equal to the standards established for other children.[36]

These remembered and uncovered acts of resistance stand as sites of memory, the documentary evidence of the ongoing struggle against racism, and for human dignity.

Historical context was the canvas for this story, but contemporary witnesses—the teachers, the students, the community leaders—gave it life, dimension, and meaning based upon their lived experiences. Their faces, their bodies, and their memories became the landscape of *The Little Black School House*. What the people who appeared in this film or who were involved in the decades-long fight for justice for former residents of the Black community of Africville, a village destroyed in the 1960s by the city of Halifax in the name of urban renewal, and for which the Halifax has now formally apologized, remember, they remember for all Canadians.[37]

In Nova Scotia, the multi-generational advocacy around educational concerns has led to successful, historic changes within the educational system and governmental agencies: designated seats for African Nova Scotians on every school board; a provincial advisory council to the Minister of Education; the African Canadian Services Division in the Nova Scotia Department of Education; a government minister responsible for African Nova Scotian Affairs with a fully staffed office; and credit courses in African Canadian Studies, Grade 11, and English 12: African Heritage are open to all Nova Scotian students at the high-school level. Yet parents and educators, while applauding these valuable, long overdue institutional developments, caution that *we are not there yet*. Much remains to be done to ensure that, as Dalhousie Law School Professor Michelle Williams says, "whatever they [children] can dream they can do."[38]

Notes

1   Du Bois, W.E.B. (1903:11). *The Souls of Black Folk*. Chicago, IL: A.C. McClurg & Co. Retrieved 1 November 2010 from: http://www.forgottenbooks.org/info/9781606801611.

2   Backhouse, Constance (1999:250–252). *Colour-Coded: A Legal History of Racism in Canada, 1900-1950*. Toronto, ON: The Osgoode Society for Canadian Legal History by University of Toronto Press.

3   Walker, J.W. St. G. (1980:107). *A History of Blacks in Canada: A Study Guide for Teachers and Students*. Hull, QC: Minister of Supply and Services Canada. For a contemporary, comprehensive discussion of the history of African Canadians see: Walker, J.W. St. G. (1999). African Canadians. In Paul Magocsi (ed.). *Encyclopedia of Canada's Peoples*. Toronto, ON: University of Toronto Press.

4   Lenetta Tyler taught for a term at Fredericton, New Brunswick's Elm Street School in 1929. The school had no bathroom and the children had to collect wood for the stove. The school covered grades one to five. Tyler, Lenetta (2003). Research interview. Development Report for *The Little Black School House*. In Saskatchewan and Alberta, where the migration of African people from Oklahoma took place at the turn of the century, the new settlers set up their own schools. A small community developed north of Maidstone in the Eldon district of Saskatchewan c. 1908. Although there were enough families for a school, local authorities were reluctant because it would mean that Black and white children would be housed together. Eventually a school was set up in 1915 but the boundaries were such that white children were excluded. After the out migration of the Black settlers in the 1920s, the school ceased to be segregated. In Alberta, Black families settled near Athabasca in the Amber Valley area, where by 1913 they had built their own school, which continued into the 1950s. Calgary writer Cheryl Foggo's memoir *Pourin Down Rain*, chronicles what it was like growing up Black in Western Canada where her family has lived for four generations. Foggo, Cheryl (1990). *Pourin Down Rain*. Calgary, AB: Detselig Enterprises Ltd.–Temeron Books Inc. For further information on the settlement of Oklahoma Blacks in western Canada see also: http://www.albertasource.ca/blackpioneers/history/articles/index.html

5   "That Canada should desire to restrict immigration from the Orient is regarded as natural, that Canada should remain a white man's country is believed to be not only desirable for economic and social reasons, but highly necessary on political and national grounds." Cited in: Mackenzie, W.L. (1908). W.L. Mackenzie King's report on his mission to England to confer with the British authorities on the subject of immigration to Canada from the Orient, and immigration from India in particular. Sessional Papers 1908, No. 36a:5–10 (retrieved 1 November 2010 from: http://www.collectionscanada.gc.ca/immigrants/021017-119.01-e.php?&document_code=021017-81&page=1&referer=021017-2410.01-e.html&section_code=pp-passage&page_nbr=69 4&&&&PHPSESSID=0q7kfuavkua5l6h81i-cool2704). See also James Walker's (1980:144) "African-Canadians," in Magocisi's *Encyclopedia of Canada's Peoples* for details on the 1911 Order in Council prohibiting "Negroes" from entering Canada, and on the impact of the 1910 immigration act on Black immigration to Canada.

6   Winks, Robin, W. (1969). Negro School Segregation in Ontario and Nova Scotia. *Canadian Historical Review* 50(2):164-191. See also: Backhouse (1999:250–252).

7   In March 2007 a white teacher in a school in Charlottetown, Prince Edward Island, appeared in blackface in a video made by three teachers and shown at a staff meeting. It mocked a member of the staff who was of African descent. The CBC quoted the principal as saying, "It's a minor incident gone awry" (retrieved from: http://www.cbc.ca/canada/prince-edward-island/story/2007/03/09/blackface-teacher.html). Two incidents of people wearing KKK outfits made national news between 2007 and 2010. First, for Halloween in October 2007, three students came to Cornwall Collegiate Vocational School wearing KKK garb and at least one carried a noose (retrieved

29 December 2010 from: http://www.cbc.ca/canada/ottawa/story/2007/11/01/ot-kkk-071101.html); second, the first prize winner in the Campbellford, Ontario, Legion October 2010 Halloween costume party was dressed as a Klansman, carrying a Confederate flag and rope with a noose, at the end of which was a man in blackface. See: KKK costume at legion Halloween party disgusts many in Ontario town. (2010, November 2). *The Globe and Mail* (retrieved 11 January 2010 from: http://www. theglobeandmail.com/news/national/ontario/kkk-costume-at-legion-halloween-party-disgusts-many-in-ontario-town/article1783090/). Furthermore, a cross-burning on the lawn of an inter-racial couple in Hants County, Nova Scotia, in February 2010 generated much national attention and outrage. It is imperative to state that these last two events caused much public outcry and disgust and, in Nova Scotia, a major public rally in support of the couple. Along with the widespread outrage that surrounded the suspension of an Ontario minor hockey coach for taking a stand against racial taunts directed at one of his players, these public responses may be significant indicators that some attitudes are shifting (retrieved 29 December 2010 from: http://www.cbc.ca/canada/nova-scotia/story/2010/02/22/ns-cross-burning-hants-country.html). For evidence of shifting attitudes, see: Allen, K. (2011, January 6). After suspension, coach returns to ice a little wiser. *The Toronto Star*. Retrieved 11 January 2011 from: http://www.thestar.com/news/article/917741--after-suspension-coach-returns-tp-ice-a-little-wiser

8   See Backhouse (1995:15). Backhouse argues that Canadians maintain a sense of "racelessness" that is in direct contrast to the historical record. Her exhaustive examination of "hundreds of statutes and thousands of judicial decisions that use racial constructs as a pivotal point of reference" lead her to conclude that, " Collectively, these legal documents illustrate that the legal system has been profoundly implicated in Canada's racist history. Legislative and judicial sources provide substantial evidence to document the central role of the Canadian legal system in the establishment and enforcement of racial inequality." Historian James W. St. G. Walker also addresses this subject in: Walker, James W. St. G. (1997). *"Race", Rights and the Law in the Supreme Court of Canada*. Waterloo, ON: The Osgoode Society for Canadian Legal History and Wilfrid Laurier University Press.

9   United Nations (1948). Universal Declaration of Human Rights, G.A. res. 217A (III), U.N. Doc A/810 at 71 (1948). Retrieved 2 November 2010 from: http://www.un.org/en/documents/udhr/index.shtml

10   Cited in Thomson, Colin A. (1986:102). *Born With A Call: A Biography of Dr. William Pearly Oliver, c.m.* Dartmouth, NS: Black Cultural Centre for Nova Scotia. A paper written by Dr. William P. Oliver in 1949 offers a compelling snapshot of the status of Black people in Nova Scotia at the time and was presented at a meeting of the Canadian Humanities Council in Halifax. The paper is both direct and candid. He listed the number of people in various jobs and discussed the poor educational opportunities arising from the segregated school such that, at the time of writing, he stated: "During the 135 years of their settlement here, there is a record of only nine negro university graduates, and of these nine only three can really be called direct descendants of the early settlers." Oliver, W.P. (1949:296). Cultural Progress of the Negro in Nova Scotia. *Dalhousie Review* 29(3):293-300. Interviewed for *The Little Black School House*, nurse and business owner Geraldine Browning, who grew up in East Preston, Nova Scotia, states that after Grade 8, it was the end of the road in the segregated school; students had to travel far from their communities to enter Grade 9.

11   See: Winks (1969:172). Negro school segregation in Ontario and Nova Scotia. *Canadian Historical Review*. Backhouse cites a number of historical legal cases in Ontario where officials used different tactics to prevent Black children from attending the common schools. See especially: Backhouse (1999:414).

12   McCurdy, Howard, M.D. (2007). Interview, *The Little Black School House*.

13 Harding-Davis, Elise (2007). Interview, *The Little Black School House*.

14 Henry, Annette (1993). Missing: Black self-representations in Canadian educational research. *Canadian Journal of Education/Revue canadienne de l'education* 18(3):206–222. See also her detailed reference list which includes: Braithwaite, Karen (1989). The Black student and the school: A Canadian dilemma. In S. Chilungu and S. Niang (eds.). *African Continuities/L'heritage African*. Toronto, ON: Terebi: 195–216; and, Lewis, Stephen (1992, June) Consultative Report on Race Relations. Toronto, ON: Ministry of Citizenship. For Nova Scotia, see: The Black Learners Advisory Committee (BLAC) (N.S.) (1994). *BLAC Report On Education*. Halifax,NS: Black Learners Advisory Committee.

15 In Nova Scotia, individuals such as Delmore "Buddy Daye", Pearleen and William Oliver, and Carrie Best were challenging formal and informal exclusion of Black people from educational opportunities, employment, housing, and public services. From challenging a barbershop's refusal to cut a young boy's hair to the protest over racist material in the school curriculum, these leaders were forthright and outspoken. Pearleen Oliver launched two challenges, one against the colour bar that prevented Black women from entering nursing, the other for the removal of the text, "Little Black Sambo," from the province's schools. She was successful in both actions. In 1944 she worked with community leader, Mr. B.A. Husbands, who on behalf of the Coloured Citizens' Improvement League, wrote to then premier A.S. MacMillan objecting to the book *Little Black Sambo* used in Nova Scotia's schools: "Whereas the little children of our public schools get their introduction to the colored race as far as public education is concerned, at an impressionable age, in the grade 2A, reader; And whereas the references in the story of "Black Sambo" appearing where it does, holds the colored race up to ridicule, causing deep pain among our children, and presenting our race in such a manner as to destroy respect: Therefore be it resolved that the Provincial Department of Education be asked to eliminate this objectionable material from the text book. And be it further resolved that the story be substituted by the authentic history of the colored people and stories of their great men and their contributions to Canadian Culture." Excerpted from: Colored Citizen's Improvement League (1944). Letter to A.S. MacMillan (1944). Halifax, NS: Nova Scotia Archives and Records Management (NSAARM).

16 Christel N. Temple discusses the sankofa concept in: Temple, C.N. (2010:127). The emergence of Sankofa practice in the United States: A modern history. *Journal of Black Studies* 41(1):127–150. doi:10.1177/0021934709332464

17 Fabre, G. and R. O'Meally (1994:8, 15). Introduction. In G. Fabre and R. O'Meally (eds.). *History and Memory in African-American Culture*. New York, NY: Oxford University Press: 3–17.

18 See James W.St.G. Walker's "African Canadians", especially sections on Migration and Arrival and Settlement. For a detailed examination of slavery in Canada, see: Smith, T. Watson (1899). *The Slave in Canada, Collections of the Nova Scotia Historical Society, For the Years 1896–98*. (Vol. X). Halifax, NS: Nova Scotia Printing Company (retrieved 12 January 2011 from: http://www.acrosscan.com/books/slavery-canada/). For slavery in French Canada, see: Trudel, Marcel (2004). *Deux siècle d'esclavage au Québec. Suivi du: Dictionnaire des esclaves et de leurs propriétaires au Canada française sur CD-ROM*. Avec la collaboration de Micheline D'Allaire. [Cahiers du Québec.] Montréal, QC: Éditions Hurtubise HMH Ltée.

19 Settling Canada: Underground railroad (no date). *Historica Minutes*. Retrieved 2 November 2010 from: http://www.histori.ca/minutes/minute.do?id=10166

20 Cooper, Afua (2006). *The Hanging of Angélique: The Untold Story of Canadian Slavery and the Burning of Old Montreal*. Toronto, ON: Harper Perennial. Burial sites include the Redhead Cemetery in Guysborough County, Nova Scotia, Priceville, in Grey County, Ontario, and a place marked by a large stone, called "Nigger Rock," in St.-Armand,

Quebec. Filmmakers Jennifer Holness and David Sutherland directed a documentary film, titled: *Speakers for the Dead*. Holness, J. (Producer) and Sutherland, D. (Director). (2000). *Speakers for the Dead* [Film]. National Film Board of Canada. This film deals with the Priceville site.

21 Davis, Elise Harding (2007). Interview, *The Little Black School House*.

22 Sparks, Judge Corrine (2007). Interview, *The Little Black School House*.

23 Preston Petition, 11 November 1820: RG 1 Vol. 422, doc. 22. Nova Scotia Archives and Records Management (NSARM); Windsor Petition, 13 February 1845: RG5, Series P, Vol. 74, #51. NSARM

24 After the reunion, my late mother, Dr. Marie Nita Waldron Hamilton, who was president of the group, steered a project to compile short biographies of the various teachers; her colleagues published it after her death. See Evans, Doris and Gertrude Tynes (1995). *Telling the Truth: Reflections: Segregated Schools in Nova Scotia*. Hantsport, NS: Lancelot Press Limited; Hamilton, Sylvia D. (Director/Writer) (1992). *Speak It! From the Heart of Black Nova Scotia* [Film]. Canada: National Film Board of Canada.

25 Hamilton, Sylvia D. (Director/Producer). (2007) *The Little Black School House* [Film]. Grand Pre, NS, Canada: Maroon Films Inc.

26 See: *Brown v. Board of Education of Topeka*, 347 U.S. 483 (1954)

27 African United Baptist Association (AUBA) (1948:18). Minutes of the AUBA. Author's personal files. Acadia University Archives, Wolfville, Nova Scotia, has a collection of AUBA minutes dating from 1854 when the organization was founded. Nova Scotia Archives and Records Management also holds some original copies of minutes from AUBA meetings.

28 The documentary was filmed in the following locations: Halifax, Dartmouth, Cherrybrook, Five Mile Plains, Inglewood, Guysborough, and Antigonish Counties, Nova Scotia; Toronto, Windsor, and Amherstburg, Ontario.

29 Guysborough Elder (2007). Interview, *The Little Black School House*.

30 Larkin, Lois (2007). Interview, *The Little Black School House*.

31 Haines, James (2003:19). Research interview. Development report for *The Little Black School House*.

32 Knockwood, Isabelle, with Gillian Thomas (1992:27, 56). *Out of the Depths: The Experiences of Mi'kmaw Children at the Indian Residential School at Shubenacadie, Nova Scotia*. Lockport, NS: Roseway. For an examination of the impact of European colonization on the Mi'kmaq, see Elder Dr. Daniel N. Paul in: Paul D.N. (2006). *We Were Not the Savages: Collision Between European and Native American Civilizations*. (3rd ed.). Halifax, NS: Fernwood Publishing.

33 Regarding Toronto's Africentric school, see: Toronto District School Board documents (available at: http://www.tdsb.on.ca/SchoolWeb/_site/ViewItem.asp?siteid=10423&m enuid=24893&pageid=21547). On Black student achievement in Toronto see: Brown, R. S. and E. Sinay (2008). 2006 *Student Census: Linking Demographic Data with Student Achievement—Executive Summary*. Toronto, ON: Toronto District School Board (retrieved 12 January 2011 from: http://www.tdsb.on.ca/_site/ViewItem.asp?siteid=1 72&menuid=28147&pageid=24206). For Nova Scotia, see: BLAC (1994). The BLAC site contains the original report and a recent review and status update. On Wade Smith, see: Knox, Carsten (2007, June 7). A matter of principle. *The Coast*. Retrieved from: http://www.thecoast.ca/halifax/a-matter-of-principle/Content?oid=960870

34 See Stanley, J. Timothy (1990). White supremacy, Chinese schooling, and school segregation in Victoria: The case of the Chinese students' strike, 1922-1923. *Historical Studies in Education/Revue d'histoire de l'education* 2(2):287-305.

35 For a discussion of the Chatham case, see: Shadd, Adrienne (2007). Interview, *The Little Black School House*. See also: Shadd, Adrienne (2007). "No back alley clique": The campaign to desegregate chatham's public schools, 1891-1893. *Ontario History*

XCIX(1):77–95. Finally, see: States, David (2003). Research Interview. Development report for *The Little Black School House.*

36 Elise Harding Davis, Dr. Howard McCurdy, and former student, Elrita Mulder, discuss the successful campaign to close SS 11 in *The Little Black School House.* The school was closed and students went to the new school in 1965, the next academic year. In 1964, references to race were removed from the Ontario provincial legislation through an amendment introduced by Leonard Braithwaite, an African Canadian member of the Ontario Legislature. Nova Scotia changed its legislation in 1954 to remove references to race; however, the segregated schools did not all close at that time since individual school districts were in charge of school consolidation. The last segregated school to close was in 1983 in Guysborough County, one of the locations featured in *The Little Black School House.*

37 Within the span of three months in 2010, Canadians witnessed two public apologies made in Nova Scotia. On 24 February 2010 the City of Halifax apologized for the destruction of the community of Africville. (The apology, the terms of the agreement reached with the Africville Genealogy Society, and a backgrounder may be found at: http://www.halifax.ca/africville/). Also in 2010, the Province of Nova Scotia announced an official apology and a free pardon to the late Viola Desmond for her wrongful imprisonment. Ms. Desmond had been thrown in jail in 1946 for sitting in the white section of a New Glasgow movie theatre. A free pardon, rarely used, is granted on the advice of the lieutenant-governor and is given in the case of wrongful convictions. See Government of Nova Scotia (2010, August 16). News Release: New Glasgow Presented with Free Pardon, Record of Conviction. Halifax, NS: Premier's Office. Retrieved 12 January 2011 from: http://www.gov.ns.ca/news/details. asp?id=20100816003

38 See: Nova Scotia Department of Education, African Services Division (ACSD) (available at: http://acs.ednet.ns.ca); Office of African Nova Scotian Affairs (ANSA) (available at: http:/gov.ns.ca/ansa/whoweare.asp); Council on African Canadian Education (CACE) (available at: http://www.cace.ns.ca); see also: Williams, Michelle (2007). Interview, *The Little Black School House.*

Meera Margaret Singh

George, 30" x 40", c-print

Patricia, 30" x 40", c-print

Eddie, 30" x 40", c-print

Avia, 30" x 40", c-print

Joanne, 30" x 40", c-print

Evelyn and Nikki, 30" x 40", c-print

Meera Margaret Singh was born in the Canadian prairies to an East Indian father and an Irish/German mother. As a mixed-race child, she had a strong desire from an early age to explore not only her own cultural background, but customs, ideologies and religions in a more global context. This led to her first degree from the University of Manitoba in Anthropology (1997). Upon completion of this degree, she spent two and a half years living, working and travelling throughout Asia. With a camera in hand, she quickly realized that her interest in displacement (cultural, geographical,psychological) could all be explored creatively. She returned to Canada and completed a BFA in Photography (2004) from the University of Manitoba and then an MFA (2008) from Concordia University, Montréal, Québec. Meera has been the recipient of several residencies and awards, including a Toronto Arts Council Visual Arts Grant (2010) and a Canada Council for the Arts production/creation grant (2009). She has been selected to participate in a residency at the Banff Centre; as the McCain Artist-in-Residence at the Ontario College of Art in Toronto; as the summer resident at the Centre for Innovation in Culture and the Arts in Canada in Kamloops, British Columbia; as a scholarship winner participating in the Magnum Workshop with international photographer Alessandra Sanguinetti; as a selected artist in an international residency with renowned contemporary German photographer Thomas Struth at the Atlantic Centre for the Arts in Florida. Meera's work has been included in numerous exhibitions and festivals in Canada and the United States. She is currently an instructor in the Photography department at the Ontario College of Art and Design.

Beyond Imaginings: Photography from the Greenbelt

The following is an email conversation between photographer Meera Margaret Singh and editor Ashok Mathur conducted over the months of October and November, 2010. The photographs presented here are part of the Farmland *series, created as a commission for the* Beyond Imaginings *exhibition.*

AM: Meera, can you begin by describing how this portrait project came into being? I know your professional history includes a good deal of creating photographic portraits, shot on film and transferred to digital, so perhaps you can give us a bit of this background as a lead-in to this particular project.

MMS: I recently relocated to Toronto and was asked by Harbourfront Centre's Head of Visual Arts, Patrick Macaulay, to put together a proposal for a photographic project that he was curating in conjunction with the Greenbelt Foundation. The exhibition, entitled *Beyond Imaginings*, was meant to highlight the diversity in Ontario's Greenbelt: 1.8 million acres of permanently protected green space, farmland, wetlands, and communities. I was thrilled to explore this area of land in order to gain a better understanding of my new surroundings.

Having worked predominantly with portraiture, I was interested in photographing people who worked the land in the Greenbelt. Most of my recent work has addressed my interest in how cultural, physical, geographical, and emotional ideas of displacement and suspension can be explored photographically.

For the Greenbelt exhibition, I continued working with these concepts, focusing upon migrant workers, immigrant farmers, and women farmers in the Greenbelt. I wanted to explore some of the complexities inherent in the relationships between the workers and this area of land. I proceeded to create a series of photographic portraits that addressed both connections and disconnections between individuals and their surrounding landscape. After meeting numerous individuals and learning of their relationships to the Greenbelt as well as their relationships to their various homelands, I was able to create what I consider to be "based on true events" narratives, as opposed to 100% documentary work.

AM: I'm intrigued by this concept of "based on true events" as it seems critical to your work in this instance. Can you elaborate on this vis-à-vis what you term purely documentary work?

MMS: After pursuing a degree in Anthropology and then entering into the visual arts, I was fascinated by the concept of 'documentary' work. It was, in fact, this genre of photography that drew me to the medium in the first place. At the time, I had spent three years living and travelling in Asia. I photographed incessantly during that time, particularly when I was in India, as I was researching/searching into my own cultural heritage along with my family's religious ideologies and practices. I wanted to absorb everything, to forget nothing. I thought the camera could help me document all of this.

When I returned to Canada and began my Bachelor's of Fine Art degree, my work invariably began to shift. I was no longer as interested in describing the world "as I saw it." Instead, I wanted to explore the world as I imagined it. I think this is where the traditional practice of social documentary photography, in the vein of Lewis Hine or Henri Cartier-Bresson[1] moves from being a platform to describe and assist the dispossessed or the marginalized and can suddenly shift in postmodern times, to becoming a source of contention. Artistic and journalistic intentions aside, the position of the documentary photographer has historically been that of a privileged interloper looking into a world that is "other." This is not to discredit the outcome of such works. Documentary photographs such as Nick Ut's photograph of the girl running through the streets of My Lai in Vietnam as her flesh burned from the effects of napalm, became *the* iconic image of the Vietnam War.[2] Images such as this had their place in making change. I believe that documentary work is necessary, while it is also necessary for it to be analyzed. Perhaps some of the problematics here stem from photography's position as a 'truth-telling' medium, offering up a direct view into reality. But whose reality? These questions have always drawn me into the complexities of documentary work. They have also made me extremely hesitant to ascribe my working methods as such.

My camera and my imagination are inextricably linked, so much so that I can only label my work as "based-on-true-events." The recipe is there for social documentary work: an interest in humanity, in difference, in the marginalized. However, my intention is not to reduce an individual, in this instance, to 'a migrant worker,' or to 'an immigrant farmer.' I am not looking to get deep into the individual to dissect an issue such as migrant labour in Canada and look at it from all angles photographically. Clearly, I am interested in each individual I photograph, interested in how their faces will speak to their history, without that ever really being confirmed. To clarify, if I were to bring light to my process by equating it to writing, I would say that I work with a fact, a social issue, and then decide to write a short story about a character I've created that would speak to the layered issue at hand.

In this instance, I have an immense interest in migration, in displacement (culturally, socially, geographically) in one's relationship to the earth/soil, and our relationship to food and food production. Once I started researching this, I discovered the complexities of how the land in Canada was used for food production, how much sacrifice was made from the migrant workers who worked this land.

I am drawn to this "reality." I have an idea of how I feel about this issue and yet, with each individual I actually meet and converse with, I see a further angle to the story. This is where things shift for me and I begin to move away from traditional definitions of documentary work. I begin to move away from trying to describe an overarching statement about a situation. I then briefly speak with each participant and decide that I want to describe a *feeling* more than a *truth*. In a way, I'm opting for semiotic ambivalence, a multiple read.

I am reminded of Martha Rosler's essay *In, Around, and Afterthoughts*,[3] where she articulates that documentary photographers should strive to find a balance in one's observation of the realities of another and one's own personal point of view and that this can only be done by using an analytic framework that proposes solutions to the difficulties inherent in photographic representations of "other."

So where does this balance lie? For me, it lies in this grey zone between documentary and fiction, where there is room for contemplation and wonder.

AM: In an earlier incarnation, we were titling this book, *The Land We Are*, a recognition that those of us who immigrate, or whose families have immigrated, to this country, inhabit the physical landscape in a number of ways. There are, of course, vast differences between rural and urban, just to mention one of the many expressions of different migratory experiences. Can you tell us what you felt was particularly significant for your photographic subjects who are, to generalize, working very closely with and upon the land?

MMS: Being a first-generation Canadian, I have witnessed the effects, intricacies, and sacrifices of immigration firsthand. I believe this was what drew me to create work around this theme. I cannot speak for the subjects I worked with. However, I did hear time and again how spending eight months of the year in Canada and four months in one's homeland created an extreme duality in terms of notions of "homeland," "home," and "family." What happens when most of your life is spent with your co-workers in a foreign land as opposed to your spouse and children? What I heard often were the terms "second home," "second family." What I also heard from numerous men was that they chose to sacrifice their relationships with their children for their child's education. Not a single worker I encountered was in Canada because they felt connected to the land. Their connection to the land is an economic one. Were they not making enough to support their families, they would not choose to be here. I feel, in this instance, that the utopian view of one's relationship to the land begins to crumble in the face of migration and market economies.

Again, I cannot speak for each participant. In all honesty, I feel I would need more time with them and would also need to provide quotations. The overall sense of home/family/sacrifice seemed synonymous with a sense of disconnect. A disconnection from one's homeland, from a sense of "home," from family, from one's family history, and from one's roots. This seems like it would move beyond one's landscape and right into one's core and psyche. When I was photographing, I often had a vision of Frida Kahlo's painting *The Two Fridas*[4] in my head. It was as though there was a splitting of self that occurred with each participant when we were interacting. There was this nostalgia for home, a longing for family. There was often a stoicism as well, a conviction that this was the 'right' thing to do for a greater good (economically). It was the *only* thing to do in the face of a tenuous economy. From a personal and photographic point of view, I was interested in seeing if this sense of displacement and dislocation could be created or witnessed on film. I am fascinated in how the body retains experience and how gesture or expression can reveal the effects of one's personal history. When someone discusses the idea of having a 'second home,' I think of this sense of duality, this 'neither here–nor–there' (or perhaps 'both here and there') existence, and I wonder if I can even begin to describe that in images. I suppose this is a challenge I'm still working through.

AM: I know from experience that the camera can create a distance between the photographer and subject, the apparatus itself acting as a type of screen or veil to separate the two. But it can also act as a conduit, a medium of sorts, that rather than inhibiting intimacy, enhances it. Can you describe how your experience as a photographer might develop that sense of greater connection with your subject—in essence, how do you feel the act of photography helps you communicate with your subjects and, further, how does the end result help you communicate with the world? An addendum to this: through the farmland project, what have you learned vis-à-vis the question of community, communion, and reconciliation?

MMS: My work on *Farmland* has really allowed me to explore that grey zone that exists between the realms of documentary and fine art photography. While there is always a desire to connect and convey in my work, this project was not solely personal and definitely possessed many social, economic, and cultural layers inherent in it. Despite the conceptual framework being quite specific, the project did not begin nor end with the actual image. The image became almost secondary to hearing about these lived experiences.

The camera gives me licence to access communities and individuals I might not otherwise have the opportunity to meet. It can definitely create distance, as you suggest, but my experience has always been otherwise. I think this has to do with my emphasis on process as opposed to final product. I am completely immersed in the shooting process and this is really where I find most of the joy in photography. The camera often acts as a backstage pass into someone's world. It tends to house a sort of legitimacy. People often place trust in the photographer if they are working in an intimate context. What I mean is that when a photographer and a subject are one-on-one, there is a complex exchange that revolves around a significant amount of trust. The subject cannot see what I see, and therefore surrenders some control in how they are being represented. This seems minute but I find it magnanimous. Each time someone works with me, I have immense gratitude, as I know that it is more than a moment that is being exchanged, but that unarticulated trust.

To be frank, I was surprised at how so many workers, without hesitation, agreed to be a part of my project. Diane Arbus once said, "A lot of people, they want to be paid that much attention and that's a reasonable kind of attention to be paid."[5] I had a strong sense that most people enjoyed being focused upon, for even a brief period of time. I feel the camera allows for this. It's one thing when someone looks at you, it's another thing when they ask if they can look at you through a lens. There's a sense of magnification there: a magnified moment, a magnified attention that is being placed upon an individual. Unlike a video camera rolling, the still camera clicks and describes that mere fraction of a second. This is what is most compelling to me as a photographer and what ties together notions of communion, intimacy, and reconciliation in concept and form: a pause in history and a stilling of time that asks for pause, reflection, celebration or apology, contemplation and for wonder.

Notes

1 Lewis Wickes Hine (1874-1940) and Henri Cartier-Bresson (1908-2004) are considered to be among the greatest portraitists.
2 Nick Ut took his famous My Lai photograph in June 1972, which earned him a Pulitzer prize.
3 Rosler, M. (2006). In, Around, and Afterthoughts (on Documentary Photography). In *Martha Rosler, 3 Works*. Halifax, NS: Martha Rosler and The Press of the Nova Scotia College of Art and Design: 61-93.
4 Kahlo, Frida. *The Two Fridas (Las dos Fridas)* [painting]. C.1939. Collection Museo de Arte Moderno, Consejo Nacional para la Cultura y las Artes-Instituto Nacional de Bellas Artes, Mexico City.
5 Cited in the Museum of Contemporary Photography website. *Diane Arbus (American, 1923-1971)*. Retrieved 27 November 2010 from: http://www.mocp.org/collections/permanent/arbus_diane.php

Section 2: Across

Jamelie Hassan and Miriam Jordan

Born in Canada of Arabic background, **Jamelie Hassan** is based in the southern Ontario city of London, Ontario. She is a visual artist and activist and, since the 1970s, has created a body of work that is intensely driven by an engagement in both local and international politics and cultures. Her interdisciplinary installations, writing, and curatorial projects explore personal and public histories. Her works are in major public collections and she is the recipient of numerous awards including the Governor General's Award in Visual and Media Arts (2001). Jamelie's engagement with film, arguably more than any other medium, demonstrates the importance of community in her practice. A film program, curated by Miriam Jordan and Julian Haladyn, contextualizes her film projects and includes the publication *The Films and Videos of Jamelie Hassan* edited by Julian Haladyn and Miriam Jordan, with essays by Laura U. Marks and the editors (Blue Medium Press, 2010). A survey exhibition of her work *Jamelie Hassan: At the Far Edge of Words* organized by Museum London, London, Ontario, (spring 2009) and the Morris and Helen Belkin Art Gallery, University of British Columbia, Vancouver, (spring 2010) is circulating nationally.

Miriam Jordan is a First Nation artist, writer, and curator. Her artwork has been exhibited internationally, including in the travelling exhibition *Oh, So Iroquois* curated by Ryan Rice; her work is in the collection of The Woodland Cultural Centre. As a writer she has contributed to such publications as *Topia*, *C Magazine*, *Parachute*, *On Site Review*, and *Film-Philosophy* as well as chapters in *Stanley Kubrick: Essays on His Films and Legacy* (2007), and *Critical Approaches to the Films of M. Night Shyamalan: Spoiler Warnings* (2010). Her most recent project is *The Films and Videos of Jamelie Hassan*, a curated program and publication produced with J. Haladyn that examines Hassan's use of moving image art forms. Jordan is presently pursuing a Ph.D. in Art and Visual Culture at the University of Western Ontario, where she teaches courses in visual arts.

Parallel Histories

Jamelie Hassan and her maternal grandfather 1968 / 1921

Jamelie Hassan

1840
The Oneida Nation in New York was facing certain annihilation and began their migration to other parts of the United States of America and Canada. They bought land south of the Thames River in southern Ontario. By the twentieth century, the Oneida Nation in New York, which had once held six million acres of land, had only 32 acres left.[1]

1876
Introduction of the *Indian Act of 1876* turned Indians into legal wards of the Canadian government.

1894
Amendment to the *Indian Act* made education compulsory for native children.[2]

December 29, 1890
Some three hundred unarmed Sioux, mostly women and children, were massacred by the United States Cavalry at Wounded Knee Creek, South Dakota, USA.[3]

Miriam Jordan and her maternal grandfather 1994 / 1943

Miriam Jordan

1828

Under the missionary zeal of the Church of England, the Mohawk Institute finds its beginnings in 1828 as the Mechanics' Institute for boys from the nearby Six Nations Reserve. In 1831 the school is re-conceived as a boarding school for boys who were to be taught farming or some other trade. In addition to learning useful skills they spent their mornings reading, writing, and learning their catechism by rote. In 1834 the school opened its doors for girls as well. These feminine charges were kept separated from their brothers and cousins and were taught the basics of housekeeping along with the same basic primer as the boys.[1]

The New England Company translated the Bible into Mohawk to ease their First Nation charges into both English and Christianity. This was part of an ongoing process of translation that began in the early days of European colonization. In the eighteenth century at Fort Hunter, New York, my sixth great-grandfather on my grandmother's side, Joseph Thayendanegea Brant, translated the Gospel of St. Mark into Mohawk.[2] After migrating from New York State to the Haldimand Tract in Upper Canada, Brant completed his translation of the *Mohawk Prayer Book*. Eventually, these Mohawk texts would fall into disuse when children were prohibited from speaking their native tongues while at school. This often meant

Figure 1."The Snowball," Sioux Falls, South Dakota. [Hussein Shousher/Sam Hallick behind the counter, on left.] Image courtesy of Hassan Archives

1900

Lac La Biche, a French word which means "doe", is a remote community in northern Alberta. Arab immigration to the Lac La Biche region, the land of the Cree Nation, has the highest population per capita of Lebanese people in North America. Lac La Biche, a village of less than 3,000, was the second community to establish a mosque in Canada.[4] It was also one of the locations of over 130 Indian residential schools that operated in Canada.

1901

Hussein Shousher/Sam Hallick, maternal grandfather of Jamelie Hassan, departed from his family in the village of Kar'oun, in what was then Greater Syria under Ottoman rule, and travelled to North America arriving at Ellis Island, New York. Upon his arrival, like many others, he had to deal not only with a change of landscape but also a name change. His name was changed to Sam Hallick. The following decade he travelled through Canada and then back into the USA, finally settling in Sioux Falls, South Dakota, where he opened an ice cream parlor called "The Snowball" (Figure 1).

Hussein Shousher's life story, like many other Arabs who immigrated to North and South America, involved journeys across vast territorial space and into remote locations that brought Arabs in close contact with the way of life of Indigenous populations. These earlier Arab travellers, at the time of their arrival to Canada in the late nineteenth and early twentieth centuries, did not represent the powers of the British Crown. In fact, these travellers were fleeing from military occupations and the threat of war. Their own histories were likewise shaped by losses due to colonialism.

Figure 2. Iroquois Chiefs from the Six Nations Reserve reading Wampum belts (~1870s)
[Left to right: Joseph Snow, Onondaga Chief; George Henry Martin Johnson, Mohawk Chief; John Buck, Onondaga Chief; John Smoke Johnson, Mohawk Chief; Isaac Hill, Onondaga Chief-fire keeper; John Seneca Johnson, Seneca Chief.] Image courtesy of Library and Archives Canada

that children would return home to their families unable to speak to their parents. Now, the Mohawk Bible is a mere relic from a time when my ancestors could often speak more than one tongue of the varied languages of their tribes: Mohawk, Seneca, Oneida, Tuscarora, Onondaga, and Cayuga.

1844

Reverend Abraham Nelles, principal of the Mohawk Institute, wrote the following lines about my great-grandmother's grandfather when he was eighteen: "Jacob Johnson, was dismissed on account of an infirmity which rendered him a disagreeable companion for the other children; he is a steady well-behaved young man."[3]

As I read this I found myself wondering just what this "infirmity" was. I recalled the Infirmities section in the 1871 Census of Canada that asked if the individual listed was "Deaf and Dumb," "Blind," or of "Unsound Mind." A slight revision in 1891 required enumerators to find out if residents were "Unsound of Mind"; this hardly seems to be an improvement from the 1861 Census of Canada inquiring about "Lunatics or Idiots." It is in this same year that census takers concerned themselves with line 13: "Colored Persons, Mulatto or Indian."[4]

In most years both government and church were concerned with the various religions that were popping up on the reservation. Some of the Haudenosaunee were Baptist, others were Methodist, Church of England, or Presbyterians, and, of course, there are the Pagans. The Six Nations Council objected to the usage of this latter term when they met with W.F. Webster, a representative of the Anglican Church, in 1908. Mr. Webster, in response to their complaint, wrote in his report to his superiors that even he had to agree a less derogatory word was needed.[5]

Figure 3. Sioux Falls, South Dakota (1920)
[Includes: Hussein Shousher/Sam Hallick with his
son Mike Hallick, on right.]
Image courtesy of Hassan Archives

Figure 4. Six Nations House, Tuscarora
Township, Brant County, Ontario (~1890s)
Image courtesy of Library and Archives Canada

1914

Hussein Assaf/Alex Hassan, my father, departed from his village of Baaloul, in what was then Greater Syria under Ottoman rule. He arrived in southern Ontario where he settled in London, Ontario.

The Arab men who had travelled to Canada in the late 1800s to early 1900s, like many Asians, had often worked outside the dominant commerce of colonial Canada, which was controlled by British or French interests. Montreal was an important connecting site for many of the young men who were outfitted with suitcases, which contained sewing items, notions, textiles, and carpets. Working their way across the country as peddlers was often the financial start for many of these travellers. Many, like my maternal grandfather and my father, travelled into southern Ontario. Some journeyed farther west, eventually working closely with native communities in the fur trade in such places as Lac La Biche; others took jobs with the railroad or on farms.

1921

Hussein Shousher/Sam Hallick with his son Mohammed (Mike) Hallick returned to his village of Kar'oun, which was, at that time, part of the post–World War I newly expanded borders of Lebanon under a French mandate government.

1932

Hussein Shousher/Sam Hallick died in Kar'oun. His surviving family members included his wife, Fatima, pregnant with their fifth child. His oldest daughter, my mother, was named Ayshi, after his wife. His wife later died in South Dakota and was survived by her one son Mohammed (Mike) Hallick, who was born in the United States (Figure 3).

1938

Hussein Assaf/Alex Hassan returned to his village of Baaloul, met and married Ayshi Shousher, daughter of Hussein Shousher/Sam Hallick.

1939

Hussein Assaf/Alex Hassan and Ayshi Shousher Hassan left Lebanon and travelled to Canada, arriving by train to London, Ontario. This was where they began their life together, raising eleven children.

Leafing through census records from multiple years I look for Jacob's name and find that he is a farmer, and there are no affirmative checkmarks in the section labeled "Infirmities." He lives with his older sister, Elizabeth, who, like him, attended the Mohawk Institute. In March 1840, Principal Nelles reports that Elizabeth has earned ten tickets for good conduct. Though he could read and spell well, sing several hymns, and answer short questions on the catechism, Jacob earned no tickets for his conduct.

Jacob is the grandfather of George Johnson. George is the maternal uncle of my grandfather's mother, Minnie Mae. It is this uncle that my maternal grandfather reports that he is living with on his border-crossing card in 1952 when he moves from Ohsweken, Ontario, to Buffalo, New York.

1871
Living two houses away in Tuscarora Township from siblings Jacob and Elizabeth Johnson in 1871 is Eliza Jack, who is twenty. She is living with Margaret Hill and Zachariah Johnson, and their two children, Charlotte and James. Perhaps Eliza is helping to care for the children, if she is this doesn't last long as a year later one of her charges, Charlotte Johnson, is listed as a student at the Mohawk Institute.[6] Aside from a brief mention in a school report Eliza disappears from the records.

In 1861 her teacher at the Mohawk Institute, Thomas Griffiths, writes in his half-year report that she is taught sewing with the other girls at the school. In addition, she learns catechism, reads the Testament, writes in block letters, and can do simple addition.[7]

This same year a photograph was taken of six chiefs. It shows the gathered men reading wampum belts. One of the chiefs is my fifth great-grandfather on my grandmother's side. His name was Isaac Hill or *Kawenenseronton*. His hair is cut short and he is dressed in European clothes. In his hands is what looks like a two row wampum belt. I wonder what his interpretation of this belt was (Figure 2).

1908
After visiting the Grand River Reserve and its residential school, Mr. W.F. Webster writes in his report for the New England Company in 1908 the following observations: "former pupils of the Mohawk Institute are reluctant to send their own children there because they consider the discipline is too strict."[8]

During this same visit the Six Nations Council conveys a message through Webster to the New England Company. They ask the Church to account for the sale of tribal lands without the consent of the people. The Speaker of the Council, Chief John C. Martin, also chides Webster for neglecting to compensate Six Nations for this omission. This makes me laugh when I read it because the Anglican Church, in its carefully edited history of the Mohawk Institute, states the following (conveniently omitting to mention their own role):

1949

After World War II and changes to immigration laws, there began another wave of migration into Canada from Asia, including Lebanon and other parts of the Arab world.

1950

Fatima Shousher, my grandmother, was finally given permission to immigrate with her sons to London, Ontario. This was after repeated sponsorship requests by my parents were refused. Some of my early artwork examines my family archives and addresses the immigration policy of Canada during the 1950s. Through my research I found letters denying my relatives entry into Canada. These refusals were based on racial categories of "Asian" that pointedly articulate a policy of systemic racism against Asians.

Growing up in southern Ontario in the city of London, I was obviously conscious of my Arab identity but also conscious that my reality was in proximity to the neighbouring Oneida community. My father took us on Sunday drives, travelling on gravel side roads, which led to the Oneida settlement 22 kilometres outside London. The Oneida farmers in this agricultural heartland of southern Ontario offered us woven baskets full of apples and pears and beaded necklaces made by Oneida women.

The nurturing of friendships and solidarity that my parents had with First Nation communities was reflected in their other political allegiances, including working throughout the 1950s in support of anti-colonial Algeria in its resistance to France's colonialism and also in support of Palestinians after their dispossession in 1948.[5]

Figure 5. Jamelie Hassan's ceramic book *Orientalism* (2004)
[Reproduction of Edward Said's book *Orientalism* in a display case with various objects in the exhibition *Orientalism and Ephemera*, curated by Hassan, at Art Metropole, Toronto]. Image courtesy of Krista Buecking

The Haldimand Tract … was conveyed to the Six Nations in 1784. This large parcel of 385,000 hectares straddled the Grand River, 10 km on each side, from its source near Dundalk, Ontario, to its outflow at Lake Erie. In later years, this land grant would be substantially reduced by colonial decree and through contested agreements with the Canadian government. As well, smaller portions were sold off by band leaders, under questionable circumstances. The disposition of the Six Nations lands has remained controversial to this day.[9]

1943

I have one photograph of my maternal grandfather.

My grandmother sent it to me in the mail after I asked her in a letter if she would give me a photo of him. A few weeks later an envelope arrived in the mail. Folded in with her handwritten letter, written in shaky script, was a creased photocopy of a young man in uniform. Two words were written across the bottom of the page in her hand: Grandpa Styres. I looked at the image and I see my face and my mother's reflected back at me. So this is my grandfather. The empty space in my nebulous family history finally has a face and a name.

Figure 6. Miriam Jordan's painting *Nature/ Morte* (2005)
[On display in the exhibition First Nations Art '06 at the Woodland Cultural Centre, Brantford.] Image courtesy of M. Jordan

I read through the rest of my grandmother's letter, but she offers no more information about my grandfather. Though I am disappointed that she doesn't tell me more of her history, I am surprised that she has given me even a photocopied image of him and a scrawled last name. But this repeats a pattern for us when speaking about our family. Once when I asked for a picture of my uncle, who died when I was twelve, she again sent me a photocopy of him dressed in his US Marine Corps uniform and wrote nothing about him. Silence shrouds both of these reproductions of my male relatives in their military uniforms, both their faces fresh and young as they are sent off to war. I know how difficult it was for her to speak of the past and our family.

1953

Jane Elm from the Oneida Settlement and many of her female relatives were a constant presence in the Hassan household at 26 Erie Avenue. I have a memory of being ill and waking from a fevered sleep with the desire to paint. Jane Elm and one of her daughters are taking care of me. I am quarantined alone in my large bedroom, which I normally share with my three older sisters. In the morning I ask for paint and something on which to paint. Jane returns to my room with a tray of brilliant colours in little china cups and a sheet of cardboard. I do a fingerpainting on the cardboard with these brilliant paints. When I recover from my illness and am allowed out of bed, the first thing I do is go into the kitchen and search through the cupboards for the ingredients the paints were made with, which I cannot find. This is one of the first memories I have of the desire to paint. How the paint was made to this day remains secret.

1955

The first Islamic convention in Canada is hosted in London, Ontario. My family participated with other community members in organizing this historic event (Figure 7).

1967

I travelled to Lebanon for the first time, met many aunts and uncles on both my mother's and father's side of the family who continued to live in neighbouring villages in the Bekaa, Lebanon. I enrolled and studied art at the Lebanese Academy of Fine Art (ALBA) in Beirut and worked at the American University Hospital as a nursing aid.

1968

I often stayed with my aunt and uncle in the small mountain village of Baaloul in the Bekaa Valley. In the early hours of the morning, as I would wait for my bus to take me to Beirut where I was attending art classes, I was often greeted by three elderly women, who were baking bread and who would invite me to take my breakfast with them. As I sat within the domed space of the traditional clay oven, my eyes burning from the rising smoke, I could see the amused expression that passed between the women. As tea with bread, cheese, and apricot jam were offered to me, one of the old women would laugh, give me a gentle pinch on the arm, and say, "you think you are the true Canadian but we are the true Canadians." While I did not understand what was meant by her words, their laughter, their expression, and especially the pinch stayed with me over the years. A decade later my brother, Ottawa-based writer Marwan Hassan, was to add another piece to this puzzle. He travelled to Lebanon in 1979 to the same village of Baaloul and stayed with my aunt and uncle. This is what he learned: two Cree sisters had met and married two Arab men, who had emigrated from Lebanon to Canada in the early 1900s. Marwan wrote of one of these men:

Figure 7. Still from Jamelie Hassan's video *The Oblivion Seekers* (1985)
[Television news clip of Jamelie as a young girl dancing at the 1955 Islamic convention in London.] Image courtesy of Hassan Archives

Figure 8. Miriam Ahmet-Allah Jordan (1974)
[Rug with Arabic text in background.] Image courtesy of M. Jordan

I tuck the photocopy of my grandfather away and forget about it until I see it reproduced again in his obituary, which my mother gives me many years later. Reading it from *The Eastern Door,* I see that the photograph was taken in 1943 when my grandfather was eighteen and before he is shipped off to participate in the Dieppe offensive.

September 1947

It is a hot summer evening in the mid-90s when my sister tells me part of the story. We are smoking in the apartment we shared on Bay Street. It was a short walk past Marshall McLuhan's house to the university where we were both students.

"Do you know who our grandfather is?" She asks me.

"No." I reply.

"He's a Styres."

The name rings a bell and I ask her, "Is he the one in Montreal who sent Mom that letter telling her not to contact him again?"

"Yeah, that's him. He's Mom's father."

Like my sister I have counted back the months from my mother's birth and figured out that she was conceived in September 1947. My grandparents' parents were friends and wanted the two to marry, but they refused.

We both shake our heads at the same time in frustration at the collective efforts of our mother and her family not to talk about her absent father. Together they stonewalled any discussion on the topic. We all knew not to talk about him.

When I was growing up I sometimes wondered if he was in jail, like a few of my relatives who periodically turned up out of nowhere. They were hugged and kissed by the family, and then they disappeared for years, lost in the confines of some faraway silent prison.

1952

After many hours spent scrolling through microfiche files, records, and census indexes and books, I find a confirmation of my grandfather's existence; a border-crossing card from the Peace Bridge dated 1952. This is not his first trip to Buffalo. He identifies himself as an ironworker. The address that he gives for his residence is on College Street in Buffalo, New York. My grandfather is staying with George Johnson, his mother's uncle.

The typed words provide information on Grandfather Styres' back-and-forth journey between Ohsweken and Buffalo. On the reserve he lived with his father and mother: Clifford Styres and Minnie Mae Martin. His grandmother is Isabel Jane Johnson. She was born in 1877 to Ezra and Eliza Kelly Johnson. Isabel Jane

After the first world war, homesick and not in good health, he longed to return to the old country. His Cree wife and the Canadian born children remigrated with him. About sixty years later this old woman I had met was that West Cree Woman, an Arabic speaking Muslim living in the little mountain village of her dead husband. Her sons in turn had migrated to South America sending the grandchildren back to the village in the summers to be with her, their Arab, Muslim grandmother who, as you can tell, was a true Canadian.[6]

1971
Closing of the Mohawk Institute Residential School in Brantford.

1972
Founding of the Woodland Cultural Centre on Six Nations of the Grand River Territory, adjacent to the main building of the residential school built in 1904, replaces the earlier building destroyed in a fire (allegedly) set by the students.

1978
Edward Said's *Orientalism* is published.[7]

1988
Cultural diversity became Canada's state policy with the enactment of the *Multiculturalism Act*.

1988
Wampum belts functioned within the complex system of traditional forms of Indigenous government. Tom Hill, Seneca scholar and artist and former Director of the Woodland Cultural Centre, initiated an examination of the wampum belts when eleven belts were repatriated to the community. An exhibition was created at the Woodland Cultural Centre to both celebrate and give the Six Nations Iroquois Confederacy members an opportunity to learn of the wampum belts' relevance to continuing systems of self-government and political power.

The catalogue accompanying the exhibition explains the meaning of the belts, such as *Gus-wen-tah*, which "consists of two parallel rows of purple wampum beads on a white background. The three rows of white beads which separate the course of the two peoples stand for peace, friendship and respect—elements which both keep the peoples at a distance and which bind them together."[8] Hill goes on to reveal that the *Gus-wen-tah* Wampum Belt is a treaty belt in which the purple and white beads illustrate that there are two distinct cultures—the Haudenosaunee and the British government—and that each would respect the other's ways.

1989
Opening of the new location of the Museum of Civilization in Gatineau, Quebec, showcases the museum's building designed by First Nation architect Douglas Cardinal. Since its opening this museum has become one of Canada's most

is fourteen years older than her younger brother George; both siblings were born on the reserve. Their mother is listed on various Canadian Census forms as either Indigenous or Irish. Like so many of his ancestors before him (and many of the descendants of the Haudenosaunee in the future), Uncle George travels south through the lands that have sheltered his people for thousands of years. After crossing the Niagara River he settles in Buffalo. It is there that George opens his door to his sister's son, welcoming my maternal grandfather into his home. My mother is living in Buffalo at this time with her mother. She saw her father only once when she was a small child.

Flipping the card over I see a note on the back saying that Grandfather Styres presented a letter from the Department of Citizenship and Immigration attesting that he is a member of the Upper Cayuga No. 427 tribe of Six Nations.

1974
I have a photograph of myself from when I was one. I am sitting in a rocking chair holding my first cat in my lap, her stomach bulges with kittens. Behind me on the wall is a rug covered with Arabic text. My father converted from Christianity to Islam before I was born. I was born on his twenty-fifth birthday so he named me Miriam Ahmet-Allah Jordan. My first name is his mother's name, while my middle name is Arabic for "Gift of God" (Figure 8).

People are always surprised to hear of the religious persuasions of my family members both past and present. There is an enduring assumption that because I am First Nations my ancestors and I are "godless pagans." Surprise ensues when I correct this stereotype by revealing that a Dutch pastor, Godfrey Dellius, converted my Mohawk ancestors in New York to Christianity. My tenth great-grandmother on my grandmother's side is Lydia Karanonodo, and she was among the first group of Mohawks to be baptized by Dellius in the church located at North Albany, New York, on 11 July 1690.[10] This is merely the first of many adaptations by my ancestors to European culture. What has resulted from the exchanges between Natives and colonists is a rich heritage of First Nations and immigrant culture that has become inextricably bound together. In these mutual exchanges, I am reminded of the *Gus-wen-tah* Wampum Belt and how it represents the binding together of two distinct cultures in a common land and the hope that both Native and settler would respect each other's traditions and sovereignty.

Later, when I am twenty, my mother and I return from London, Ontario, where I am attending university, to her house in Upstate New York. At the border we both present our Status Cards. The border guard looks at my full name on my card and says to me, "This isn't an Indian name!"

I respond by asking him, "What is an Indian name?"

الیس آیلند، نیویورك

Ellis Island,
New York

پیتربورو، اونتاریو

Peterborough,
ONT.

وینیپیك، مانتوبا

Winnipeg,
Manitoba

Jamelie Hassan's "Geographical Snowballs" (2010)
[Adapted from elements from Hassan's installation
in *Across Borders* (1996) at Artspace, Peterborough,
an exhibition that included the work of Shelley Niro
and Catalina Parra.] Image courtesy of Hassan

القرعون · لبنان

Karoun, Lebanon

ساينت بول · مينسوتا

St. Paul,
Minnesota

جلنكو

Glenco

outstanding national institutions—a Canadian landmark. It is recognized both for the originality and beauty of its architectural design and for the major collection of Aboriginal art and culture that is housed within its walls.

September 1990

Kahnawake and Kanesatake/Oka Crisis, the longstanding dispute over land at Oka ended after 78 days of an armed standoff between the Mohawks and the Quebec police and the Canadian army. In this dispute the city of Oka wanted to use the land to expand the Oka golf course.[9]

October 1990

Indian Summer, the last official project of the artist-run centre Embassy Cultural House, is organized. This exhibition was presented in bookstore locations on Richmond Street in London, Ontario, and the Woodland Cultural Centre. It included artists Joane Cardinal-Schubert, Florence Ryder, Daryl Chrisjohn, and Robert Frechette's images from behind the barricade at Oka.

Daryl Chrisjohn was one of the makers of replica wampum treaty belts, which are in the collection of the Woodland Cultural Centre. The Chrisjohns were Oneida descendants of those survivors who had travelled up into southern Ontario from New York after the American Revolution.

1992

Travelling Theory, the first exhibition of contemporary art from Canada to the Middle East, was presented at the Jordan National Gallery of Fine Arts in Amman. It was co-curated by independent curator Fern Bayer and myself, in partnership with the McIntosh Gallery, the University of Western Ontario, London, Ontario.[10] An extensive cultural program and exhibition were inspired by one of Edward Said's essays in his book, *The World, The Text, and the Critic*.[11] It was also the first major contemporary art exhibition in Canada to focus on the Middle East after the 1990 Gulf War.

1993

The Anglican Church of Canada made its formal apology to Native people.

1995

Gerald McMaster, in his capacity as curator at the Museum of Civilization, curates the XLVI Biennale di Venezia representing Canada with an exhibition by Métis artist Edward Poitras.[12]

October 2001

The Lands within Me: Expressions by Canadian Artists of Arab Origin exhibition opened at Canada's Museum of Civilization in Gatineau, Quebec. As the artworks were being assembled and installed in September 2001, the 9/11 attacks happened in the United States. The museum director, Victor

He replies, "You know something like Pocahontas."

My mother and I are both silently containing our indignation as he hands back our cards and waves us on.

1991

In my last year of high school, when I am still living in Upstate New York, my father tells me he wants to show me something. After promising not to say anything he opens a thick file labelled "Indian Status" and pulls out a letter.

My father explains that this is a letter replying to my mother, who had contacted her father, Mr. Styres, asking him to help his grandchildren regain their status, which had been taken away when she married my father, a white man. In 1985 the Canadian government passed Bill C-31, reversing years of discrimination against First Nations women, and their children, who were stripped of their status.

I read the letter addressed to my mother. My grandfather's lawyer threatens my mother with legal action if she contacts him again.

I find myself disgusted by this faceless man who has to hide behind lawyers to speak to his daughter. I know without asking that my mother is both mortified and wounded by this letter from her father.

2005

I visit my aunt and uncle at the Six Nations Reservation; I call her aunt though she is my mother's first cousin. Her mother, my grandmother's sister, has died recently. A few weeks before I had attended my great-aunt's funeral feast, which was held at my aunt's house, an Elder speaks in what I subsequently learn is Oneida, a language that I cannot speak, in part, because my grandmother and her parents were not permitted to speak it.

Later as I sit at the kitchen table my cousin tells me how she and her siblings grew up with Status Cards that labelled them as members of different tribes. I am not surprised, as I have heard this before, but then she tells me that I am Oneida and not Mohawk as my Status Card states. I am startled and pained by this news. Even before I regained my status my family told me that I was Mohawk. This is a result of the Canadian government's attempt to erase the history of First Nations women by enforcing patrilineal descent. The Haudenosaunee traditionally follow a matrilineal line of descent, with children taking the tribal and clan affiliation of their mother. This was a concerted effort on the part of the Canadian government and churches to diminish the power of First Nations women who traditionally controlled the allocation and usage of land of their tribes. My grandmother and her full siblings are labelled as Mohawk

Rabinovitch, in response to these attacks on our neighbour, made a decision to "postpone indefinitely" the exhibition. After considerable protest on the part of the artists and activists and the direct intervention of then Prime Minister of Canada Jean Chrétien, the museum director was forced to reverse his decision. The exhibition opened as planned.[13]

2002
National Gathering on Aboriginal Artistic Expression, the first in a series of three forums, was held in Ottawa.

2003
Minister's Forum on Diversity and Culture was held at the Museum of Civilization. I was one of the members of the advisory committee with Alanis Obomsawin, who served on the committee for one year, which resulted in a two-day forum that brought together more than 500 participants, both government and heads of Canadian cultural institutions with activists, to discuss and create a plan of action for progressive government initiatives to support responsible cultural policy.

Significantly, diaspora and migration in Canada cannot be understood without speaking of Aboriginal people and their vital role and relationship to immigrant populations. These narratives of the relationship between non-European immigrant communities in Canada and Aboriginal people have been largely absent from the official histories of the nation-state.

2005
Anishinaabe artist Rebecca Belmore was selected to represent Canada at the Venice Biennale; the curators were Jann L.M. Bailey, Kamloops Art Gallery, and Scott Watson, Morris and Helen Art Gallery, University of British Columbia.

5 June 2008
I received an invitation from Phil Fontaine, National Chief of the Assembly of First Nations, to attend the ceremony and the Statement of Apology to the former students of the Indian residential schools on Parliament Hill, Ottawa, Canada.

11 June 2008
Prime Minister of Canada Stephen Harper rose in the House of Commons and apologized, on behalf of the government of Canada, to all Survivors of Canada's Indian residential school system. This historic apology, as Phil Fontaine, National Chief of the Assembly of First Nations, wrote, "will contribute to the healing and reconciliation for all Survivors and all Canadians."[14]

by the Canadian government because their father, Harold Porter, is Mohawk. This is how I became a Mohawk.

2006

During the spring of 2006 I presented several of my paintings in an exhibit at the Woodland Cultural Centre (Figure 6). I invited my mother and grandmother to attend the opening. We met outside the museum on Mother's Day, which coincided with the opening. My husband and I made the trip from London to Brantford via car. As we neared the museum we drove past the Mohawk Chapel, which functioned primarily as the chapel for students attending the Mohawk Institute.

Various members of my family have been baptized or married in the Mohawk Chapel. My great-great-grandfather Charles Porter's parents, Ellen Powless and Nicodemus Porter, were married in the chapel in 1870. Nicodemus Porter's brother, Joseph, likewise married Ellen's older sister, Catharine Powless, in this same chapel. Their son, Joseph Porter Jr., was thirteen when the principal of the Mohawk Institute listed him as a student in third form at the Mohawk Institute in a report to the New England Company dated 30 June 1872. Joseph Jr., the first cousin of Charles, is one of a group of male students of whom the principal complains: "Their speaking Indian so much among themselves when at play, or when out of school, is one of the greatest hindrances to their progress at school. We do what we can to induce them to talk English, *without compulsion.*"[11]

The Mohawk Institute itself became part of the Woodland Cultural Centre in 1972. The imposing brick of the old building currently houses administrative offices and a research centre. Next to the school is the newer building of the museum, which functions as an exhibition space for Iroquoian and Algonkian people.

As we got out of our adjacent cars my grandmother stared at the three-storey building that towered over us.

She said quietly to me, her eyes not meeting my gaze, "Oh, this is the Mush Hole. I wondered where it was. My, my…," she paused and hesitated, "um, friends told me about it."

"Did you go to school here?" I ask touching my grandmother's shoulder, which is trembling.

She doesn't answer me. I ask her again and she responds by pointing to the trees behind the school and says to me, "There are children buried out back."

It is only after she is dead that I find out my grandmother was referring to her half-siblings who were sent to the Mohawk Institute because their father Harold and their mother Maybelle could not take care of them.

2009

Jeff Thomas, artist and curator, in response to the Caledonia Blockade, organized the exhibition *Home/land and Security*, which presented both Native artists and non-Native artists in the context of the Six Nations, the Grand River, and community histories at the Render Gallery of the University of Waterloo and other public sites.

March 22, 2010

Chief Justice Murray Sinclair, Chair of the Truth and Reconciliation Commission, gave a talk in London at the University of Western Ontario on the challenges facing the Commission. The majority of those present were from neighbouring First Nations communities, including the Oneida Settlement.

Notes Hassan

1 Campisi, J. (1988:45, 61). The Oneida Treaty Period, 1783-1838. In J. Campisi and L.M. Hauptman (eds.). *The Oneida Indian Experience: Two Perspectives.* Syracuse, NY: Syracuse University Press.

2 General Synod Archives of the Anglican Church of Canada (2008). The Mohawk Institute—Brantford, Ontario. Retrieved 20 July 2010 from: http://www.anglican.ca/rs/history/schools/mohawk-institute.htm

3 Eye Witness to History (1998). Massacre At Wounded Knee, 1890. Retrieved 20 July 2010 from: http://www.eyewitnesstohistory.com/pfknee.htm

4 Information found at the Alkareem Mosque (in Lac La Biche) website. Retrieved 20 July 2010 from: http://www.laclabicheregion.com

5 For a brief overview of this history see: El Ali, M. (2010). Overview of Palestinian Forced Displacement in and from Lebanon 1948-1990. *Al majdal* 44(Summer/Autumn): 22-28.

6 Hassan, Marwan (1997:69). Matamoros, Palm tale two: A true Canadian. *West Coast Line* 31(2):66-71.

7 Said, Edward W. (1978). *Orientalism.* New York, NY: Pantheon Books.

8 Woodland Cultural Centre (1989:7-8). *Council Fire [exhibition catalogue]: A Resource Guide.* Brantford, ON: Woodland Cultural Centre.

9 York, Geoffrey and Loreen Pindera (1991). *People of the Pines.* Toronto, ON: Little, Brown & Company Ltd.

10 The artists from Canada in the *Travelling Theory* exhibition included Ron Benner, Stan Denniston, Janice Gurney, Jamelie Hassan, Robert Houle, Lani Maestro, Robert McNealy, Marianne Nicolson, and David Tomas. A special issue of *Harbour: Magazine of Art & Everyday Life,* 2(1), on the exhibition and symposium *Travelling Theory* was co-published by the McIntosh Gallery (University of Western Ontario, London, Ontario) in 1992.

August 2009

My mother visits me in London, Ontario, coming from her home in Buffalo. She hands me an obituary for her father, breaking a long-standing silence between the two of us.

In the obituary, Ross Montour writes of my grandfather's war experiences: "He never liked to talk about it and if he did would become very emotional."[12]

There are many things that my grandfather did not like to talk about. But he is not the only one who was silent. This short history of my grandfather and grandmother is a hard history to write because so much of it has been wilfully silenced. It is a silence enforced by our families and ourselves, but it is also a silence imposed upon us by governments and churches intent on denying our histories and our continued existence. The objective of residential schools as late as 1920 was as Duncan Campbell Scott declared, "I want to get rid of the Indian problem ... Our objective is to continue until there is not a single Indian in Canada that has not been absorbed into the body politic, and there is no Indian question, and no Indian department."[13] If healing and reconciliation are to truly happen, we must speak of our own histories and note the censored histories of those who walk beside us.

Notes Jordan

1   Between 1831–1969, the Diocese of Huron authorized enrolment from 15 to 185 students. See General Synod Archives of the Anglican Church of Canada (2008). The Mohawk Institute—Brantford, Ontario. Retrieved 30 November 2010 from: http://www.anglican.ca/rs/history/schools/mohawk-institute.htm

2   Johansen, Bruce Elliot and Barbara Alice Mann (eds.) (2000:31). *Encyclopedia of the Haudenosaunee (Iroquois Confederacy)*. Westport, CT: Greenwood Press.

3   Graham, Elizabeth (1997:52). *The Mush Hole: Life at Two Indian Residential Schools*. Waterloo, ON: Heffle Publishing.

4   1861 Census of Canada, line 13, Tuscarora, Brant, Ontario.

5   Webster, W.F. (1908). New England Company. *Report of Mr. W.F. Webster upon his Visit to the Mohawk Institute, Brantford, and the Grand River Reserve, Canada*. London, UK: Spottiswoode & Co.

6   See the 30 June 1872 NEC Report in Graham (1997:216).

7   Graham (1997:216).

8   Webster (1908:13).

9   See General Synod Archives of the Anglican Church of Canada (2008). The Mohawk Institute.

10 Sivertsen, Barbara J. (2006:22). *Turtles, Wolves, and Bears: A Mohawk Family History*. Westminster, MD: Heritage Books.

11 Graham (1997:218).

12 Montour, Ross (2007:story 4). Dieppe survivor passes. *The Eastern Door* 10(15).

13 Government of Canada (1920:54, 63). Report of the Special Committee of the House of Commons examining the Indian Act amendments of 1920 (Duncan Campbell Scott testimony on 30 March 1920). Library and Archives Canada, RG10, volume 6810, file 470-2-3, part 7.

11 See Travelling Theory in Said, Edward W.
    (1983). *The World, The Text and the Critic.*
    Cambridge, MA: Harvard University
    Press.
12 "Métis is a self-defined term meaning
    more than a mixed white-Indian ancestry.
    It refers to a distinctive sociocultural
    heritage and describes communities,
    social customs, conventions, traditions."
    See: McMaster, Gerald (1995). *Edward
    Poitras: Canada XLVI Biennale di
    Venezia.* Hull, QC: Canadian Museum of
    Civilization: 35, footnote 13.
13 Kaouk, Aïda (ed.) (2003). *The Lands Within
    Me: Expressions by Canadian Artists of
    Arab Origin.* Gatineau, QC: Museum
    of Civilization. Worthy of note for this
    context regarding Lebanon was that of
    the twenty-two artists in the exhibition,
    seven of the artists who participated
    have origins or family origins from
    Lebanon: myself, Hannah Alpha, Mirella
    Aprahamian, Yasser Badreddine, Rawi
    Hage, Jayce Salloum, and Camille
    Zakharia.
14 Fontaine, Phil, National Chief, Assembly
    of First Nations (2008). Email invitation to
    author to attend ceremony and Apology
    on Parliament Hill, Ottawa, Canada,
    dated 5 June 2008.

Miriam Jordan
Gus-wen-tah (2010)

Renisa Mawani

Renisa Mawani is Associate Professor of Sociology and Founding Chair of the Law and Society Minor Program at the University of British Columbia (2009–2010). She is a socio-legal historian who works on the conjoined histories of Asian migration and settler colonialism. She has published widely on law and coloniality and legal geography, and her articles have appeared in journals including: *Law/Text/Culture*; *Social and Legal Studies*; *Social Identities*; *Theory, Culture, and Society*; and *Cultural Geographies*. Her first book, *Colonial Proximities: Crossracial Encounters and Juridical Truths in British Columbia, 1871-1921* (UBC Press, 2009), details the dynamic encounters between Aboriginal peoples, Chinese migrants, mixed-race populations, and Europeans in the late-nineteenth and early-twentieth centuries and the epistemic truths and modes of governance these contacts produced. Her second book (in progress) is a transnational history of the Komagata Maru, its place in anti-colonial struggles in India and across the British Empire.

Cross Racial Encounters and Juridical Truths: (Dis)Aggregating Race in British Columbia's Contact Zone

[*Originally published: Mawani, R. (2007/08). Cross-Racial Encounters and Juridicial Truths: (Dis)Aggregating Race in British Columbia's Contact Zone.*[1] *BC Studies 156/157:141–171. Content has been reproduced in its entirety but formatted in the style of this publication.*]

On 27 August 1890, Indian Agent William Henry Lomas submitted his annual report to the Superintendent of Indian Affairs, Ottawa. Here, he informed his superiors, as he did each year, of the progress made among the Indians of the Cowichan Agency. While there was nothing particularly extraordinary in his recollection, it is precisely the quotidian nature of his comments that warrant closer investigation:

> There is little change in the Indians living in Victoria and Nanaimo. Some are hardworking and steady, having considerable amounts in the saving banks; others are constantly fined for being in possession of intoxicants, and the police records for any year will prove that it is almost impossible to prevent the sale of liquor in small quantities to the town Indians. Women go out to white houses to wash and char, and are given occasional drinks of spirits, and in nearly every case become people who will spend all they earn in spirituous liquor, obtaining it at any cost. *A greater part of this traffic is done by the lower class of Chinese, but I am sorry to say that merchants of high standing often connive at the trade, and Indians living at a distance from the cities can often leave with large quantities of liquor in their canoes—sometimes hidden in their boxes of biscuits, sometimes in flasks and soda water bottles, and again in bottles that once contained Worcester sauce.*[2]

Focused on the banalities of the everyday, Lomas' report offers an important glimpse into crossracial encounters and their flourishing conditions on Canada's west coast. While recognizing that colonialism thrived on interraciality, through labour, mobility, and the circulation of commodities, for example, he viewed these contacts to be potentially dangerous, particularly for aboriginal peoples. Interraciality, he warned, furnished native communities with opportunities to access and consume intoxicants, thwarting their progress towards modernity and civilization. But for Lomas and others, not all contacts were equally disconcerting. As the quote above suggests, it was encounters between aboriginal and Chinese populations that proved especially troublesome. Precisely because these races were so putatively different—Indians were thought to be undeveloped and in need of protection and the Chinese were perceived to be conniving and dangerous—interactions between them, Lomas insisted, were sure to unsettle and possibly even subvert colonial rule.[3]

Narratives of interraciality and heterogeneity, like the one above, raise important questions about what we know and have yet to learn about British Columbia's colonial contact zone. Although the colonial archive is littered with government reports and correspondence that echo Lomas' observations about the persistent and perilous contacts between Chinese, aboriginal peoples, and those of mixed-race ancestry, genealogies of Indigenous-European relations and of Chinese migration to Canada's west coast have, for the most part, been written as distinct and separate.[4] This is not to suggest that questions about crossracial encounters have not yet been asked or are entirely new. The Fraser River Gold Rush, as Jean Barman explains, rapidly transformed the demography of Canada's west coast: "British subjects," she writes, "suddenly found themselves jostling Americans, blacks, Chinese, Germans, Italians, Jews and Spaniards on the streets of Victoria."[5] Barman and others have offered us critical insights into the prevalence of interracial relations in historical British Columbia.[6] However, we still know little about how migration from China produced new geographical proximities and altered existing configurations of colonial knowledge and power. While we know that crossracial encounters were pervasive, we still have much to learn about these interactions, the epistemic fields they drew from, and the forms of governance they inspired.

This paper explores some of the ways that Chinese migration to British Columbia shifted terrains of colonial power, creating new anxieties and exigencies for Indian Agents, missionaries, and legal authorities. To be clear, this paper focuses less on the physical encounters between Chinese and aboriginal peoples and instead tracks how the arrival of Chinese migrants, from the late nineteenth century onwards, unsettled the region's racial topography. Frequent contacts between Chinese and aboriginal peoples, like the ones lamented by Indian Agent Lomas, produced renewed racial knowledges and forms of legality. Chinese migration to British Columbia, I argue, forced colonial agents to redraw boundaries between aboriginal peoples and Euro-Canadians in ways that generated new meanings of racial difference and new constellations of racism. In the pages that follow, I explore the ways in which colonial authorities responded and reacted to the arrival and presence of the Chinese (including fear, contempt, and resentment) and how these reactions influenced their existing repertoire of colonial knowledges about racial superiority and inferiority. The growing presence of Chinese along Canada's west coast activated concerns about interraciality and racial purity and in so doing created conditions in which Indian Agents, missionaries, and legal authorities could hone and clarify their existing racial taxonomies. By contrasting migrants from China with aboriginal peoples and with African-Americans south of the border, colonial authorities produced racial differences through a matrix of uneven knowledges, including commonsense, criminal statistics, and legal truths.

While British Columbia's prevailing racial field was undoubtedly shaped by local conditions, the epistemic grids that underpinned it were also informed by a transnational and circuitous movement of peoples and ideas. To make sense of the growing Chinese presence, authorities often borrowed racial grammars from the United States and constituted new racial epistemologies and points of comparison in the process. These racial distinctions were not merely descriptive but were highly politicized. The first function of state racism, as Foucault has argued, was aimed at "separating out the groups that exist within a population....into the subspecies known precisely as races."[7] Ultimately, racial classifications enabled the colonial state to create and reinscribe differences between seemingly different racial groups while at the same time determining biopolitical futures: distinctions between "good"/ "bad" and "assimilable"/ "unassimilable" populations enabled the state to determine who could remain in the settler regime and under what conditions and who was to be expelled and eliminated.[8] Whereas fears about labour informed these prevailing concerns, the putative threats posed by Chinese labourers and merchants, as Indian Agent Lomas suggests, were not about economic questions alone but about biological ones that centered on the health and longevity of aboriginal peoples, and ultimately, of the settler regime.

The *Royal Commission on Chinese Immigration* (1885) and the *Royal Commission on the Liquor Traffic* (1894) provide evidence from which it is possible to analyze questions about competing racial truths and colonial racisms.[9] These commissions serve as important sources of legality because they show how law and social policy inform, produce, and draw upon existing "knowledge formats."[10] These two Commissions can tell us about the changing racial fields of heterogeneity and interraciality in British Columbia, the epistemologies that informed the region's racial topography, as well as law's complicity in their production. How did colonial administrators make sense of the growing population of migrants from China? What sorts of racial vocabularies did they borrow and from where? In what ways were the Chinese and their epistemic and material relations forged against other racialized populations, most notably "Negroes" and "Indians"? And how did these comparisons produce renewed forms of racisms? In answering these questions, albeit in a preliminary way, I draw from several statistical tables detailing crime rates as well as from the testimony of select witnesses. My focus on numbers and narratives is twofold;

first, to highlight the multiple "knowledge formats" through which juridical racial truths have been historically produced, and second, to explore how epistemologies about racial superiority and inferiority have gained an objectivity and neutrality that persists in our contemporary historical moment.[11] Numbers, as many scholars have now argued, have been perceived as "modern facts" that are situated beyond social, legal, and historical circumstances, a perception that has obscured the *politics* of enumeration.[12]

Historians and others have drawn on the *Royal Commission on Chinese Immigration* (1885) to document the ways in which early Chinese migrants were constituted as antithetical to whiteness and to white settlement.[13] Although the *Royal Commission* is filled with numerous examples, of how the Chinese were defined against other racial populations as well as the movements of racial knowledges across the Canada-US border, few have explored how the Chinese were inserted into a broader racial field and how their racial identities were forged against other populations deemed racially inferior. These questions can offer rich insights into the emergence of state racisms and their dynamic, competing, and contested fields. Through comparisons with African-Americans and aboriginal peoples, witnesses who testified before these Commissions created a range of disparate and contradictory racial knowledges. These truths were integral to dominant conceptions of the "Chinese" as both a juridical category and as a racially inferior population that was (dis)placed along the margins of historical British Columbia. In statistical tables and in witness testimony, "Whites," "Negroes," "Indians," and "Chinese," were constituted not only as discrete races but as populations that were socially, morally, and physically incompatible and thus in need of separation and racial management. What becomes evident when we think comparatively are the ways in which racial categories and their epistemic fields shifted at critical historical junctures when the colonial state was thought to be imperiled. The presumed unassimilability of migrants from China was often undergirded by concerns about white labour as many scholars have argued, but their *foreignness* was also informed by Orientalist truths about the Chinese as a "cunning" and "despotic" race who threatened the state's efforts to improve and assimilate vulnerable aboriginal peoples.[14]

By bringing racial heterogeneity and interraciality to the fore, this paper is also an attempt to unsettle historiographies of race and racisms in western Canada's colonial contact zone by locating these discussions within a wider global frame.[15] Too often, scholars writing about British Columbia have approached Canada's most westerly province as though it were truly at the "edge of empire," a region physically and intellectually cordoned off from other parts of the world.[16] Although colonialism was always rooted in temporal and spatial specificities, empire was also a *global* phenomenon that linked diverse and disparate geographical locales within a wider terrain of power and knowledge.[17] Colonial authorities in what is now British Columbia drew from a range of racial epistemologies and strategies of management which were often borrowed from other contexts, including the US.[18] While these truths about race were adapted to the local demands and rhythms of colonial rule, what these dynamics reveal is the continuous interplay between the local and the global, the universal and the particular. Before examining these movements, let me first offer a few brief and contextualizing comments about colonialism and its racial truths.

Colonial Knowledges and Racial Typologies

> Knowledge means rising above immediacy, beyond self, into the foreign and distant—Edward Said[19]

Colonial knowledges, as anthropologists Bernard Cohn and Nicholas Dirks have long argued, were as central to maintaining British rule and command in India as were military and economic power.[20] Across the British Empire, from India to western Canada, colonial administrators relied on a range of "investigative modalities" to generate truths about colonial populations who were not only geographically distant, as the epigraph from Edward Said suggests, but also close, proximate, and immediate.[21] Surveys, censuses, cartographic practices, and classificatory schemas enabled colonial agents to know and order the foreign and the unknowable and to conceptually and literally map their newly acquired territories. While colonial knowledges, including statistics, often produced "countable abstractions" of people, they also facilitated racial divisions *between* populations, distinguishing those who might optimize or maximize life in the colonies from those who might endanger it.[22] For Edward Said, the production of colonial epistemologies and categories was both contingent upon and generative of modern truths about race, including origins, classifications, and destinies.[23] However, knowledges of racial inferiority and superiority were not neatly organized along the Orient/ Occident binary, and thus, were not as consistent or unified as Said initially suggested.[24] On the contrary, racial epistemologies were arranged along a grid of uneven and shifting coordinates which generated a conflictual, contested, and ambiguous field. It was precisely the elasticity and uncertainty of racial difference that rendered these distinctions so tenacious and resilient.[25]

Despite many criticisms of his Eurocentric focus, Foucault's speculative insights about state racisms provide us with important conceptual tools for rethinking the colonial encounter and its regimes of racial truth. Colonial readings of Foucault have certainly expanded our understandings of biopolitics and its alternative genealogies; however, there are still conceptual gaps surrounding questions of state racism, or more accurately state *racisms*.[26] Although Foucault's comments about "the human race of races, the distinction among races, the hierarchy of races" all imply an underlying heterogeneity, his analytic, as it stands, does little to further our assessments about colonialism and its diverse, and competing epistemological foundations.[27] The colonies were indeed locales where a racial episteme was cultivated, but racial differences were never ordered against Europeanness alone. As I discuss in the following sections, colonial administrators drew *numerous* distinctions between white and non-white populations. It was precisely through these multiple comparisons that they identified a hierarchy of races, one that carried high political stakes. To be sure, the colonial encounter did not produce a singular, homogenous, or static state racism that was then directed uniformly at the colonized, but generated a range of *state racisms* that distinguished populations through a dynamic repertoire of internal and external differences.[28] In British Columbia, the phenotypical, moral, and cultural characteristics ascribed to "Indianness," and "Chineseness" enabled Indian Agents and missionaries to distinguish these populations and to determine their place in the settler regime.

The racial logics deployed by colonial officials along Canada's west coast fractured the colonizer/ colonized divide in significant ways. From the nineteenth century onwards, administrators used different modalities of juridical knowledges including crime statistics, legal cases, and commissions of inquiry, to mark and divide not only the European from the Indian but also from the Chinese. In their attempts to count and compile an archive of crime statistics for instance, judges, police officers, and local bureaucrats generated a racial order which rendered "Whites," "Indians," "Chinese," "Half-Breeds," and "Negros" to be discrete and immutable species whose differences were not only biologically innate and ineradicable but whose being was physically, morally, and affectively incompatible. Thus, for Agent Lomas, the "Indian" had a weakness of the will and was prone to drunkenness while the "Chinaman" had a racial predisposition to corrupt vulnerable aboriginal peoples through the sale of liquor.[29] Separating the population into races was in part about calculating risks, which of these communities might enhance British Columbia's emerging society and which ones might inhibit it. Whereas missionaries and Indian Agents along Canada's west coast often perceived the futures of native peoples with optimism, that many could be improved and eventually assimilated, they viewed the Chinese to be antithetical to western values and dangerous to both whites and Indians. Unlike aboriginal peoples, many insisted that the Chinese were a population that could not easily (or ever) be absorbed into British Columbia.[30]

From the nineteenth century onwards, racial distinctions between indigenous and European were routinely institutionalized in juridical practices. "Lawfare," as John Comaroff describes it, was central to empire— as a coercive instrument of colonial power, a site of counterinsurgency, and a locus of knowledge production.[31] Not engaging with questions of colonialism directly, Ian Haney-Lopez has used American naturalization cases to illustrate how judges drew upon scientific and commonsense knowledges to make legal distinctions between whites, "Negroes," and those migrant populations who could not easily fit into the black/white paradigm.[32] What Haney-Lopez illustrates is that law was not only historically implicated in racial knowledge production, but that law's truths were followed by serious material consequences, defining who had access to racial privilege, property, and ultimately, citizenship.

Importantly, legal knowledges were not produced in the courtroom alone.[33] Commissions of inquiry were also sites of "lawfare" where truths about racial difference were newly constituted, debated, and in some cases, legislated.[34] From the nineteenth century onwards, Royal Commissions, as inquiries into specific social problems, were integral to the production and accumulation of legal knowledges, both in the metropole and in administrative and settler colonies.[35] In Canada, commissions enabled the Imperial, Dominion, and in some cases the provincial governments to generate information that would not only provide documented "facts" about particular and pressing social and moral issues but which would eventually form the basis for further inquiry and for legislation and social policy. But these knowledge-producing machines were integral to the making of juridical racial truths as well. Government commissions, as John Comaroff tells us about colonial South Africa, were not in the business of documenting reality but were in the practice of creating it. Commissions of inquiry generated ethnological knowledges about the racial populations they investigated, giving "bureaucratic currency and practical reality to the categorical structures and cultural divisions that formed the emerging ethnoscape."[36] Both the *Royal Commission on Chinese Immigration* (1885) and the *Royal Commission on the Liquor Traffic* (1894) drew upon statistics, legal and scientific expertise, and on commonsense knowledges to generate racial truths about Chinese, African-American, aboriginal, and mixed-race communities.[37] By appointing Royal Commissions to investigate Chinese immigration and the liquor trade in Canada, the Dominion government constituted each of these to be *moral problems* that required not only the accumulation of knowledge but also legal and political solutions aimed at restricting Chinese immigration.

The Royal Commissions each drew upon an "epistemological pluralism" that incorporated the expertise and commonsense views of its witnesses as well as the "objectivity" of numbers, including crime statistics and court data.[38] Although both Commissions were, to some extent, informed by prevailing ideas of "unfree labour" that were circulating in the US and up the west coast, the Commissioners and witnesses generated their own racial distinctions - between Chinese and aboriginal peoples, for example - that were geographically and politically localized.[39] Despite the different substantive foci of the two Commissions, there were apparent and important continuities. The Chinese were characterized in both reports to be a race that was not only distinct from and inferior to whites, but that was inherently different from and in some cases a danger to *internal populations* including "Negroes" and "Indians."[40] In the following two sections, I examine these variegated racial knowledges, their movements across the Canada-US border, and the ways in which they galvanized additional juridical "facts" in support of Chinese exclusion.

Moving Beyond Black and White: *The Royal Commission on Chinese Immigration* (1885)

The *Royal Commission on Chinese Immigration* (1885) was appointed by the John A. Macdonald government on 4 July 1884. Macdonald selected Dr. Justice J.H. Gray, of the Supreme Court of Canada, and Dr. Joseph Chapleau, secretary of state, to investigate "all the facts and matters connected with the whole subject of Chinese immigration, its trade relations as well as the social and moral objections taken to the influx of Chinese people into Canada."[41] Their mandate was to generate "proof" of whether legal restrictions on Chinese immigration, similar to those enacted in British Columbia and then disallowed by the courts, were in the best interests of the country.[42] The Commissioners fulfilled these directives quickly. Shortly after their report was published, Chapleau himself initiated a Bill to "Restrict and Regulate Chinese Immigration into the Dominion of Canada." The Bill, which was approved that same year, enabled the Dominion government to begin its lengthy campaign aimed at restricting and eventually prohibiting migration from China, first through the head taxes and subsequently the *Chinese Immigration Act* of 1923 that ended large-scale migration to Canada.[43]

Historians and others have used this inquiry to document the ways in which early Chinese migrants were constituted as antithetical to the western values of work and morality. In her important book, *Vancouver's Chinatown*, Kay Anderson draws from the report to track how politicians and labour organizers in British Columbia constructed the Chinese as a discrete and distinct race. "Almost every one of the forty-eight BC witnesses invited to testify on the Chinese presence in the province," she writes, "traded freely in the language of racial types, racial instincts, and racial apathy."[44]

While Anderson's point is a critical one, her own book did not trace "the language of racial types," but focused specifically on how government officials created Chineseness against Europeanness, both epistemically and geographically. The commissioners and witnesses did view the Chinese to be foreign, unassimilable, and inferior, but these racial distinctions were never determined against whiteness alone. Nor were their ideas about race geographically bound. If colonialism opened perilous possibilities for intermixture across racial divides, as Indian Agent Lomas remarked, then the colonial encounter became the formative moment when racial categories were determined across a shifting grid of difference, one that placed the Chinese in a comparative frame that was repeatedly trafficked across the Canada-US border.[45]

Throughout the Royal Commission's report, migrants from China were constituted in ambivalent and contradictory ways, both as industrious workers whose presence was necessary to build the economy and infrastructure of a young Canada but whose foreignness threatened the emerging nation. To make sense of these recent arrivals and their effects on white settlement witnesses did not construct racial grammars anew. Instead, many drew upon an established archive of racial difference that proliferated in California, Oregon, and Washington and was emergent along Canada's west coast. Those who described labourers from China as racially inferior made their determinations across a range of comparisons that included whites and blacks. In so doing, many inserted the Chinese into an existing configuration of racial knowledges.[46] In some ways this is hardly surprising as the Commissioners took much of their evidence from witnesses in San Francisco and in other US cities along the coast. But, my interest is in tracking how knowledges of blackness that pervaded the Royal Commission informed other epistemic connections that were then transformed in the process. The racial lexicon that underwrote the testimony of witnesses enabled Indian Agents, missionaries, and legal authorities in British Columbia to characterize the Chinese as a race that not only posed an economic threat to whites but also a biological and moral affront to aboriginal peoples.

Although the Royal Commission on Chinese Immigration has been the subject of much scholarly debate, one area that has received significantly less attention has been the statistical tables. Like censuses and other enumerative devices, these tables provide important political insights as to how populations were racially defined, classified, and ordered, and how these determinations changed over time. Enumeration, as many scholars have argued, figured centrally in colonial biopolitics.[47] While numbers were instrumental in "making up people," and in producing distinct racial bodies, counting also generated aggregates or populations that demanded different modes of governance, ranging from improvement and civilization (aboriginal peoples) to deportation and expulsion (Chinese migrants).[48] Despite that documenting race carried a presumed objectivity, counting was in and of itself a "formalizing racial governmentality" that operated both bureaucratically and administratively, generating new racial identities, social relations, and configurations of power in the process.[49]

In their investigations into the social and moral objections to Chinese immigration, the Commissioners not only canvassed testimony from various constituencies but also solicited crime statistics from local authorities. The tables they produced tell us perhaps less about the criminal propensities of the Chinese relative to the deviant impulses of other races and more about the constitution of nineteenth century juridical-racial categories and taxonomies. Specifically, the table entitled "Return of Convicts Sentenced in the Supreme Court of British Columbia to the British Columbia Penitentiary" (Table I) illustrates the racial heterogeneity of the colonial contact zone and its comparative logics. The table was organized along five "races": "Chinese," "Indians," "Half-Breeds," "Negroes," and "White." The taxonomic logic of the table is not entirely clear as the categories were not alphabetically indexed. Reading the table as a grid that descends in order from top to bottom and left to right thus raises questions about prevailing racial orders. Were the categories deliberately arranged in a descending order of civility, or through other schematic principles? The outer placement of "Chinese" and "White" not only forged epistemological relations between these populations but also those in-between.

Although the categorical arrangements are ambiguous, one thing is clear; the racial breakdown did not fully reflect the demographics of British Columbia. In the nineteenth century, Canada's west coast was home to a large white, aboriginal, and mixed-race population.[50] The inclusion of "Negroes" is surprising given that the black community in Canada's most westerly province was relatively marginal, a point that is reflected in the absence of black offenders below.[51] Instead of dismissing this as an error or aberration, I approach the table as an artifact that might provide us with critical insights into local and inchoate taxonomies and the wider forces that shaped them.

Although British Columbia did not have a significant black population and slavery did not mark the Canadian nation as it did in the US, the persistent movements of workers, labour organizers, and politicians between California and British Columbia contoured emergent racial truths in important ways. Discussions of blackness and of slavery, as I elaborate further on, inadvertently shaped and undergirded debates about the putative threats that "unfree" Chinese labour posed to whites. More significantly, they also informed discussions about the dangerous influences that the "corrupting" Chinese had upon aboriginal peoples, through the sale of liquor, for instance.

The testimony of witnesses further illustrates the significance of racial grids and crossracial comparisons. Debates about the Chinese and their perilous effects on labour and white superiority were often located within global conversations about race. James P. Dameron, a lawyer and resident of California, situated his comments of the Chinese accordingly. Informed by an article in the *Popular Science Monthly*, he rehearsed a familiar but contentious argument about racial evolution, one that substantiated monogenesis over polygenesis, that the world's races had only one origin.[53] "Mankind is divided into four different groups," he explained. "First, the black; next the red; next

Table I: Return of Convicts Sentenced to the Supreme Court of British Columbia to the British Columbia Penitentiary[52]

Race					Crime Committed	Sentence	When Sentenced	Where Sentenced
Chinese	Indians	Half-Breeds	Negroes	White				
1					Larceny	2 years	March 13/80	New Westminster
				1	Shop-breaking	2 years	Aug 23/80	Victoria
				1	Rec'g Stolen goods	5 years	Aug 23/80	Victoria
				1	Embezzlement	2 ½ years	Aug 23/80	Victoria
1					House breaking	5 years	Sept 20/80	Richfield
1					Wounding with Intent	2 ½ years	Sept 20/80	Richfield
				1	Larceny	2 years	Oct 1/80	Quesnelle
1					Shop-breaking	2 years	Oct 11/80	Clinton
	1				Larceny	3 years	Oct 18/80	Kamloops
		1			Killing Cattle	5 years	Oct 18/80	Kamloops
				1	Larceny	5 years	Oct 18/80	Kamloops
1					Assault with Intent	7 years	Oct 25/80	Lytton
	1				Larceny	2 years	Oct 25/80	Lytton
				1	Larceny	2 years	Oct 29/80	Yale
1					Stabbing	10 years	Oct 29/80	Yale
1					Aiding, abetting	10 years	Oct 29/80	Yale
	1				Larceny	2 years	Nov 10/80	New Westminster
7	3	1	0	6				

Source: Royal Commission on Chinese Immigration (1885), pp. 391–393.

the brown, and last, the white. Modern scientists have gone on and divided mankind into twelve cases, or twelve different groups." The origins of these races, whether four or twelve, he insisted, could be traced to Caucasians, who were the most civilized and superior of all.[54] Although the race-crime table did not consistently follow Dameron's evolutionary model, placed as the outer-most column, whites could indeed be read as the origin of the species.

Informed by a Darwinian logic, Dameron elaborated his points about racial superiority and its instability. The Mediterranean and Mongolian races, he conceded, were "the most highly developed, surpassing all other human species in numbers of individuals."[55] Although the Mongols had reached an elevated stage of progress relative to the other races, Dameron was quick to qualify that "the Mediterranean or Indo-Germanic species have, by means of higher development of their brain, surpassed all other races and species in the struggle for life, and have already spread the net of their dominion over the whole globe." For Dameron, fears about Chinese migration to California were about labour and much more: they represented a crucial struggle over life. These "hardy Mongolians, with their peculiar civilization have met us at the Golden Gate, and have begun the contest for ascendancy," he explained.[56] Because the Chinese were so eager and willing "to work more hours and live on less, live on what a white laborer would starve on," to "throw open the country to their immigration," he cautioned, "the European would in a few years mean to be overrun, so that the white man would have to emigrate, or begin a *war of the races*."[57] His emphasis on life, race, and war, draws striking parallels to Foucault's claims about biopolitics. For many white colonists, struggles over Chinese labour were indeed biopolitical, raising questions about how these foreigners might affect the lives of whites, not in economic terms alone, but also in moral and biological ones.

At the same time that witnesses like Dameron inserted the Chinese into a global racial field, others located their presence within prevailing concerns about blackness and slavery. Many witnesses who testified made explicit and implicit references contrasting the Chinese with African-Americans. While these comparisons have received some attention from American scholars, few have questioned how Chinese migration to Canada was informed by these wider discussions.[58] Given that many Chinese migrated to British Columbia from California, and that Canadian authorities frequently consulted their American counterparts, as the Royal Commission makes clear, we need to think more carefully about these transnational connections and how they shaped racial knowledges and exclusionary practices along Canada's west coast. As Ann Laura Stoler reminds us, comparison was a cornerstone of colonial politics. "Colonial regimes," she explains, "were not hegemonic institutions but uneven, imperfect, and even indifferent knowledge acquiring machines." Thus, "[c]olonial bureaucracies" were "invested in selective comparison with other polities: with highlighting their similarities to some and differences from others."[59] In nineteenth century British Columbia, these comparisons between Chineseness and blackness figured prominently in the production of local juridical racial truths.

In some ways, connections between African-Americans and the Chinese were a product of empire's global reach. Both slavery and indentured labour were inextricably linked to the development and expansion of imperialism and capitalism. In the mid-nineteenth century, Chinese migration, as many scholars have argued, enabled authorities in the American west and south to solve a pressing dilemma, to advocate freedom for slaves on the one hand, while maintaining a cheap, surplus, and expendable labour force, on the other.[60] Like African-Americans, Chinese labourers, although indentured and thus not fully enslaved, were continually referenced as "slave labour" that was equally if not more demoralizing to white superiority. John Swift, a long-time resident of San Francisco, claimed that the "influx of the Chinese has had a *worse effect upon the respectability and dignity of [white] labor than slavery had in the south*."[61] Objections to Chinese labour, Swift claimed, were even more intense than was opposition to slavery: "There is a stronger feeling here against the Chinese than there is in the south against negroes [sic]," he opined. For Swift, these distinctions were, in part, about future effects and possibilities: "I would rather have negro slavery today" he explained, "for negroes [unlike Chinese] are born in the country and at least take an interest in it."[62]

The comparative frames that witnesses evoked in their discussions about the Chinese and African-Americans, as Swift's testimony suggests, often centered on the question of legal status. In American jurisprudence, racial distinctions were frequently made on a continuum between whiteness (freedom) and blackness (unfreedom). As a result of this binary, US judges were often faced with vexed questions as to how they should classify the "other races."[63] Immigration law became pivotal in securing distinctions between different racial populations. "The law," as historian Mae Ngai explains, "established a quota system that classified the world's population according to nationality and race, ranking them in a hierarchy of desirability for admission into the United States."[64] These legislative enactments did not only order those racial groups seeking entry into the US as "good"/ "bad" and "desirable"/ "undesirable" but also structured their relations with domestic racial populations. The "foreignness" of the Chinese became an important marker of difference that was not only intended to distinguish Chineseness from whiteness but also from the internal specter of blackness that so deeply shaped American society.[65]

In his testimony to the Royal Commission, Henry Haight, the former Governor of California, evoked this foreign/ domestic distinction. "The negroes of California are very respectable, decent people," he explained.[66] Although Haight insisted that African-Americans were "ignorant," it was their legal status and their seeming permanence that opened up possibilities for development and assimilation. While both blacks and Chinese were inferior to whites, the marked difference between them, Haight and others suggested, had to do with question of entry point and ultimately legality; that the Chinese truly did not belong and could be sent back to their country of origin, while "Negroes," who were initially brought to the US as slaves were now long-time inhabitants who had nowhere to go back to, and thus, were aspiring to adapt to American life.[67]

In marking the Chinese as foreign and unassimilable, many witnesses emphasized those putative cultural and moral sensibilities that positioned them against African-Americans. Mr. Slanson, a court reporter for the *Oregonian,* a leading newspaper in Portland, argued that the Chinese were a detriment to society's morals. The Chinese, he claimed, would "steal whenever they get a chance, and are very much like the old-time down-South negroes [sic] from a police point of view."[68] Slanson's views were not uncontested. Others insisted that the Chinese lacked a morality that could often be found among blacks. For Morris Estee, a lawyer and long-time California resident, the Chinese were "more intelligent" than other races but "would not make good citizens, any more than slaves would make good citizens if they were honest."[69] In drawing these connections, Estee placed himself in an awkward position. Who was worse, the Chinese coolie or the slave? "In some respects they [Chinese] are inferior to the negro [sic], and in some respects they are far superior," he explained. While Estee raised questions about the honesty of slaves, he thought them to be morally superior: "as to their morality, there is no comparison [between the two]: *the negro is vastly more moral than the Chinese here*."[70] Questions about Chinese migrants and their putative immorality assumed a parallel logic in British Columbia. Discussions about the Chinese as "cunning," "deceptive" and "despotic," as I discuss in the following section, were mobilized throughout the late nineteenth century to emphasize the threats they posed to aboriginal peoples and to further justify their exclusion from Canada.

As the evidence above indicates, many witnesses who appeared before the Royal Commission did insert Chinese migrants into a wider logic of race that drew epistemic connections with African-Americans. While this racial grammar was undoubtedly linked to global capitalism, slavery, and European superiority, knowledges about Chineseness were localized differently along the Pacific Northwest. In British Columbia, where race and racisms have such different histories how are we to make sense of this spectre of blackness? By eliciting testimony from witnesses in California and up the coast, the languages of race that were transported to Canada's west coast were similar to those flourishing south of the border. Whereas legal authorities counted and calculated criminal cases in ways that took stock of black offenders as Table I indicates, discussions about Chinese labour in Canada were also structured along a universal logic of "free" versus "unfree." Canadian authorities perceived Chinese labour as threatening to British Columbia's emerging settler society precisely because the Chinese were thought to be enslaved and indentured workers who were undercutting white ones. In his testimony to the Royal Commission, Malcolm Sproat described the Chinese as a race that was in "abject slavery...to custom and tradition" and "in a state of low animal apathy."[71] These "degrees of unfreedom" not only made it difficult if not impossible for the "Canadian unskilled workman" to compete, but activated and renewed an older racial vocabulary that was constituted through the trans-Atlantic slave trade.[72]

Importantly, the racial epistemologies that this grammar generated not only shaped and organized colonial labour relations in California, but also in British Columbia where politicians continually cautioned one another about the demoralizing effects that labour from China would have upon white lives. But Chinese migrants were thought to compromise nation and its racial futures in other ways as well. Between his comments about "abject slavery" and "low animal apathy," Malcolm Sproat explained these threats as follows:

> The substantial grievance of the white settlers in the province, from the social and political point of view....is that while burdened with a mass of uncivilized Indians whose numbers exceed their own, an additional enormous mass of ignorant and debased aliens, male adults without families, and absolutely without any capabilities for citizenship [the Chinese], are forced upon them, in remorseless disregard of their well-being and of the repeated resolutions and acts of their legislature.[73]

The growing Chinese presence may indeed have increased the white man's racial burden, as Sproat suggests above; however, the Chinese, as Indian Agent Lomas and others cautioned, also endangered the future of white settlement in other ways: large-scale Chinese migration created close interracial proximities that unsettled state initiatives to domesticate and assimilate the "mass of uncivilized Indians." It is to these points that I now turn.

Disaggregating Race: *The Royal Commission on the Liquor Traffic* (1894)

By the time the *Royal Commission on Chinese Immigration* had published its report in 1885, the Chinese had been firmly constituted as a population that was not only inferior to whites but also distinct from and incompatible with other racial populations. The Chinese, as Malcolm Sproat and many others argued, could never successfully be absorbed into British Columbia's settler society. Not only did they undermine the value of white labour, but as witnesses who appeared before the *Royal Commission on Chinese Immigration* (1885) claimed they manifested other "racial defects," including a disregard for truth and a propensity to commit crime.[74] By the 1890s, it was precisely these fears about the putative immorality and sinister influences of the Chinese that raised pressing concerns for colonial authorities. This threat was about white settlement and much more: if Chinese migrants continued to enter the country, Indian Agents and law enforcers cautioned, their presence would not only corrupt whites but might potentially devastate aboriginal peoples. As Indian Agent Lomas' annual report warned, the Chinese - labourers and merchants alike - were directly implicated in supplying intoxicants to Indians, a condition that assailed at the very heart of colonial rule.

Concerns about Chinese men supplying liquor to Indians became commonplace throughout the late nineteenth century. While Indian Agents and police constables circulated and exchanged these fears in government memos, correspondence, and in legal cases, their sentiments were especially pronounced in the *Royal Commission on the Liquor Traffic* (1894). Unlike the *Royal Commission on Chinese Immigration* (1885), which was mandated to investigate the effects of Chinese immigration, an issue that was contentious but not completely divisive, this commission was confronted with deciding the vexed question of prohibition, an issue so controversial that even the federal government had long evaded it. Briefly, the Royal Commission was formed in 1891 to assess the practicality of national prohibition at a time when this issue was fiercely contested. Chaired by Sir Joseph Hickson, the Commission had several mandates: to determine the extent of the liquor traffic in Canada, to decide upon the implementation of the *Canada Temperance Act*, and to assess whether a national policy of temperance was desirable and even achievable. Although the Commission declared at the outset that its intention was *not* to evaluate the moral aspects of liquor use but to investigate the commercial and social interests surrounding licensing and law enforcement, its report created and reinforced a prevailing moral order to which racial truths were critical.

Like the *Royal Commission on Chinese Immigration* (1885), numbers figured centrally in the production of racial knowledges. Not only did numbers forge the Commission's evidence providing truths about race, but statistical data was deployed to demonstrate a causal relationship between race and crime, even when these claims could not be numerically supported. In the British

Columbia section, race-crime tables were evoked by the Commissioners and witnesses as a way of emphasizing the dangers of Chinese immigration. Henry William Sheppard, the Superintendent of the Victoria City Police, submitted two numerical tables to the Commission extracted from his department's Annual Report for 1891. The tables, one summarizing criminal cases before the Victoria Police Court and the other documenting convictions (see Table II and III below), were published in the appendices of the Royal Commission but served as important reference points in witness testimony. Instead of highlighting other relevant characteristics (such as gender and age, for example), the tables divided those arrested and convicted of various crimes, including drunkenness and supplying liquor to Indians, into three racially distinct taxonomies: "all except Indians and Chinese," "Indians," and "Chinese."[75] Unlike the *Royal Commission on Chinese Immigration*, Victoria police authorities were no longer concerned with documenting the offences of "Half-breeds" or "Negros," even though the former had long been accused of supplying intoxicants to aboriginal peoples.[76] Rather, crime, and the liquor problem in particular, were now divided amongst the province's three most numerically significant populations.

Sheppard presented these tables to the Commissioners as though they were "facts" available for government use in their raw form. These numbers implied that Victoria's police authorities did not make any racial determinations but simply gathered and recorded observable racial differences between those convicted for liquor-related and other offences.[77] Despite this seeming impartiality, many scholars have told us that knowledge production does not take place outside of social circumstances but is in effect a social and political process. Even numbers as knowledge formats are never impartial or neutral but are generated through and require a set of interpretive conditions.[78] As Nikolas Rose has argued, numbers do not simply record a preexisting reality but are constitutive of it.[79] The aggregation of race, in these tables and others, not only produced and ordered racial identities in hierarchical from but also created social conditions that became central to colonial governance: the need to protect vulnerable Indians from the sinister influences of the Chinese.

Like other knowledge producing processes in nineteenth century colonial contexts, the mapping of crime was inextricably linked to the mapping of race.[80] By organizing crime statistics through race, colonial agents, including Victoria's police authorities, were able to constitute distinct populations that were both homogenized and homogenizing, "species" who displayed specific external and internal traits that enabled the colonial state to watch, govern, and in some instances remove them from the emerging settler society (through incarceration, for example). Like the table in the *Royal Commission on Chinese Immigration*, the categories above were organized racially rather than alphabetically, as "all except Indians and Chinese," "Indians," and "Chinese." These taxonomies constituted the distinctions between Indians, Chinese, and others as real, tangible, and significant, while the categorical arrangements suggested an operative hierarchy that connected these taxonomies in a racially ordered logic. The making of juridical categories was not then a descriptive process of representation but was established on specific assumptions about the origins, characteristics, and evolution of human nature. Racial discourse, David Theo Goldberg insists, "includes a set of hypothetical premises about human kinds (e.g., 'the great chain of being,' classificatory hierarchies, etc.) and about the differences between them (both mental and physical)."[81] By creating a racial matrix, the Victoria Police submitted tables that represented "All except Indians and Chinese," "Indians," and "Chinese" as distinct and knowable races whose racial identities and propensities towards crime were relative and relational. Indians and Chinese were not only populations who exhibited biological differences that made them distinguishable but also moral and mental traits that rendered them socially and affectively incompatible and thus in need of segregation.

Table II: Victoria, BC, Convictions for Offences Committed in 1891

Nature of Offence	Committed by all except Indians and Chinese	Committed by Indians	Committed by Chinese	Total
Assault	30	8	4	42
Infraction of City By-laws	136	---	39	175
Drunkenness	406	175	1	582
Gambling	29	---	12	41
Infraction of Public Morals Act	36	---	5	41
Supplying Intoxicants to Indians	29	---	2	31
Vagrancy	42	---	4	46
Possession of Intoxicants	---	35	---	35
Other offences	96	3	12	111
Total	804	221	79	1,104

Table III: Summary of All Cases before the Victoria Police Court

Nature of Offence	Committed by all except Indians and Chinese	Committed by Indians	Committed by Chinese	Total
Convicted in police court	801	221	79	1,104
Sent for Trial	31	2	6	39
Discharged	231	28	31	290
Grand Total	1,066	251	116	1,433
Total cases before court for drunkenness	423	182	1	606

Source: Royal Commission on the Liquor Traffic (1894), Appendix No. 11, pp. 669.

In other numerical tables compiled during the same period, the first category, "all except Indians and Chinese," was a category often used to describe whites. In the *Royal Commission on Chinese Immigration*, a similar table was submitted by Charles Bloomfield, the Commissioner of Victoria Police. Detailing those cases that were heard in Victoria's Police Court, Bloomfield's classifications were as follows: "Whites," "Indians," and "Chinese." Below the table was a note: "In this statement, under the heading of whites, are included all others than Chinese and Indians."[82] Here, whiteness was defined through negation, representing a heterogeneity that included other racial populations but which also captured European nationalities and ethnic differences.[83] But by the turn of the century, white became a category in and of itself. Given the growing racial diversity of British Columbia, the negative category of whiteness could no longer adequately contain ethnic and cultural distinctions and instead was narrowly defined in ways that signified a range of moral proclivities including, habits, customs, lifestyles, and the ability to self-govern. In British Columbia as in other administrative and settler colonies, whiteness became "a state of being."[84]

Unlike Europeans, who were deemed to have a nationality and thus a history, the classification of "Indians" and "Chinese" characterized these populations as *racial species* that were marked by few internal differences. Counting, as Arjun Appadurai has told us about the Indian census, did not only produce types and classes, but also created "homogenous bodies (within categories) because number, in its nature, flattens idiosyncrasies and creates boundaries around those homogenous bodies as it performatively limits their extent."[85] By counting bodies, police authorities did more than erase and flatten heterogeneity, including regional and linguistic differences. Through their taxonomic schemas, administrators inadvertently placed these racial populations into what Anne McClintock has described to be "anachronistic space," a space that was "prehistoric, atavistic...irrational," and outside of history. To be clear, I am in no way suggesting that Indians and Chinese were ascribed the same or even similar racial characteristics. What I am pointing to is how authorities constituted these "races" as static, unchanging, and homogenous populations, who for different reasons were deemed to be "inherently out of place in the historical time of modernity."[86] While Indians were outside of history because they were not yet morally developed, the Chinese were thought to be lacking in those necessary characteristics— freedom, civility, and justice - which were emblematic of European modernity.

From the late nineteenth century onwards, colonial administrators frequently drew figurative and literal boundaries between Indians and Chinese, borders that were fortified through the problem of intoxicants and intoxication.[87] In the Royal Commission's report, witnesses traded on commonsense ideas about aboriginal peoples and Chinese migrants as racially discrete and as differentially and unevenly implicated in British Columbia's illicit liquor problem. While aboriginal peoples suffered from a weakness of the will that was evident in their over-consumption of alcohol and in their public displays of drunkenness, the Chinese, who many argued did not normally consume liquor, were among those held responsible for the persistent intoxication amongst aboriginal communities. "Considering the number of Chinamen and others who try all means in their power to sell intoxicants to the Indians," remarked Indian Agent McTiernan in 1883, "it is surprising that there is not more drunkenness among them."[88]

Numbers alone were unable to substantiate the Commission's production of racial truths, however. From the tables above it is clear that the overwhelming convictions for all offences, including drunkenness and supplying intoxicants to Indians, were committed by those classified as "all except Indians and Chinese." As Table 1 indicates, 406 offenders in this category were convicted for drunkenness compared to 175 "Indians" and 1 "Chinese." These figures were consistent with the convictions for supplying intoxicants to Indians; 29 "all except Indians and Chinese" were convicted compared with 2 "Chinese." While this category encompassed whiteness as a negative and flexible category it also worked politically to obscure white crime. Given the "facts" produced through enumeration, how could authorities continue to deploy racial narratives about "drunken Indians" and "cunning Chinese traffickers"?

In late nineteenth century British Columbia, the "drunken Indian" had become a well-known "fact" that was rarely questioned or contested. While there was little consideration as to whether this presumed defect was biological, environmental or developmental, many agreed that aboriginal peoples might exhibit self-control once they reached the appropriate level of maturity and civility.[89] This idea that Indians could not withstand the effects of alcohol became commonsense knowledge which informed and legitimized a range of prohibitory statutes including various sections of the *Indian Act*, that Indians needed to be prohibited from consuming liquor and that sobriety was critical to enfranchisement and citizenship.[90] Many witnesses who appeared before the Commission both drew upon and reinforced these truths. Take for example the testimony of Samuel Drake, the Sheriff of Nanaimo. While Drake conceded that an "Indian is a pretty decent fellow when he is sober, as most of them are," he explained but "when they get drunk they seem to lose all respect for the rights of any other party in their neighborhood." They are "capable of doing things when they are drunk,"

Drake added, "that they would never do when sober."[91] But while Indians could be redeemed through moral training and sobriety, colonial authorities were less convinced about the possibilities for Chinese migrants.

Throughout witness testimony, allegations about the Chinese and their involvement in the illicit liquor trade emerged frequently. Those who were called to testify expressed greater concerns about migrants from China, and their involvement in the liquor traffic, than they did for any other racial groups. The two Commissioners, Judge McDonald and Dr. Reverend J. McLeod, who queried witnesses in British Columbia routinely asked whether the Chinese consumed liquor and if they supplied it to aboriginal peoples. While some who testified described the Chinese to be a "sober race," others insisted they were intemperate but were successful in evading the gaze of authorities as "a great deal of their drinking is done in their homes."[92] Colonial agents were less divided about the role of Chinese migrants in the sale of liquor, however. Many Indian Agents and missionaries lamented that Chinese men were devastating aboriginal communities by supplying them with intoxicants. As Indian Agent Phair reported to his superiors, there "are two or three Chinamen here [Lillooet] who I believe get their living by selling liquor to Indians but they are so cunning that its [sic] almost an impossibility to prove them guilty."[93] This rhetoric about "drunken Indians" and "cunning" Chinese was so widely circulated that these racial truths over-determined the numerical evidence submitted by Superintendent Henry Sheppard.

At the Commission's hearings, Judge McDonald questioned Sheppard on his Annual Report as follows:

> I observe there were 406 cases of drunkenness according to your report? —*Yes*
>
> I observe the cases of Indians number 231?—*Yes*
>
> And of those 175 for being drunk?—*Yes*
>
> In the cases of the Indians, did you try to find out where they got the liquor?—*Yes. The Chinese generally got it for them.*
>
> Did you succeed in making cases?—*In a few cases.*
>
> You had 29 convictions?—*Yes, for supplying them.*
>
> Were the persons so convicted licensed?—*No.*
>
> They were unlicensed?—*Yes.*
>
> Out of 175 cases of Indians, there were 29 convicted the second time?—*Yes.*[94]

This exchange is interesting for several reasons. First, McDonald's questions were informed by a particular set of racial assumptions. Clearly, he was unconcerned about the documented distribution of liquor offences as displayed in the two tables, that it was mainly whites who were convicted for supplying liquor to Indians and for intoxication. Instead, his questions seemed to be guided by persistent racial knowledges about "undeveloped" Indians who were unable to self-regulate and who routinely became intoxicated, and those "duplicitous" Chinese men who were guilty of supplying them with alcohol. These perceptions were reinforced by Sheppard. When he was questioned by Dr. Reverend McLeod, he led the Commissioners to conclude that all convictions for supplying liquor to Indians were made against Chinese men:

> I noticed that when you mentioned cases of sale of liquor to Indians, you said there were 29 cases and the persons sold illicitly?—*A Chinaman would meet an Indian and go in and get a bottle of liquor for himself, and he would give it to the Indian.*
>
> So they supplied Indians by the bottle?—Yes.[95]

For those who read the Commission's report without referencing the tables, Sheppard's testimony only confirmed dominant racial truths about the dangers that Chinese men posed to aboriginal populations. When Judge McDonald asked Wellington Dowler, a clerk employed at the Victoria Police Court, as to whether "other people are sent into saloons to get liquor for the Indians," he responded as follows: "Yes, mostly Chinamen. They are the people who violate the law."[96]

Although the Commissioners and witnesses generated a series of knowledges about racial populations and the liquor problem in British Columbia, these truths about "drunken Indians" and Chinese migrants who worked as immoral entrepreneurs had much deeper epistemological roots. The Royal Commission's production of racial subjectivities did not only generate new ideas about racial difference but drew from and activated truths that were circulating across the border. The Chinese migrant who threatened white labour and was putatively inferior to African-Americans in the mid-nineteenth century, was in later years demonized for the biological dangers he posed to aboriginal peoples. While the inherent immorality and dishonesty of the Chinese was distinguished against the "ignorance" of the "Negro" in California, in British Columbia, these qualities of Chineseness were constituted against the presumed vulnerability of aboriginal peoples. Although fears of Chinese labour continued to underwrite anti-Chinese racism along Canada's west coast, by the late nineteenth century Indian Agents and police authorities lamented the Chinese for other reasons, including their penchant to sell liquor to Indians. These crossracial contaminations, many argued, not only threatened the moral and physical well-being of aboriginal communities but also the longevity of British Columbia's settler regime. The protection of white and aboriginal lives could only be accomplished through Chinese exclusion.

Conclusions

In *Culture and Imperialism*, Edward Said urges us to speak about the past and present effects of empire through "overlapping territories" and "intertwined histories."[97] This essay has taken Said's challenge seriously. First, by focusing on the production and proliferation of juridical racial truths in late nineteenth century British Columbia, I have tried to highlight the "overlapping territories" of Canada and the US by tracking a transnational and circuitous language of race. And second, drawing from the two Royal Commissions, I have explored, albeit in a preliminary way, one *epistemic* thread in the "intertwined histories" of aboriginal-Chinese encounters. Large-scale Chinese migration to British Columbia reconfigured colonial relations between aboriginal peoples and Euro-Canadians, a point made by Indian Agent Lomas in his 1890 Annual Report. These new contacts, proximities, and exigencies, including the illicit sale of liquor, prompted authorities like Lomas to rethink their prevailing epistemologies of race. Similarly, to make sense of the growing Chinese presence, witnesses who testified before the Royal Commissions on Chinese Immigration and on the Liquor Traffic drew upon a much older racial lexicon of slaver, and in so doing, produced a distinct and localized racial grid. By contrasting the Chinese against African-Americans and aboriginal peoples, witnesses created a new population that was putatively dangerous, not only to whites, but also to these internal Others. For many Indian Agents and legal authorities, the protection of aboriginal peoples and the longevity of white settlement in British Columbia could only be secured through Chinese exclusion.

Said's invitation to explore "overlapping territories" and "intertwined histories" of empire serve as useful methodological directives for rethinking state racisms. For Foucault, racism is integral to the modern state. The "modern state," he writes, "can scarcely function without becoming involved with racism at some point."[98] By tracking the interdependencies of racial knowledges, their convergences and entanglements, we can begin to unravel the *multiplicity of state racisms* and the contradictory conditions upon which they thrived. Racial thinking, as Ann Laura Stoler remind us, "harnesses itself to varied progressive projects and shapes the social taxonomies defining who will be excluded from them."[99] In late nineteenth century British Columbia these progressive projects not only included the making of a settler regime but one that was premised on the improvement and assimilation of aboriginal peoples, a project that many argued would be compromised by the Chinese. These charges, as I have suggested above, were underwritten by distinct racial truths that rendered the Indian to be "vulnerable" and the Chinese to be "cunning" and "despotic." Emphasizing "overlapping territories" and "intertwined histories" thus might offer us critical insights into the multiple, diverse, and contested field of racial knowledges, their inconsistencies, and contradictions. The hope is that by disaggregating the heterogeneity of racial truths, we can begin to understand the logics and structures that have made modern state racisms so resilient.

Notes

1   Pratt, Mary Louise (1992:6-7). *Imperial Eyes: Travel Writing and Transculturation*. New York, NY: Routledge. I am drawing the term "contact zone" from Mary Louise Pratt. Throughout this essay, I use the term "colonial" to reference a set of power relations as opposed to a specific political formation. Earlier versions of this paper were work-shopped at the "Refracting Pacific Canada Conference" held at UBC (2007, March) and at the UBC Sociology Faculty Workshop (2008, January). I would like to thank participants at both events for their comments/ questions. Many thanks are due to Henry Yu and Bob McDonald for their invitation and for very useful editorial and substantive suggestions, and to the two anonymous reviewers for their challenging questions and comments. Finally, I am grateful to Shelly Ketchell for her invaluable research assistance.

2   *Canada Sessional Papers*. No. 18, 54, 1891, 105. Lomas to Superintendent of Indian Affairs, 27 August 1890. My emphasis.

3   Mawani, Renisa (under review). *Cartographies of Colonialism*. This argument is developed more fully in book monograph.

4   In the *Royal Commission on the Liquor Traffic* (1894) many witnesses and legal authorities lamented the interactions between the Chinese and Aboriginal peoples. This is a point that repeatedly emerges in late nineteenth century police reports. See Mawani, *Cartographies of Colonialism*, especially Chapter 4.

5   Barman, Jean (2007:68-69). *The West Beyond the West: A History of British Columbia*. Toronto, ON: University of Toronto Press.

6   Harris, Cole (1997). *The Resettlement of British Columbia*. Vancouver, BC: University of British Columbia Press; Like Barman, Cole Harris has also documented the various racial and ethnic groups who resided in nineteenth century British Columbia. On interraciality more generally see also Jean Barman and Bruce McIntyre Watson, (Summer 1999). Fort Colville's Fur Trade Families and the Dynamics of Aboriginal Racial Intermixture in the Pacific Northwest. *Pacific Northwest Quarterly* 90(3):140-53; Barman, Jean (1999, July) What a Difference a Border Makes: Aboriginal Racial Intermixture in the Pacific Northwest. *Journal of the West* 38(3):14-20; What I am arguing here is that we need to explore how these histories were intertwined and the types of racial knowledges and modes of exclusion they engendered.

7   Foucault, Michel (2003:255). *Society Must be Defended: Lectures at the College de France, 1975-1976*. New York, NY: Picador.

8   Foucault (2003:254-256). Biopolitics, as Foucault has argued, is contingent upon distinguishing good races from bad ones. A crucial part of biopolitical futures is life and death. Foucault explains that death is not only biological but may also be political.

My evocation of expulsion here is not biological but social, cultural, and spatial. Aboriginal peoples were expelled onto reserves, for example.

9   *Royal Commission on Chinese Immigration Report and Evidence* (Ottawa, 1885). Hereinafter *Royal Commission on Chinese Immigration. Royal Commission on the Liquor Traffic* (Ottawa, 1894). Hereinafter, *Royal Commission on the Liquor Traffic.*

10 On "knowledge formats" see Valverde, Mariana (2003). *Law's Dream of a Common Knowledge.* Princeton: Princeton University Press, especially Introduction.

11 Valverde (2003:23); Rose, Nickolas (1999: Chapter 6). *Powers of Freedom: Reframing Political Thought.* Cambridge: Cambridge University Press. For a critique of numbers see Rose.

12 Appadurai, Arjun *(1996). Modernity At Large: Cultural Dimensions of Globalization.* Minneapolis: University of Minnesota Press, especially Chapter 6; Poovey, Mary (1998). *A History of the Modern Fact: Problems of Knowledge in the Sciences of Wealth and Society.* Chicago: University of Chicago Press; Rose (1999: Chapter 6).

13 There is now a voluminous literature on Chinese migration that draws in part from the *Royal Commission on Chinese Immigration* (1885). The classic texts include, Anderson, Kay (1991). *Vancouver's Chinatown: Racial Discourse in Canada, 1875-1980.* Montreal & Kingston: McGill-Queen's University Press; Roy, Patricia E. (1989). *A White Man's Province: British Columbia Politicians and Chinese and Japanese Immigrants, 1858-1914.* Vancouver, BC: University of British Columbia Press; Ward, Peter (1990). *White Canada Forever: Popular Attitudes and Public Policy Towards Orientals in British Columbia.* Montreal & Kingston: McGill-Queens University Press.

14 Arguments about labour have been prolific. Two examples include Roy (1989); Saxton, Alexander (1995). *The Indispensable Enemy: Labor and the Anti-Chinese Movement in California*, Second Edition. Berkeley, CA: University of California Press.

15 Clayton, Daniel (2000:5). *Islands of Truth: The Imperial Fashioning of Vancouver Island.* Vancouver, BC: The University of British Columbia Press. Daniel Clayton has described BC history to be "positivist in tone and provincial in outlook."

16 Perry, Adele (2001). *On the Edge of Empire: Gender, Race, and the Making of British Columbia, 1849-1871.* Toronto, ON: University of Toronto Press; Harris, Cole (2004:165-182). How did Colonialism Dispossess? Comments from an Edge of Empire. *Annals of the Association of American Geographers* 94. See Perry, this is now a familiar description of British Columbia. Cole Harris seems to be emphasizing the specificity of British Columbia in his essay. This is precisely what I am arguing against.

17 Thomas, Nicholas (1994:66). *Colonialism's Culture: Anthropology, Travel, and Government.* Princeton: Princeton University Press.

18 Stoler, Ann Laura (ed.) (2006). *Haunted by Empire: Geographies of Intimacy in North American History.* Durham: Duke University Press. US history is not often thought of in the context of empire and colonial/ postcolonial studies.

19 Said, Edward (1979:32). *Orientalism.* New York, NY: Vintage Books.

20 Cohn, Bernard (1996:3). *Colonialism and its Forms of Knowledge.* Princeton: Princeton University Press; Dirks, Nicholas (1996:i-xvii). In Bernard Cohn, *Colonialism and its Forms of Knowledge.*

21 Cohn (1996:5).

22 Appadurai (1996:117). I have taken the quote "countable abstractions" from Appadurai.

23 Said (1979:232-233).

24 Ahmad, Aijaz (1992). *In Theory: Classes, Nations, Literatures.* New York, NY: Verso. There is now a longstanding literature that critiques *Orientalism* for essentializing the Orient/ Occident distinction and for glossing other social relations that shifted the content, intensity, and effects of Orientalism. The most famous of these is made by Ahmad, especially Chapter 5.

25 Mahmud, Tayyab (1998-1999:1228). Colonialism and Modern Constructions of Race: A Preliminary Inquiry. *University of Miami Law Review* 53.

26 See Mbembe, Achille (2003). Necropolitics. *Public Culture* 15(1):11–40; Moore, Donald (2005). *Suffering For Territory: Race, Place, and Power in Zimbabwe*. Durham: Duke University Press, especially Introduction; Stoler, Ann Laura (1995). *Race and the Education of Desire: Foucault and the Colonial Order of Things*. Durham: Duke University Press.

27 Foucault (2003:255).

28 Stoler, Ann Laura (1997:183–206). Racial Histories and their Regimes of Truth. *Political Power and Social Theory*,11. For a very useful discussion of the multiplicity of racisms and the internal and external characteristics of racial essences.

29 Valverde, Mariana (1998:162–170). *Diseases of the Will: Alcohol and the Dilemmas of Freedom*. Cambridge, MA: Cambridge University Press. On Aboriginal peoples as weak-willed.

30 The unassimilability of the Chinese comes up repeatedly in the *Royal Commission on Chinese Immigration* (1885). See also Anderson (1991:44–55).

31 On "lawfare" see Comaroff, John (2001:306). Colonialism, Culture, and the Law: A Foreward. *Law and Social Inquiry* 26(2).

32 Haney-Lopez, Ian (1996). *White by Law: The Legal Construction of Race*. New York, NY: New York University Press.

33 Backhouse, Constance (1999). *Color Coded: A Legal History of Racism in Canada, 1900-1950*. Toronto, ON: University of Toronto Press; Walker, James (1997). *"Race," Rights and the Law in the Supreme Court of Canada: Historical Case Studies*. Ontario: Wilfred Laurier University Press. Constance Backhouse and James Walker have written about the legal construction of race in Supreme Court cases in Canada. Much of the critical race literature in the US does not problematize the colonial in discussions of race and law. Mahmud's, "Colonialism and Modern Constructions of Race," is an exception.

34 See Comaroff (2001:306).

35 On commissions of inquiry see Ashforth, Adam (1990). *The Politics of Official Discourse in Twentieth-Century South Africa*. Oxford: Clarendon Press; Frankel, Oz (2006). *States of Inquiry: Social Investigations and Nineteenth Century Print Culture in Britain and the United States*. Baltimore, MD: Johns Hopkins University Press; Stoler, Ann Laura (2002). Colonial Archives and the Arts of Governance. *Archival Science* 2:87–109.

36 Comaroff, John (1998:332). Reflections on the Colonial State, in South Africa and Elsewhere: Factions, Fragments, Facts, and Fictions. *Social Identities* 4(3).

37 Those of mixed-race ancestry or "Half-Breeds" as they were commonly called referred to people of Aboriginal and European ancestry. For a discussion of this juridical category, see Mawani, Renisa (2000). In Between and Out of Place: Racial Hybridity, Liquor, and the Law in Late Nineteenth and Early Twentieth Century British Columbia. *Canadian Journal of Law and Society* 15(2):9–38.

38 "Epistemological pluralism" comes from Valverde (2003: 15). On the interactions between common knowledge and science in law see also Haney-Lopez (1996:5–9).

39 Merry, Sally Engle (2000: 131–136). *Colonizing Hawai'i: The Cultural Power of Law*. Princeton: Princeton University Press. Writing about Hawaii, Sally Merry has noted that missionaries perceived Chinese men to pose a danger to Native Hawaiians. These discourses, she argues, were imported from California.

40 In the *Royal Commission on Chinese Immigration* (1885), the foreignness of Chinese migrants was often contrasted against internal Others, including Aboriginal peoples and African-Americans. I elaborate on this point in the following two sections.

41 *Report of the Royal Commission on Chinese Immigration* (1885:vii).

42 Ward (1990:38).

43 *Chinese Immigration Act*, SC, 1923, c.38.

44 Anderson (1991:45).

45 Chang, Kornel (2007). *Transpacific Borderlands and Boundaries: Race, Migration and State Formation in the North American Pacific Rim, 1882-1917*. University of Chicago:

Unpublished PhD Dissertation; Lee, Erika (2002). Enforcing the Borders: Chinese Exclusion along the borders with Canada and Mexico, 1882-1924. *The Journal of American History* 89(1):54-86. There is a growing interest in the Canada-US borderlands.

46 Kim, Claire Jean (1999:106). The Racial Triangulation of Asian Americans. *Politics and Society* 27(1). Claire Jean Kim's "field of racial positions" is useful here.

47 Appadurai, Arjun (1996:133).

48 Hacking, Ian (2002). *Historical Ontology*. Cambridge: Harvard University Press, Chapter 6. "Making up people" comes from Ian Hacking's famous essay of the same title.

49 Goldberg, David T. (1997:30-32). *Racial Subjects: Writing on Race in America*. New York, NY: Routledge.

50 Barman, Jean (2007:429). Barman details the racial and ethnic breakdown of the province as follows. 1871: British/ Continental European 23.7% (8,576); Asian 4.3% (1,548); Aboriginal (est) 70.8% (25,661). 1881: British 29.6% (14,660); Continental European 5.0% (2,490); Asian 8.8% (4,350); Aboriginal (est) 51.9% (25,661). See Barman, Table 5.

51 Killian, Crawford (1978). *Go Do Some Great Thing: The Black Pioneers of B.C.* Vancouver, BC: Douglas & McIntyre; Winks, Robin (1997). *The Blacks in Canada: A History*. Montreal & Kingston: McGill-Queen's University Press. A search of the *Annual Reports of the Inspector of Penitentiaries* reveals that "black" and/ or "Negro" was not used in other provinces. The two provinces that used this category sporadically were Manitoba (1891, 1897) and British Columbia (1895). A term that was used more frequently in other places was "colored." See Annual Report of the Inspector of Penitentiaries. *Canada Sessional Papers*, 1880/1881-1900.

52 The original table published in the *Royal Commission on Chinese Immigration* covers 1880-1884. I have only included 1880 and have modified the table to exclude names of offenders/ judges. There were no "Negroes" recorded for 1880, one for 1881, one for 1882, none for 1883, and three for 1884.

53 On monogenesis and polygenesis see Robert Young, Robert (1995:9-13). *Colonial Desire: Hybridity in Theory, Culture, and Race*. London: Routledge.

54 *Royal Commission on Chinese Immigration*, 350.

55 *Royal Commission on Chinese Immigration*, 350.

56 *Royal Commission on Chinese Immigration*, 351.

57 *Royal Commission on Chinese Immigration*, 351, my emphasis.

58 See for example Jung, Moon-Ho (2006). *Coolies and Cane: Race, Labor, and Sugar in the Age of Emancipation*. Baltimore, MD: Johns Hopkins University Press; Kim (1999); Lowe, "The Intimacy of Four Continents;" Okihiro, Gary *(1994). Margins and Mainstreams: Asians in American History and Culture*. Seattle, WA: University of Washington Press. Interestingly, albeit unsurprisingly, few of these scholars discuss these relations in terms of colonialism.

59 Stoler, Ann Laura. Tense and Tender Ties: The Politics of Comparison in North American History and (Post) colonial Studies. In Ann Laura Stoler (ed.). *Haunted by Empire:* 55-56.

60 For discussions about the Chinese in the American south see Jung (2006).

61 *Royal Commission on Chinese Immigration*, 339, my emphasis.

62 *Royal Commission on Chinese Immigration*, 339.

63 Haney-Lopez (1996).

64 Ngai, Mae (2004:17). *Impossible Subjects: Illegal Aliens and the Making of Modern America*. Princeton: Princeton University Press.

65 Kim (1999:109). Kim makes a similar point about foreignness. However, by arguing that Asian immigrants were seen as superior to Blacks, she glosses over important contradictions which I would argue are precisely what sustain racisms.

66 *Royal Commission on Chinese Immigration*, 239.

67 For a similar argument see Erika Lee, Erika (2003:31). *At America's Gates: Chinese Immigration During the Exclusion Era, 1882-1943*. Chapel Hill: University of North Carolina Press.

68 *Royal Commission on Chinese Immigration*, 175.

69 *Royal Commission on Chinese Immigration*, 345.

70 *Royal Commission on Chinese Immigration*, 345, my emphasis.

71 *Royal Commission on Chinese Immigration*, 166–167.

72 I am citing Ann Stoler who is paraphrasing Lisa Lowe's arguments in the same volume. See Ann Laura Stoler. Intimidations of Empire: Predicaments of the Tactile and Unseen. In Stoler (ed.). *Haunted by Empire*: 11.

73 *Royal Commission on Chinese Immigration*, 166.

74 McLaren, John (1999: 423–442). Race and the Criminal Justice System in British Columbia, 1892-1920: Constructing Chinese Crimes. In G. Blaine Baker and Jim Phillips (eds.). *Essays in the History of Canadian Law: Volume VIII: In Honor of R.C.B. Risk*. Toronto, ON: University of Toronto Press.

75 *Royal Commission on the Liquor Traffic*, Appendix No. 11, 669. In the *Annual Report of the Inspector of Penitentiaries*, age, gender, ethnicity, and other factors were recorded. See note 49.

76 Mawani, Renisa (2000).

77 Poovey (1998). Poovey makes this point that numbers appear to be beyond interpretation and analysis. See Poovey, especially Introduction.

78 Rose (1999:Chapter 6).

79 Rose (1999:212).

80 Brown, Mark (2001:345–368). Race, Science, and the Construction of Native Criminality in Colonial India. *Theoretical Criminology* 5(3).

81 Goldberg (1997:47); (Malden: Blackwell, 1993).

82 *Royal Commission on Chinese Immigration*, 388.

83 Goldberg (1997:181).

84 Goldberg (1997:171).

85 Appadurai (1996:133).

86 McClintock, Anne (1995:40). *Imperial Leather: Race, Gender, and Sexuality in the Colonial Contest*. New York, NY: Routledge.

87 Anderson (1991); Harris, Cole (2002). *Making Native Space: Colonialism Reserves, and Resistance in British Columbia*. Vancouver, BC: University of British Columbia Press. These literal boundaries are evident in the creation of reserves and of Chinatowns.

88 *Canada Sessional Papers* 4(47), 1884, 4-45-4-46. McTiernan to Superintendent, August 15, 1883.

89 Campbell, Robert (2004, September:1–104). A 'Fantastic Rigmarole': Deregulating Aboriginal Drinking in British Columbia, 1945-62. *BC Studies* 141; Valverde (1998).

90 *An Act to Amend and Consolidate the Laws Respecting Indians*, 1876, Chapter. 18, s.79, s. 86.

91 *Royal Commission on the Liquor Traffic*, 555.

92 *Royal Commission on the Liquor Traffic*, 534.

93 British Columbia Archives, GR-0429, Box 1 File 9. C. Phair to Attorney General, October 1880.

94 *Royal Commission on the Liquor Traffic*, lines 39269-39280, 479, my emphasis.

95 *Royal Commission on the Liquor Traffic*, lines 39302-39303, 480, my emphasis.

96 *Royal Commission on the Liquor Traffic*, lines 39192-193, 476.

97 Said, Edward (1994:61). *Culture and Imperialism*. New York, NY: Vintage Books.

98 Foucault (2003:254).

99 Stoler (1995:9).

Rhose Harris-Galia

Coming up North was not a long-term plan. It was supposed to be only for a year or two at the most, and then move to warmer climes... like Ottawa. Ten years later, **Rhose Harris-Galia** is still in Iqaluit, Nunavut. Having moved to Canada as a live-in caregiver in 1999, Rhose found her way to Iqaluit in October 2000 when job prospects were limited in Edmonton. Her first thoughts of "Where in the world am I?" were quelled by the warm welcome and easygoing nature of both her employers and the community. After receiving her permanent residency card, she immediately took the Canadian Registered Nurses Examination and passed. In December of 2002, she started work as a casual employee at what is now called the Qikiqtani General Hospital. She worked several jobs in addition to this, which included working at the Children's Group Home, as a customer service agent/supervisor for First Air, and even as a security guard at the airport. Her various occupations kept her in touch with different aspects of the Iqaluit community and introduced her to many of the city's residents. She decided to go full-time at the Hospital in 2006. She and her partner Mathew bought a house in 2004 and were married in 2007. They still reside in Iqaluit with their two-year old son, Brian Daniel.

Arctic Bayanihan[1]

Ask anyone in most of the industrialized countries in the world if they have ever met or seen a Filipino at work and the answer will most likely be "Yes." We are everywhere, doing everything, in every field—from private homes to being in the public eye, from housework to teaching, from the oil fields to the hospitals. The global Filipino community has quietly and yet most assuredly grown exponentially, making Filipinos one of the busiest and most well-known labour communities in the world to be found in every nook and cranny where there is work to be found. And one of those nooks happens to be latitude 63°44'N and longitude 68°31'W—better known as the City of Iqaluit, capital city of the Canada's newest territory, Nunavut.

The Iqaluit Filipino community is a mixture of Filipinos from all walks of life, from the zero generation immigrants who are the first of their kin and clan to come to North America, to those who were born and raised in Southern Canada. There are those from the southern Philippines to the far northern islands, urbanites and those with rural roots. One might wonder how such a diverse group manages to live and integrate themselves into a community that is not only the complete opposite of home environmentally, but also a community that is mainly populated by Inuit, a people unique and distinct from every other Aboriginal nation in Canada. A very brief look at the history of the Philippines can help answer this question.

The Philippines had a rich culture long before the Spanish came in the mid-1600s. The trade between different Southeast Asian nations helped contribute to its prosperity, and also paved the way to its diversity. People from Indonesia, Malaysia, Taiwan, and China came and shared their own cultures and formed an identity uniquely Filipino. This integration of cultures held true upon the arrival of the Spaniards in 1521. For over 300 years, the Spaniards put their stamp on the Filipino identity in a multitude of ways, *from* politics, education, to religion. Then came the Spanish–American War, which resulted in the Philippines falling into American hands and leading to the Philippine–American war.[2] The Americans contributed even more to the Filipino make-up, their main contribution being improved literacy and education for the masses. Then came World War II and the Japanese occupation, which was bloody, but mercifully brief. After all these conquerors, all these different nations laying claim to the Philippines, she finally won her freedom in 1946.

It is inevitable that a nation that has been conquered or taken over by another will have scars that would take generations to heal. Memories are long, and more so if that nation's culture is forcibly stifled and the people prohibited from living their lives as they have always known. So what happened to the Filipino psyche? What came out as the Filipino identity after having been under so many conquerors, well-intentioned or not? Are we Spanish? American? Japanese? The answer: yes, we are all of these. And no, we are none of these. The plethora of contributing nations, conquerors and traders alike, turned the Filipino Culture into a delightful and complicated mix of East and West.

The Filipino culture is a combination of cultures that baffles most people, and is difficult to explain and pinpoint, even by Filipinos themselves. We take the best that other nations can contribute and make it our own. For instance, the Spaniards brought in Christianity, and the end result was that the Philippines became the largest Catholic nation in Southeast Asia. But our Catholicism also leaves room for the old beliefs that have been handed down from generation to generation: the strong belief in saints, and angels, spirits appeased by offerings and candles. While the pagan system of beliefs faded away into history, it did not disappear completely. Instead, it adapted to the new faith that had forced its way into the country, which made a new faith that took the best of both worlds and made it their own.

Another good example is the language. Filipino is one of two official languages of the Philippines, the other being English. Filipino is mostly based on *Tagalog*, which is the dialect of the Philippines' central region. But Filipino is also a language that incorporates Malay, Chinese, English, Spanish, and even Latin. You would be hard-pressed to find anyone who speaks undiluted Tagalog in the cities, but in the rural areas of Central Luzon,[3] the older generation can be found using words that the younger generation would not be able to define.

Generation after generation, Filipinos were subject to a foreign power that imposed their own rules and their own culture. There was definite resistance to colonialism and foreign occupation, but in the midst of this, a distinct Filipino character took hold and bloomed. As a nation, Filipinos learned from their oppressors, observed, and eventually adapted to their presence. The old ways merged with the new and a balance of the two was found. It is this adaptability that is the hallmark of the Filipino. Wherever we go, whatever we do, we adapt to our new homes and make these our own. We manage to find a place in the community, without forcing our own practices, but instead, finding a way for our culture to meld with the existing environment we find ourselves in.

This holds true even as far North as Nunavut, Canada. I can think of no other place that is as geographically, environmentally, and culturally different from the Philippines as the Arctic; warm versus cold, tropics versus tundra, center of trade versus as isolated as they come. And yet here one will find a flourishing Filipino community that has grown quietly and managed to join with the Inuit community.

I was what most of my countrymen jokingly refer to as "fresh off the boat" when I moved to Iqaluit in 2000. At the time, there were only a handful of Filipinos in the Arctic, and my employer was quick to introduce me to them. One of them lived no more than five kilometres from my childhood home. She, too, still had family overseas and was working on having them move to Canada. The other Filipinos had already brought family over, or had gotten married and started families of their own. It was odd, to say the least, to see people who had been born and raised in tropical climes living and working in one of the world's harshest environments. But work we did, and more; the Filipino community has grown from that handful to almost a hundred in 2010.

There are Filipinos who have been here for twenty years, and more keep coming. What is it about this particular community that makes them stay? Several have given their opinions regarding this, and if one looks closely enough, it turns out the Inuit community is not as far removed from the Philippine community at all.

The main similarity is the most obvious one: we look alike. Perhaps there is something to the Bering Strait theory, which suggests that somewhere early on in humankind's history, Eurasians crossed a land bridge into what is now North America. It is easy enough to believe that one clan went one way and the other stayed and went southward. I was always mistaken as an Inuk when I first arrived, and it holds true to this day. There is the dark skin that tans readily, black hair, and the dark eyes that don't quite have the obvious epicanthic folds. Facial characteristics like shape, bodily characteristics such as build, height, and so on strongly indicate a possible genetic connection that has yet to be examined.

If one listens hard enough, parallels with the language are noticeable as well. There are a few words that when loosely translated have identical meanings (for example, *taima* and *tama na* mean "that's enough"*)*. There are also words that are mere homonyms (for example, *mammianaq* and *mamaya na* mean "sorry" and "later," respectively). It would take a keen linguist to find out just how close the two, Inuktitut and Filipino, truly are.

The strong sense of community is another similarity between the two. Whether or not you know your neighbour in the Philippines, if a tragedy occurs next door and you have been sharing the same wall for generations, you will help your neighbour. Entire communities band together during rough times. There is no difference in the Inuit culture. If there is a loss in the family, young or old, the entire community goes into mourning. Family members are comforted by neighbours regardless of whether their last chat was two weeks or two months prior.

The sense of oneness holds true in joyful occasions as well. Fiestas are frequent in the Philippines, and one can walk into a family's backyard during holidays and partake of the food, regardless of whether or not one is related. The Inuit tradition of a community feast is exactly the same. Everyone partakes of the food that is set out, whether it is harvested from the sea, land, or the nearest grocery store.

There is one more strong similarity between the two cultures that stands out. It is the strength of faith. A Baptist sector, a Baha'i sector, and even Jehovah's Witnesses are part of the Northern religious make-up. But the main denominations are Anglican and Roman Catholic. More than one Filipino has stated that it is this strong belief that binds them to the community. It is a common denominator that helps with not only adjusting to a life away from home, but it also helps in the initial presentation of the Filipinos into the community. Individuals and families are introduced, and eventually these groups meet socially outside of the Church setting. More than one Filipino I interviewed admitted that the community spirit that started in the churches helped them know the local community better, and the ties that started therein extended to the Inuit homes and social circles.

Offshoots of the church gatherings are the extended meetings that occur outside of regular Sunday services. Bible readings occur in different church members' homes. These evolved from both prayers and potlucks, where people gather together to catch up with each other, into impromptu healing circles where problems slowly came to the forefront. While there are numerous gatherings within the Inuit community that are similar, healing ministries and fellowships are of common interest in both cultures and is another bond that connects the two.

But from a very personal perspective, I also see a difference when it comes to emotions. I see Filipinos as open with their emotions and problems when surrounded by those closest to them. We are undeniably emotional in the privacy of our homes, and where problems arise where tears are inevitable, we are, for the most part, open to talk about problems regardless of how red-rimmed our eyes may become. We easily ask for assistance when needed, especially if there are problems with violence, no matter how big or small. However, my own experiences with the Inuit are different as I often see them as more private when it comes to airing problems and I have not witnessed detailed discussions around addictions in the family or histories of abuse. From what I have seen, most of the Inuit will only open up regarding these issues if prompted by a counsellor, close family, or in extreme circumstances, alcohol and the law. There are groups nowadays comprised of church folk, and people can come when they wish just to express their feelings, air their issues, and talk without fear of repercussions. They can cry, they can laugh, they can console, and it serves as a way to recognize problems, talk about issues, and perhaps slowly encourage them to consider it not a weakness to speak of these issues, but a strength. From my cultural perspective, I see this as a beginning of sorts for a group that has held itself in check emotionally for so long. It is difficult to hear stories and not want to tell someone to take it a step further and reach out for assistance, but the fact is, it is a big enough step to have those with issues trust someone enough to open up. Change is slow, but if given half a chance, it might come in the form of growing self-awareness and a discovery of self-worth. Perhaps it is not so farfetched that such actions can help any community to change and heal.

The Filipino Community has indeed flourished in Canada's northern climes. Baffin Island is not the only place where we can be found. We can be found in Cambridge Bay, Rankin Inlet, Yellowknife, and in smaller communities as well. It is our capability to adapt that makes us strong enough to move from our comfort zones and thrive in an environment that, while geographically polar opposites (pardon the pun), is not that different from the smaller *barangays*[4] and farms from our home. Asked to reflect on how we as a community managed to integrate ourselves into the Inuit landscape, the answer is not just found in our history. It is not just because we come from a culture that melds with others and morphs into a distinct personality. We were welcomed, never truly treated as outsiders despite the obvious fact that we were. We were not from the North, and we were definitely 'from away,' as some would put it. The welcome had a lot to do with the fact that perhaps, in essence, we are simply meeting up with a community very much like ours, which has helped us feel at home. The process is constantly evolving, and the community is growing and adapting day by day.

If there was one thing Inuit can discover from their Filipino brethren, it is perhaps the realization that while we are in the twenty-first century, they do not need to give up their way of life, their language, their culture. If they look into the annals of history, there is something to be learned: that while one's culture is indeed distinct, there is nothing to stop them from adapting to the modern world. Take advantage of what technology affords them: a global sounding board at the tips of everyone's fingers. Inuit culture is rich, but many are afraid it is slowly fading. This does not need to happen. It will take generations, but it only takes one person, one family, or one community to show the rest that Inuit culture can adapt, it can adjust and blend with the modern world and not lose its distinct identity. They can survive the pains of the past and make the future their own.

There are key values that we Filipinos can learn from our Inuit counterparts as well. These can be summarized into what Inuit call *Inuit Qaujimajatuqangit*, more commonly known as "IQ Principles."[5] It is loosely understood and translated as "Inuit traditional knowledge" and values that have been passed down from generation to generation. In the past few years and since the creation of Nunavut, the Inuit community has tried its best to explain this abstract concept in a more concrete manner. If one looks it up, one will find varied descriptions and breakdowns of what IQ Principles are. IQ shows us that the values of Inuit revolve around caring for each other, teamwork and community building, resourcefulness, innovativeness, and respect for people, the land, and resources. It is a set of teachings and resources handed down from Inuit Elders, now in written form, and are used to guide the new and upcoming generations.

Is it as simple as this, though? Can we read the IQ Principles and say, "Yes, this is so obvious"? All I need to do is commit it to memory. These principles were handed down from times past, and still are dynamic in such a way that it can adapt and adjust to what the changing times bring. The IQ Principles teach not only Inuit but everyone that the Elders knew how to take care of their land, their people, and their community and that these methods and lessons must be held true in order for the community to grow.

Sharing ideas between the Filipino and Inuit community is indeed not too difficult. The cultures are closer than most think, and communicating with each other goes deeper than the written and spoken word. Our similarities are more obvious than our differences, and it makes for a wonderful blend of East and West in the Far North.

Notes

1 *Bayanihan* is a Filipino term taken from the word *bayan*, referring to a nation, town or community. The whole term *bayanihan* refers to a spirit of communal unity or effort to achieve a particular objective.

2 Dumindin, A. (2006). *Philippine-American War, 1899–1902* [online book]. Retrieved 4 November 2010 from: http://philippineamericanwar.webs.com/

3 Central Luzon (also known as Region III) is located north of Manila, the nation's capital, on the Philippine's largest island.

4 A *barangay* is similar to a village and is headed by the smallest local government unit.

5 See "Inuit Qaujimajatuqangit (IQ)" from the Government of Nunavut website. Retrieved 30 November 2010 from: http://www.gov.nu.ca/hr/site/beliefsystem.htm

Sid Chow Tan

Born in China and a baby paper son (illegal) immigrant to Canada in 1950 following the repeal of Chinese exclusion, **Sid Chow Tan** is a descendant of pioneer adventurers. Raised in small-town Saskatchewan by grandparents, a graduate of the University of Calgary and nearly forty-year resident of Metro Vancouver, Sid has been active for nearly three decades in community media and redress for the Chinese head tax/exclusion laws. Growing up the youngest in the only Chinese family in town, Sid's politics is informed by a life of anti-racism and social justice activism, occasionally resulting in civil disobedience and arrest. His first recollection as an activist is a grade seven school debate supporting universal health care. Since then, he has helped found and build organizations in Vancouver and across Canada to fill community and personal needs. A freelance media producer and community organizer, Sid's current community service includes national chairman of the Chinese Canadian National Council and founding and current director of Head Tax Families Society of Canada, ACCESS Association of Chinese Canadians for Equality and Solidarity Society, National Anti-Racism Council of Canada, Downtown Eastside Community Arts Network, Downtown Eastside Neighbourhood Council, W2 Social Enterprise Café Society, CMES Community Media Education Society, and W2 Community Media Arts Society, soon to be operating a multi-purpose multi-platform media arts centre in the historic Woodward's building. Father to a son and daughter, his art is activism and his trade is in organizing.

Aiyah![1] A Little Rouse of Time and Space

Even with testimonial witness and record, historians still make educated guesses to fill in the gaps. When there are no witnesses and records to history, one can only imagine. Yet with imagination, the divination of grand meaningful historical events is possible, and the minutia within. So it is with "A Little Hoy Ping on the Prairies" and "Gim and Ruby," stories of the meeting between my Grandfather and Indigenous people in what would be his final resting place on the great plains of North America.

What follows are two tellings of the story of a seminal moment for our family. The narrative account is my response to a call for submissions for a Chinese Canadian National Council online history and culture project five years ago. The dialogic account is my ongoing personal effort, manifesting partly in Gold Mountain Turtle Island, a collaborative First Nations and Chinese opera in development by the Carnegie Community Centre in the Downtown Eastside of Vancouver, British Columbia. Both efforts are rooted in my belief that First Nations and the Chinese in Canada must look to the future for a fair telling of their history.

There are many people to thank for their encouragement: my children and their children, their partners, the mother of my children and our grandchildren, my friends and frequent critics Anne-Marie Sleeman, Leah Kaser, Jim Wong-Chu, Victor Wong, Sean Gunn, and Elwin Xie. Special thanks to Rika Uto and Ethel Whitty of the Carnegie Community Centre, Donna Spencer of the Firehall Arts Centre, and collaborators Renae Morriseau, Michelle La Flamme, and Shon Wong of the First Nations/Chinese Opera project. For my Grandparents, Chow Gim (Norman) Tan and Wong Nooy Tan. May their sleep soothe.

1) A Little *Hoy Ping*[2] on the Prairies

Ah Yeh (paternal grandfather) had good luck. His survival in Canada came with the close friendships formed with the local Cree and Métis clans of the great plains of Gum San (Gold Mountain/North America). To these Aboriginal and Native brothers and sisters, our family thanks you.

Ah Yeh's early life in Canada was loneliness and hard work. He silently cursed the racist exclusion law (1923–1947)[3] that separated him from his new wife and recently born son. It would be a quarter of a century before he could be reunited with his wife here in Canada. Then they would wait nearly another quarter of a century before their only child and his family could join them.

Mercifully, opening and running a café supplanted the loneliness. He often thought of the money he borrowed for the head tax and starting his café. Then would silently curse again the racist law that required only Chinese people to pay a tax to come to Canada. He always wondered why he and all other Chinese were required to pay a tax that was enough to buy two houses. Europeans got free land to farm. He knew the obvious answer. Oh well, he thought, at least the government allowed him to hire Indian women to help waitress and wash dishes. A law forbade him and other Chinese business owners from hiring white women.

Every day, Ah Yeh hoped for enough business so there was money to send back to and support his family in China. The two-elevator Saskatchewan town Ah Yeh had opened shop in had an Indian Agency. This manifest of the so-called 'white man's burden' doled out ammunition, snare wire, and food vouchers for Indians living on reservations. Most of the Indian reservations were within a day's walking distance to the Post Office where the Agency was located.

A childhood playmate lived in a suite on the third floor of the town's federal and largest building because his parents did the cleaning and fixing. The boast of the town is the second oldest continuous operating courthouse in Canada built next to the historic provincial Land Titles office. Two blocks away, upstairs in the Town Hall, was reputedly the grandest opera house on the Canadian prairies when built.

Another childhood playmate lived south of us, across a vacant lot with his 'in-town' relatives. Ah Yeh eventually bought and renovated the solidly built house and also built a house on the vacant lot. My friend was a local Cree band chief's son, and we would often walk to school together in those carefree days of life. Our facial features and hair were similar and our friendship playful. This welcomed a little Hoy Ping in the territory of the mighty Cree Nation of Saskatchewan near Sweetgrass and Red Pheasant.

Ah Yeh often swapped cash for the food vouchers the Indians received. Over the years, his café slowly became both a retail store and a small wholesale food outlet to the nudge–nudge wink–wink of special redemption-for-voucher locals. During the winter, his garage behind the store was often an overnight stop for those too drunk or tired to make the long trip home to the reservation. Many hunters, Indian and whites, would bring seemingly waste parts of bears, deer, moose, and other wild animals in exchange for food and cash. Ah Yeh would dry and prepare the parts, selling them for medicinal purposes to the knowing.

Fast forward 50 years later...

When I was naughty or didn't study Chinese, Ah Yeh would call me a *mong gok doy* (lost kingdom boy), meaning the loss of country and culture. In reality, he was referring to Aboriginal people, defeated by the superior firepower, Europeans who stole their land and then tried to erase their language and culture. It was Ah Yeh's rule that my adopted brother and I had to speak Chinese in the back of the store where we ate and slept. The penalty for not speaking Chinese? A knuckle duster ring on the skull. Ouch! Ah Nging (paternal grandmother), who carried me to Canada as a baby 'paper son'—illegally—in 1950, also called me a *mong gok doy* along with expletives and endearments. Her penalty for not speaking Chinese? The ear grab. Ouch!

Ah Yeh often used the story of how young Indians lost their language and culture to try to convince my brother and me of what would befall us if we did not have Chinese reading and writing skills. My answer to his preachings? Then as now, never having been the sharpest knife in the drawer, I rebelled against his old-fashioned ideas—comics, rock and roll, and later a clandestine firecracker, condoms, and cigarettes franchise among my friends. One thing led to another—girls, cars, university, et cetera. Some Hoy Ping language survives with me though, thanks to Ah Yeh's knuckle dusting and Ah Nging's ear grabs. Ah Yeh gave Chinese names to my children, the first of our family line to be born in the Gold Mountain after a century and a half of struggle. Sadly, my grandparents did not live to see my first grandchild—the fifth generation of our Tan branch of the Chow family tree to be living in Canada.

Ah Yeh showed wisdom but was aloof, my being Ah Nging's baby Buddha. As a boy, a child really, Grandfather at age ten was already imbued with the spirit of the Kwan Kung—righteousness, devotion, and loyalty—when he offered to look after a rich man's cows so his older sister would not be sold. Whenever Ah Nging told this story, she would cry. Her husband was a man who jumped at the chance to *dow jee foo*—go to land of perpetual toil—at age nineteen. Without any classroom schooling, Ah Yeh eventually taught himself to read and write Chinese and a little bit of English too. Because he gave locals credit for food and goods, his story of times and spaces is memorable and prescient: simply, a Canada that excluded him for most of his life but within it, a people who welcomed him.

Ah Yeh explained we are the people of *jung gok*—the middle or centre kingdom. It is natural for an affinity to exist between middle and lost kingdoms, more so since both had suffered under *hun mor gok*—the kingdom of the red hairs. Now called *ying gok*, the 'red hairs' is in reference to British and white English speakers who evidently ate a lot of carrots. The Chinese 'ying' character here means 'heroic and dashing.' Hey, police then were known as *look yee*—green coats—because green was the uniform colour of immigration officials. Ah Yeh's take on the British was to adopt the name Norman because they had defeated the Anglos.

There is no written record of when the middle and lost kingdom crossed paths in historic Battleford, Saskatchewan—at one time the site of the territorial government of most of what is now western Canada. Almighty Voice is a legend here. Louis Riel had spent time in the Fort Battleford jail, as did Cree leaders Chiefs Poundmaker and Big Bear. Wandering Spirit was among the six Cree and two Assiniboine men hung for insurrection within the fort's stockade, the largest mass hanging in Canada since Confederation. Norman of the Hoy Ping clan of the middle kingdom, driven to this land by hunger, arrived to seek opportunity.

In my mind, Ah Yeh's seminal meeting with the Cree was simple, solemn, and about respect, consent, and trust. He would have introduced himself by saying he was pleased to meet the leaders of the Red Pheasant and Sweetgrass clan of the Cree people.

"Welcome to my café. My name is Norman and I am a cook. Together we can prosper so I can bring my wife and son to live among you. We have a common racist enemy so let us help each other. Like me, you do not have the vote so are treated as second class. We will talk more about this after you taste my cooking."

"Your face and words tell us you are a brother. Your offer to feed us shows you are generous and respectful. I am Len, chief of the Red Pheasant. We welcome you as our brother," says the apparent commander of the men of the Red Pheasant and Sweetgrass. He nods to those closest to the outside door, and two big tubfuls of fresh fish and game, a sack of potatoes, and a mix of vegetables are brought, deposited in the kitchen.

Norman turns the radio on and instructs the men to help themselves to coffee. Len and Norman go to the kitchen. Here Norman purposefully amazes the chief with his deftness and flourishes with axe, meat cleaver, and knife in cutting and preparing the bounty. Len asks Norman if he'll teach him how to cut and chop like him. They both begin work on the feast of fusion— likely venison chop suey, roast wild duck with potatoes, fried and steamed fresh pickerel, and goldeye. Of course there would be rice and soy sauce.

Norman's cooking is clearly a hit with the Cree men, even though they tease Len that it is women's work. When most are done eating, three young Cree women arrive with more game and potatoes. They take away the leftover food, tasting and giggling all the while clearing the tables, washing the dishes, and cleaning the kitchen. Norman seems beguiled by one woman apparently in charge, and his new Cree brothers notice. She smiles, he smiles, everyone smiles. Later, Norman lets them all know he is the sole support for his extended family in China whom he misses very much. Slowly, everyone leaves except Len.

"My sister Ruby smiles at you because she needs a job. Her husband has run off," Len says to Norman, who brings out a bottle of scotch and two glasses. Len shakes his head from side to side, lifting his coffee cup. "Whiskey poisons my people. I do not drink it. Ruby raises her son alone because her boy's father loves whiskey too much. Ruby is a good woman and does not drink whiskey anymore."

"I understand," acknowledges Norman, pouring Len another coffee and himself a three-finger drink and lighting a cigarette. "Whiskey is the small warmth at the end of a long work day. Soothing if I do not drink more than a small glass or two. Your sister is a good worker. I need help with the weekend lunch and dinner trade and will treat her fairly."

Norman ran his café and store for nearly fifty years, over twenty-five without Nooy, his wife and their son, Wing, because of Canada's racist exclusion law against us Chinese. When asked about this, he looks towards the back wall shrine of Kwan Kung, patron protector of warriors, writers, and artists, facing the front door. Then he looks upward as towards heaven and thanks the local Indians and Métis for their friendship. Ah Nging coughs. Ah Yeh then gives a thumbs up and in a warrior's voice proclaims, "*Lo wah kiu ho sai lai*"—old overseas Chinese number one.

Ah Nging chuckles saying, "Ho yeah, ho yeah"—good stuff, good stuff.

Grandfather and Grandmother, I will never forget you.

2) Gim and Ruby

Cree Territory, inside the Wah Kiu Café, Battleford, Saskatchewan, at the junction of the Battle and North Saskatchewan River. A seminal meeting. Gim, the restaurant owner, is scrubbing the counter and readying the café to open. Vince, a Cree carver, enters. Gim introduces himself.

G: Welcome. My name Gim. I am cook. You are my first customer. What your name?

V: I'm Vince, a carver with no money but can make a trade. I will give you...

G: Vince, first you eat. I treat you. You want coffee?

V: Yes, thanks...can I have bacon and eggs, sunny up, fried potatoes with onions?

G: Okay. Coffee coming up...cream and sugar?

Vince nods. Gim gives Vince his coffee and exits to the kitchen. Ruby enters, exchanges pleasantries with Vince as Gim enters shortly after.

G: Good morning. Coffee?

V: Gim, my sister Ruby, eh. Ruby, this is Gim. He's a cook.

R: Nice to meet you. I just finished coffee at home.

V: No you didn't. We don't have any coffee at home. That's why I came here. Gim, Ruby would love a coffee but she's like me—no money. Pretty sad, eh?

G: No problem. Nice meet you Ruby. You are first woman here. Good for coffee...bacon and eggs too.

R: Thank you Gim. That's nice name. Does it mean anything?

G: How you like eggs? Onion fried potatoes?

R. Eggs over easy. Yes, fried onions in pan fries.

G: In Chinese, Gim mean gold. My father hope. Find gold. Get rich.

Gim exits to the kitchen. Two people come in. Gim takes a while to notice so Ruby pours coffee as Gim enters. They look at each other and smile. Ruby walks up to Gim and pushes him into the kitchen.

R: Two bacon, eggs, and pancakes. One over easy, one scramble. Thought I would help. Don't really have anything better to do except talk to Vince, and I do that all day.

G: Thank you. I cannot pay you, but feed you, teach you to cook.

R: Don't have to pay me...yet. I'll work for food for Vince and me...and tips.

G: You hired. We talk later. For Vince...bacon, egg.

More people come in. Ruby shouts meal orders to Gim and clears and helps Gim wash dishes. Finally the breakfast trade slows down. Ruby fixes a plate, pours herself coffee and refills Vince's cup, sits down, and begins to eat. Gim enters.

V: Sit down a bit. Your breakfast special is a real hit. Cheap and fast, that's it, eh?

G: Fast. Eggs, pancakes, toast...fast cook. Keep bacon, sausage, ham, and potatoes ready to warm. Special too cheap I think?

V: Think too much work for you maybe. You cook fast but serve slow. If Ruby wasn't helping you, you'd be in trouble.

R: Gim said he can't pay me but can teach me to cook...Chinese food too. I can keep the tips. Deal is you and I can eat here.

G: Ruby good help. Vince, you right...need help. Cannot pay now. When business better, pay Ruby. Now I send money to wife, daughters in China first. Canada government hate Chinese. Make us second class. Not let wife, children come to Canada.

V: The government haven't done Ruby and me any good, eh. We have a common racist enemy so let us help each other. Like me, you do not have the vote so can be treated as second class.

R: Oh Vince, don't you have anything else to do? Complaining about something you can't do anything about doesn't help. Gim is making a living for his family. He doesn't complain, works hard, looks after his family. That's honourable. There's nothing better than that.

G: Please, what mean honourable?

R: You are good man. Honest. You work hard, look after your family.

G: I try. Not too good. Work hard yes. Save money no. Maybe someday go back home.

V: Your face and words tell us you are a brother. Your offer to feed us shows you are generous and respectful. You are welcome, you are a brother. How good a cook are you, eh?

G: I cook anything, make good.

V: How about venison, moose meat? Fish?

G: Please, what venison?

R: Deer meat.

G: You bring, I show you. I cook Chinese style. Maybe show everyone.

R: Me too? Will you show me?

G: That deal. I show you cook. You help. I make money, you make money. We eat good, get rich. You think?

R: I think yes. Vince, go get us some venison and fish. Come on, make yourself useful.

Vince leaves. Gim and Ruby look at each other and smile. Then Gim starts singing.

Getting Good and Fast
I'm cook to make a buck
And feel it's a noble task
Keeping hungry people fed
Getting good then fast.
You ready the sausage, ham and bacon
Eggs and toast take no time to cook
You ready the potatoes and porridge
And always give the coffee a look.
Just when you think you can relax
And sit down and rest awhile
There's lunch specials to prepare
More coffee to pour with a smile.
I cook to make a buck
And feel it is a noble task
Keeping a hungry people fed

Getting good then fast.
I make do with what's at hand
Wild duck cooked black bean sauce
Venison steak, stew with potatoes
Steamed fish green onion ginger toss.
A hundred recipes in my head
Boston, banana coconut cream pie
Bread, donuts and cinnamon rolls
To fill a stomach and leave a sigh
I cook to make a buck
And feel it's a noble task
Keeping hungry people fed
First getting good then fast.

R: You are really something.

G: I go cook. You help lunch special. Soya sauce chicken, beef stew, and rice. Lots work do.

R: Besides carving, Vince loves hunting and fishing the most. Good hunter and fisherman. We always have lots of meat and fish, mostly venison and goldeye fish.

G: Maybe roast venison, steam fish for dinner special.

Gim exits to the kitchen. Ruby clears tables, makes coffee, then goes to the kitchen where Gim is washing dishes. They are both smiling from ear to ear. Ruby helps Gim put away dishes and start food preparation.

R: Why did you come to be here?

G: Father-in-law own café. My duty, make café, make money. How you say? Honourable.

R. Must be hard. You miss your wife and kids?

G: Ruby, you honourable. You good woman. Nothing better than that.

R: You don't know me Gim. You don't know me at all.

G: You pretty. Have boyfriend? Yes?

R: Have many boyfriends. Too many. All boys, no men. Boys no good. I want a good man.

G: Yes, miss family. Miss much.

Ruby continues working as Gim exits to the storeroom. Sound of a flute. Ruby seems mesmerized, exits to the storeroom. Gim is sitting on his bed playing a flute. Ruby starts swaying to the music. From the dining room, a customer's voice.

C: Anybody here? Are we too late for breakfast?

R: (*Entering*) We do breakfast all day. Would you like a coffee?

Weeks pass. Vince is now procurer of meat, fish, and local fruits and vegetables for Wah Kiu Café. Gim shows his skills in pastry. His specials of wild game and fish are a modest success and talk of the town. There is playfulness in their work, particularly around the knife work Gim shows Ruby. Often, at the end of the day, Gim plays his flute as Ruby dances, with much giggling and ai-yaah-ing. Provisions arrive from out of town.

G: Lap Cheng. Lap cheng.

R: What's that?

G: Chinese sausage. From Vancouver. Very very tasty.

R: They are shrivelled and dry.

G: When steamed, gets big, very tasty. Chinese sausage best...steam, sweet.

R: Sweet, eh? Chinese sausages are sweet. I can't wait to try... (*giggle*). When was last time your Chinese sausage was steamed?

G: Please, don't know what you say.

R: Sorry, a joke. Bad joke... (*giggle*). You are a good man. Honourable. Ain't nothing better than that.

G: Make special for you. Make for honourable woman. Chop Chinese sausage, pork, chestnuts...steam. Very good. Special fried rice for you. We eat good.

R: Thank you Gim. Maybe make just before we close. We eat together. Chinese sausage, steamed and sweet... (*giggles and kisses Gim*).

G: Ten years ago...

R: What?

G: Wife steam sausage. Ten years ago. Last time.

Notes

1   *Aiyah* is an exclamation in Chinese. It is used as a sigh or "oh, oh" or "wow man."

2   *"Hoy Ping"* literally means "open peace" and is the name of a district in southern China. This story was first published as an online essay at the Asian Canadian Culture Online Project website: http://www.ccnc.ca/accop/index.php?section=content/essays/essayMain.php&sub=content/essays/sidTan/sidTan.shtml

3   See: *The Chinese Immigration Act* (1923). S.C., c. 38.

Ronald Lee

Ronald Lee is a Romani Canadian, born in Montreal. He is a journalist and author and, from 2003 to 2008, he taught a spring seminar, "The Romani Diaspora in Canada," at New College, University of Toronto, as part of the Equity Studies Program, Department of Humanities. He is a founding member, former executive director, and Chairman of the Board of Directors of the Roma Community Centre, in Toronto. Registered in 1998, the Centre assists Romani newcomers to Canada with their social integration and serves as a cultural centre that organizes ethnic Romani events for the local Romani community. The Centre also helps to acquaint other Canadians with Romani culture, music, history, and their situation in the refugee-producing countries prior to the admission of these countries to the EU. Its aim is also to assist with the social self-empowerment of Romanies in Canada. This is a non-governmental, Romani organization whose members are mostly Roma, and the Romani language is often used at meetings. He has three published works to date. The first, *Goddam Gypsy,* a semi-autobiographical novel about Romani life in Montreal and Canada in the 1960s (Tundra Books, 1971) is also published in Spanish, German, and Czech translations; it is now republished under its original title, *The Living Fire* (Magoria Books). The other two works include *Learn Romani* (University of Hertfordshire Press, 2005), an 18-lesson self-study course of *Kalderash* Romani, and *Rromano-Alavari: Romani-English Dictionary* (Magoria Books, 2010). His current manuscript, *The Gypsy Invasion: Romani Refugees in Canada 1997–2006,* is currently being revised and updated for publication. It is based on his experience in Toronto working with Romani refugees, immigration lawyers, and the Immigration and Refugee Board since the Czech-Romani refugees arrived in Canada in 1997 and with later refugee groups from Hungary, Romania, Bulgaria, and elsewhere in central/eastern Europe. He has also written numerous newspaper and magazine articles about Roma in Canada and, more recently, about the Romani refugee situation in Canada. As well, Ronald has written scholarly articles in academic publications such as Chapter 9, of *Gypsy Law: Romani Legal Traditions and Culture* (University of California Press, 2001), which was originally published as an article. Ronald has also lectured extensively for colleges and universities, both in Canada and in the US, as well as in the Toronto area, for public and private elementary and high schools. As a folk musician, he also performs locally with other Romani musicians at Romani cultural events.

The Attempted Genocide and Ethnocide of the Roma

Canadian visitors to Europe often see dark-skinned people begging on the streets of large cities, clustered in parks or waiting around food distribution centres. Dejected men, women in long skirts and bandanas and children of all ages— families on the move—fleeing from there and unwanted here. They might look like Native people to Canadian tourists, but they are not. They are Roma, the victims of apartheid, hatred, and rising fascism—the dispossessed of Europe.

A historical overview

The Roma,[1] or "Gypsies," originated as composite groups of Hindu *Kshatriya* recruited from vassal states in northwestern India by the Ghaznavid Muslim invaders under Mahmud Ghazni in the early eleventh century.[2] Thousands of Indians considered useful were forcibly or voluntarily removed to Ghaza in what is now Afghanistan during this period. The Roma, descended from those Hindu troops called *ghulam*,[3] and their supporting camp followers, wives, and children[4] were sent to Khurasan in eastern Persia (Iran) as ethnic contingents of the multi-ethnic army serving as occupation and garrison troops.

In 1040, the Ghaznavids were defeated by the Seljuk Turks at the three-day Battle of Dandanqan in Khurasan, and the surviving Indian troops and camp followers fled westward to Armenia.[5] From there, they were forced to relocate to Cilicia in western Byzantium after the Battle of Ani in 1064 when the Armenians were defeated by the Seljuks in their expansion westward. A large number of Armenians, accompanied by Hindu troops and camp followers, fled to a new homeland in Cilicia provided by their fellow Christian Greeks of the Byzantine Empire. In 1071, the Byzantines in turn were massively defeated by the Seljuk Turks at the Battle of Manzikirt, and the Roma then came under the rule of the Sultanate of Roum (or Rum), also called Iconium.

In Anatolia, the former Indians gradually evolved into a composite people speaking the common Sanskrit-based military koïné with additions of Persian words used by Hindu troops in the Ghaznavid service.[6] This became the only native language of the ancestral Romani group in Anatolia and was subject to input from Greek, Armenian, and other languages of the region.

A new people, the *Romiti* (or Roma), evolved from the Hindu refugees from Khurasan and a new language developed from their military koïné.

Over time, groups of Roma drifted from Anatolia into the Balkans on their own westward migration, or they arrived accompanying the invading Ottoman Turks as auxiliaries[7] beginning by the twelfth century. By the early fifteenth century bands of Romanies began to appear all over Christian Europe. According to written records of the period,[8] these bands consisted of a hundred or more people under the leadership of men who termed themselves "counts" or "dukes" of Little Egypt. Artist Jacques Callot left illustrations of one such band with which he travelled from France to Italy in the early seventeenth century. His illustrations show richly dressed leaders on fine horses accompanied by followers consisting of mounted men armed with the latest weaponry of the period, including wick fire muskets, and with horse-drawn carts and women and children on foot. This was the period of the religious wars in western Europe, and what Callot is probably showing is a band of Roma armed for self-defence and possibly heading to join the army of some military leader.[9]

By this period Roma had entered European history albeit misidentified as "Egyptians," most likely based on the practice of some of these early groups of Roma in Europe to claim they were Egyptian Christians on a pilgrimage of atonement for having denied Christ in order to escape death by the Muslim invaders of Egypt.[10]

At first the Catholic states of Europe believed their story, which was backed up by the fact that many Roma told them they had come from Little Egypt (*Kleine Aegipter* in German) in the Middle East, which was then part of the empire of the Muslim Mamluk rulers of Egypt.[11] Free conduct passes were issued by popes and rulers of various countries, alms were forthcoming and, for a short time, Roma were treated like members of a sovereign nation referred to as "Egyptians." Their "dukes" and "counts" were entertained by kings and noblemen, but this idyllic state was not to continue for long. As the Catholic hegemony of Europe disintegrated with the Protestant Reformation and the Renaissance, nation-states in central and western Europe evolved. Roma were now seen as undesirable interlopers, non-productive members of society, potential criminals, heathens, and sorcerers.[12] In most European countries, both Catholic and Protestant, Roma were condemned as "pagans" and "non-believers."

Local priests spread the false story that the Roma had been "blacksmiths" in Palestine and had forged the nails used in the Crucifixion. They accused the Roma as being co-murderers of Christ along with Jewish accomplices. At this date, the ancestors of the Roma had not left India. The Roma, in turn, came up with a now widely known counter-legend about a Romani blacksmith who stole the fourth nail thus sparing Jesus a little extra agony and, for this, Christ blessed them and gave them the right to steal to earn their living.

To the Church, white was good and Christian and black was evil and satanic. The dark-skinned Roma were seen as "imps of Satan." They professed to be Christians but they never attended Mass or paid tithes to the Church. They (we) were also accused of cannibalism.[13] The mere thought of cannibalism to a Romani person is ludicrous. Outsiders or non-Roma to traditional Roma (which we all probably were back then) are seen as sources of contamination. For a Romani person to eat a non-Romani person would be like a Brahmin eating a Shudra in India.[14]

What was totally unknown to the outside world was that Romanies actually followed a non-crafted folk religion that had its roots in Hinduism with overtones of other belief systems, somewhat like voodoo or Santeria. Unlike crafted religions—which have unalterable dogmas, doctrines, appointed priests or ministers, holy books, and established places of worship—folk religions require little, with only a belief system and simple ceremonies followed by the community as a whole. Among Vlach-Romani speakers, this is referred to as the *Romaniya* or *Pochitayimos-Rromano* and among other Romani groups as *Romanipen/Romanipe*.[15] This lack of visible religious paraphernalia and ignorance of the Romani culture and spiritual beliefs has caused centuries of persecution and human suffering throughout Europe by zealous fanatics dedicated to forcing us to conform to their belief systems. While outsiders knew the Roma spoke an unintelligible language, samples of which were occasionally recorded,[16] writers constantly stated that what we spoke was not a legitimate language but some made-up gibberish or even the local non-Romani thieves' jargons called *argot* in France, *germania* in Spain, and cant or the Vulgar Tongue in England.[17] Thus, we were denied even our own language. As late as the twentieth century, many non-linguist politicians during the communist era declared Romani not to be a viable language worthy of development and preservation.[18] Even today, Romani still has to be recognized as a legitimate minority language by all the countries of the EU. The Canadian government does not list Romani as a minority language, we are the missing patch from the quilt of the multicultural mosaic and are totally absent from Canadian history books.[19] Hundreds of thousands of Roma have lost their language. For the estimated three to four million who have retained it, in Europe and in the Americas, Romani has now become a threatened language after surviving for a thousand years in spite of all attempts to obliterate it along with its speakers.

By the seventeenth century, Roma gradually began to lose their earlier status as a distinct people or members of a legitimate nation and were reduced to the level of vagabonds and undesirable elements of the local populations like the indigenous Masterless Men and other non-Romani itinerants. The persecution of the Romani people was now well underway.[20] Banishments, executions, pogroms, whippings, mutilations, and shipment to the colonies of the maritime countries of Spain and Portugal, later France and Britain, were all methods designed to drive the unwanted "Egyptians" and the later Other-defined "gypsies" from their boundaries into neighbouring states.[21] These then applied their own inhuman methods to drive them somewhere else where they were equally unwelcome. Many Roma managed to escape the pogroms and persecution thanks to the poor communication methods, the greed of local officials who could often be bribed, and the existence of wilderness and uninhabited regions of forests and mountains. Roma would also escape by travelling at night and by living near borders that gave easy access to two or more jurisdictions.[22]

The Roma were thus forced to adopt a culture of survival that took many forms in different countries: commercial nomadism in the emerging nation-states to avoid settling and becoming targets for the rulers, and settlements around castles or villages in the feudal countries of central/eastern Europe, often under the protection of the nobility. Here they became sedentary artisans, entertainers, and agricultural workers. Others were nomadic entertainers, artisans, or horse traders; they would apply any work stratagem that enabled them to survive. In the vassal states of Wallachia, Moldavia, and Transylvania (now Romania) Roma were enslaved until the *Slobuzheniya* or Emancipation in 1855 to 1856.[23]

Slavery in the Romanian Principalities of Moldavia and Wallachia had been until then a national institution—slaves bought and sold like cattle, families separated, young women sexually exploited by their owners, and severe punishments inflicted for minor infractions administered by the owners. Enslavement of Roma also existed in a non-institutionalized way in some other countries like Czarist Russia, Austria-Hungary, Spain, and even Scotland. Roma convicts were sent to the galleys of France and Spain, and the English shipped Romani bond slaves to the thirteen colonies, Barbados, and Jamaica. During this period and later, Roma in western Europe were never very numerous compared to the vast concentration of Roma in the Ottoman Empire in the Balkans, in Czarist Russia, and in the Austro-Hungarian Empire.[24] Thus the greater part of the Romani nation escaped the persecutions of the western European nation-states and German petty kingdoms.

By the eighteenth century, these persecutions gradually subsided and were replaced by harassment, laws limiting commercial nomadism, fines, imprisonment, registration of nomads, and other forms of growing state control, except in some of the German states where pogroms and "Gypsy hunting"[25] by noblemen were common, even in the so-called Age of Reason.

In the sprawling empires of feudal Europe, Roma were tolerated, allowed to exist, but never accepted as a legitimate people with an ancestral language and culture. In some countries, aristocrats, orientalists, and wealthy dilettantes saw Romanies as curiosities and studied our language and lore in a racist, paternalistic attempt to capture this Gypsy Lore for posterity. This began with Heinrich Grellman in 1783[26] and continued with his successors through the British-based *Gypsy Lore Society*[27] to the modern academic neolorists of the twenty-first century.

This toleration continued in some countries[28] until the Nazi Genocide of the Second World War,[29] which was followed by communist ethnocide in the attempted total assimilation of Roma into the general proletariat. The self-contained free-market economy of the Roma was declared "reactionary," and our traditional trades, skills, and economic base were destroyed in one generation. Nomadism was outlawed and the self-supporting commercial itinerant element among the Roma was forced to settle.

For those already sedentary in their own settlements, they and the former itinerants were provided with menial jobs in factories, agriculture, or some other menial job in the system. They were provided with all the rights and benefits of any other citizen and their standard of living improved as they were being de-cultured and assimilated. This resulted in their children becoming an urbanized sub-proletariat unable to fend for themselves when communism collapsed and the new democracies emerged.

Unable to resume their now forgotten self-sustaining, self-generated economy, most Roma then became the victims of a massive welfare culture in the former Soviet Bloc countries. The communist laws protecting them from persecution disappeared and skinheads, neo-nationalists, and fascists emerged from the woodwork to create new scapegoats out of the Roma to replace the pre-war Jews who had been decimated by their Nazi forerunners during the Holocaust.

Little interest has been shown in this ongoing crime of cultural ethnocide perpetrated against us by rulers, national governments, and institutions since our appearance in Christian Europe in the fifteenth century.[30] Whether one uses a gas chamber to commit genocide or commits ethnocide or cultural genocide by sending the children of the ethnic minority to a boarding school to be educated by strangers in a language and culture not their own, the result is the same. The language, culture, and self-identity of the group ceases to exist and the ethnic group is left alive but obliterated as a culture.

Beginning with the Byzantines who misnamed us *Athinganoi/Atsinganoi* after an earlier group of Persian refugee mystics—which gave rise to terms like *tsigani*, *cigani,* and as on—we have been misnamed and misidentified from the beginning. One ploy used by rulers was to simply order Roma out of the country under threat of pain of death as in France under the Edict of 1612, the German states, the Netherlands, Britain, and elsewhere or to declare us a non-people by legislating *gitanos* out of existence in Spain[31] or renaming us *Ujmagyar* (New Hungarians) in Hungary[32] and ordering us to settle and become ethnic Spanish or ethnic Hungarians. We were often forbidden to marry one another and, at the same time, forbidden to marry the local population.[33] Our language, culture, and native dress were outlawed almost everywhere. In Austria–Hungary under Empress Maria Theresa, Romani children were kidnapped by her royally empowered kidnappers to be brought up as good Christian Hungarians. This did not work out as planned but it had a destructive effect on the language and culture of Hungarian Roma. Her son Joseph II extended her policy throughout the empire, but his successors did not pursue the kidnapping policies with the same vigour, so the policy lapsed.[34]

But the Empress set the pattern for the forcible taking of Romani children, which has continued throughout Europe ever since in one form of another. According to oral histories, in Britain and other countries of western Europe children were often taken from destitute Romani families by local authorities and placed in orphanages run by religious organizations. One state-sponsored child-snatching organization was in Switzerland. From 1926 until 1973 the Catholic Swiss agency *Pro Juventute* ran a program called "Operation Children of the Road." Unknown numbers of Romani and children of non-Romani itinerant groups were placed in Catholic orphanages or with Swiss families. Even after the closure of this organization, it was reported that about one hundred of these children still remained incarcerated in clinics and institutions as late as 1988.[35] In communist Czechoslovakia, children were also taken from their families and placed in state orphanages and boarding schools.[36]

History Repeating – The Present State

When I visited Romani refugee camps around Rome in 2001, Roma in the camps and Italian activists, such as photojournalist Stefano Montesi and American journalist Kate Carlisle of European Roma Rights Centre in

Budapest, informed me that when Romani women with their children were arrested for begging, the police often took the better-looking and healthier children and placed them for adoption by Italian families.[37] When Czech and Hungarian Romani refugees arrived in Toronto and the surrounding area from 1997 onward, our Roma Community Centre volunteers discovered that Romani children were taken by the Ontario Catholic Children's Aid Society in Hamilton and placed in foster homes. This usually happened when the fathers were detained or arrested as suspects in some petty crime or immigration problem and the mother was unable to obtain enough welfare to feed herself and the children and was then arrested for shoplifting food. No attempt was made by the Catholic Children's Aid to place these children in Romani foster homes nor did they feel the need to do this so as not to destroy the cultural heritage of these children. Instead, these children were railroaded into the general foster care system.

In July 2006, I received a telephone call from a Canadian-born Romani mother in Toronto who almost lost her children to the Toronto Catholic Children's Aid Society when a school principal notified them that the children's mother was operating a psychic-advisor parlour on Bloor Street. The Children's Aid people were ready to remove the children because they felt they were being exposed to Satanism and witchcraft. I advised the mother to see a civil rights lawyer at the University of Toronto Law Clinic where she eventually received the necessary legal assistance to prevent the removal of her children.

On 8 March 2010, Premier of Slovakia Robert Fico announced his intention to create a program that would "gradually put as many Roma children as possible into boarding schools and gradually separate them from their life they live in the settlements."[38] His stated reasoning was that this would prevent the next generation from being unable to "integrate." He failed to mention that his plan goes against the United Nation's *Universal Declaration of Human Rights*, which guarantees rights to culture and language. Based on the tragic experience with Native children sent to boarding schools in Canada, this will in all probability destroy the Romani culture and language in Slovakia if it becomes law. It will also ensure that these de-cultured Roma of the future will still be hated and persecuted by white Slovaks as their parents and for the same reason—the color of their skin and the Romaphobia of Slovaks in general. This cannot be legislated out of existence.

The solution should be to work constructively to empower the Roma themselves, which will allow them to have an equal say in their future as citizens and to improve the settlements, currently these are worse than the shantytowns in Third World countries.[39] Svinia is typical of the hundreds of similar settlements in Slovakia built under communism with ersatz materials and shoddy labour and left to decay after 1990. Members of Canadian Native groups who saw a film on this at private educational showings have commented that the conditions of the Roma in Svinia, one of hundreds of such settlements, were much worse than those on any Native reserve in Canada. The Slovak proposal has come under criticism from Amnesty International and other agencies in Europe, including the European Commission on Human Rights. EU membership includes a declaration by member states that they will uphold the United Nation's *Charter of Human Rights and Freedoms*.[40]

Despite the fact that Roma and Sinti,[41] like Jews, were singled out as victims of the Nazi Holocaust on racial grounds and that an estimated one and a half million were murdered,[42] we have vanished from the Holocaust according to the US Holocaust Memorial Council. The Council currently does not have a single presidential-appointed Romani member since the presidency of Jimmy Carter, who had appointed Dr. Ian Hancock who followed William A. Duna who was appointed by Ronald Reagan.[43] We have been conveniently vaporized among "the others," reduced to anonymous background spear carriers in this tragic Nazi opera of mass murder.

Roma have also vanished from the educational systems worldwide. Romani schoolchildren are unable to learn anything about their own history and culture and are becoming assimilated as they pass through the assimilating school system and its Other-required prerequisites. Romani slavery in the former principalities has been flushed down the memory tube of Romanian history. Roma simply do not exist in school textbooks anywhere until university level, where some courses are beginning to be offered on Romani studies to now-assimilated Romani students.

What children do read are kindergarten versions of the adult fantasy literature. This adult pabulum began in the form of novels beginning with Cervantes,[44] through Victor Hugo[45] to George Borrow[46] and a host of asinine armchair imitators to D.H. Lawrence[47] and Erich von Stroheim[48] to Canada's Robertson Davies[49] and Charles de Lint.[50] These misinformed authors have written an endless series of novels romanticizing and fictionalizing the "Gypsies" they had never met. Collectively, they have created a generic mythological "Gypsy" that feeds on itself like the generic African "native" or North-American "Indian" of novels and Hollywood films. The advent of the celluloid Moguls has also served as the *coup de grâce* of the reality of the Roma, and this has been ably followed by television prime-time fantasy, popular songs like *Gypsies, Tramps and Thieves* by Cher, and other manufactured mass-culture trash like the plastic Esmeralda doll with her plastic caravan and plastic dancing bear, nicely packaged as part of the massive commoditization of a money-making mythical "Gypsy" culture.

Recent documentaries like *The Gypsy Child Thieves,* which aired on CBC's *The Passionate Eye* on 25 October 2010, showed only one of the symptoms of the much greater problem: the Romani history of slavery in what is now Romania, historical persecution, the Nazi Holocaust, communist assimilation policies in central/eastern Europe, past and current unacceptable high rates of unemployment for Roma that result in high poverty levels, imposition of state welfare cultures, discrimination in education and in the housing market, and the general undeclared state of apartheid during this EU Decade of Roma Inclusion (2005–2015). The halfway point shows this to be more of the Decade of Roma Exclusion. Rather than choosing to air one of the many existing documentaries that might show something of the problem facing the Roma and our history, the CBC chose to go for a sensational tabloid shocker portrayal of one of the major symptoms affecting Roma from Romania worthy of Randolph Hearst's yellow journalism, but failed to point out that these criminal gangs are a minority and not representative of all Roma in all countries in or outside the EU, including native-born Roma in the Americas. Targeting such a symptom is the equivalent of exposing a headache when the problem is an historical brain tumour resulting from European xenophobia, the Nazi Holocaust, communist assimilation policies, and a welfare culture imposed on Roma in the so-called new democracies.

Compounding this type of media irresponsibility and negativity is the decision of President Sarkozy of France to deport Roma refugees living in France, mainly from Romania and Bulgaria, because of an incident in a Romani camp in France that resulted in violence. The violence was mainly committed by itinerant workers who were French citizens and not foreign Roma. All Roma living in France who are members of EU states but are not French citizens were also included in this deportation order, which only offered a small stipend to the deportees.[51] This resulted in the deportation of over a thousand Roma, mainly from Bulgaria and Romania, and the destruction of 128 camps. A French court blocked the deportation of seven Roma claiming that they were not a threat to public order.[52] After condemnation from members of the French cabinet and government, Brussels, and the Vatican, Sarkozy agreed to follow the directives of EU membership and, in return, France was allowed to exercise control over its own immigration policies.

In the village of Ostrovanya in Eastern Slovakia, a wall has been erected around the Romani settlement on the outskirts of the village to separate the Roma from the non-Romani villagers. The wall, partially financed by the villagers themselves, now prevents Roma from easy access from their settlement into the village shopping area, medical services, and the local school. The wall has aroused criticism, including Prime Minister Iveta Radicova who stated that the wall would not solve anything.[53]

The end result of all this is that the average person anywhere in the world sees "Gypsies" either as thieves just waiting to "gyp" you or as romantic creatures of fiction, semi-mythological beings, or just anybody who abandons the moral restraints of law-abiding "people like us" and who travels around wearing an earring and playing the fiddle, leading a life of hedonistic abandon. Any one of us can become a "Gypsy." Books worth reading are not read by general readers, while popular coffee-table books about "Gypsies" are full of mythology and misinformation.

When my Romani Diaspora in Canada course was first offered in 2003 at New College, University of Toronto, an article appeared in *The Varsity* entitled "You Say Roma I say Tomato." Random questioning of grad students on campus about who Roma were resulted in the students not understanding what was meant by the question beyond the City of Rome and Roma tomatoes. When asked about Gypsies, the answers were "extinct," "thieves," "costumes you wear on Halloween" (mainly females), "people who travel around," and "women who tell fortunes." Not one student identified either Roma or Gypsies as a valid ethnic group with an origin from India.

After surviving centuries of genocide, an estimated fifteen million people of a nation of worldwide Romani people without a country are now potentially in grave danger of becoming victims of cultural ethnocide.[54]

Notes

1   Roma is a plural proper noun in the Romani language common. It cannot be used in the singular in English as in "He/she is a Roma." The media uses the plural "Romas," which is also incorrect. The proper adjective is Romani, which can also serve as a noun. He/she is Romani would be correct or he/she is a Romani. Roma generally refers to the Roma of central/eastern Europe and the Americas. Gypsy is in the same category of unacceptable definitions as "Indian," "Eskimo," and "Negro"— words created and employed by dominating colonial societies to define what were considered "racial inferiors."

2   Hancock, Ian (2002:7, 10–11). *We are the Romani people: Ame sam e Rromane džene* (first published 1992). Hatfield, UK: University of Hertfordshire Press; Marsh, Adrian (2008:42, 69–70). *No Promised Land: History, Historiography & the Origins of the Gypsies.* Thesis: submitted for consideration for the degree of Doctor of Philosophy to

the school of Humanities, University of Greenwich: Istanbul & London; Lee, Ronald (2007:56-57, 63-64). The Romani Diaspora in Canada (NEW 343H1: course pack). University of Toronto, Toronto, ON.

3   Rishi, W.R. (1974:vi). *Multilingual Romani Dictionary*. Chandigarh, India: Roma Publications, Indian Institute of Romani Studies, University of Chandigarh; Lee, Ronald (2009). A New Look at Our Romani Origins and Diaspora. Retrieved 20 January 2011 from: http://kopachi.com/articles/a-new-look-at-our-romani-origins-and-diaspora-by-ronald-lee/#more-43

4   Nicolle, David (1996:191). *Medieval Warfare Source Book: Christian Europe and its Neighbours*. London, UK: Brockhampton Press. This was a common structure in Indian and other medieval armies even in Europe in the seventeenth century.

5   Hancock (2002). Not all of the Hindu troops and camp followers in Khurasan would have been at the battle but would have migrated to Armenia when they learned of the Ghaznavid defeat. Hancock theorizes that some Hindu *ghulam* may have been recruited by the victorious Seljuks, but would have ended up with the rest in the Sultanate of Rum eventually.

6   Hancock, Ian (2000:1-13). The Emergence of Romani as a Koïné Outside of India. In T.A. Acton (ed.). *Scholarship and the Gypsy Struggle: Commitment in Romani Studies*. Hatfield, UK: University of Hertfordshire Press (retrieved 9 December 2010 from: http://www.radoc.net/radoc.php?doc=art_b_history_koine&lang=en&articles=true); Hancock (2002:140-41).

7   Marushiakova, Elena and Vesselin Popov (2001:16-24). *Gypsies in the Ottoman Empire: A contribution to the history of the Balkans*. Hatfield, UK: University of Hertfordshire Press.

8   Fraser, Angus (1995:67-71). *The Gypsies*. Oxford, UK: Blackwell Publishing; and Crowe, David M. (1994:33). *A History of the Gypsies of Eastern Europe and Russia*. New York, NY: St. Martin's Press.

9   Les Gravures de Jacques Callot (1621), Bibliotèque Nationale, Paris in Fraser (1995:141). German illustrations from the same period show similar groups of armed Roma. There are also many other references to Romani soldiers serving in various European armies during this period and later, suggesting that the *Kshatriya* tradition among these early Roma was not entirely forgotten. Gronemeyer, R. and Georgia. A Rakelmann (1988). *Die Zigeuner: Reisende in Europa*. Köln: DuMont Buchverlag. See illustration by Guler von Weinek (1606).

10 Hancock (2002:29).

11 Hunt, Yvonne (1999:72-73). Yiftos, Tsinganos: Λ Note on Greek Terminology. *Journal of the Gypsy Lore Society* Series 5, 9(1):71-78; Soulis, G.C. (1961:148). The Gypsies in the Byzantine Empire and the Balkans in the late Middle Ages. *Dumbarton Oaks Papers* 15:141,143-165. Roma were also often confused with other non-Romani itinerants following a similar way of life. For more on this confusion, see Fraser (1995:35).

12 Fraser (1995:67-71).

13 Crowe (1994:39).

14 Lee (2001:203, 208). The Rom-Vlach Gypsies and the Kris-Romani. In W.o. Weyrauch (ed.). *Gypsy Law: Romani Legal Traditions and Culture*. Berkley and Los Angeles, CA: University of California Press. Romani cannibalism could never have happened. Our own folk religion would have prevented it. See Lee for description of the *marime* code of the Roma. Also see Fraser (1995:161, 195, 248).

15 Lee (2001:188-230); Hancock (2002:70-76).

16 Boorde, A. ([1542] 1870:217). *The Fyrst Boke of the Introduction of Knowledge*. M. Barnes, F.J. Furnivall (eds.). London, UK: Early English Text Society, N. Trübner & Co. (retrieved 9 December 2010 from: http://www.digitalbookindex.org/index.cgi). The first such recording of Romani was in England by Andrew Boorde where he gives some recorded sentences of "Egipt speche" or Egyptian Speech.

17 Grose, F. (1796:F). *A Classical Dictionary of the Vulgar Tongue. The Third Edition, Corrected and Enlarged*. London, UK: Hooper and Wigstead. It was widely believed that this Vulgar Tongue or Thieves' Latin was the actual language of Romanies in Britain. The dictionary itself attributes this jargon to "Gypsies."

18 Fraser (1995:161); Crowe (1994:59).

19 The US Census Bureau does list Romani as a minority language in the US.

20 Hancock, Ian (1987:53–60). *The Pariah Syndrome; An account of Gypsy Slavery and Persecution*. Anne Arbor, MI: Karoma Publishers Inc.

21 Fraser (1995:161).

22 Hancock, Ian (2004, November 5). Diaspora Populations and the role of Intellectuals, Workshop at the Institute for Diaspora Studies, Northwestern University. Norris University Center, Evanston Campus, Evanston, IL; Fraser (1995:148–154).

23 Hancock (1987:11–29, 49–60).

24 Because these empires were patchwork quilts of multiple ethnic groups and religions, the Roma were just one more, and nomadic Romani groups could usually travel all over these empires; thus they avoided the persecution they were subjected to in the nation-states of western Europe.

25 Hancock (1987:58); Fraser (1995:147).

26 Grellmann, H.M.G. (1783). *Ein historischer Versuch über die Lebensart und Verfassung, Sitten und Schicksale dieses Volks in Europa, nebst ihrem Ursprung*. Dessau and Leipzig. (2nd edition, Göttingen, 1787). Trans. by M. Raper (1787). *Dissertation on the Gipsies, being an Historical Enquiry, concerning The Manner of Life, Economy, Customs and conditions of these People in Europe, and their Origin*. 2nd edition, 1807. London, UK: G. Bigg.

27 Founded in 1888 in Britain.

28 Hancock (1987:58–88). Germany and Switzerland continued their very harsh laws against nomadic Sinti and Roma between the two World Wars.

29 While the total number of Romani victims of the Nazis and their puppets will never be known, the original estimate of 500,000 is far too low. Newer estimates suggest as many as well over a million were killed. Records exist only for those killed in the camps who were identified with a "Z" for *Zigeuner*. Untold thousands were murdered in the conquered countries and some of the puppet states. Statistics just do not exist. The late Dr. Sybil Milton, Senior Historian of the US Holocaust Memorial Council (USHMC) estimated the total number at a million and a half. This figure is also the estimate arrived at by the International Organization for Migration (IOM). Hancock, I., email letter dated 12 January 2011 posted on Roma_in_ Americas list serve at: Roma_in-Americas@yahoogroups.com

30 Lemkin, Raphael (1944:79). *Axis Rule in Occupied Europe: Laws of Occupation – Analysis of Government Proposal for Redress*. Concord, NH: Rumford Press. By ethnocide or cultural genocide, I am using the term to define the destruction of a culture, from Greek *ethnos* and Latin *cide* to mean the destruction of the culture of a people as opposed to genocide, the destruction of the people themselves. Genocide, defined by Raphael Lemkin in 1943, means "the destruction of a nation," and the United Nation's 1951 Convention on the Prevention and Punishment of the Crime of Genocide defines it as acts committed against "national, ethnical, racial or religious" groups. With this in mind, ethnocide can then be defined as a crime motivated by ethnicity, "Us and Them" or "Us and the Others" syndrome, a dichotomy that contains dangerous and potentially fatal possibilities, from forcibly relocating the group through ethnic cleansing by the State to where they are equally unwanted to violent suppression of language and culture as opposed to genocide that involves the murdering of the members of the ethnic group in questions.

31 Fraser (1995:161).

32 Fraser (1995:156).

33 Fraser (1995:157).

34 Crowe (1994:77–78); Fraser (1995:156–157).

35 The Swiss Gypsies: the jenisch. From the Switzerland.isyours.com website: http://isyours.com/e/guide/graubunden/jenisch.html

36 Many of the Romani refugees arriving in Canada that I interviewed and who grew up in these orphanages knew nothing of their Romani ethnicity, were persecuted as Roma in the Czech Republic because of their Romani appearance, and were unable to reconnect with their fellow Roma who retained their culture and language.

37 This information also appears in the Canadian documentary *Suspino: A Cry For Roma* (2003). Directed by G.D. Kovanic. Bowen Island, BC. Tamarin Productions. 72 mins. DVD Distr. by Bullfrogfilms.

38 Slovakia says Roma kids "must be taken" from homes for "integration." *World Bulletin*. Retrieved 2 December 2010 from: http://www.worldbulletin.net/news_print.php?id=55199

39 *The Gypsies of Svinia* (1998). Directed by J. Paskievich. Ottawa, ON: National Film Board of Canada. 95:31 min., VHS, DVD.

40 Goldirova, Renata (2010). Brussels cautions Slovakia over boarding schools for Roma. *euobserver.com* 12.03.2010 @ 18:16 CET. Retrieved 2 December 2010 from: http://euobserver.com/9/29665

41 The Sinti are the Romani people who migrated to the German-speaking regions of western Europe and are now also located in France, Italy, and elsewhere. The word *Sinti* is probably derived from German *Reisende,* which means "travellers."

42 The sources for this estimate are from the late Dr. Sybil Milton, senior historian of the US Holocaust Memorial Council, and the International Organization for Migration (IOM). Both references were provided by Dr. Ian Hancock, University of Texas at Austin in a personal email letter dated 14 January 2011.

43 US President Obama has not shown any interest to date in appointing a Romani member, again, despite letters urging him to do so.

44 Cervantes, Miguel de (1613). *La Gitanilla* (The Little Gypsy Girl). By this date Roma had been living in Spain for barely one hundred years, and *La Gitanilla* seems to be the first novel to feature Romani characters.

45 Hugo, Victor (1831). *Notre Dame de Paris* first English translation by Frederic Shoberl (1834) as *The Hunchback of Notre Dame.*

46 George Borrow was the first Victorian author to really introduce "genuine Gypsies" to the reading public. The following were all devoted to "Gypsies " and their language: *The Zincali* (1841), *The Bible in Spain* (1843), *Lavengro* (1851), *The Romany Rye* (1857), and *Romano Lavo-lil, word-book of the Romany* (1874). Borrow also introduced the term Romany to English readers.

47 Lawrence, D.H. (1930). *The Virgin and the Gipsy.* New York, NY: Knopf.

48 Stroheim, Erich von (1935). *Paprika the Gypsy Trollop.* New York, NY: Universal Publishing.

49 Davies, Robertson (1981). *The Rebel Angels.* Toronto, ON: MacMillan of Canada.

50 De Lint, Charles (1985). *Mulengro A Romany Tale.* New York, NY: Ace Fantasy Books.

51 Saltmarsh, M. (2010). Sarkozy toughens on Illegal Roma. *The New York Times Reprints.* Retrieved 6 December 2010 from: http://www.nytimes.com/2010/07/30/world/europe/30france.html?_r=1&pagewanted=print

52 Bloomberg News/International Herald Tribune, September 1, 2010, French court blocks deportation of Roma.

53 Slovakian council in Ostrovany funds wall to isolate Roma community. *The Times* [online]. Retrieved 6 December 2010 from: http://www.timesonline.co.uk/tol/news/world/europe/article7031373.ece

54 Ian Hancock provided the estimate that there is between 10 and 12 million Roma in Europe and the rest of the eastern Hemisphere and between 2 and 3 million in all of north and south America, with more in South America than in North America. Private email letter to the author, 14 January 2011.

Bonita Lawrence and Enakshi Dua

Bonita Lawrence (Mi'kmaw) is Associate Professor in the Department of Equity Studies, York University, where she coordinates the Undergraduate Program in Race, Ethnicity and Indigenous Studies. Her research and publications have focused primarily on federally unrecognized Aboriginal communities and urban, non-status, and Métis identities, as well as exploring the complex relations between Native peoples and racialized settlers. She has published *"Real" Indians and Others: Mixed-Blood Urban Native Peoples and Indigenous Nationhood* (University of Nebraska Press and UBC Press, 2004). With Kim Anderson, she has co-edited a collection of Native women's scholarly and activist writing entitled *Strong Women Stories: Native Vision and Community Survival* (Sumach Press, 2003) as well as guest-editing "Indigenous Women: The State of Our Nations" (*Atlantis: A Women's Studies Journal* 29(2), Spring, 2005). Other publications include "Reclaiming Ktaqumkuk: Land and Mi'kmaq Identity in Newfoundland" in *Speaking for Ourselves: Environmental justice in Canada* (UBC Press, in press); "Indigenous Peoples and Black People in Canada: Settlers Or Allies?" (with Zainab Amadahy) in *Breaching the Colonial Contract: Anti-Colonialism in the US and Canada* (Springer Publishing, 2009); "Indigenous And Restorative Justice: Reclaiming Humanity And Community" (with John Usher) in *International Perspectives on Restorative Justice in Education* (Centre for the Study of Crime, Restorative Justice and Community Safety, in press); and "Decolonizing Antiracism" (with Enakshi Dua) in (*Social Justice* 32(4), 2005). Her upcoming work, *Fractured Homeland: Land and Identity in Federally-Unrecognized Algonquin Communities in Ontario*, examines Algonquin identity and struggles to protect the land in the face of a comprehensive claims process. Bonita is a traditional singer who continues to sing with groups in Kingston and Toronto at Native social and political gatherings.

Enakshi Dua is Associate Professor in the School of Women's Studies at York University, Toronto. She teaches feminist theory, anti-racist feminist theory, post-colonial studies, development studies, and globalization. She is the co-editor of *Scratching the Surface: Canadian Anti-racist Feminist Thought* (Women's Press, 1999). Her research includes projects that focus on the historical construction of the categories of nation, race, and gender in Canada. Other research includes immigration processes, women and health, equity policies, criminalization, and the racialization of masculinity and femininity, globalization, and biodiversity. She has over twenty years of experience in anti-racist feminist organizing at the community level, and has held administrative positions that deal with feminist, anti-racist, and equity issues within the academy.

Decolonizing Anti-Racism

[*A similar version of this article was published as: Lawrence, B. and E. Dua (2005). Decolonizing Antiracism.* Social Justice *32(4):120–143. This was a special issue entitled "Race, Racism and Empire: Reflections from Canada." Guest Editors: Narda Razack, Enakshi Dua, and Jody Warner. Content has been reproduced in its entirety but formatted in the style of this publication.*[1]]

Introduction

In continuous conversations over the years, we have discussed our discomfort with the manner in which Aboriginal people and perspectives are excluded within anti-racism. We have been surprised and disturbed by how rarely this exclusion has been taken up, or indeed, even noticed. As a result of this exclusion, Aboriginal people cannot see themselves in anti-racism contexts, and Aboriginal activism against settler domination takes place without people of colour as allies. While anti-racist theorists may ignore contemporary Indigenous presence, Canada certainly does not. Police surveillance is a reality that all racialized people face, and yet Native communities are at risk of direct military intervention in ways that no other racialized community in Canada faces.[2]

This paper represents a call to post-colonial and anti-racism theorists to begin to take Indigenous decolonization seriously. Because we are situated differently in relation to decolonization and anti-racism, we are beginning with our own locations.

> **Bonita:** *I first encountered anti-racism and postcolonial theory when I began attending university, in my early thirties. While I have looked to anti-racism, as I earlier looked to feminism, to "explain" the circumstances that my family has struggled with, both sets of perspectives have, ultimately, simply been part and parcel of an education system that has addressed male and white privilege but ignored my family's Indigeneity.*
>
> *To say this is to also acknowledge that a number of factors—notably immigration and urbanization—have already been at work in*

delineating relations between Aboriginal people and people of colour. Back in the sixties, when Canada was overwhelmingly white, my mother, who was Mi'kmaq and Acadian, clearly felt marginalized and inferiorized by Anglo-Canadians and ostracized by many French-Canadians. In the city, she welcomed the new presence of people of colour as potential friends and allies, and saw our struggles for survival and adaptation to the dominant culture in common. At the time there were not many of us, Aboriginal people or people of colour, brown islands in a white sea.

Fast forward to 2005. For many Native people in Eastern Canada, the urbanization and assimilation pressures of the 50s and 60s meant that our parents married white people. This same interval featured large-scale immigration of people of colour. So now, as urban Native people, we are tiny paler islands floating in a darker "multicultural" sea. Over the past 15 years or so since Oka, in common with many urban mixed-bloods, I've struggled to learn about my own Indigeneity. In this context, my light skin separates me from the people of colour that my mother would have viewed as allies. There is nothing new about racial ambiguity among mixed-bloods of any background. But for Aboriginal peoples in Canada, something else is at work here—the generations of policies specifically formulated with the goal of destroying our communities and fragmenting our identities.

For years, I have witnessed the result of these policies, as my family, my friends, and many of my Aboriginal students struggle with our lack of knowledge of heritage brought about by our parents' silence, the fact that our languages were beaten out of our grandparents' generation, that we may have been cut off from access to the land for generations, that we may know little of our own ceremonies, and that ultimately our Indigeneity is either validated or denied by government cards that certify "Indian" status. None of these policies or their repercussions are topics for discussion at anti-racism conferences. It is difficult not to conclude that there is something deeply wrong with the manner in which, in our own lands, anti-racism does not begin with, and reflect, the totality of Native peoples' lived experience—that is, with the genocide that established and maintains all of the settler states within the Americas.

And yet, to even begin to address decolonizing anti-racism, I have to acknowledge first of all that I am one of only a handful of Aboriginal scholars within academia; as such, I am routinely asked to "speak for" and represent Indigeneity to outsiders in a manner that is inherently problematic. Because of this, I must always begin by referencing the traditional elders and community people—and other Indigenous scholars—for whom Indigenous rather than academic knowledge is most central and who would begin by asking "what does post-coloniality and anti-racism theory have to do with us?" An academic paper addressing these issues is therefore aimed primarily at anti-racism scholars and activists, who for the most part are not Indigenous. More problematically, it uses the rhythms and assumptions of academic discourse, without cultural resonance or reference to Mi'kmaw or other specific Indigenous frameworks. As such, my fear is that this paper will continue to homogenize Indigenous peoples in all their diversity into a singular and meaningless entity known as "First Nations people" to outsiders, in exactly the manner that is currently common within anti-racism discourse. These tensions, between who I can make claims to speak for, how I am speaking in arguing academic theory, and to whom I am speaking, in this paper, remain ongoing.

Ena: *I came to Canada as a sixteen year old. I was born in India, and en route to Canada we resided in the United States. In all three contexts, I came across references to Aboriginal peoples. In India, people wondered of another place where people were also called Indian. Growing up in the United States and Canada I was bombarded with colonialist history. From school curriculum to television programmes to vacation spots, a colonialist history of conquer and erasure was continually reenacted. I resided in a city in which the main streets were named after Aboriginal leaders and communities. As the houses that we resided in exited onto these streets, such naming of space was important as it inserted us as settlers into the geography of colonialism. Much of this made me uncomfortable. I was given similar history of India and other Indians, and I knew that this history was not accurate. I was vaguely conscious that the lives of Aboriginal people and people of color were being shaped by the same processes. I saw myself as allied with Aboriginal people. However, what I did not see was how I may be part of the on-going project of colonization. I did not place myself in the processes which produced such representations, nor relations.*

My experiences with racism, sexism and imperialism led me, as a young women, to become engaged in a project of developing anti-racist feminism, a site in which I hoped we could look at the ways in which different kinds of oppressions intersected. However, in looking back I realize that we failed to integrate on-going colonization into this emerging body of knowledge. For example, I edited a collaborative book project, in which a number of anti-racist feminist scholars explored the intersections of "race" and gender. At the time, I felt that we were doing a good task of centering Aboriginal issues. We began the anthology by examining the ways in which Aboriginal women had been historically racialized and gendered. There was another article that examined questions of Aboriginal self-government. In looking back I would suggest that we failed to make Aboriginality foundational. We did not ask those who wrote on work, trade unions, immigration, citizenship, family, etc., to examine how these institutions/relationships were influenced by Canada's on-going colonisation of Aboriginal peoples. While more recently I have turned to cultural theory, critical race theory, and post-colonial studies, my fear is that, as I did in my earlier work, these approaches also fail to center the on-going colonisation of Aboriginal peoples.

Where do I come to this paper? As an attempt, as someone committed to anti-racist feminist struggles, to examine my complicity in the on-going project of colonization. My complicity is complex. First as an inhabitant of Canada, I live in and own land that has been appropriated from Aboriginal peoples. As a citizen of Canada, I have rights and privileges that are not only denied to Aboriginal peoples collectively, but have been deployed to deny Aboriginal rights to self government. Second, as someone involved in anti-racist and progressive struggles, I am wondering about the ways in which the bodies of knowledge that I have worked to build have been framed in ways that contribute to the active colonization of Aboriginal peoples. I need to read, write, teach, and be politically active differently.

Despite our different positioning, experiences and concerns, we have reached a common conclusion—that anti-racism is premised on an ongoing colonial project. As a result we fear that rather than challenging the on-going colonization of Aboriginal peoples, Canadian anti-racism is furthering contemporary colonial agendas. We will argue that anti-racism theory participates in colonial agendas in two ways; first by ignoring the on-going colonization of Aboriginal peoples in the Americas, and second by failing to integrate an understanding of Canada as a colonialist state into anti-racist frameworks. In this paper, we are seeking ways to decolonize anti-racism theory. Our goal, in writing this, is to begin to lay the groundwork which might make dialogue possible among anti-racist and Aboriginal activists.

What does it mean to look at Canada as Colonized Space?
What does it mean to ignore Indigenous sovereignty?
We will be arguing that anti-racist and post-colonial theorists have not
integrated an understanding of Canada as a colonialist state into their
frameworks. It is therefore important to begin by elaborating on the actual
means through which colonization in Canada as a settler society has been
implemented and is being maintained. We also need to reference how
Indigenous peoples resist this ongoing colonization.

Settler states in the Americas are founded on and maintained through
policies of direct extermination, displacement, or assimilation, all premised
to ensure that Indigenous peoples ultimately disappear *as* peoples, so that
settler nations can seamlessly take their place. Because of the intensity of
genocidal[3] policies that Indigenous people have faced and continue to face,
a common error on the part of anti-racist and post-colonial theorists is to
assume that genocide has been virtually complete, that Indigenous peoples,
however unfortunately, have been "consigned to the dustbin of history"[4]
and no longer need to be taken into account. And yet such assumptions are
scarcely different from settler nation-building myths, whereby "Indians"
become unreal figures, rooted in the nation's pre-history, who died out and
no longer have to be taken seriously.

Being consigned to a mythic past or "the dustbin of history" means being
not allowed to change and exist as real people in the present. It also means
being denied even the possibility of regenerating nationhood. If Indigenous
nationhood is seen as something of the past, the present becomes a site
where Indigenous peoples are reduced to small groups of racially and
culturally defined and marginalized individuals drowning in a sea of
settlers—who do not have to be taken seriously. At the heart of Indigenous
peoples' realities, then, is nationhood. Their very survival depends on it.

To speak of Indigenous nationhood is to speak of land as Indigenous, in
ways that are neither rhetorical nor metaphorical. Neither Canada nor the
United States—nor the settler states of "Latin" America for that matter-which
claim sovereignty over the territory they occupy have any legitimate basis
at all to anchor their absorption of huge portions of that territory.[5] Indeed,
Indigenous peoples' nationhood is acknowledged in current international
law as the right of inherent sovereignty—the notion that peoples who have
been known to occupy specific territories who have shared a common
language, a means of subsistence, forms of governance, legal systems, and
means of deciding citizenship are, in fact, nations—particularly if they have

entered into treaties, since, as Churchill notes, treaty relationships are only entered into between nations.[6]

In contrast, as a settler state, the legal system in Canada has been premised on the need to pre-empt Indigenous sovereignty. The legal system does this through the assertion of a "rule of law" that is daily deployed to deny possibilities of sovereignty and to criminalize Indigenous dissent. Because this rule of law violates the premises on which treaties were signed with Aboriginal people, the Supreme Court occasionally is forced to acknowledge the larger framework of treaty agreements that pre-date assertions of Canadian sovereignty.[7] For the most part, however, court decisions have historically been a chief instrument of disenfranchisement of Aboriginal peoples. In recent times they have served both to enlarge the scope of the potential for a renewed relationship between the Crown and Aboriginal peoples and to drastically curtail those possibilities.

It is important to understand the manner in which Native rights to land were legally nullifed in Canada, and when this changed. In 1888, because of a court decision known as *St. Catherines Milling and Lumber*,[8] Aboriginal peoples' rights to the land were ruled as being so vague and general that they were held to be incapable of remedy. This legal decision codified in law that Aboriginal peoples were on a path to extinction; the only way that "Indians" could acquire legal rights was to assimilate into Canadian society.

The relationship between Canada and Aboriginal peoples was redefined by the *Calder* decision[9] in 1973, which clarified that Canada had a legal obligation to recognize the rights that Aboriginal peoples have to their traditional lands, to redress where these rights had been violated, and to enter, belatedly, negotiations with Aboriginal nations in regions where no treaties had been historically signed. Canada's response to this obligation, however, was to deliberately maintain a colonialist stance. Instead of seriously entering into new relationships with Indigenous peoples based on equal stature, Canada unilaterally created a policy whereby Aboriginal peoples have to formally submit a "land claim" in order to redress land theft. The land claims process, then, far from being "progressive," involves Canada refusing to negotiate with Indigenous peoples as equals, and instead asserting the right to control how their own land theft from Indigenous peoples should be redressed. The fundamentally colonial nature of the process is masked by liberal pluralist notions that Native peoples are an "interest group" whose "claims" must be measured against the needs of other "groups" of citizens.

After the *Calder* decision, other important developments had potentially huge consequences for Indigenous nations' relations with Canada. Most notably, in 1982, Section 35 of the *Constitution Act* recognized and affirmed existing Aboriginal and treaty rights, as originating prior to colonization, and which included future rights that may be recognized in land claims or other agreements. From the start, however, there was little clarity about what this would mean. Jurisdiction over the land in the Constitution Act remained divided up between Canada and the Provinces under Sections 91 and 92, as they had since Confederation. Given this pre-emptive division of power, where could space be made for Aboriginal jurisdiction over lands?

The courts could have addressed these changes in positive ways. Instead, in the 1990s, a number of important court decisions were instrumental in drastically curtailing the promises of *Calder* and Section 35. For example, *Van der Peet*[10] clarified that Aboriginal rights were not general and universal, and therefore would have to be proven by each band specifically for their own territories; these rights would also be restricted to pre-contact practices.[11] Meanwhile, *Delgamuuk*[12] began the process of defining the content of Aboriginal title, in highly restrictive ways.[13] Because of these and other recent decisions, Aboriginal rights are being delineated without the political and cultural framework of an Aboriginal government,[14] and without the cultural/spiritual framework at the heart of Indigenous societies.

Large portions of territory, particularly in British Columbia, but also in Quebec and the Maritimes, are currently claimed by Canada without formal land-based treaties ever having been signed. Since *Calder*, Canada should have been formally negotiating new treaties; however, instead it has been consolidating its hold on these territories through the comprehensive claims policy. Given the inherent colonial nature of the land "claims" process, it is perhaps not surprising that land claims settlements are exercises in "municipalization." Returning any land is never on the agenda. Instead, cash awards are offered to "sweeten" the status quo, in exchange for Nations formally assuming the status of municipalities. The cash settlements may enable communities to have some resources to repair some of the worse excesses of colonialism; it does not, however, enable them to recreate a new future. As Taiaiake Alfred succinctly sets out, Canada's basic policies of assimilation and destruction remain unchanged. The government continues to divest responsibility for the effects of colonialism on Aboriginal peoples while holding tight to their land base and resources, redefining without reforming, and further entrenching in law and practice the real basis of its power.[15]

The immediacy of the problem facing Aboriginal peoples in Canada is that the status quo of a colonial order continues to target them for legal and cultural extinction, while continuing to undermine the viability of communities through theft of remaining lands and resources.[16] Aboriginal people need to re-establish control over their own communities, which means that land must be returned to them, to render communities viable and to rebuild nationhood, and a legal framework be reached whereby Aboriginal peoples' existing and returned lands come under their own authority. This means a total re-thinking of Canada, where sovereignty/self-determination is on the table, not as a concept to pay lip service to, but as fundamental to Indigenous survival. Anti-racist theorists, if they are truly progressive, must begin to think about what their personal stake is in this struggle, and about where they are going to situate themselves.

We also need a better understanding of the ways in which Aboriginal peoples resist ongoing colonization. At the core of Indigenous survival and resistance is reclaiming a relationship to land. And yet, within anti-racism theory and practice, the question of land as contested space is seldom taken up. From Indigenous perspectives, it speaks to a reluctance, on the part of non-Natives of any background, to acknowledge that there is more to this land than being settlers on it, that there are deeper, older stories and knowledge connected to the very landscapes around us. To acknowledge that we all share the same land base and yet to question the differential terms on which that land base is occupied is to become aware of the colonial project that is taking place around us.

Indigenous stories of the land are both spiritual and political, and encompass tremendous longevity. For example, Mi'kmaki, the "land of friendship." which encompasses what is now called the Atlantic provinces, was viewed by the Mi'kmaq as a sacred order, flowing from the Creation story which moves seamlessly from mythical time into historical time around the end of the last ice age.[17] Mi'kmaki is "owned" in a formal sense only by unborn children in the invisible sacred realm;[18] however, its seven regions are also traditionally governed by a Grand Council or Mawiomi, and it has historically been part of the Wabanaki Confederacy, a larger geopolitical unit extending into what is now the northeastern United States. At still another level, in an effort to resist invasion, in 1610 the Mawiomi negotiated a Concordat which consolidated Mi'kmaki formally as a Catholic republic under Rome.[19] All of these spiritual and geopolitical relations, past and present, connect Mi'kmaq people with Mi'kmaki.

It is not just the imprint of ancient and contemporary Indigenous presence that these lands carry. Focusing on the land also reveals important gaps between western and traditional knowledges that shape how we see these relationships to land. For example, for many Native peoples, land is connected to language in deep and profound ways. As Jeannette Armstrong explains, from her own people's perspective:

> As I understand it from my Okanagan ancestors, language was given to us by the land we live within … . The Okanagan language, called N'silxchn by us, is one of the Salishan languages. My ancestors say that N'silxchn is formed out of an older language, some words of which are still retained in our origin stories. I have heard elders explain that the language changed as we moved and spread over the land through time. My own father told me that it was the land that changed the language because there is a special knowledge in each different place. All my elders say that it is land that holds all knowledge of life and eath and is a constant teacher. It is said in Okanagan that the land constantly speaks. It is constantly communicating. Not to learn its language is to die. We survived and thrived by listening intently to its teachings-to its language-and then inventing human words to retell its stories to our succeeding generations… In this sense, all Indigenous peoples' languages are generated by a precise geography and arise from it.[20]

There are implications to this linking of land and language and memory and history, both for Indigenous peoples and settlers. For Indigenous peoples, part of their profound strength that has helped them to maintain their identity despite five centuries of colonization is the fact that they have maintained knowledge of who they are because of longstanding relationship to the land. On the other hand, for settlers, Indigenous peoples re-mapping traditional territories to earlier names, earlier boundaries, and earlier stories, has a profoundly unsettling effect. It reveals the Canadian nation as still foreign to this land base. It clarifies that even after five century of colonization, the names that the colonizer has bestowed on the land remain irrelevant to its history. It calls notions of settler belonging-as whites OR as peoples of colour, based simply on notions of Canadian citizenship, into question.

Cherokee theologian Jace Weaver has asserted that until postcolonial theory takes seriously both the collective character of Native traditional life, and the importance of specific lands to the cultural identities of different Native peoples, they will have little meaning for Native peoples.[21] In the next section, we will begin to examine more succinctly how post-colonial and anti-racist theory fails to address Aboriginal people's presence and concerns.

How has Anti-Racism/Post-colonial theory been constructed on a colonising framework?
We would like to start by pointing out that in our discussion we will refer to a vast body of literature - critical race theory, post-colonial theory and theories of nationalism. Notably this is a diverse body of literature, with many different arguments. And notably it has been subject to many critiques.[22] However, in our reading, this diverse body of literature shares crucial ontological

underpinnings—all of these writers fail to make Indigenous presence and ongoing colonization, particularly in the Americas, foundational to their analyses of race and racism. As a result, we fear that there is a body of work that is not only implicitly constructed on a colonising framework, but also participates in the on-going colonisation of Aboriginal peoples.

We would like to elaborate on this argument by exploring five areas where international critical race and post-colonial theory has failed to make Indigenous presence and colonization foundational. First of all are the ways in which Native existence is erased through theories of race and racism which exclude them. Secondly there are the ways in which theories of Atlantic diasporic identities fail to take into account that these identities are situated in multiple projects of colonization and settlement on Indigenous lands. Thirdly, there are the ways in which histories of colonization are erased through the writings of the history of slavery. Fourth, there are the ways in which decolonization politics are equated with anti-racist politics. Finally, there are the ways in which theories of nationalism contribute to the ongoing delegitimization of Indigenous nationhood. While often theorising the British context, these writings have been important for shaping anti-racist/post-colonial thinking throughout the West.

Let us begin by looking at the ways in which critical race theorists often erase the presence of Aboriginal peoples. We have chosen Stuart Hall's essay "The West and the Rest." In this essay, Hall introduces a post-colonial approach to "race," racialised identities and racism. He locates the emergence of "race" and racism in the historical emergence of the constructs of "the West and the Rest." In doing so he points to the ways in which the inhabitants of the Americas figure centrally in the construction of notions of the West. He also makes the connections between the colonisation of the Americas and Orientalism. Moreover, the strength of Hall's chapter is that in elaborating a theory of "race," he makes the links between colonialism and knowledge production, between the historical construction of the idea of "race" and the present articulations of "race."

Despite these strengths, Hall fails to examine the ways in which colonialism continues for Aboriginal peoples in settler nations. Indeed he posits colonialism as something that existed in the past, and as something that is restructured as "post-colonial." For example, in commenting on the last of five main phases of expansion, Hall defines "the present, when much of the world is economically dependent on the West, even when formally independent and decolonized."[23] There is a surprisingly lack of any mention of the parts of the world that have not been decolonised. As a result, Aboriginal peoples become relegated to a mythic past, whereby their contemporary existence and their struggles for decolonisation are not only erased from view, but through such erasure denied legitimacy. Moreover, there is no exploration of how the on-going colonization of Aboriginal peoples shapes contemporary modes of "race" and racism in settler nations (including those settler nations located in the Caribbean where those of African and Asian descent have established political authority). Rather, the relationship between colonialism and the articulation of "race" is limited to the ways in which the colonial past is rearticulated in the present. We would ask what are the consequences of such omissions, for Aboriginal peoples in settler societies, and their struggles for nationhood. In what ways do such omissions distort our understanding of the processes of "race" and racism?

We can see a similar ontological assumption about colonialism and Indigenous peoples in theories of Atlantic diasporic identities. In exploring diasporic identities in the Americas, most theorists fail to ask, let alone explore, the ways in which these identities have been articulated through the colonisation of Aboriginal peoples, or the ways in which the project of appropriating land shaped the emergence of black/Asian/hispanic settler formations. We have chosen Paul Gilroy's influential text, *The Black Atlantic*, to illustrate this.

In *The Black Atlantic*, Gilroy sets out to explicate two interrelated projects; first to rethink modernity via the history of the black Atlantic and the African diaspora , and second to examine the ways in which diasporic discourses have shaped the political and cultural history of black Americans and black people in Europe.[24] However, in exploring the history of the Black transatlantic, Gilroy does not make any significant reference to Indigenous peoples of the Americas or Indigenous nationhood. Similar to Hall, when Gilroy does make reference to Indigenous peoples or colonisation it is to locate them in the past. For example, in one of the few references to Indigenous peoples, Gilroy states "Striving to be both European and Black requires some specific forms of double consciousness... If this appears to be little more than a roundabout way of saying that the reflexive cultures and consciousness of the European settlers and those of the Africans they enslaved, the "Indians" they slaughtered, and the Asians that they indentured were not, even in situations of the most extreme brutality, sealed hermeneutically from each other, then so be it.[25] Referencing Indigenous peoples solely as those who were slaughtered not only suggests that Indigenous people in the Americas no longer exist, it renders invisible the contemporary situation and struggles of Indigenous peoples, and perpetuates the myths of the Americas as an empty land.

In contrast, James Clifford, in *Routes,* extends Gilroy's work on diasporic identities. Importantly, Clifford opens up the possibilities of exploring the ways in which Indigenous leaders/theorists have shaped Black counterculture, as well as the ways in which black counterculture may be premised on a colonising project. He suggests that "for the purposes of writing a counter history in some depth... one can imagine intersecting histories." In addition, Clifford acknowledges the presence of Indigenous peoples, and their struggle for decolonisation. As he points out, "Tribal or Fourth World assertions of sovereignty and 'first nationhood' do not feature in histories of travel and settlement, though these may be part of the Indigenous historical experience."[26]

However, a closer examination of Clifford's treatment of both of these issues is disappointing. In dealing with the question of how diasporic claims intersect with other histories, Clifford fails to make any significant reference to Indigenous writers, leaders, or resistance movements. Rather he references Jewish, Islamic, and South Asian histories in the making and critique of modernity.[27] Thus, while Clifford makes the important argument that diasporic visions cannot be studied in isolation from each other, he does not ask how these diasporic visions, the processes of constructing home away from home, are premised on the on-going colonization of Indigenous peoples.

Moreover, when it comes to integrating issues of Indigenous sovereignty, we find a curious ambiguity. On one hand Clifford notes that "it is clear that the claims made by peoples who have inhabited the territory since before recorded history and those who arrived by steamboat or airplane will be founded on very different principles."[28] But rather than elaborating such principles, Clifford's attention is much more focused on asserting that Aboriginal peoples are also diasporic, an investigation that leads him to raises what he see as ambiguities in Indigenous nationhood. For example, in contrasting Indigenous and "diasporic" claims to identity, Clifford suggests that Indigenous claims are primordial. As he stated, Indigenous claims "stress continuity of habitation, Indigeneity, and often a 'natural' connection to the land" while "diaspora cultures, constituted by displacement, may resist such appeals on political principle."[29] Such a characterisation of Indigenous claims not only ignores the contemporary political, social and economic realities of Indigenous peoples, but also fails to address the ways in which diasporic claims are premised on a colonising social formation. Thus, despite opening up the possibility of asking how diasporic identities articulate with or resist colonization projects, Clifford fails to take into account that these identities are situated in multiple projects of colonization and settlement on Indigenous lands.

We can see a similar erasure of colonialism and Indigenous peoples in writings on slavery. Writers such as Gilroy, Clifford and others have emphasized the ways in which the enslavement of Africans has shaped European discourses of modernity, European identity, and contemporary articulations of racism. As Toni Morrison powerfully states, "Modern life begins with slavery."[30] While we do not contest this importance of slavery, we wonder about the claim that modernity began with slavery, given the significance of colonialism and Orientalism in constructing Europe's sense of itself as modern. As importantly, the claim that modernity began with slavery rather than the genocide and colonisation of Indigenous peoples in the Americas that of necessity preceded it again erases Indigenous presence. The vision that is evoked is one where the history of racism begins with the bringing of African peoples to the United States and Canada as slaves.

We also ask how such theorising about slavery fails to address the ways in which modes of slavery, and the anti-slavery movement in the United States, were premised on earlier and continuing modes of colonisation of Indigenous peoples. For examples, whose land was the "40 acres" to be carved out of? How do we take account of the fact that President Lincoln signed the order for the largest mass hanging in US history, of thirty-eight Dakota men, because of an uprising in Minnesota, during the same week that he signed the Emancipation Proclamation?[31] Such events not only suggest connections between the anti-slavery movement and the on-going theft of Indigenous land and forced relocation or extermination of its original inhabitants, but also points to a resounding silence among anti-slavery activists, women's suffragists, labour leaders and ex-slaves such as Frederick Douglas about land theft and Indigenous genocide. Such silences suggest that these diverse activists may have had something in common—an apparent consensus that the insertion of workers, white women, and blacks into American (and Canadian) nation-building was to continue to take place on Indigenous land, regardless of the cost to Indigenous peoples. We would suggest that the relationship between slavery, anti-slavery, and colonialism is obscured when slavery is presented as the defining moment in North American racism.

Thus, as we can see, critical race and post-colonial scholars have fairly systematically written on-going colonisation out of the ways in which racism is articulated. This has erased the presence of Aboriginal peoples and their on-going struggles for decolonisation, as well as not allowing for a more sophisticated analysis of migration, diasporic identities, and diasporic countercultures. What is equally disturbing is that when we look at the few scholars who do include Aboriginal peoples and decolonization into their theoretical frameworks, decolonization politics are equated with anti-racist politics. We would like to suggest that such an ontological approach places decolonisation and anti-racism within a liberal-pluralist framework, a framework that decenters decolonisation.

An example of this is Frankenberg and Mani in their classic article on the possibilities and limits of post-colonial theory. Notably, these authors attempt to analyse slavery, racialisation, and identity in conjunction with colonization. Importantly they acknowledge the limits of applying the term post-colonial to white settler societies. In particular, Frankenberg and Mani note that the term is unable to take in to account the forms of anti-racist and Aboriginal struggles in the United States: "the serious calling into questions of white/Western dominance by the groundswell of movements of resistance, and the emergence of struggles for collective self-determination most frequently articulated in nationalist terms."[32] In contrast they suggest the term post-civil rights may be more applicable. As they state, "Let us emphasis that we use the term 'post-Civil Rights' broadly to refer to the impact of struggles by African Americans, American Indian, La Raza and Asian-American communities… collectively producing a 'great transformation' of racial awareness, racial meaning, racial subjectivity."[33]

While Frankenberg and Mani clearly take seriously the need to bring on-going colonisation into anti-racist and post-colonial theory, our concern is that they place de-colonisation struggles within a pluralistic framework. As a result, decolonization struggles become one component of a larger anti-racist struggle. Such pluralism, while utopian in its intentions, both marginalises decolonisation struggles, and continues to obscure the complex ways in which people of colour have participated in projects of settlement. In contrast, we would suggest that on-going colonisation and decolonisation struggles need to be foundational in our understandings of racism, racial subjectivities, and anti-racism.

The final issue that we will address is the manner in which theories of nationalism render Indigenous nationhood unviable, which has serious ramifications in a colonial context. For nations that have for centuries been targetted for physical and cultural extermination, and have faced further fragmentation through identity legislation, the post-colonial emphasis on deconstructing nationhood[34] simply furthers Indigenous de-nationalisation. Such deconstructions can ignore settler state colonization[35] or theorize, from the outside, about how communities "become" Indigenous solely because of interactions with colonialist nationalist projects,[36] which evaluates Indigeneity through social construction theory if Indigenous nations' own epistemologies and ontologies do not count. More problematic still are works which denigrate nationalism as representing only technologies of violence[37] or a reification of categories that can result in a degeneration into fundamentalism and "ethnic cleansing."[38] Or there is the simple dismissal of so-called "ethnic absolutism" as increasingly untenable cultural strategy[39] which calls into question the very notion of national identity. None of these perspectives enable Indigenous peoples in the Americas to envision any future that does not involve continuous engulfment by the most powerful colonial order in the world, and their continuous erasure, since Columbus, from global international political relations.[40] In this respect, postcolonial deconstructions of nationalism appear to be premised on what Cree scholar Lorraine Le Camp calls "terranullism," the erasure of ongoing post-contact Indigenous presence.[41] Perhaps it is not surprising that from these perspectives, decolonization, nationhood, and sovereignty begins to appear ridiculous and irrelevant, impossible and futile.[42]

For Aboriginal peoples, postcolonial deconstructions of nationalism simply do not manifest any understanding of how Aboriginal peoples actualize nationhood and sovereignty despite the colonial framework enveloping them. As Oneida scholar Lina Sunseri notes, Indigenous nationhood existed prior to Columbus, and when contemporary Indigenous theorists on nationalism explicate traditional Indigenous concepts of nationhood, they re-define the concept of nation itself, by moving beyond a linkage of nation to state and/or modernity and other European-based ideas and values. [43]

In summary, then, critical race and post-colonial theory sytematically erases Aboriginal peoples and decolonisation from the construction of knowledge about "race," racism, racial subjectivities, and anti-racism. We have argued that such erasure has profound consequences. It distorts our understanding of "race" and racism. It distorts our understanding of the relationship that people of colour have to multiple projects of settlement. It posits people of colour as innocent[44] in the colonization of Aboriginal peoples. As a result, the way in which people of colour in settler formations are also settlers, who have settled on lands that has been stolen, is not addressed. It ignores the way in which people of colour have complex relationships to settler projects. While on one hand they are marginalized, on the other hand they may have at particular historical moments been complicit with ongoing land theft and colonial domination of Aboriginal peoples. It distorts our writing of history. And this erasure is important because it excludes Aboriginal people from the project of anti-racism—and indeed, from history.

While it is problematic that international scholarship refuses to address settler state colonization and Indigenous decolonization, it is even more problematic that the same epistemological and ontological frameworks are reproduced in Canadian anti-racism theory, which is written on land that is still colonized.

The failure of Canadian anti-racism to make colonization foundational has meant that Aboriginal peoples' histories, resistance, and current realities have been segregated from anti-racism. In this section, we would first of all like to explore how this segregation is reflected in theory, and its implications for how we understand Canada and Canadian history. Secondly, we would like to complicate our understandings of how people of colour are located in the settler society.

The segregation of Aboriginal peoples' knowledge and histories of resistance from anti-racism is manifested in a number of ways. In most anti-racism conferences, Aboriginal organizations are not invited to participate in organizing and shaping the focus of these conferences. As a result, Indigeneity is given only token recognition. Aboriginal ceremonies are deployed in a performative manner to open the conference (regardless of the meaning of these ceremonies for the elders involved). One Aboriginal speaker is usually invited as a plenary speaker. A few scattered sessions may address Indigeneity, but these sessions are attended primarily by the families and friends of Aboriginal presenters; they are not seen as intrinsic to understanding race and racism. Aboriginal presenters at these sessions are sometimes challenged to re-shape their presentations to "critical race" frameworks; failure to do so means that the work is seen as "simplistic". In our classes on anti-racism, token attention--normally one week--is given to Aboriginal peoples, and rarely is the exploration of racism placed in a context of ongoing colonization. In anti-racist political groups, Aboriginal issues are placed within a liberal pluralist framework where not only are they marginalized, but furthermore, they are juxtaposed to other, often contradictory struggles, such as that of Quebec sovereignty.

These practices reflect the theoretical segregation that underpins them. Our understandings of Canada and Canadian history are currently fundamentally flawed by the widespread practice within anti-racism scholarship of ignoring Indigenous presence at every stage of Canadian history. The picture that is drawn, then, is of Canadian history replete with white settler racism against immigrants of colour. If Aboriginal peoples are mentioned at all it is only at the point of contact, and then only as generic "First Nations." a term bearing exactly the degree of specificity and historical meaning as "people of colour." The "vanishing Indian" then, is as alive in anti-racism scholarship as it is in mainstream Canada.

A classic example of this is James Walker's 1997 text *"Race," Rights and the Law in the Supreme Court of Canada,*[45] which considers four historic Supreme Court rulings that were instrumental in maintaining racial discrimination and anti-semitism in Canada. Disturbingly, legal decisions affecting Native peoples are ignored in this text. By comparison, Constance Backhouse's 1999 work *Colour-Coded: A Legal History of Racism in Canada, 1900-1950,*[46] goes a long way towards filling this gap. In this text, Backhouse addresses crucial cases such as the legal prohibition of Aboriginal Dance, the Re: Eskimos case which ruled on whether "Eskimos" were legally "Indians," and other instances of colonial and racial discrimination in the law, against Aboriginal peoples and people of colour. The picture that develops from Backhouse's approach is a much more in-depth view of the embeddedness of racism in a regime that is frankly colonial. Unfortunately, this kind of inclusive perspective is all too rare.

These practices of exclusion and segregation reflect the contradictory ways in which peoples of colour are situated within the nation-state. On the one hand, they are marginalized by a white settler nationalist project, and yet on the other hand, as citizens, they are invited to take part in ongoing colonialism. Because of this, people of colour have a complex relationship to Indigeneity. In this section we explore the dynamic interaction between people of colour, Indigeneity, and colonialism.

We will argue that people of colour are settlers. While there are broad differences between those who were taken here as slaves, those who are currently migrant workers, those who are refugees without legal documentation, and those who have emigrated and obtained citizenship, people of colour live on land that is appropriated and contested, and where Aboriginal peoples are denied both nationhood and access to their own lands. In this section, we want to examine three different ways in which in which, as settlers, people of colour participate in or are complicit in the ongoing colonization of Aboriginal peoples. First, there are the ways in which the histories of settlement of people of colour have been framed by racist exclusion. Missing in these accounts are the ways in which the settlement of people of colour has taken place on Indigenous land. Secondly, there are the ways in which, as citizens, peoples of colour have been implicated in colonial actions. And finally, there are current and ongoing tensions, between Aboriginal peoples and people of colour, notably around areas of multiculturalism policy and immigration.

Let us begin by looking at the history of settler formation in Canada and the ways in which people of colour have been situated and participated in the colonial project. Certainly the project of the Canadian nation state was one of white settlement, which displaced Aboriginal peoples and targetted them for physical and cultural extermination to open land for settlers, while marginalizing and restricting the entry into Canada of people of colour. Much of Canadian anti-racist scholarship has attempted to document the exclusions and marginalizations of people of colour from the emerging nation. However, this work does not examine the ways in which the entry of people of colour into Canada put them in colonial relationships with Aboriginal peoples.

For example, to speak of Black loyalists in Nova Scotia being denied the lands they were promised, or being awarded poor lands that whites did not want[47] without referencing who was being forced off the territories they were attempting to settle is to entirely erase the bloodiest interval of genocide in Canadian history.[48] The Black settler population in Nova Scotia, ex-slaves with few options, were largely denied the opportunity to appropriate Native land, so that many eventually left for Sierra Leone.[49] However, to speak of the loss of Black land rights without referencing who was being exterminated in order to "free up" the land for settlement is to be complicit in erasing genocide.

Another example is how the "head tax" and other legislation and policies which restricted non-European immigration in Western Canada are decontextualized from the suppression of Cree and Blackfoot peoples after the 1885 rebellion.[50] It was not until Native peoples on the plains were militarily subjugated that settlement of newcomers became possible, and only then were restrictions needed to ensure that the settler population that replaced Native peoples would be white. To efface this history of bloody repression and focus solely on those whose presence eclipsed Native realities, no matter what the levels of discrimination they faced, is not only segregationist—it is highly inaccurate in the history it tells.

Native eyes were always present, watching each wave of newcomers—white, Black, or Asian—establish themselves on their homelands. Their removal needs to be written into the histories of racist exclusion that peoples of colour faced—not in a cursory way, as in a meaningless generic statement that "First Nations were here before the settlers"—but with a least some specific information as to how the lands where people of colour settled were removed from the control of *specific* Indigenous nations.

Further complicating the ways in which people of colour have participated in colonial projects is through their understanding of themselves as colonists. For example, in challenging the early twentieth century discourse of whiteness and nation, South Asian male migrants constructed a parallel discourse in which they referred to themselves as colonists and defined their project in Canada as one of constructing an Indian colony.[51] Other groups, such as Japanese Canadians and Jewish Canadians, also deployed the discourse of colonization to situate themselves within a white settler formation.[52]

There are also recent ways in which, as citizens, peoples of colour have been implicated in colonial actions. An example is the ways in which people of colour who had citizenship rights participated in constitutional reform which denied Aboriginal peoples' efforts to fundamentally reshape Canada in ways that would have addressed aspects of decolonization. The Charlottetown Accord proposed constitutional changes that included a number of important features for Aboriginal peoples, including the recognition of Aboriginal governments as a third order of government in Canada; a definition of self-government in relation to land, environment, language, and culture; and representation in the Senate. While the Accord was the result of years of negotiations between Aboriginal leaders and the Canadian government, the government proposed that it be ratified through a national referendum. In essence, all Canadian citizens, including people of colour, were invited to decide on whether the Canadian government should honour its commitments to Aboriginal peoples.[53] We do not know how, or even whether, people of colour voted with respect to the Charlottetown Accord. However, this example serves to illustrate the complex relationship that people of colour have to a settler society. Those that had citizenship rights in Canada were in the position to make decisions on Aboriginal sovereignty, decisions which should have been made by Aboriginal peoples. Notably, anti-racist groups failed to note this contradiction.

Perhaps the most difficult and contentious area where Aboriginal realities are effaced by the interests of people of colour is with respect to immigration and multiculturalism. Aboriginal theorists and activists, particularly in Canada, have largely been silent about this issue, which reflects the discomfort and ambivalence that many Aboriginal people feel when official policies and discourses of multiculturalism and immigration obscure Native presence and divert attention from their realities, and when communities of colour resist their marginalization in ways that centre their realities and render Aboriginal communities invisible. Canadian language policy is a classic example where multiculturalism policy outweighs redressing assaults on Indigenous languages. Funding is provided first for "official" languages and then for "heritage" languages; only then are the remaining dregs divided up among the fifty-odd Indigenous languages in Canada currently at risk of extinction in the face of ongoing cultural genocide.

The reality is that ongoing settlement of Indigenous lands, whether by white people or people of colour, is still part of Canada's nation-building project, and is still premised on the displacement of Indigenous peoples. At present, with respect to immigration, Aboriginal peoples are caught between a rock and a hard place: either get implicated in the anti-immigrant racism of white Canadians that has always targeted Native peoples for extinction, or support the struggles of people of colour that fail to take seriously the reality of ongoing colonization. What is often overlooked by anti-racist activists is that *Delgamuukw* clearly set out instances where Aboriginal title could be infringed (in other words, limited or invalidated) by continuing immigration.[54] Canada's immigration goals, then, can be used to restrict Aboriginal rights. Anti-racist activists need to think through how their campaigns can pre-empt Aboriginal communities establishing title to their traditional lands. This is particularly important with recent tendencies to advocate for open borders. The borders in the Americas are European fictions, restricting Native peoples' passage as well as that of peoples of colour. However, to speak of opening borders without addressing Indigenous land loss and ongoing struggles to reclaim territories is to divide communities that are already marginalized from one another. The question which needs to be asked is how opening borders would impact on Indigenous struggles to reclaim land and nationhood

There is a need for scholarship that ends practices of segregation, and attempts to explore the complex histories of interactions between peoples of colour and Aboriginal peoples. How did the [creation of the multiculturalism policy in 1971 ...] connect with Canada's attempt [...] to pass the White Paper [1969] to do away with "Indian" status and Canada's fiduciary responsibility to status Indians? To what extent did Black-Mi'kmaq intermarriage in Nova Scotia represent a resistance both to extermination policies against Mi'kmaw people and the marginalizing of Black loyalists? What were the interactions between Chinese men and Native communities during the building of the Canadian railroad? Are there policies that connect the denial of west coast Native fishing rights with the confiscation of Japanese fishing boats during the internment? In what ways did people of colour support or challenge the various policies used to colonise Aboriginal peoples? What were the moments of conflict, and moments of collaboration?

In asking these questions, we are asking that anti-racism theory examine the ways in which people of colour have contributed to the settler formation. Note that we are not asking that every anti-racism writer will become an "Indian expert." This is not desirable. It is also not expected that books on Black, or South Asian, or East Asian histories in Canada would extensively focus on Aboriginal peoples. But in speaking of histories of settlement, there is a need for an explicit awareness and articulation of the intersection of specific settlement policies with policies controlling "Indians". What is needed is to recognize on-going colonisation as foundational. What is sacrificed, of course, in such clear rendition of the bigger picture, is any notion of the innocence of people of colour in projects of settlement and colonial relations.

Summary: Taking on Decolonization

This paper has addressed the multiple ways in which post-colonial and anti-racist theory has maintained a colonial framework. In summary, we would like to suggest the following areas as topics to be taken up.

1. Aboriginal sovereignty is a reality that is on the table. Anti-racist theorists need to begin talking about how they are going to place anti-racist agendas within the context of sovereignty and restoration of land.

2. Taking colonization seriously changes anti-racism in powerful ways. Within academia, anti-racist theorists need to begin to make ongoing colonization central as to how knowledge is constructed about race and racism. They need to learn how to write, research, and teach in ways that account for Indigenous realities as foundational.

3. While we have focussed this paper on anti-racism theory, it is also important to discuss the ways in which anti-racist activists have failed to make the on-going colonization of Indigenous peoples foundational to their agendas. We would suggest that most anti-racist groups fail to include Indigenous concerns, and when they do so, they too employ a pluralist framework. There is a strong need to begin discussions, between anti-racist and Aboriginal activists, around how to frame claims for anti-racism in ways that do not disempower Aboriginal peoples.

This paper has been written in the hopes of facilitating dialogue between anti-racism theorists and activists and Indigenous scholars and communities.

In reflecting on what it means to have such a dialogue, we need to think through the process of how we wrote this paper. We chose to write it in one voice, rather than coming from our different perspectives (Bonita rooted in Indigenous perspectives, Ena in anti-racism and post-colonial theory) because we wanted to go beyond a pluralistic method of simply presenting our different views without attempting a synthesis. For Ena, working in a collective voice meant attempting to take on Indigenous epistemological frameworks and values, a process that was difficult and incomplete. For Bonita, working in a collective voice enabled Indigenous concerns to be placed front and centre within anti-racism, instead of attempting to critique anti-racism from the outside. However, because we framed the dialogue as a critique of existing trends in posti-colonial and anti-racism theory, this meant that centring issues within Indigenous frameworks was sacrificed. As we worked within the framework of anti-racism and post-colonial theory, we continually struggled over the fact that Indigenous ontological approaches to anti-racism, and the relationship between Indigenous epistemologies and post-colonial theory could not be addressed.

In reflection, we have learned that engaging in a dialogue between anti-racism theorists/activists and Indigenous scholars/communities requires talking on Indigenous terms. Aboriginal people may find little relevance in continuing to debate anti-racism and post-colonial theory which not only excludes them but lacks relevance to the ongoing crises which Aboriginal communities face. They may, rather, wish to begin with the realities of contemporary colonization and resistance. They may wish the conversation to take place within Indigenous epistemological frameworks and values—addressing culture, traditional values, spirituality—as central to any real sharing of concerns. For true dialogue to take place, anti-racist theorists cannot insist on privileging and insisting on the primacy of post-colonial or critical race theory as ultimate "truths."

A final word must be said about anti-racism *within* Native communities. While Aboriginal peoples have fought long and bitterly to resist the racism shaping Canada's colonial project, colonial legislation of Native identity has had profound implications for how Aboriginal communities have been racialized and the forms that racism can take within Native communities. This paper has focused on addressing the ways in which anti-racism as we now know it needs to be decolonized. For Aboriginal peoples, a further direction may be to ask how Aboriginal communities would shape an anti-racism project in ways that are relevant to the violence that colonization has done to Indigenous identity. The legacy of cultural genocide and legal classification by "blood" and descent means that Aboriginal peoples must work to find their way through a morass of "racial thinking" about very basic issues relating to Native identity and nationhood. Their ways of doing this may move between retraditionalization and deconstruction, between Indigenous and western ways of addressing how Indigenous identity has been reduced to biology. Most of all, it means finding ways of working "with a good heart."

Wel'alieq!/Thank you.

Notes

1 This project represents an equal collaboration between both authors, but the choice to put Bonita Lawrence's name forward first was explicitly political. Because this paper names anti-racism as part of a colonial project, and challenges the positioning of peoples of colour as innocent of colonizing relationships, both authors struggled with a sense that Bonita Lawrence would face greater criticism and marginalizing from anti-racism circles if her name was put in first place, than Enakshi Dua would, as a woman of colour with a long history of anti-racism theory and activism. We decided to challenge these practices by situating the Aboriginal person first in the title.

2 Razack, Sherene (2004:147). *Dark Threats and White Knights: The Somalia Affair, Peacekeeping, and the New Imperialism.* Toronto, ON: University of Toronto Press. The spectre of "Native unrest" appears to have haunted the Canadian government since the 1885 uprising, so that the military is usually on the alert whenever Native activism appears to be spreading. As Sherene Razack has noted, the Canadian government, in sending the Airborne Regiment to Somalia in 1993, was highly aware that they might not have enough military power left at home in the event that the country was faced with another Oka.

3 Lemkin, Raphael, in Ward Churchill (1994:12–13). *Indians Are Us? Culture and Genocide in Native North America.* Toronto, ON: Between the Lines Press. The meaning of the term "genocide", as coined by Raphael Lemkin in 1944, during the discussions leading to the United Nations Genocide Convention, was given as follows: "Generally speaking, genocide does not necessarily mean the immediate destruction of a nation, except when accomplished by mass killing of all the members of a nation. It is intended rather to signify a coordinated plan of different actions aimed at destruction of the essential foundations of the life of national groups, with the aim of annihilating the groups themselves. The objective of such a plan would be disintegration of the political and social institutions, of culture, language, national feelings, religion, and the economic existence of national groups, and the destruction of personal security, liberty, health, dignity, and the lives of individuals belonging to such groups . . . Genocide has two phases: one, destruction of the national pattern of the oppressed group: the other, the imposition of the national pattern of the oppressor"

4 Spivak, Gayatri (1994, May). Presentation at University of Toronto.

5 Churchill, Ward (1992:411). *Struggle for the Land: Indigenous Resistance to Genocide, Ecocide and Expropriation in Contemporary North America.* Toronto, ON: Between the Lines Press.

6 Churchill (1992:19–20).

7 Coates, Ken (2000:7). *The Marshall Decision and Native Rights.* McGill-Queen's University Press. In the 1999 Marshall decision, for example, concerning the rights of Mi'kmaw people in the Maritimes to fish, the courts upheld the integrity of 18th century treaties between Britain and the Mi'kmaw nation as superceding the authority that Canada had vested in such institutions as the Department of Fisheries and Oceans.

8 The *St. Catherines Milling and Lumber* case involved a dispute between Canada and the Province of Ontario over timber revenues. Canada, in its defence, invoked the federal government's relationship to Aboriginal peoples; however, the decision, in Ontario's favour, defined Aboriginal rights virtually out of existence, stating that Indigenous people merely had a right to use their land, and that legally this right was no more than a "burden" on absolute Crown title, like a lien that must be discharged before land can be legally acquired. For over a century after this case, every Native litigator was forced to argue against this ruling, drastically limiting the possibilities for asserting Indigenous peoples' rights to their territories.

9 With *Calder*, the Nisga'a people took British Columbia to court for recognition of their
   rights to their traditional lands which they had petitioned about for over a century.
   The Supreme Court, on appeal, denied their title on narrow procedural grounds, but
   ruled that there is a pre-existing Aboriginal right and title to the land that does not
   flow from any rules enacted by a non-Aboriginal government.

10 Mainville, Robert (2001:26). *An Overview of Aboriginal and Treaty Rights and
   Compensation for their Breach*. Saskatoon, SK: Purich Publishing Ltd. When Dorothy
   Van der Peet, a member of the Sto:lo Nation charged with violating the Fisheries Act,
   asserted that these restrictions violated her Aboriginal rights as defined by Section
   35, the Supreme Court decision began the process of defining how Aboriginal rights
   would be interpreted in the courts.

11 Mainville (2001:29).

12 Mainville (2001:32). The original case involved the claim by the Gitksan and
   Wetsowe'ten Houses to ownership and jurisdiction over the entire 58,000 square
   kilometres of their traditional landbase in central British Columbia. Their tireless
   attempt to have elders address the courts on their own terms, using oral traditions as
   "proof," was summarily dismissed by the B.C. court. When the case was appealed to
   the Supreme Court, however, the court decision, without actually addressing Gitksan/
   Wetsowe'ten self-government, defined Aboriginal title simply as the right to exclusive
   use and occupancy of the land rather than outright political control.

13 Persky, Stan (1998:19). *Delgamuukw: The Supreme Court of Canada Decision on
   Aboriginal Title*. Vancouver/Toronto: Greystone Books (Douglas & McIntyre);
   Macklem, Patrick (2001:103–104). *Indigenous Difference and the Constitution of
   Canada*. University of Toronto Press. As part of the ruling, a stringent set of criteria
   were developed which had to be met to prove title The court also demanded that land
   covered by Aboriginal title could only be used for land-based activities that were part
   of the court's vision of a "distinct" relationship between Aboriginal peoples and the
   land. For example, any form of resource development in ways that the courts deem to
   be contrary to the nation's "traditional" activities was prohibited; finding new ways
   to survive in the face of ongoing colonization is not "permitted" under *Delgamuukw*.
   Finally, Aboriginal title has been conceptualized within a narrow frame of collective
   ownership/use that is not constitutive of an Indigenenous nation's identity such as
   Canadians enjoy with Canada.

14 Monture-Angus, Patricia (1999:120). *Journeying Forward: Dreaming First Nations
   Independence*. Halifax, NS: Fernwood Publishing.

15 Alfred, Gerald Taiaiake (1999:xiii). *Peace Power and Righteousness: An Indigenous
   Manifesto*. Oxford University Press.

16 St. Germain, Jill (2001). *Indian Treaty-Making Policy in the United States and Canada,
   1867–1877*. Toronto, ON: University of Toronto Press. At present, all existing Indian
   reserves in Canada combined are still less than the acreage of one-half of the Navajo
   reservation in Arizona.

17 Henderson, James (Sa'ke'j) Youngblood (1997:16). *The Mi'kmaw Concordat*. Halifax,
   NS: Fernwood Publishing.

18 Henderson (1997:32).

19 Henderson (1997:87).

20 Armstrong, Jeannette (1998:175-6, 178). Land speaking. In *Speaking for the
   Generations: Native Writers on Writing*. Tucson, AZ: University of Arizona Press.

21 Weaver, Jace (1998:20–21). From I-hermeutics to we-hermeneutics: Native Americans
   and the postcolonial. In Jace Weaver (ed.). *Native American Religious Identity:
   Unforgotten Gods*. Maryknoll, NY: Orbis Books: 1-25.

22 See for example: Ahmad, Aijaz (1992). In *Theory: Classes, Nations, Literatures*. London:
   Verso; Chambers, Ian and Lidia Curti (eds.). (1996). *The Post-Colonial Question*.
   London: Routledge Press; Frankenberg, Ruth and Lata Mani (1992). Cross-currents,

crosstalk: Race, 'post-coloniality' and the politics of location. *Cultural Studies* 7(2):292–310; McClintock, Anne (1997). No Longer in a Future Heaven: Gender, Race, and Nationalism. In Anne McClintock, Aamir Mufti, and Ella Shohat (eds.). *Dangerous Liaisons: Gender, Nation, and Postcolonial Perspectives*. Minneapolis, MN: University of Minnesota: 89–112; Parry, Benita (1987). Problems in current theories of colonial discourse. *Oxford Literary Review* 9(1–2):27–58.

23 Hall, Stuart (1996:191). The West and the rest: Discourse and power. In Stuart Hall, David Held, Don Hubert, and Kenneth Thompson (eds.). *Modernity: An Introduction to Modern Societies*. London: Open University: 184–224.

24 Gilroy, Paul (1993:17). *The Black Atlantic: Modernity and Double Consciousness.* Cambridge, MA: Harvard University Press.

25 Gilroy (1993:2–3).

26 Clifford, James (1997:252). *Routes: Travel and Translation in the Late Twentieth Century.* Cambridge, MA: Harvard University Press.

27 Clifford (1997:267).

28 Clifford (1997:253).

29 Clifford (1997:252).

30 Gilroy (1993:308).

31 Cook-Lynn, Elizabeth (1996:63). *Why I Can't Read Wallace Stegner and Other Essays: A Tribal Voice*. Madison, WI: University of Wisconsin Press.

32 Frankenberg and Mani (1992:480).

33 Frankenberg and Mani (1992:480–481).

34 Grewal, Inderpal and Caren Kaplan (1994). *Scattered Hegemonies: Postmodernity and Transnational Feminist Practices*. Minneapolis, MN: University of Minnesota Press; Penrose, Jan (1993). Reification in the name of change: the impact of nationalism on social constructions of nation, people and place in Scotland and the United Kingdom. In Peter Jackson and Jan Penrose (eds.). *Constructions of Race, Place and Nation*. London: UCL Press: 27–49; Anderson, Benedict (1991). *Imagined Communities: Reflections on the Origin and Spread of Nationalism*. London and New York: Verso; Hall, Stuart (1994). Cultural identity and diaspora. In P. Williams and L. Chrisman (eds.). *Colonial Discourse and Postcolonial Theory*. New York, NY: Columbia University Press: 392–403.

35 Anderson (1991).

36 Anderson (1991); Warren, Kay (1992:189–219). Transforming memories and histories: The meanings of ethnic resurgence for Mayan Indians. In Alfred Stepan (ed.). *Americas: New Interpretive Essays*. New York, NY: Oxford University Press.

37 Nixon, Rob (1997:69–88). Of Balkans and Bantustans: Ethnic cleansing and the crisis in national legitimation. In Anne McClintock, Aamir Mufti, and Ella Shohat (eds.). *Dangerous Liaisons: Gender, Nation, and Postcolonial Perspectives*. Minneapolis, MN: University of Minnesota.

38 Penrose (1993); Nixon (1997).

39 Hall, Stuart (1996). When was 'the post-colonial?' Thinking at the limit. In Iain Chambers and Lidia Curti (eds.). *The Post-Colonial Question: Common Skies, Divided Horizons*. London: Routledge, quoted in Weaver (1998:14).

40 Venne, Sharon (1998). *Our Elders Understand Our Rights: Evolving International Law Regarding Indigenous Rights*. Theytus Press.

41 Le Camp, Lorraine (1998). Terra Nullius/Theoria Nullius—Empty Lands/Empty Theory: A Literature Review of Critical Theory from an Aboriginal Perspective. Unpublished manuscript, Department of Sociology and Equity Studies, Ontario Institute for Studies in Education.

42 Cook-Lynn (1996:88).

43 Sunseri (2005).

44 Razack (2004:10, 14). Sherene Razack has theorized that a critical way in which power relations can be ignored is when individuals assume that they can stand outside of hierarchical social relations, and therefore are innocent of complicity in structures of domination. She has also noted that individuals are often involved in a "race to innocence," where they emphasize only their own subordination and disregard how they may simultaneously be complicit in other systems of domination. When we disregard how systems of oppression interlock, it is relatively easy to focus on our own oppression and disregard where we are privileged over others.

45 Walker, James W. St. G. (1997). *"Race," Rights and the Law in the Supreme Court of Canada: Historical Case Studies*. Osgoode Society for Canadian Legal History and Wilfred Laurier University Press.

46 Backhouse, Constance (1999). *Colour-Coded: A Legal History of Racism in Canada, 1900-1950*. Osgoode Society for Canadian Legal History and University of Toronto Press.

47 Hill, Daniel G. (1981:10, 63–64). *The Freedom Seekers: Blacks in Early Canada*. Toronto, ON: Stoddart Publishing; Walcott, Rinaldo (1997:35-36). *Black Like Who? Writing/ Black/Canada*. Toronto, ON: Insomniac Press; Mensah, Joseph (2002:46). *Black Canadians: History, Experiences, Social Conditions*. Halifax, NS: Fernwood Press.

48 Paul, Daniel N. (2000:182–184). *We Were Not the Savages: A Mi'kmaq Perspective on the Collision between European and Native American Civilizations. 21st Century edition.* Halifax, NS: Fernwood. Mi'kmaw people fought the English for over a century, up and down the eastern seaboard in conjunction with other allied nations of the Wabanaki confederacy. With the eighteenth century peace treaties came a concentrated campaign of extermination efforts by the British Crown, including the posting of bounty for the scalps of Mi'kmaq men, women, and children in 1744, 1749, and 1756 and accompanying "scorched earth" policies to starve out the survivors, the absolute denial of land for reserves for most of a century after asserting military control in 1763, and finally, the accompanying spread of epidemics which brought the Mi'kmaq people, to near-extinction. Daniel Paul notes that by 1843, only 1300 were left of a people whose numbers had been estimated as between 30,000 and 200,000. The most concentrated interval of extermination efforts were those that immediately preceded the settling of loyalists, white and Black, in Nova Scotia.

49 Mensah (2002:47).

50 Miller, J. R. (1989:190-194). *Skyscrapers Hide the Heavens: A History of Indian-White Relations in Canada*. University of Toronto Press; (Stonechild and Waiser, 214-237); Carter, Sarah (1997:186-193). *Capturing Women: The Manipulation of Cultural Imagery in Canada's Prairie West*. McGill-Queen's University Press. The implementation of pass laws, the policing of reserves by the Northwest Mounted Police, the outlawing of spiritual ceremonies, and other policies which strengthened the heavy hand of the "Indian Agent," the erroneous labelling of twenty-eight Cree bands as traitorous and the starvation policies implemented against them, the mass hanging of eight Cree men and the imprisonment of approximately 50 other Crees that accompanied the hanging of Louis Riel and the crushing of the Metis, the denial of matrimonial rights and the labelling of Aboriginal women as prostitutes in efforts to drive Native women out of white settlements—all these actions were necessary to subjugate the Indigenous people of the prairies.

51 Dua, Enakshi (2002). 'Race' and Governmentality: The Racialization of Canadian Citizenship Practices. In Debi Brock (ed.). *Making Normal: Social Regulation in Canada*. Harcourt Brace.

52 For Jewish Canadians see Canadian Jewish Alliance, *Annual Report*, 1917. For Japanese Canadians see *Winnipeg Free Standard*, p1, June, 1916.

53 The Accord was subject to intense debate, particularly the sections on Aboriginal self government. These sections were questioned first by Aboriginal women's

organizations and then by national feminist groups, as they were seen to potentially prevent gender rights within Aboriginal communities through the potential the Accord granted to Aboriginal governments to opt out of the *Charter of Rights and Freedoms*. Since the Charter was seen as a protector of Aboriginal women's rights, granting government powers to Aboriginal communities was seen as a potential threat to Aboriginal women. An argument was made that self government was present in the accord as a new right rather than a recogition and affirmation of an existing right, and therefore should be challenged. The platform of the national feminist organization, the National Action Committee, therefore stated that the "Charlottetown Accord is a bad deal for Aboriginal women." Notably, NAC failed to address the significance of the accord with respect to Aboriginal decolonization. Rather, gender rights were seen as paramount, even in relationship to Aboriginal self-government. In 1992, Canadians voted against the accord. Nationally, fifty-four percent of the votes cast opposed the Accord.

54 Persky (1998:20).

Robinder Kaur Sehdev

Robinder Kaur Sehdev is a first-generation immigrant currently residing on Anishinabe territory. She was raised in Cree, Dene, and Métis territory (Fort McMurray, Alberta) where treaty talk, settler racism, and the capitalist "development" imperative significantly shaped her understanding of belonging, community, and colonialism. She is a non-Indigenous affiliate of the Indigenous Studies Research Network based in Brisbane, Australia. She holds a Ph.D. in Cultural Studies from York and Ryerson universities where she researched the involvement of popular cultural representational practices in the normalization of the myth of the innocent settler state. Robinder is editor of a special issue of the *Canadian Journal of Law and Society* on Canada's Truth and Reconciliation Commission with Dr. Rosemary Nagy. Her current research asks how the concept of sovereignty is conceptualized and taken up by anti-racist feminists seeking solidarity with Indigenous peoples in Australia and Canada. This research queries the possibilities of developing social justice, specifically feminist, alliances across colonial differences. She has taught extensively in critical Indigenous, race, and feminist studies.

People of Colour in Treaty

If recent activist action is any indication, there appears to be a growing desire for solidarity between Indigenous and non-Indigenous people of colour.[1] There are logical reasons for this, as both communities can share in meaningful conversations about how racism influences our lives and shapes our communities. From such conversations comes the potential to develop new strategies of resistance and renewal rooted firmly in our lived experience with racial injustice. I recognize that the desire for solidarity needs to be the subject of some analysis: How pervasive are these solidarities? Under what circumstances do they arise? Who builds and maintains them? These are all important questions to investigate as the mechanics of solidarities between Indigenous and non-Indigenous people of colour would shed important light on how decolonial and anti-racist politics are *done* in the context of systemic racism and the discourses of inclusion and tolerance that are so favoured in our liberal democracy. However, the purpose of my writing here is much more basic. In this paper I offer a simple argument, directed toward other people of colour who, like me, wish to acknowledge and disrupt colonial violence that produced residential schooling, recognizing that it is not incidental to the racism we experience. Our belonging on this land is made possible by treaty, and it is therefore incumbent on us to reconsider our strategies for social justice with treaty in mind. We have played a crucial part in nation formation, but this is a settler nation whose borders extend to absorb Aboriginal people without regard for their sovereignty.

The strategies of confronting racism that people of colour (the "our" and "we" of this paper) employ must reflect these realities. We must also recognize our implication in colonial processes even while they deeply (and detrimentally) affect us. Our current strategies of confronting systemic racism that code our communities as outside of the nation or inconsequential to its well-being are, therefore, insufficient for addressing the particular violence directed toward Aboriginal people. Without succumbing to the paralysis of guilt or self-pity, which often shifts attention from challenging oppression to easing consciences, we must recognize our conflicted position as marginalized settlers and treaty citizens.

Power and complicity

Shifting currents of power are brought to bear on our lives; thus our sense of self is produced through power. Writing from an anti-racist feminist perspective, Sherene Razack notes that we cannot confidently speak of "women's experience" because there is no single experience and no universal woman.[2] We all navigate different power contexts that position us as subordinate, complicit, or oppressive in complex and often unpredictable ways. Thus a woman can be both subordinate and oppressor at once:

> For example, think of the migrant woman of colour, who, once in Canada becomes "temporary foreign worker," "underemployed," "minority," "marginal," and "settler" all at once. Not only does her sense of self shift with the shifting forces at work around her, demanding her to respond in partial and in varied ways, but in these shifting configurations of power come shifting communities, networks of knowledge, history and tradition. Sometimes these relationships are productive and help her to achieve some sense of [community,] self and justice, and sometimes they are exploitative and abusive. Regardless, layer upon layer they impinge on her sense of self in relation to others.[3]

There is no such thing as the innocent subject whose hands are unsullied by power. Razack writes that "[w]hen we pursue ... shifting hierarchical relations, we can begin to recognize how we are *implicated* in the subordination of other women."[4] She notes that given the interactive nature of power, even those of us who strive to be attuned to power and justice are deeply implicated in the oppression of others.

This does not mean that social justice work is pointless or that power is so relative that its abuse fundamentally means nothing; this acknowledgement calls upon us to shift our attention from the quest for innocence to the dynamics of power in which we are located and act upon. This also exposes the process nature of power and oppression where the marginalized are called upon to ensure the domination of others on the margins, and where oppression is realized institutionally and individually. The denial of personal accountability on the basis of a lack of direct personal or ancestral action will not wash here. Even if my ancestors had no direct role to play in residential schools, I am nonetheless their beneficiary. While the power at work here is socially constructed, it is undeniably a material reality. In other words, power and power hierarchies *matter* in immediate and visceral ways, and so we must direct our attention to the power contexts that produce us as simultaneously marginal and dominant. Exposing power and oppression as *processes* means that they are not de facto states of being. This leaves the possibility for justice open and this is a potentially productive place to work from.

When I was a student, a professor asked those of us non-Aboriginal students to consider the privileges we enjoyed in Canada.[5] This was a hard task for me as I saw more burdens than privileges. I saw racist violence, alienation, glass ceilings, tokenism, and accusations of fundamentalism and terrorism. And even though I continue to see and experience racism in varied ways, I benefit from settler privileges. The right to earn a living from the land, to build a home (physical and metaphorical) anywhere in this country, and to be a citizen are only a few examples of how settlers are privileged. These privileges came from treaty with Aboriginal nations, without whose recognition settlers would have no right to build homes, govern themselves, move freely, or earn a living here. Aboriginal and non-Aboriginal people are, as J.R. Miller says, not "leaving any time soon."[6] He urges politicians to respect this and leave aside their polemics in favour of cooperation. "They also would be doing the country an enormous favour by getting behind efforts to educate the non-Native public about treaty rights through public education and curriculum reform."[7] In short, settlers are "treaty people" too, even if popular logic declares treaty to be exclusive to Aboriginal people. Shortly, I will outline how some Aboriginal political philosophers and legal scholars explain treaty and treaty relationships, but I would now like to turn to the ways that relationships and plurality are invoked and managed in the Canadian nation in relation to residential schools.

The Prime Minister's apology for residential schools indicates the need to collectively shoulder the responsibilities of apology and reconciliation, and it indicates the opening of a space to discuss community, collective responsibility, and the scope of the offered apology. In Prime Minister Harper's own words, "on behalf of the Government of Canada and all Canadians, I stand before you, in this Chamber so central to our life as a country, to apologize to Aboriginal peoples for Canada's role in the Indian Residential Schools system." He then endorsed the Truth and Reconciliation Commission's role of educating the nation about residential schools, stating that "[i]t will be a positive step in forging a new relationship between Aboriginal peoples and other Canadians, a relationship based on the knowledge of our shared history, a respect for each other and a desire to move forward together with a renewed understanding that strong families, strong communities and vibrant cultures and traditions will contribute to a stronger Canada for all of us."[8] What the Prime Minister proposes is no less than the formation of a new relationship where the distinctness of our communities, families, and cultures will be respected. Compelling though this image is, Harper has demonstrated a lack of commitment to this new relationship and, as Chrisjohn and Wasacase argue, his government is ideologically in line with those that instituted residential schools.[9] Moreover, the language of harmony and tolerance that Harper invokes brings to mind the language of multicultural inclusion and skirts the matter of profound structural change that would enable a true commitment to good relations. As Razack has argued, one cannot acknowledge difference without confronting domination.[10]

The relationship between the state and non-Aboriginal people of colour is deeply fraught, marked by structurally entrenched inequality. Prior to groundbreaking work on historical struggles for citizenship and national recognition,[11] one might mistakenly believe that people of colour are recent additions to the national fabric. Indeed, when non-Aboriginal people of colour are invoked in public discourse, it is often within the multicultural frame, which ignores the historic diversity of Canada and the profound power imbalances that shaped it. Multiculturalism is a liberal social contract of tolerance for cultural difference within a nation. But tolerance is not anti-racism and it will not end racism.[12] Anti-racism demands an analysis of the ways that racial oppression is systemically embedded, thereby denaturalizing it and moving us closer to its destabilization. In other words, its eyes are set on power whereas multiculturalism looks to cultural harmony without the imperative of systemic change. Multiculturalism allows the nation to remain recognizable and intact. This does not permit racial justice or a new and just relationship with Aboriginal people.

Despite official multiculturalism's failures, people of colour have often been invoked to provide the gloss of racial and cultural harmony for a nation rooted in oppression. But this gloss is thin; as many critical race theorists have noted,[13] Canada is a settler nation, rooted in colonial ideologies of governance, land tenure, and the law. Indeed, colonization is a global matrix (after all the British empire alleged that the sun did not set on its flag), and many non-Aboriginal people of colour hail from nations left deeply scarred by its legacy. Through migration our ancestors and we have sworn allegiance to Canada and the Queen of England. This is a deeply conflicted position to be in since the colonization of nations across the globe was carried out in the name of European, if not specifically British, empire. Not only is this a terrible irony to leave one nation blighted by colonialism only to swear an oath of allegiance to its figurehead, but it compels us to consider the different relationship with the state that sets Aboriginal and non-Aboriginal people of colour apart (set apart, but not in opposition). Non-Aboriginal people of colour are not sovereign on this land. While our connection to this land might be important it is not critical to our languages, stories, knowledge systems, and selves. And, importantly, we have not entered into treaty with the Canadian state; rather, we have submitted to the state's authority, even while we may contest it. This is not so with Aboriginal nations, which are linked with the Canadian state and the colonial empires before it through treaty.

Treaty relationships

One expression of domination in Canada occurs with the imposition of equivalences that, in effect, would level the very difference that distinguishes First Nations' sovereignty from the ethnic, linguistic, or cultural rights of other minorities. The language of a state-to-state relationship is often used to communicate the intact sovereignty of Aboriginal nations and distinguish their unique position vis-à-vis the state, but this is tricky language. Nationalism and sovereignty are often understood in Eurocentric terms, which assume that its definitions are universal while variations are something less than "true" nationalism and sovereignty. This simply is not the case. Aboriginal sovereignty and nationality are distinct and affirmed in treaties made with European newcomers.

To First Nations, the gesture of national accommodation and inclusion does not even begin to address the fundamental problems of imposing a settler national structure on an existing state-to-state relationship. Legal scholar and citizen of the Chicksaw Nation, James (Sakéj) Youngblood Henderson begins from the fundamental position that treaties formed between First Nations and the British Crown affirm First Nations' sovereignty. He argues that the imposition of Canadian settler nationalism in the form of Canadian citizenship threatens to undermine Aboriginal sovereignty that "transforms the sacred homeland of Aboriginal nations" into a space where ethnic difference is paraded in the service of "Euro-Canadian self-congratulation and individualism."[14] Henderson writes:

> These *sui generis* sovereigns are the ancient law of the land, and they are embedded in Aboriginal heritages, languages, and laws. They were distinct from the European traditions of aristocracy and sovereignty. They reflect a distinct vision of how to live well with the land with other peoples by consent and collaboration. The diversity within Aboriginal sovereignty reveals a generation of holistic orders that were designed to be consensual, interactive, dynamic, and cumulative ... They are intimately embedded in Aboriginal worldviews, ceremonies, and stories, as expressed by the structure and media of Aboriginal languages and art. They reveal who First Nations are, what they believe, what their experiences have been, and how they act. In short, they reveal Aboriginal humanity's belief in freedom and order.[15]

Aboriginal politics exercise a philosophy of relations that Huron–Wendat historian Georges Sioui describes as "circular" philosophies.[16] Circular philosophies recognize the interrelatedness of the human and the land, animal, water, spirit, and plant worlds. This necessitates the making of treaties that formalize these relationships and ensure that they are properly cared for. Just as a circle has no end, treaty is a process to be made and reaffirmed. It is recursive. The potential to recover neglected relations or repair abused ones is therefore alive.

Contrary to the settler myth that Aboriginal people were ignorant of treaty-making practices until Europeans introduced them, it was European newcomers who needed to be versed in Aboriginal treaty practices. Treaties between Aboriginal and European nations were governed by the Covenant Chain of Silver (communicated in Gus Wen Tah, or Two Row Wampum). According to Métis historian David McNab:

> The Covenant Chain is an Aboriginal concept of relationships in their totality which have included, among other things, cultures, diplomacy and trade. The Chain, which was adopted by the Dutch, the French and then the English, was originally wrought in iron and then in silver; it was a metaphor for the partnership, or covenant, meaning a sacred agreement, between the Aboriginal and European nations in all matters regarding their mutual relationship.[17]

Peace, respect, and friendship were the basis of all subsequent treaties, or in McNab's words, "This was the original meeting ground."[18] The Covenant Chain of Silver ensures that all treaties re-affirm this relationship, and it communicates the recursiveness of the treaty-making process; left unpolished, silver will tarnish, thus a shining chain is the sign of a good treaty relationship.

Traditions and stories surrounding treaty are meant to educate everyone about the relationships entered into and communicated by treaty. These are sacred relationships. Cree reverend and moderator Stan McKay describes the spiritual significance of treaty: "Treaty talks were about sharing the sacred land, and that required prayerful preparation. The treaty negotiations were understood to be tripartite. The talks involved the Creator, the Queen's representatives, and the Aboriginal peoples."[19] McKay notes that the involvement of the spiritual world in the treaty process was lost on settler society, which wrongly understands treaty to mean the imposition of agreements by a powerful body onto a comparatively powerless one. This is a disempowering, reductive, and overwhelmingly popular view of treaty. Such a view fails to recognize treaty-making practices as a vitally important part of Aboriginal spiritual and political life as well as a critical avenue for historical and contemporary Aboriginal political action. Failing to recognize the significance of treaty to Aboriginal political philosophies and practices amounts to another act of colonization.

Treaty as a space of solidarity

Residential schools were instituted under the pretense of fulfilling the government's treaty obligations. Cree citizen and founding president of the Federation of Saskatchewan Indian Nations, John Tootoosis, explains that when they made treaty with settlers, Aboriginal leaders stipulated that their children be educated in settler ways of knowing and doing so they and future generations could "compete on an equal basis."[20] The government's response came in the form of residential schools. "The government violated deeply the spirit and intent of this most important (to the Indians) promise. The "education" provided was immediately subordinated to the conversion process and religious indoctrination."[21] Residential schooling, like other state strategies of cultural genocide and colonial violence, did profound violence to treaty relationships made between First Nations and the Crown. In this context, returning to treaties as a space that might enable cooperative action can risk a return to such abusive practices, but it also turns a critical eye on the colonial mechanisms that worked to diminish and transform treaty into a smokescreen for genocide. Commitment to good treaty relationships opens a critical space for challenging the quotidian and institutionalized operation of power that produced residential schools and kept them in operation. After all, good treaty relations will never be maintained through the status quo.

The Crown represents non-Aboriginal people's interests in treaties with Aboriginal nations, but as I have said, the Crown has violated the rights of its non-white citizens (indeed, throughout the country's history, citizenship was exclusively granted to white people) despite repeated promises of multicultural inclusion. We, people of colour that is, have metaphorically and literally challenged the borders of the Canadian state, and we recognize that the state is not natural and immutable, but susceptible to (incremental, glacial) change.

In an effort to identify and analyze colonialism's role as the structuring mechanism of oppressions in settler nations, some anti-racists have articulated their accountability to the sovereignty of Aboriginal nations.[22] This commitment to Aboriginal sovereignty serves as a useful way of linking the work of challenging race and racism to Aboriginal political struggles, foregrounding the imperative to decolonize and restore Aboriginal sovereignty. This is useful and insightful work; however, given the colonization of Aboriginal knowledge systems and the historical failure of non-Aboriginal people to appreciate the depth and breadth of Aboriginal philosophies, we cannot assume that anti-racists (and I count myself among them) understand Aboriginal sovereignty in Aboriginal terms. I am not saying that Aboriginal knowledges are unknowable, but that colonial ideology is pervasive.

Sovereignty is a debated concept among Aboriginal philosophers and activists. Scholar and activist Aileen Moreton–Robinson,[23] citizen of the Quandamooka Nation, argues that sovereignty *matters* in material and embodied as well as public, political, and cultural ways. She questions the ways that Aboriginal sovereignty and politics are represented and opportunistically used by settler political and cultural institutions and power holders. Noting the diminishment of Aboriginal knowledge and political systems, Kanien'kehaka political philosopher Taiaiake Alfred warns that the notion of Aboriginal sovereignty is often grafted onto its European counterpart along with its attendant notions of state, governance, and borders.[24] This colonial strategy suggests that Aboriginal political and knowledge systems are derivative of their European counterparts, thus decolonial uses of sovereignty are severely curtailed. Cherokee feminist activist and scholar Andrea Smith recognizes the colonial uses of and abuses to sovereignty but argues that the concept need not be shackled to its European definition.[25] Rather, she argues for an Indigenous understanding of sovereignty that is non-statist, non-hierarchal, and takes direction from Indigenous women activists who express an inclusive, relational, and spiritual vision of sovereignty. Sovereignty is a contested and politically urgent concept, and the complexity of these debates suggest that when Aboriginal and non-Aboriginal activists talk of sovereignty, they are not speaking about the same thing.

I am in favour of organizing on the basis of a shared interest in treaty and treaty relationships over a mutual commitment to sovereignty because treaty is the basis of relationships and for non-Aboriginal belonging on this land, not because sovereignty is irretrievable from colonial versions while treaty is somehow unaffected. Both treaty and sovereignty have been subject to sustained colonial violence. Treaty is important to non-Aboriginal people of colour and anti-racist politics because it is the ground upon which residential schools are condemned, the apology is criticized, and redress is sought. Treaty is also the space that the state has attempted to appropriate and empty of meaning. The turn to treaty is important also in terms of solidarity formation between Aboriginal and non-Aboriginal people of colour because it presents the possibility to develop discursive spaces where we can begin to explore our relationship with one another within a settler and racist state.

We might begin to develop this discursive space by exploring why people of colour have been written out of, perhaps forgotten in, the treaty relationship between the Crown and Aboriginal nations. This is another way of asking how colonial power alienates non-Aboriginal people of colour from our relationships with Aboriginal people. In theory, the Crown represents our (people of colour) interests, thus we are already in relationship with Aboriginal peoples. That *en masse* we do not know this reflects the dominant strategy of including (or perhaps absorbing) us when it suits the status quo, and it certainly suits the status quo to present the image of a contrite, though unified, and so stable settler nation. A stable settler nation is a nation resistant to actually cultivating a good treaty relationship with Aboriginal nations. From the marginalized settler's side of this relationship, the Canadian state is in need of substantial change. Multicultural inclusion was presented to us as the healing salve, but it offers surface relief, not substantive change, and so we must resist the vacant conciliatory language and the parade of ethnic difference. Treaties are adaptable enough to last such critique and reconstitution on the settler's end; those formed between Aboriginal nations and the Dutch, for example, were transferred to subsequent imperial interests. Anti-racist action and people of colour must continue to challenge the Aboriginal–white dichotomy that pervades the literature and that "whites out" people of colour from the establishment of settler states.

So what's a person of colour to do? The critical thing in my view is to focus attention on decolonizing treaty. In other words, we need to turn from an understanding of treaty as a historical artifact, based in European notions of rights and freedoms, and move toward Aboriginal philosophies of treaty as a process of *making and keeping* good relations. We, people of colour, must refuse the myth that treaty does not concern us. We belong here not because Canada opened its doors, but because Aboriginal nations permitted settler governance on their lands. Finally, we must identify as treaty citizens and so refuse the liberal strategies of tolerance and inclusion of difference at the expense of the more difficult task of formative change. After all, treaty is the space where power is negotiated.

Notes

1   As I write, the Toronto chapter of the activist network, Defenders of the Land, is preparing for "Indigenous Sovereignty Week 2010: Indigenous Resistance and Renewal" (21–28 November 2010), which features a workshop called "Indigenous Solidarity for People of Colour." There are other networks that work to establish solidarities between Indigenous and non-Indigenous people of colour. For example, INCITE! a feminist activist network of women of colour and Indigenous women across Turtle Island focuses on solidarity formation for anti-violence.

2   Razack, Sherene H. (1998:159). *Looking White People in the Eye: Gender, Race, and Culture in Courtrooms and Classrooms.* Toronto, ON: University of Toronto Press.

3   Sehdev, Robinder Kaur (2010:118). Lessons from the bridge: On the possibilities of anti-racist feminist alliances in Indigenous spaces. In L. Simpson and K. Ladner (eds.). *This Is an Honour Song: Twenty Years since the Blockades.* Winnipeg, MB: Arbeiter Ring Publishing: 105–123.

4   Razack (1998:159).

5   I will always be grateful to Patricia Monture for turning her classroom into a space of creative anti-colonial dreaming.

6   Miller, J.R. (2009:306). *Compact, Contract, Covenant: Aboriginal Treaty-making in Canada.* Toronto, ON: University of Toronto Press.

7   Miller (2009:306).

8   On 11 June 2008 Prime Minister Harper offered a full apology on behalf of Canadians for the Indian residential school system in Ottawa, Ontario. Retrieved from: http://pm.gc.ca/eng/media.asp?id=2149

9   Chrisjohn, R. and T. Wasacase (2009). Half-truths and whole lies: Rhetoric in the 'Apology' and the Truth and Reconciliation Commission. In G. Younging, J. Dewar, and M. DeGagné (eds.). *Response, Responsibility, and Renewal: Canada's Truth and Reconciliation Journey*. Ottawa, ON: Aboriginal Healing Foundation: 219-229.

10 Razack (1998).

11 For examples, see: McKittrick, K. (2002). "Their Blood is There, and They Can't Throw it Out": Honouring Black Canadian geographies. *Topia: Canadian Journal of Cultural Studies* 7:27-37; Ward, W.P. (2002). *White Canada Forever: Popular Attitudes and Public Policy Toward Orientals in British Columbia* (3rd ed.). Montreal, QC: McGill-Queen's University Press.

12 Bannerji, H. (1997). Multiculturalism is … anti-anti-racism: A conversation with Himani Bannerji. *Kinesis*: 8-9.

13 See: Bannerji, H. (2000). *The Dark Side of the Nation: Essays on Multiculturalism, Nationalism and Gender*. Toronto, ON: Canadian Scholar's Press, Inc.; Razack, Sherene H. (2002). Introduction: When place becomes race. In S.H. Razack (ed.). *Race, Space, and the law: Unmapping a White Settler Society*. Toronto, ON: Between the Lines Press: 1-20; Stasiulis, D. and R. Jhappan (1995). The fractious politics of a settler society: Canada. In D. Stasiulis and N. Yuval-David (eds.). *Unsettling Settler Societies: Articulations of Gender, Race, Ethnicity and Class*. London, Thousand Oaks, New Delhi: Sage: 95-131.

14 Henderson, J.S.Y. (2002:416). Sui Generis and Treaty Citizenship. *Citizenship Studies* 6(4):415-440.

15 Henderson, J.S.Y. (2008:21). Treaty governance. In Y.D. Belanger (ed.). *Aboriginal Self-Government in Canada: Current Trends and Issues* (3rd ed.). Saskatoon, SK: Purich: 20-38.

16 Sioui, Georges (1999). *Huron-Wendat: The Heritage of the Circle*. (Trans. J. Brierley). Vancouver, BC: University of British Columbia Press.

17 McNab, David (1999:8). *Circles of Time: Aboriginal Land Rights and Resistance in Ontario*. Waterloo, ON: Wilfrid Laurier University Press.

18 McNab (1999:11).

19 McKay, Stan (2008:110). Expanding the dialogue on truth and reconciliation—In a good way. In M. Brant Castellano, L. Archibald, and M. DeGagné (eds.). *From Truth to Reconciliation: Transforming the Legacy of Residential Schools*. Ottawa, ON: Aboriginal Healing Foundation: 103-115.

20 Cited in Goodwill, J. and N. Sluman (1984:27). *John Tootoosis*. Winnipeg, MB: Pemmican Publications.

21 Goodwill and Sluman (1984:27).

22 See: Lawrence, B. and E. Dua (2005). Decolonizing antiracism. *Social Justice* 32(4):120-143; Thobani cited in Khan, S. (2007). The fight for feminism: An interview with Sunera Thobani. *Upping the Anti: A Journal of Theory and Action* 5. Retrieved 6 December 2010 from: http://uppingtheanti.org/journal/article/05-the-fight-for-feminism; Razack (2002); Razack (1998); Nicoll, F. (2004). Reconciliation in and out of perspective: White knowing, seeing, curating and being at home in and against indigenous sovereignty. In A. Moreton-Robinson (ed.). *Whitening Race: Essays in Social and Cultural Criticism*. Canberra, AU: Aboriginal Studies Press: 17-31; Nicoll, F. (2000). Indigenous sovereignty and the violence of perspective: A white woman's coming out story. *Australian Feminist Studies* 15(33): 368-386. doi:10.1080/713611981

23 Moreton-Robinson, A. (2007). Introduction. In A. Moreton-Robinson (ed.). *Sovereign Subjects: Indigenous Sovereignty Matters*. Crows Nest, AU: Allen & Unwin: 1-11.

24 Alfred, Taiaiake (2009). *Peace, Power, Righteousness: An Indigenous Manifesto* (2nd ed.). Don Mills, ON: Oxford University Press.

25 Smith, Andrea (2008). *Native Americans and the Christian Right: The Gendered Politics of Unlikely Alliances*. Durham, NC: Duke University Press.

Srimoyee Mitra

Srimoyee Mitra is a performance artist, curator, and writer. She completed her M.A. in Art History at York University, Toronto, in 2008. Since then she developed a multidisciplinary installation entitled *Let's Talk, Get to Know Each Other Better, We Are All Human* (2008–2009) in collaboration with the Art Gallery of Ontario's Youth Council. Her performance *Becoming a Canadian Citizen at the AGO and Thinking About Contemporary Art* premiered at the Extra-Curricular: Between Art and Pedagogy (February 2010) conference at the University of Toronto and has been included at the Shift: Dialogues on migration in contemporary art symposium (April 2011), McKenzie Art Gallery, Regina. Her performances have been featured in venues as diverse as Carla Garnet Project in *NightLight*, Nuit Blanche (Lansdowne) in 2007, and *Toronto Free Broadcasting* (September 2009) curated by Maiko Tanaka and Chris Lee. Her recent curatorial projects include *Crossing Lines: An Intercultural Dialogue* (29 November 2009–23 January 2010) at the Glenhyrst Art Gallery of Brant, Brantford, and *Reply All* (May 2008), an online collaborative project commissioned by SAVAC (South Asian Visual Arts Centre) and Art Metropole. Srimoyee has worked as a writer for publications including *Time Out Mumbai*, *Art India*, and *The Indian Express* newspaper in India. Since 2008, she has been working as the Programming Co-ordinator at SAVAC (South Asian Visual Arts Centre) in Toronto, where she currently lives and works.

Learning Through Crossing Lines:
An Intercultural Dialogue

Introduction

On 11 June 2008 I watched the live coverage of the Canadian government's apology to the First Nations, Métis, and Inuit peoples of Canada at the Alternator Gallery for Contemporary Art in Kelowna, Territory of the Syilx Nation, in British Columbia. The atmosphere was charged with emotions and anticipation as I was seated amid national and international Indigenous and non-Indigenous media artists, filmmakers, cultural workers, curators, and policy-makers. That afternoon I felt as though I had witnessed a landmark moment in Canadian history. In particular, the piercing words by the president of the Native Women's Association of Canada, Beverly Jacobs, stayed with me. As she accepted Prime Minister Harper's apology, Jacobs responded with a candid question: "What is it that this government is going to do in future to help our people?"[1] Jacobs's frankness elucidated the innate dilemma of the rhetoric of moving on and bridging cultural gaps that surrounded the apology in Canada.[2] She held not only the Canadian government, but also the entire polity accountable for the intergenerational losses suffered by the First Peoples. I understood Jacobs's question as a public examination of the government's intentions: was the government prepared to go beyond a simplistic model of apology and forgiveness to one where the Truth and Reconciliation Commission also set forth a process of transformation that engaged in a fundamental critique of colonialism in Canada?[3] I found it curious that the multicultural reality of Canadian society was left out of the apology. Instead it was framed as a simple binary relationship between European settlers (the perpetrators) apologizing and seeking forgiveness for their actions in the past from the First Nations, Métis, and Inuit peoples (the victims). While the mandate of the reconciliation process emphasized the intergenerational trauma experienced by Indian residential school Survivors and their families,[4] it minimized the collective responsibility of non-Indigenous people in Canada, whose foundations are also intrinsically linked to the Crown. Thus, by excluding more recent and multiracial immigrant perspectives from the apology, the government situated the need for initiating the truth and reconciliation process simply to deal with its actions in the past. It glossed over the systemic colonial barriers that still limit the scope for developing cross-cultural dialogues and collaborations among Indigenous, non-

Indigenous, and immigrant communities and reinforce the disconnections and nonchalant attitudes of the general public.

Back at the Alternator Gallery, the mood was dramatically different. A diverse community of artists, practitioners, scholars, and organizations had all gathered there for a four-day national conference and festival of the Independent Media Arts Alliance. Entitled "On Common Ground,"[5] the conference paid tribute to the history of Indigenous media art practices in Canada. The conference showcased the range, diversity, and complexity within contemporary Indigenous media art practices and highlighted the importance of these contributions to contemporary Canadian media and visual art. The panel discussions and social events surrounding the symposium facilitated formal and informal opportunities to learn, discuss, and exchange ideas, strategies, and conversations on issues relevant to media art practice in Canada from an Indigenous framework. The mobilization of cross-cultural perspectives on media art practices fostered mutual respect and empathy. What the government had failed to facilitate institutionally was happening on a small-scale and grassroots level. It reinforced my belief in the potential of contemporary art to bypass the complacency of bureaucracy and established structures of discrimination. The potential of cultural production to innovate, heal, and develop alternate sites of agency and collectivity changed my understanding of its necessity irrevocably. It led me to a profound realization of my intergenerational responsibility as a young artist, writer, and curator. "On Common Ground" imagined a different Canadian society, one in which the fraught and unequal distribution of systemic advantages and disadvantages among the settler, immigrant, and Indigenous communities was examined critically and its implications were reckoned with by a broad audience. As a recent migrant from India, this conference opened my eyes to the complexities and differences of the experiences of colonialism and marginalization experienced between a person of Indigenous backgrounds and myself, even though we shared the same name—"Indian." It forced me to re-evaluate my role in Canadian society located between dominant Euro-American and Indigenous cultures. Do immigrants perpetuate the brutal legacy of colonialism established by European settlers when we migrate to Canada? Can Indigenous communities and immigrants work towards a framework of decolonization that transforms the social, political, and cultural landscape and empowers us to coexist peacefully along with the dominant cultures with dignity and mutual respect?

South Asians and First Peoples epitomize the complexities of coexistence between Indigenous and non-Indigenous communities in Canada. As two communities that share the same name, their histories and experiences of

"Indianness" differ widely. "Indian" is a loaded term in Canada, as it is linked inextricably to the harmful crimes committed by the colonial regime to assimilate and alienate the First Nations, Métis, and Inuit peoples in Canada with the establishment of the Ministry of Indian Affairs, Indian Residential Schools in 1860, and finally the *Indian Act* in 1876. The systemic socio-economic barriers and intergenerational loss and displacement of cultures, communities, and identities are still pervasive within contemporary Canadian society today. South Asians migrated to Canada since the early twentieth century as British colonial subjects before India, Pakistan, and Bangladesh had emerged as sovereign states. They also bore the consequences of cultural and intergenerational loss, fragmentation, and marginalization in a fundamentally colonial and racist society. Over the years, the immigration policy in Canada has expanded dramatically and is reflected in the multicultural reality of urban centres. According to Statistics Canada, South Asians constitute the largest immigrant group. While the presence of the South Asian demographic has been largely accepted in the mainstream popular culture, in our post-9/11 world of tight border security and suspicion, and of economic, war, and environmental refugees, poor immigrants continue to face discrimination on racial and socio-economic grounds if they get in. There are parallels as well as differences then that exist between the ideas and experiences of displacement

Top, middle, and bottom installations: Afshin Matlabi, *Natives* (2009) (front view); Ali Kazimi, *Shooting Indians: A Journey with Jeff Thomas* (rear view); and Bonnie Devine, *New Earth Braid* (2009). All shown in the exhibition *Crossing Lines: An Intercultural Dialogue* (2009–10).

and marginalization, home, belonging, cultural traditions, and continuity that shape the contemporary experience of South Asian migrants and the First Peoples of Canada. Yet I was surprised to find very limited scopes of interactivity or knowledge exchange between immigrant and Indigenous communities and negligible government infrastructure that facilitated such processes. Consequently, I found myself thinking about the possibility of building intercultural dialogues based on the impacts of colonialism and discrimination between both communities. Inspired by the gathering in Kelowna, I wondered if it was possible to develop events to raise awareness and build solidarity, trust, and empathy towards one another.

In 2009 I had the opportunity to curate an exhibition at the Glenhyrst Art Gallery of Brant, located next to the Six Nations of the Grand River Territory and home to a burgeoning South Asian community. Encouraged by my taste of an alternate society, one that was conscious and engaged, based on Indigenous cultural values and principles at the On Common Ground conference, I hoped this experience would inform my curatorial practice. I developed a thematic framework for the exhibition that was relevant to the history, culture, and demographic of the city and explored the possibilities of building mutual understanding, trust, and solidarity through cross-cultural dialogues between South Asian immigrants and the First Peoples in Canada.

When I started working on this exhibition I did not know much about the complex histories of the Six Nations of the Grand River Territory. I was uncomfortable speaking about the project, and, in particular, I struggled to use appropriate language that was bereft of jargon or rhetoric. Much of my research and what I learned took place through informal and lengthy conversations with the artists who participated in *Crossing Lines: An Intercultural Dialogue*.[6] As I learned about the history of Brantford and Six Nations from different Indigenous and non-Indigenous perspectives, I worked through my discomfort of being an outsider and unaware to develop a deeper understanding of Canadian history. The eventual exhibition examined the issues of connection and disconnection and sites of intersection and divergence that exist between the so-named "Indian" communities in Canada. I invited eight artists from different Indigenous and South Asian backgrounds to explore the possibility of developing cross-cultural dialogues by examining ideas of loss and displacement from their diverse experiences. In the next section I will discuss the artworks made by each of the artists and their strategies for building cross-cultural dialogues.

Jeff Thomas, *A Conversation with Edward S. Curtis, #7 Medicine Crow Wearing a Hawk Hide Headdress (Crow Nation c. 1908)* (2009).

Re-imagining Indians

When Indian filmmaker Ali Kazimi and Iroquois photographer Jeff Thomas started working on *Shooting Indians: A Journey with Jeff Thomas* in 1997, photography was the common language between them. In the film, Kazimi takes the viewer on an intimate journey through Jeff Thomas's art practice while using an autobiographical approach that reveals Kazimi's personal history as a South Asian immigrant. Most enlightening is Kazimi's candid narration of his own misconceptions when he had started working on the film, as it opens up the relatively unexamined space of dialogue between an immigrant and First Nations artist. Their collaboration addresses the limitations of language and stereotypical representations that frames the presence (and absence) of the First Peoples' and immigrants' experiences in the master narrative of Canadian history. After visiting the Six Nations of the Grand River Territory with Thomas, Kazimi notes that while his prior assumptions were unsettled after going to the reserve, he found startling economic disparity and disillusionment. Kazimi acknowledges that his conversations with Thomas enabled him to develop a deeper understanding and respect of the context of First Nations, Métis, and Inuit experiences. Meanwhile, Thomas's ongoing engagement with the work of Edward Curtis, the twentieth century photographer and filmmaker whose artistic legacy forms the premise of the film, sets a precedent of critical inquiry into the canons of Canadian history. Kazimi and Thomas's *dialogic* approach creates a framework for questioning the existing paradigms of looking and thinking about personal histories. Together, they develop a sensitive portrayal of the contradictions of "Indianness" through the personal lens of Kazimi's diasporic history and Thomas's body of work.[7] *Shooting Indians* is an award-

Animose 1: Greg Staats,
Animose, 1996–ongoing

winning Canadian documentary film that challenges established forms
and mediums of representing immigrant and First Peoples' cultures. While
Canada's cultural landscape has changed dramatically since Kazimi and Jeff
started working on the film in 1984, the issues of stereotypes, systemic erasure,
and disconnection are still relevant.

Shooting Indians: A Journey with Jeff Thomas helped me understand the
strategy of developing cross-cultural dialogues as a process of building
trust and mutual respect. It formed the touchstone for this exhibition. As
a next-generation immigrant and cultural practitioner, I felt that it was
important to highlight and revisit the discussion started by the duo in this
exhibition. In fact, the dialogic approach developed by the artists through
the development of the film also formed one of the core principles of
Thomas's photographic practice.

Crossing Lines showcases a new work from Thomas's landmark, ongoing
series of photographs entitled *A Conversation with Edward S. Curtis*, in which
he re-contextualizes images from Curtis's 20-volume study of "The North
American Indian"[8] in a contemporary context. Entitled *A Conversation with
Edward S. Curtis, #7 Medicine Crow Wearing a Hawk Hide Headdress (Crow
Nation c. 1908)* (2009), Thomas assembles a triptych of three photographs:
two historical portraits by Curtis of Medicine Crow dressed in ornate jewelry
and a hawk carcass on his head, shot from different angles (profile and
frontal view), which flank a recent photograph of a hawk taken by Thomas at
a bird sanctuary in Coaldale, Alberta. The hawk hide headdress references
the Indigenous practices of revering animals for their special traits. The
hawk symbolizes qualities that the bird is known for such as swiftness,
agility, and precise eyesight, all of which are extremely valuable to a hunter
and warrior such as Medicine Crow. Curtis's photographs seem to capture

Animose 2; Greg Staats, Animose, 1996–ongoing

the sitter's pride in his cultural heritage in the slightly raised bridge of his nose in the profile photograph and the clarity of his direct gaze in the frontal portrait. By placing the recent photograph of the hawk in the centre, Thomas's triptych can be read to symbolize the importance and necessity of Indigenous knowledge systems to sustain our degraded environment today. Medicine Crow also symbolizes the continuity of the various streams of Indigenous knowledge that are part of our everyday lives and constitute our contemporary culture. By projecting Kazimi's film in the same room, directly across from Thomas's 16-foot-long photographic print in the gallery, I wished to address the ongoing importance of their cross-cultural dialogue in contemporary visual art discourse today.

A different form of dialogue occurs in Afshin Matlabi's drawing *Natives*, where the artist explores, from an immigrant perspective, the absence of Indigenous knowledge and subjectivities in dominant cultural history. Approaching these gaps through the lens of (mis-)representing Indigenous and immigrant people in popular culture, Matlabi portrays two figures holding specific gestures that draw the viewer's attention into the work. The figure on the right-hand side of the drawing is shown with one arm above her head holding a pose from the Indian classical dance, *Bharatanatyam*, where stylized hand gestures or *mudras* constitute an integral part of the dance vocabulary. By portraying the figure without her traditional costume, Matlabi resists the viewer's easy categorization and simplistic conclusions about the dancer's cultural identity. The figure beside her holds an open-handed gesture, which can be understood as a symbol of friendship and peace among some First Peoples. It can also be read as a universal signal to stop, perhaps alluding to the marginalization of both immigrant and Indigenous communities by the patronizing gaze of the dominant culture. The title of the work *Natives* also refers to the common and disparate histories and intergenerational traumas of colonization experienced by South Asian and Indigenous communities. Using pencil and ink on paper, Matlabi fills the background of his large-scale drawing with countless, multidirectional strokes. In particular, the erratic, bold flow of the strokes between the figures draws the viewer's attention, as they seem to break the linear flow of colour in the rest of the drawing. I understand these multidirectional strokes to symbolize a need to disturb the established ideas and assumptions shaping South Asian and Indigenous identities and cultures in the dominant narrative. The distance between the figures, holding specific and seemingly disconnected poses, can be understood as the artist's attempt to acknowledge the complexities surrounding Indigenous and migrant relations in Canada. Meanwhile, reflecting upon the brutal historical similarities of exoticization and fetishization of Indigenous and South Asian cultures by the colonial gaze, Matlabi's foregrounding of the figure referencing an Indigenous gesture demonstrates his plea to reframe the dominant cultural narrative from an Indigenous framework.

Reframing the gaze is also central to Ojibway artist Bonnie Devine, who explores the intricacies of the relations between Indigenous and non-Indigenous communities metaphorically. *New Earth Braid* is made up of reeds gathered from the banks of the Grand River in Six Nations and the outskirts of Brantford, which are used to create a 12-foot-long braid that represents the oral histories, cultures, and traditions of the First Peoples that are woven into the land. Through these simple reeds, Devine references the undocumented histories of Indigenous knowledge systems and the First Peoples' spirit of collaboration that has enabled migrants and settlers to survive and thrive in a foreign land. In contemporary society, the gesture of braiding signifies various traditions associated with women's work such as basket weaving, an Elder braiding a child's hair, and the adolescent practice of making friendship bands. In my conversations with the artist, I have learned that Devine also associates the *New Earth Braid* with the Council of Three Fires and her cultural heritage regarding the work as embodying values of diligence, compassion, and courage as the basis for cross-cultural discussions to succeed.

Roy Caussy examines the multiple and incomplete narratives that make up the canonical accounts of Canadian history. He creates rubbings of three plaques that commemorate three of the most significant moments of Brantford's history: The *Haldimand Proclamation* of 1784, The Mohawk Institute Residential School that was established in 1831 and closed in the 1970, and the founding of the town of Brantford in 1877. Each plaque presents a distinctly different perspective and approach of the history and culture of the region. By bringing them together within one gallery, Caussy simply elucidates the socio-economic, cultural, and political disparities that persist within contemporary Canadian culture. He juxtaposes these deep-rooted chasms with a melodic sound installation, in which he has recorded voices of strangers he has encountered on the streets of Brantford, to develop a resonant harmony that is made up of multiple voices and programmed to play every seven minutes. Every time the sound piece is turned on, it fills the gallery with a sense of familiarity and intimacy. In *Three-part Harmony* (2009), Caussy highlights the severe need to reinvent and rework the simplistic dominant discourse that perpetuates the alienation and marginalization of Indigenous people and newcomers in the mainstream.

Ottawa-based Ehren Bear Witness Thomas subverts the colonizing master narratives in popular culture in his invigorating videowork *Strange Homelands: Part Two*. Reflecting on the narcissism and the disconnection of our over-saturated consumer culture with multiple histories and paradigms of viewing, listening, and understanding, Thomas layers and samples personal footage with scenes from Hollywood films, Disney cartoons, pop music, and video games. He challenges linear and polarizing frameworks in the mainstream through his dynamic media art practice, based on his personal Indigenous subjectivities. Thomas's video emanates a sense of urgency to refute totalizing narratives and to shift the accepted master narrative of North American history and culture to one that is based on ideologies of social justice, freedom, and peace.

Meanwhile, Yudi Sewraj of Guyanese and South Asian heritage expands on the notions of loss, displacement, and doubt in the dominant cultural history in his video installation *Nineteen Seventy-Eight* (2009). The installation is made up of three major components: two sets of videos, one playing on old-school TV monitors and the other projected on the wall, placed on opposite sides of an opaque wooden crate and making it impossible for the viewer to experience the entire installation at once. *Nineteen Seventy-Eight* draws attention to the spatial and temporal elements of the work, opening it up to multiple subjectivities and responses. There are peepholes on different sides of the crate that enable the audience to look inside and find an abandoned couch. The videos, which display a running loop of found household objects being destroyed and swept away, seem to draw parallels with the loss of multiple narratives and histories that have been erased by the master narrative. In the video projection, Sewraj inverts the viewer's gaze onto himself, as he performs in it. Using a mimetic strategy to critique accepted paradigms and practices of everyday life, a sense of discomfort and alienation is palpable in Sewraj's absurd attempts to replicate the mundane actions of an old man that plays on a monitor inside the video. The video within a video further breaks down any sense of origin or authenticity that might legitimize the prevailing colonial master narrative that has repeatedly led to the violent intergenerational losses of language, culture, and traditions suffered by immigrant and Indigenous populations.

The experience of loss and dislocation also informs Ohsweken artist Greg Staats's ongoing series of black and white photographs entitled *Animose*. Staats embarked upon this series in 1996, a decade after he moved to Toronto, as a way of coping with the loss of his sense of belonging. The etymology of the word *Animose* comes from *anima*, meaning "breath" or "discreet presence," which personifies Staats's exploration of discarded objects through his photographs. By privileging their presence in the urban-scape through his photographs, this series provides an alternate understanding of Canadian cities and lifestyles that links his personal experiences with found and forgotten objects he encounters on the street, bus stops, and parks. Some examples include: two carpets lying on the curb, a mound of dirt heaped on the sidewalk and street, a chair sitting across a log camouflaged between tree trunks, and two bundles of sticks flung out on the street. Each of these photographs exude a strong presence and balance in their new settings. The photographs embody the serenity and vitality of oral traditions and knowledge systems that have been intrinsic to the development of Canadian culture. They also symbolize the importance of acknowledging the presence of oral traditions, ceremonies, and symbols of First Nations, Métis, and Inuit cultures and experiences in Canada as the first steps toward building cross-cultural dialogues and trust with immigrant and settler communities.

Steps toward the future

In her analysis of the current reconciliation discourse, researcher and scholar Paulette Regan has said, "we remain stuck in a mindset of denial and guilt about past wrongs in which we problematize and pathologize Indigenous peoples, seeking legal and bureaucratic solutions to a long list of 'Indian problems' and 'historical' 'claims.' In doing so, we deflect attention away from the 'Settler problem,' [and] our own complicity in maintaining the colonial status quo."[9] Critiquing the biases latent in the institutionalized structures of cross-cultural interactivity, Regan holds the willingness of non-Indigenous communities to engage with the narratives revealed through the Truth and Reconciliation Commission equally responsible in developing an effective framework that builds awareness and destabilizes the colonial mindset of the dominant culture. Cross-cultural dialogues can provide a common space for self-reflexivity, listening, and learning from the multiple histories, experiences, and narratives that remain unheard of in the mainstream. Through his series of photographic works, Greg Staats acknowledges that these Indigenous subjectivities must be the starting point of any form of cross-cultural dialogue. The dialogic approach, facilitated at the small-scale and grassroots level, becomes crucial in overcoming the government's superficial apology that has failed to acknowledge the devastating impact of past injustices that continue into the present. For newcomers to Canada, in particular, such opportunities can facilitate an effective way in understanding the complexities of Canadian histories, which will lead to nuanced ways of engaging with contemporary Canadian culture.

Altogether, the artworks exhibited in *Crossing Lines: An Intercultural Dialogue* attempt to disturb the dominant cultural history that "'misrecognizes' and disrespects [and denies] the oral histories, cultures, and legal traditions of Indigenous peoples."[10] Emerging from a minoritarian perspective, immigrant and Indigenous subjectivities of the artists are based on notions of loss and displacement, which form the starting point for building cross-cultural dialogues through the exhibition. Such a perspective challenges the colonial mindset and hegemonic narratives of a national history that legitimize the disparities and socio-economic privileges that exist between Indigenous, immigrant, and settler communities. Exploring the possibility of dialogues also provides artists (and myself) with an opportunity to re-imagine contemporary Canadian society based on ideas of collectivity, community, and mutual respect.

In retrospect, *Crossing Lines: An Intercultural Dialogue* was an enlightening experiment, a meaningful exercise, and the beginning of my exploration on the strategies of learning through dialogue and collaboration. In the process I learned about my own discomfort while working on and researching the concepts for this exhibition, with a heightened awareness of my limited knowledge of the complex histories, narratives, and traditions of diverse Indigenous communities and nations. I realized that my role and responsibility as a recent immigrant in Canada was in a constant state of flux, as it shifted between being a beneficiary, thus perpetrator, of the colonial socio-economic privileges of the dominant framework—benefiting from incentives provided to middle-class and educated immigrants for instance—on the one hand, and on the other, being vulnerable to the discriminatory and unquestionable laws of the same structures. I learned how to speak from my position of knowing and not knowing with humility and honesty as I engaged in dialogues with the accomplished and emerging artists in the exhibitions, many of whom had a strong grasp of creating collaborative and collective strategies to develop mutual trust and respect. This exhibition, in its small-scale and localized context, sought to build an ethos of communication that recognized the struggles within Indigenous and immigrant communities and to build solidarity on a personal and human level.

Notes

1 Jacobs, B. (2008:6857). Canada. Parliament. House of Commons Debates (Hansard). 39th Parliament, 2nd Session, Vol. 142, No. 110 (June 11, 2008). Ottawa, ON: Public Works and Government Services Canada. Retrieved 7 December 2010 from: http://www2.parl.gc.ca/HousePublications/Publication.aspx?Language=E&Mode=1&Parl=39&Ses=2&DocId=3568890.

2 Clark, T. and R. de Costa (2009). A Tale of Two Apologies. *Canada Watch*. Fall 2009:36–37,40. Retrieved 8 December 2010 from: http://www.yorku.ca/robarts/projects/canada-watch/

3 Regan, Paulette (2007). An apology feast in Hazelton: Indian residential schools, reconciliation, and making space for Indigenous legal traditions. In Law Commission of Canada (ed.). *Indigenous Legal Traditions*. Vancouver, BC:UBC Press: 40–76.

4 de Costa, Ravi (2009). Truth, Reconciliation and the Politics of Community: The Politics of Community and Identity: Learning from one another. University of Ottawa (May 20–22, 2009). Retrieved 25 November 2010 from: http://www.sciencessociales.uottawa.ca/communities09/en/discussion.asp

5 The On Common Ground conference took place between 10–15 June 2008, and was organized in partnership with the Ullus Collective, an Indigenous Media Arts Collective from the region, and the Alternator gallery in Kelowna, BC.

6 *Crossing Lines: An Intercultural Dialogue* was co-presented by SAVAC (South Asian Visual Arts Centre) and the Glenhyrst Art Gallery of Brant from 29 November 2009–22 January 2010. The exhibition took place at the Glenhyrst Art Gallery of Brant in Brantford, Ontario.

7 Francis, Margot (2002). Reading the autoethnographic perspectives of Indians 'Shooting Indians.' *Topia* 7:5–26. Francis first attributes the term "Indianness" on p. 11. For further discussion on this term see: Lyman, Christopher (1982). *The Vanishing Race and Other Illusions: Photographs of Indians by Edward Curtis*. New York, NY: Pantheon Books in association with the Smithsonian Institution Press.

8 Thomas's research at the National Archives revealed that when Curtis made these portraits, most of the First Peoples had lost their traditional livelihoods of hunting and fishing. Many were even banned from practising their songs, dances, and carrying out cultural practices. So, when Curtis took these photos, it gave the sitters an opportunity to dress in their cultural heritage that was being denied them by the colonial regime.

9 Regan (2007:44) [reference in original removed].

10 Regan, Paulette (2007:43).

Malissa Phung

Malissa Phung is completing a doctorate in English and Cultural Studies at McMaster University in Hamilton, Ontario. For the past three years she has been studying post-colonial cultures and Asian Canadian literature while living about 30 kilometres from the Six Nations of the Grand River. Living in close proximity to the ongoing Caledonia land claim dispute and being part of an academic community committed to teaching and writing about anti-racism and anti-colonialism have greatly influenced the scope of her dissertation project and her activist politics. Her doctoral dissertation focuses on the ways in which representations of settler work ethic in Chinese Canadian literature and documentaries can potentially reproduce existing colonial discourses used to justify settler belonging on Indigenous lands and to maintain colonial stereotypes about Indigenous peoples that imply they are undeserving of contested lands and resources that have been misappropriated from them and their ancestors. Born in Red Deer, Alberta, to ethnically Vietnamese displaced immigrants of Chinese descent, Malissa grew up mostly in Edmonton where she and her family have benefited a great deal from Treaty 6. Being the daughter of a successful hair salon owner in Chinatown—a downtown business district that intersects with an urban Indigenous population—has provided her with a complicated upbringing of racist and classist views of Indigenous peoples. In her academic and creative work, Malissa strives to unsettle these colonial views she has inherited from both her community and the dominant settler society.

Are People of Colour Settlers Too?

In their 2005 article, "Decolonizing Antiracism,"[1] Indigenous and critical race studies scholars Bonita Lawrence and Enakshi Dua point out that "there is something deeply wrong with the manner in which, in our own lands, antiracism does not begin with, and reflect, the totality of Native people's lived experience—that is, with the genocide that established and maintains all of the settler states."[2] Lawrence and Dua take anti-racist and anti-colonial academics and activists to task for overlooking and effectively erasing from their analyses and political projects the histories, epistemologies, and political claims of Indigenous people. They claim that anti-racist and anti-colonial academics and activists have failed to make the presence and ongoing colonization of Indigenous people in the Americas foundational to their analyses of race and racism. They argue that these elisions have narrowed theoretical and historical understandings of race and racism, particularly in Canadian anti-racist discourses, which can render people of colour innocent in the ongoing colonization of Indigenous people. Though people of colour have faced and still face marginalization and exclusion in Canada, Lawrence and Dua contend that people of colour are still complicit in the ongoing land theft and colonial domination of Indigenous people.

Lawrence and Dua's work compels us to think critically about how people of colour are complicit in the colonization of Indigenous people in Canada, a problem that has often been framed as a white settler–Indigenous issue. For too long now, issues of racial discrimination and exclusion that people of colour face in Canada have been framed as a separate issue from the colonial legacies that still affect the material experiences of Indigenous people today. It is as though the fact that people of colour face discrimination and exclusion in Canada somehow means that they cannot possibly contribute to the colonization of Indigenous people as well. Or, in the case of refugees fleeing from their places of origin to escape political persecution, even if they benefit as colonial settlers, how can we blame them for settling when their main priorities lie in the basic need to survive? In her groundbreaking 2007 book *Exalted Subjects: Studies in the Making of Race and Nation in Canada*, the feminist and anti-racist scholar Sunera Thobani forcefully argues that despite the magnitude of their dehumanization and exploitation, we cannot minimize the fact that immigrants and refugees are also participants in and beneficiaries of Canada's colonial project, especially when they work towards achieving equality with Canadian settler subjects, thereby placing their political status above that of Indigenous people in Thobani's triangulated theory of Canada's racial hierarchy.[3] But this issue of whether people of colour are settlers is a complicated one that requires more than just a simple recognition or acknowledgement that people of colour are complicit settlers. And so, while I agree with Lawrence and Dua's central claim that people of colour are settlers, I have some questions about the implications of this complicated argument.

If people of colour are settlers, then are they settlers in the same way that the French and British were originally settlers in Canada? And what exactly does being a settler mean? Is it a simple descriptive term—settler proper—or is it a term that carries historical legacies inflected differently by race, class, gender, sexuality, and ability? Is it a unified monolithic subject position? Or can colonial settlerhood be stratified? Do different settlers operate on different levels with regard to access to power? What is even more complicated is the question of mixed race settlers: if all non-Indigenous Canadians are settlers simply because they or their ancestors migrated to Canada, then what do we make of settlers who have Indigenous ancestors several generations removed? Can someone who easily passes as a settler choose not to be a settler? I admit these are complicated questions to ask in light of the racist and sexist legacies of the *Indian Act*'s marriage laws that used to determine and still does determine who is and who is not a status "Indian."

Though I may not have ready answers to these difficult questions, I would like to begin discussing their implications by questioning whether settlers of colour can be easily equated with white settlers. I am not disagreeing with Lawrence and Dua's main argument; I am not looking for some way to mitigate the complicity of settlers of colour. Instead I am interested in what a concept like *settler* can do, how this concept can recalibrate the methodologies and epistemologies that anti-racist and anti-colonial academics and activists use to produce knowledge and shape public discourses in Canada—necessary steps to consider as we work towards transforming Canadian policies and institutions more fully acknowledge and affirm Indigenous claims to national and cultural independence.

being a settler simply means being a Canadian, then how are all settlers equal when not all Canadians are equal? Whether a settler is of British or French or any other European descent, depending on a whole range of factors (such as time of emigration, mix of racial background and cultural heritage, the type of English or French accent with which a settler speaks), settlers benefit from the ongoing colonization of Indigenous people to differing degrees. The more assimilated a settler, the more a settler shares the dominant physical characteristics, linguistic features, and nationalistic desires of a settler society, the more a settler will be afforded the material benefits and opportunities to become productive citizens of Canada.[4] Lawrence and Dua would rightly argue that when marginalized settlers of colour organize and demand equal access to citizenship rights and benefits, they risk staking colonial claims to belong and own land and resources that have been stolen through imperial land treaties that have never been fully honoured or that have been legally misinterpreted to advantage and benefit predominantly white settlers. What concerns me, however, is how we can equate the colonial status of settlers of colour with that of white settlers—how we can talk about settlers in monolithic terms when any non-Indigenous Canadian is not necessarily first and foremost only a settler?

If we look to the literary production of white settlers in nineteenth century Canadian literature, we can trace how settlers in Canada began to conceive and imagine their settler placement and belonging on Indigenous lands. This was also a period of colonial administration and land cession treaty negotiations that began to prioritize land acquisition and control over the establishment of peace and friendship between settlers and Indigenous people, which had originally been the primary objective of the 1763 *Royal Proclamation Act*.[5] Understanding concepts of white settlerhood during this shift in Indigenous–settler relations can shed light on contemporary settler–Indigenous relationships and reveal both the similarities and differences between contemporary people of colour and these nineteenth century colonial settlers.

Nineteenth century Canadian literature was deeply invested in telling stories and devising images that worked to affirm the myth of Indigenous people as a vanishing and dying race, only to be replaced by stories and images of *Indigenized* white settlers; that is, *Indigenous* in their ability to cultivate Indigenous attributes and skills.[6] Literary scholars have attributed the colonial trope of the vanishing "Indian" to white settler desires to vacate Indigenous people from the national imaginary and to overcome the unsettling knowledge that settlers would never be indigenous to this land.[7] So to justify their right to occupy and belong in Indigenous territories, nineteenth century white settler writers, I would add, conveniently constructed a labour narrative of hard work and enterprise to self-indigenize; meanwhile Indigenous people, according to colonial stereotypes, have been constructed as lazy and lacking in industry and civility. Stereotypes about Indigenous people in Canada stem from the colonial notion of *terra nullius*: when the French first came to colonize the so-called uninhabited *New World*, they assumed that "since the Amerindians led a mobile life without settled abode, 'ranging' the land 'like beasts in the woods', they could not be classed as inhabitants according to European law."[8] In other words, since Indigenous people were seen as lazy, uncivilized, nomadic people who did not cultivate the land for profit, according to these settler colonial labour narratives, white settlers earned their right to the land that Indigenous people had apparently allowed to go to waste.

People of colour engage in this process of indigenization when they work towards achieving, or, in some cases, have managed to achieve, upward class mobility while at the same time promoting similar settler colonial labour narratives of hard work and enterprise in the face of Indigenous claims to autochthony. Assimilated people of colour can produce similar settler colonial narratives in order to emplace their settler belonging on Indigenous lands: such narratives of immigrant origins and trials and tribulations can construct people of colour as exemplary settlers who have been able to work hard to rise above their racialized immigrant origins and succeed despite all of the odds stacked against them. But successful portraits of model immigrants and people of colour also run the risk of being mobilized to either blame marginalized settlers of colour and Indigenous people for not being able to contribute to the settler society, or to blame model minorities for taking away jobs from Canadian settler subjects. I will now turn to a particular group of settlers to further address these tensions.

Chinese indentured labourers were constructed in nineteenth century Canadian culture as a "model minority" group. Stereotypes of Chinese labourers as hyper-industrious labour machines willing to work for next to nothing abound in historical records, newspapers, government publications, and immigration debates at the time. These *positive* stereotypes came hand-in-hand with negative stereotypes as Chinese settlers circulated in mainstream Canadian representations as the "yellow peril."[9] Furthermore, Chinese labourers represented a racial and moral threat to the national fabric and an economic threat appropriating resources that rightfully, it is argued, belong to hardworking industrious white settlers when, in fact, these resources more rightfully belong to Indigenous people.

For example, from the 1870s to the Great Depression, white labour leaders lobbied for restrictive and racially discriminatory immigration policies to protect the standards of living of white Canadian workers; they conceived of Asians as "degraded workers who were unfair competition to white Canadians."[10] More recently, there was also the racist W-Five news exposé, "Campus Giveaway," broadcasted on CTV in 1979 on the supposed mass displacement of hardworking white Canadians from highly competitive and lucrative programs such as pharmacy, computer science, engineering, and medicine by foreign international students, who were represented in the segment with images of Chinese Canadian university students.[11] A much more recent reiteration of the "yellow peril" discourse is the problematic coverage of a perceived Asian hyper-enrolment and unfair Asian–white competition in Canadian universities in the *Maclean's* 2010 article "Too Asian?" Stephanie Findlay and Nicholas Köhler's article sparked rigorous public debate and mobilized public calls to action from Asian Canadian citizens, academics, and activists across the nation in blog posts, newspaper articles, online commentary forums, and community meetings.[12] These long-standing racial and class inter-settler tensions suggest that there are multiple ways of being configured as an invasive settler. Although they may occupy Indigenous lands and benefit from the displacement of Indigenous people, Chinese settlers have also been figured as perpetually *foreign* or *alien*, unsettled settlers posing an invasive threat to the livelihoods of *Indigenized* white settlers. As this kind of historical analysis demonstrates, Chinese settlers cannot simply be equated with the original British and French settlers, either at the level of representation or at the level of material experience.

I have included the case of Chinese settlers in my discussion for several reasons. First of all, Canadian literary and visual representations of Chinese labour and colonial settlerhood constitute the main subject of my Ph.D. dissertation. I am interested in exploring what it means to represent the history of Chinese exclusion and marginalization in Canada and to formulate anti-racist discourses without being grounded in the history of Indigenous exploitation and oppression in Canada. Second, as a middle-class female junior academic settler born to Sino–Vietnamese immigrants in what is now known as central Alberta, I have benefited a great deal from Treaty 6.[13] This essay constitutes a reflection of my own complicity as a racialized Canadian settler subject. Because of Treaty 6, my immigrant family has been able to improve their socio-economic status and send me and my brother to university. Though I may have experienced my fair share of racial and gender discrimination throughout my life, I never had to worry about my employers making negative assumptions about my work ethic or productivity since *positive* stereotypes about Asians being hard workers and exceptional at math would exaggerate my physical and intellectual capacity. Given the inequity of these settler privileges and treaty benefits that my family and I enjoy, through my scholarly research I have come to be politically and ethically committed to undermining the ways in which anti-racist discourses regarding settlers of colour, particularly Chinese settlers, become mobilized among diasporic communities to stake claims of national belonging and acceptance.

Not only have I drawn on Lawrence and Dua's critical intervention but I have also nuanced the ways in which the entry of settlers of colour to Canada has put them in colonial relationships with Indigenous people. I recognize that relying on monolithic notions of the term "settler" runs the risk of reducing settler–Indigenous relations to overly simplistic binary models of thinking. If we lump all non-Indigenous people into a single category of settler, then do we risk erasing and subsuming the different histories and everyday experiences of settler privilege and marginalization from which white settlers and settlers of colour come from? As I said before, the questions and concerns I have been raising thus far are not meant to mitigate the complicity of settlers of colour; rather, I raise these complexities as part of a solidarity exercise that aims to recuperate the term settler as a politicized identification for white settlers and settlers of colour.[14] I am interested in invoking an anti-colonial conceptualization of the term "settler" that both recognizes non-Indigenous complicity in Canada's ongoing colonial project and stands in solidarity with the decolonization projects of Indigenous people. To self-identify as a settler rather than as a Canadian does not necessarily negate the rights and benefits of citizenship that settlers have come to accrue as a result of settler colonialism. But mobilizing all settlers to become aware of the ways in which their settler privileges are anything but natural and well deserved can constitute a first step in supporting Indigenous activism against settler domination.

I conclude this essay with an example from New Zealand/Aotearoa. *Pakeha*, the Maori word for the descendants of European colonizing settlers, came to invoke a particular form of politics in New Zealand, one which recognized Maori claims to sovereignty, was built on a revisionist conception of New Zealand's colonial history, and was sensitive to Maori claims of institutional racism within New Zealand society.[15] Somewhat equivalent to the term "settler" in Canada, the Maori word *pakeha* has been a source of contention in race politics in New Zealand. In the 1990s, non-Maori committed to an anti-racist politics began to self-identify as *pakeha* on a wider scale, whereas those who opposed the term opted for "New Zealander."[16] At one point, *this* term generated such extensive opposition that there was a call by a member of Parliament to ban public use of the word.[17]

I bring up this example of a politicized concept of settlerhood not to propose that the term "settler" can do the same political work that the Maori word does in New Zealand since the English term is rooted in a colonial language. I am merely suggesting that perhaps the term "settler" can aspire towards doing the same type of history work that the term *pakeha* does. When we identify as settlers or *pakeha*, we acknowledge where we actually come from—not here. Settlers of colour and *pakeha* of colour are already quite aware that they are not from here, or that they have never truly belonged here. But given the propensity of settlers to retell enduring labour narratives of rightful occupation and belonging on this land, thereby overwriting the fact of this land being Indigenous territory, I can only ask that political allies of Indigenous people remain vigilant and committed to working towards undermining such "self-indigenizing" narratives within their own settler communities.

Notes

1 Reprinted elsewhere in this volume.
2 Lawrence, Bonita and Enakshi Dua (2005:121). Decolonizing antiracism. *Social Justice* 32(4):120–143.
3 Thobani, Sunera (2007:16–17). *Exalted Subjects: Studies in the Making of Race and Nation in Canada*. Toronto, ON: University of Toronto Press.
4 I owe my conceptualization of settler privilege to the way in which Ross Chambers discusses white privilege as a set of cards one is dealt. He describes identity as a poker hand, "in which the value of the ace (whiteness) can be either enhanced, if one holds a couple of court cards or another ace (masculinity, heterosexuality, middleclassness...), or alternatively depreciated by association with cards of lower value (ethnicity, color, lack of education, working-classness...)." See: Chambers, Ross (1996:144). The unexamined. *The Minnesota Review* 47:141–156. Settler privilege can likewise be enhanced or depreciated, but to the degree of assimilation a settler exhibits.
5 Dickason, Olive P., with David T. McNab (2009:156–157). *Canada's First Nations: A History of Founding People from Earliest Times*. (4th ed.). Don Mills, ON: Oxford University Press.
6 Johnston, Anna and Alan Lawson (2006). Settler colonies. In Henry Schwarz and Sangeeta Ray (eds.). *A Companion to Postcolonial Studies*. Malden, MA: Blackwell: 360–376.
7 See: Goldie, Terry (ed.) (1989). Fear and temptation. In *Fear and Temptation: The Image of the Indigene in Canadian, Australian, and New Zealand Literatures*. Kingston, ON: McGill-Queen's University Press: 3–18; Johnston and Lawson (2006).
8 Dickason with McNab (2009:146).
9 The term "yellow peril" was originally devised by Kaiser Wilhelm of Germany, who used it to foster racial discrimination, and was later used to describe the supposed danger of Orientals overwhelming the West. For more on this topic in another settler society context, see: Walker, David (1999). *Anxious Nation: Australia and the Rise of Asia 1850–1939*. St. Lucia, AU: University of Queensland Press.
10 Goutor, David (2007). *Guarding the Gates: The Canadian Labour Movement and Immigration, 1872–1934*. Vancouver, BC: UBC Press.
11 Chan, Anthony B. (1983). *Gold Mountain: The Chinese in the New World*. Vancouver, BC: New Star Books.
12 For the original article, see: Findlay, Stephanie and Nicholas Köhler (2010). Too Asian? *Maclean's* 123(45):76–81. For an astute analysis of Findlay and Köhler's xenophobic article, see Jeet Heer's online commentary in *The National Post*: Heer, Jeet (2010, November 15). *Maclean's* article on Asians familiar to anti-Semites of old. *The National Post* (retrieved 29 December 2010 from: http://fullcomment.nationalpost.com/2010/11/15/jeet-heer-macleans-article-on-asians-familiar-to-anti-semites-of-old/); See also his blog-post for *The Walrus* at: Heer, Jeet (2010, November 24). Too

Brazen: Maclean's, Margaret Wente, and the Canadian media's inarticulacy about race. *The Walrus Blog*. Retrieved 29 December 2010 from: http://www.walrusmagazine.com/blogs/2010/11/24/too-brazen/

13 Signed in 1876 between delegates representing the British Crown and Plains Cree and other Indigenous people such as the Nakoda, Salteaux, and Chipewyan, Treaty 6 ceded the Indigenous territory now known as central Alberta and Saskatchewan for colonial settlement.

14 Throughout this essay, I have been employing the seemingly benign and neutral term "settler" rather than "settler-invader," which was first adopted by colonial and post-colonial scholars in the 1980s to emphasize the physical violence and representational erasure exacted on Indigenous communities that the more benign and seemingly neutral term "settler" conceals. In the Canadian context, I use the term "settler" not to mitigate these historical violences but to acknowledge Indigenous agency and sovereignty and to avoid affirming the colonial discursive myth of conquered vanishing Indigenous people when the history of Indigenous displacement and dispossession in Canada was more a result of legal imperialism than outright military conquest. See: Stasiulus, Daiva and Radha Jhappan (1995). The fractious politics of a settler society: Canada. In Daiva Stasiulus and Nira Yuval-Davis (eds.). *Unsettling Settler Societies: Articulations of Gender, Race, Ethnicity and Class*. London, UK: Sage Publications: 95–131.

15 Larner, Wendy and Paul Spoonley (eds.) (1995:51). Post-colonial politics in Aotearoa/New Zealand. In *Unsettling Settler Societies: Articulations of Gender, Race, Ethnicity and Class*: 39–64.

16 Larner and Spoonley (1995:52).

17 Larner and Spoonley (1995:52).

Henry Yu

Henry Yu was born in Vancouver. His parents were immigrants from China, joining a grandfather and great-grandfather who spent almost their entire lives in British Columbia. Descended through his mother's family from migrants who left Zhongshan county in Guangdong province in South China and settled around the Pacific in places such as Australia, Hawai'i, the Caribbean, Southeast Asia, the United States, and Canada, Henry has a particular interest in the relations between trans-Pacific migrants and Indigenous peoples. Currently, he is Director of the Initiative for Student Teaching and Research in Chinese Canadian studies and the Principal pro tem of St. John's Graduate College at University of British Columbia (UBC), as well as the Project Lead at UBC for "Chinese Canadian Stories," a collaborative project to digitally document Chinese Canadian history. He serves as a board member of the Chinese Canadian Historical Society of British Columbia and is the Co-Chair of the City of Vancouver's project: Dialogues Between First Nations, Urban Aboriginal and Immigrant Communities in Vancouver. Henry received his B.A. in Honours History from UBC and a M.A. and Ph.D. in History from Princeton University. After teaching at Princeton, University of California, Los Angeles, and Yale he returned to UBC in 2004. Henry's book, *Thinking Orientals: Migration, Contact, and Exoticism in Modern America* (Oxford University Press, 2001) won the Norris and Carol Hundley Award as the most distinguished book of 2001. He is currently working on several book projects, including one entitled *Pacific Canada* that aims to reimagine the history of Canada.

Nurturing Dialogues between First Nations, Urban Aboriginal, and Immigrant Communities in Vancouver

During 2010, I had the privilege of being involved with a unique process organized by the City of Vancouver. Recognizing that in Vancouver we stood at a historic juncture in which new immigrant communities have transformed the populations of our city, we began a conversation that we hoped would allow for the creation of a common future together for immigrant and Aboriginal communities. Moving forward meant creating a new vision of Canada that recognized a history of injustices to both Aboriginal people and non-white immigrants. This terrible history—wrought by white supremacist policies of land dispossession, residential schooling, immigrant exclusion, and racial discrimination in voting, housing, and employment—needed to be acknowledged and its legacies made widely known before a more optimistic future could be envisioned together. We hoped that if this process could be started in Vancouver, it might also inspire other cities and regions of Canada to undergo a similar process of dialogue that would help lay the groundwork for a transformation of our society.

As one of three co-chairs, along with Councillor H. Wade Grant of the Musqueam Nation and Susan Tatoosh, Executive Director of Vancouver's Aboriginal Friendship Centre Society, the Steering Committee was a diverse group of representatives from Vancouver's local First Nations of Musqueam and Tsleil–Waututh, from urban Aboriginal organizations, immigrant settlement organizations, neighbourhood houses, and academics from local universities. The Steering Committee was formed to help advise city social planner Baldwin Wong and Dialogues project coordinator Karen Fong in helping plan and implement a series of dialogue circles involving members of local First Nations, urban Aboriginal, and immigrant communities.[1] The Steering Committee recognized that many new arrivals in Canada received very little information about the history of Aboriginal people and, in particular, of the devastating effects of governmental policies such as residential schooling; therefore, through no intention of their own, they were often left only with stereotypes and the negative images of popular culture as the basis for their knowledge about Aboriginal people.

What could be generated, we wondered, if we could organize a dialogue process in which small groups engaged and thoughtful participants from Aboriginal and immigrant communities could speak and listen to each other in a safe and secure environment? How could we help begin to address the gaps of knowledge that existed, so that as our society continues to be changed by new arrivals, they can work together with First Nations and Aboriginal people on building better communities through a process of shared understanding rather than ignorance and misapprehension? Could we produce together from these dialogues a story of who we are, where we are, and who we aspire to be?

Who am I? Where am I? What is an immigrant? Who was here first?
My name in English is Henry Yu. My Cantonese name is 余全毅, and I was born in Vancouver in the year of Canada's Centennial. My maternal grandfather, Yeung Sing Yew, and his brothers and their father before them, came to British Columbia from Zhongshan county in Guangdong province in China. My parents, Yu Shing Chit and Yeung Kon Yee, came to Canada three years before I was born, joining a community of family and kin who had been crossing the Pacific back and forth for over 150 years. This is my story, my history, and I tell it this way to acknowledge that although I was born here, my family comes from somewhere else, and like all the migrants whose families came to Vancouver from somewhere else, we have made our home on the unceded traditional territory of the Coast Salish people. During the Dialogues Project, urban Aboriginal participants invariably acknowledged, during their stories of "who they were," a story at the same time about the First Nations or Métis communities somewhere else in BC or Canada or the United States from which they or their families came. This story about "where they were from" was at the same time an important acknowledgement about where they were now—that they now lived on someone else's territory as a guest.

It seems like such a simple thing to acknowledge that my family comes from somewhere else and that, except for the First Nations who were here before migrants arrived in the eighteenth and nineteenth centuries from across the Atlantic and Pacific, we are all late arrivals. But in Vancouver, in British Columbia, and in Canada in general, stories of arrival and claims about belonging are fraught with violence. Oftentimes the violence has been physical—involving the removal and abuse of bodies—but the violence has also been a very effective narrative violence, a mythic story of dispossession and possession that renders damage by distorting and celebrating the stories of some people, while silencing and erasing the stories of others.

I was born here, but when I was growing up, the history I learned in school was a collection of stories I could not recognize. "Our" story, I was told, was of people who came from across the water far away, who rode a train across a vast land and built a place called Canada. Some of those people had English names, and some of them had French names. But somehow my grandfather and great-grandfather and people with names like mine were missing. I remember, just once, hearing that the Chinese had helped build the railroad upon which the Canadians rode, but then they disappeared into silence for the rest of the story. What were they doing the rest of the time?

In the third grade, my teacher asked us to build models of either the traditional long houses or the ocean canoes of the Coast Salish people. Since I was eight years old and forbidden at home to use a sharp knife, my older brother helped me carve a canoe out of balsa wood, based upon a picture we found in a library book. I was so proud of my little carving, and after the class celebrated our achievements, I kept the canoe on my desk at home all the way into high school. Seeing it reminded me of the lesson that day in school, about how Native people had lived here before the arrival of Europeans. It was the last time in school that I remember being asked to think about the Aboriginal people in whose land we lived. What were they doing the rest of the time?

The rest of the time.

It is this silent erasure of time that tells another set of histories. Stories ignored or kept in the narrow margins in the sidebars of textbooks. Stories erased from our common past. It is not that the story of my grandfather and others like him was untold. He told it to those within the family, or to his friends, in fragments and snippets. Some of those stories involved interactions and relationships between Chinese and Aboriginal people. There was a world only glimpsed by the rest of us, a world in which the railroad that my great-grandfather and his relatives helped build ran through Indigenous communities all the way up the Fraser Canyon. And even as the Chinese finished laying the tracks in 1885 and were immediately asked to pay an onerous Head Tax in order to keep coming, they kept coming. They kept coming by the boatload in the tens of thousands year after year, working in mines, and in logging camps, and in canneries, and in grocery stores, and the farms that grew the produce for those stores, and as cooks and laundry men, and café and store owners in every small town in BC and across the Prairies all the way to Halifax.

Even as those migrants whose families had come from Europe rode the train westwards and arrived to see Aboriginal people and Chinese everywhere already, those young Chinese men like my great-grandfather walked and rode the train in the other direction, often marrying into local Aboriginal communities and creating a very different world than the one I had learned about in textbooks about "westward" expansion and settlement. When that mixed and unique world was steadily eroded and ended by the ethnic cleansing of Aboriginal people through reserves and residential schooling, and by anti-Asian immigration legislation and exclusion, the traces of memory remained within many Aboriginal communities of Chinese men who were fathers and grandfathers, and kindly local restaurant and store owners in small towns who welcomed rather than turned away all customers no matter their race. But they are only glimpses and fragments, traces of a real, lived history targeted for eradication and erased from a collective memory framed narrowly as a white settler history of the Canadian nation. We supposedly have two "Founding People" of Canada—the English and the French. But when the Canadian Confederation was invented, there were many other people already here, and the colony of British Columbia was just as much in existence as what would become Ontario and Quebec. And the presence already of Chinese, as well as Native Hawaiians and other Pacific migrants in BC, along with the complex Indigenous societies along the coast and in the interior, could not simply be erased. Stories long ignored or forgotten can be told and retold, filling the silences created by erasure.

During the opening launch reception for the Dialogues Project, a short snippet of a documentary made by the Chinese Canadian Historical Society of British Columbia (CCHSBC), entitled *Cedar and Bamboo*, was shown. The film, produced by CCHSBC board member Jennifer Lau and past board member Karin Lee, and directed by Diana Leung and Kamala Todd (who is also one of the City of Vancouver's Dialogues Circle Project Team), focused on the stories of four people of mixed Chinese–Aboriginal ancestry. The film-makers had a powerful vision of the impact that recovering these forgotten and ignored histories could make. By providing a historical context for considering the long history of engagements between Aboriginal people and immigrants who were otherwise unwelcome, the film created an important moment of mutual recognition through a shared past. Musqueam Councillor Grant, one of the three aforementioned co-chairs for the project, spoke movingly about growing up aware of his own mixed ancestry and of his pride of seeing the story of his own father, Howard Grant, featured in the film. The family history of the Grants perhaps exemplified the promise of opening up a dialogue about histories still too uncommonly told, and the challenge of what kind of shared future still awaits us.

So much of our common past is left out of what is supposed to be our common history, so that we are left with an array of uncommon stories that do not add up. One of the triumphs of a white supremacist colonial history of Canada was the mythical alchemy that made it possible for everyone who arrived from Europe to become a "Canadian," and for all those who were non-white to remain a "visible minority," forever arriving late, or a "native" forever destined to disappear. During the early twentieth century, when anti-Asian politics ruled British Columbia, the slogan used was "White Canada Forever," a phrase that meant those who were considered "white" owned not only the future, but also the past. The moment a migrant stepped off the boat in Halifax from Glasgow, even before he climbed aboard the train that might take him all the way to Vancouver, he was already a "Canadian." His "accent" would not undermine his claims to belong in the way that speaking English with an "Oriental" accent would, and still does. Despite the fact that migrants from across the Pacific arrived at the same time on Coast Salish land as those migrants from across the Atlantic, white supremacy built a sense of belonging around "whiteness." Non-English-speaking "white" migrants could gain the status of full belonging in Canada by speaking English and converting themselves to Anglophone dominance. Those who were considered non-white were not accorded the same privileges and possibilities.

Say the word "immigrant" and who do you imagine? To those Aboriginal people whose ancestors welcomed the first trans-Atlantic and trans-Pacific migrants to these shores, everyone else is a migrant to their homeland. If we are to all make a home together here, there can be no reconciliation with the inequities of our past until this simple truth is recognized. But the demographic reality of our present and future must also be taken into account. There is a "New Canada"[2] being made in the last four decades since immigration reform removed racial barriers to non-white migration. The top 10 places of birth for immigrants who arrived in Canada between 2001 and 2006 included only two European countries. The United Kingdom, which was the dominant No.1 sending nation for the first century of Canadian history, was on the list at No. 9, sending just over 25,000 new immigrants. In contrast, six of the top 10 countries were in Asia, and the top four on the list alone—the People's Republic of China, India, the Philippines, and Pakistan—accounted for two-thirds of all new migrants to Canada in that period, with the People's Republic of China sending over 155,000, India over 129,000, the Philippines over 77,000, and Pakistan over 57,000.[3]

In 2006, 83.9 per cent of all new immigrants to Canada came from regions outside of Europe, and the very moniker "visible minority" to designate "non-white" Canadians had become a questionable description, in particular to describe Canada's urban populations. Over 96 per cent of Canada's "visible minorities" live in metropolitan regions. Two main groups—South

Asians and self-identified ethnic Chinese—accounted for half of all visible minorities in Canada,[4] with each accounting for roughly one-quarter of the total. Other migrants from Africa, Latin America and the Caribbean, and Asia are remaking our society. Ethnic Chinese and South Asians account for 8 per cent of Canada's total population, and because they have settled overwhelmingly in either the metropolitan regions of Toronto or Vancouver, they have transformed those cities. Between 1980 and 2001, for instance, the largest proportion of new migrants to Canada were ethnic Chinese who came from various locations in Southeast Asia (including Hong Kong), along with migrants born in the People's Republic of China. These various ethnic Chinese migrants went overwhelmingly (87%) to the five largest cities in Canada, with 41 per cent going to Toronto and 31 per cent to Vancouver alone.[5]

What is clear is that trans-Pacific migration from Asia, as well as "visible minority" migrants in general from outside Europe, has transformed Canada in the last 25 years. Vancouver in particular has become a city in which the term "visible minority" makes no sense. In 2006, four out of 10 Vancouverites had been born outside of Canada, and five out of 10 were of Asian ancestry. Richmond and Burnaby, suburbs of metropolitan Vancouver, were comprised of 65 per cent and 55 per cent visible minorities, respectively, and 50 per cent of Richmond's population is ethnic Chinese; in Vancouver, Canada's third largest city, the "visible minority" is "white."

If the "New Canada" can be understood by looking at the changed face of Vancouver in the present, so too can the future be seen in the largely non-white faces of our youth. Visible minorities in Canada are literally the face of tomorrow—their median age in 2006 was 33 versus an average age of 39 for the population as a whole. The fast growing non-white population of our younger generations also includes First Nations and Aboriginal youth, who represent one of the fastest-growing segments of Canada's young. The future of Canada can be seen in our changing demographics, but are we ready to meet the challenges of this new world?

The Dialogues Project was meant to engage in a sharing of our pasts—who we are and where we are from—but also to create a shared understanding about who we aspire to be in the future. Nine locations were chosen as sites for dialogue, with a mix of participants selected from volunteers and those identified and invited by the Steering Committee as having valuable insights to contribute to the conversations. We strove to include both Elders and youth of Aboriginal and immigrant backgrounds in as many of the groups as possible, recognizing that wisdom and life experience blended with the fresh curiosity of the young was an important element of bridging many of the generational gaps that exist in both Aboriginal and immigrant communities. Each of the groups met three times and was guided in its discussions by one of a set of trained facilitators, led by Eric Wong, and a group of volunteer youth leaders played a prominent role with the intention of having them also lead an outreach process to broaden the process to other youth. A closing dialogue circle involving all of the groups together was held at the Vancouver Public Library, with the Mayor of Vancouver, Gregor Robertson, and several city councillors in attendance, as well as Her Honourable Adrienne Clarkson, the former Governor General of Canada, and her husband John Saul who had taken a keen interest in the Dialogues Project, with the intention of exploring how similar dialogues might take place in other sites across Canada.

After the dialogue circles ended, a series of site visits were organized. The Steering Committee believed that these were crucial for creating a sense of familiarity and welcome among the participants. Urban environments so easily become segregated spaces, and like welcoming a neighbor into one's own home, a mutual process of visitation and hospitality was seen as an organic outgrowth of the sharing of stories within the dialogue circles. At the conclusion of the Dialogues Project, some of the most interesting insights and moments will be made available in both a written and video form. Although all conversations from the circles themselves were private and kept anonymous in order to create and maintain a safe and secure atmosphere for dialogue, follow-up interviews and a summation of many of the issues brought up during the dialogues will become a valuable document that we hope will become the basis for further discussion and educational outreach, in particular, for addressing the dearth of information about First Nations and Aboriginal issues and history currently provided to new immigrants to Canada.

Even as we break the silences and speak the truth about many of the terrible things that have been done in our past, we are left with the task of trying to understand what we have in common, what we can take from our broken past, upon which we can build a shared future. Do we need a shared past in order to have a common future? I became a historian in a quest to answer this basic question, and the Dialogues Project for me is an important part of a collective, collaborative project for those sets of people whose stories have often been silenced or ignored, so that they could speak and hear each other's stories. We hoped that each of us in listening would be able to know ourselves and each other a bit better, and to generate a dialogue that created a mutual understanding of our differences as well as what we shared in common.

We remain so far away from creating together a new shared future. The settlement of land claims and treaty negotiations, and a much-needed reconciliation process, will be long and hard. But perhaps through one story at a time about who we are and where we are from, we can begin to build in a collaborative manner a new shared history, one that recognizes the painful aspects of our past, and perhaps even provides a common understanding of who we are and where we are.

Notes

1   The Steering Committee's first task was to help advise social planner Baldwin Wong on the City of Vancouver's application for a grant from British Columbia's Welcoming and Inclusive Communities and Workplaces Program (WICWP), which receives most of its funding from the federal government under the *Canada–British Columbia Immigration Agreement* (retrieved from: http://www.welcomebc.ca/wbc/service_providers/programs/welcome_program/index.page). The Dialogues Project homepage and a documentation of the process can be found at: http://vancouver.ca/commsvcs/socialplanning/dialoguesproject/index.htm

2   The information here has been adapted and/or excerpted, including statistical data, from my 2009 article: Yu, H. (2009:1012–1013). Global migrants and the new Pacific Canada. *International Journal* 65(4):1011–1026.

3   Statistics Canada, Geography Division (2007). World: Place of Birth of New Immigrants to Canada, 2006. In *2006 Census of Canada*. Romania at No. 7 was the origin of just over 28,000 immigrants. Also see: Immigration to Canada from the Asia Pacific, 1961–1996. In *Population & Immigration Statistical Report*. Vancouver, BC: Asia Pacific Foundation of Canada. (Original source: 1996 Census).

4   Chui, T., K. Tran, and H. Maheux (2007). *Immigration in Canada: A Portrait of the Foreign-born Population, 2006 Census*. Ottawa, ON: Minister of Industry.

5   Chinese Canada is not homogeneous, with a great variety of linguistic and social variation reflecting varied origins not only in Asia, but from around the globe. The same can be said of South Asians, who, like ethnic Chinese, often come to Canada as part of global diasporas that emanated from home villages decades and even centuries earlier, bringing with them to Canada a wide array of family journeys and complicated histories from around the world and over many generations. By 2006, South Asians had slightly surpassed ethnic Chinese as the largest group of "visible minorities" in Canada, but both are categories that envelop a complex spectrum of family and personal histories that cannot be reduced to simple ethno-cultural or racial categorizations. See: Guo, Shibao and Don Devoretz (2005, February). The Changing Faces of Chinese Immigrants. In *Research on Immigration and Integration in the Metropolis,* No. 05–08. Vancouver, BC: Vancouver Centre of Excellence.

Section 3: Transformation

Roy Miki

Vancouver writer, poet, and editor **Roy Miki** taught in the English Department at Simon Fraser University from the mid-1970s until his retirement in 2007. He was a specialist in North American modernist and contemporary literature, and his teaching and research focused on the critical and creative implications of anti-racist theory, cultural studies, poetics, Canadian literature, minority literature, and Asian Canadian cultural production. A *sansei* (third generation) Japanese Canadian, Roy was born in Winnipeg in 1942 only months after his family was forcibly moved to Ste. Agathe, Manitoba, from their home in Haney, British Columbia. They were directly affected by the government's wartime decision to uproot, dispossess, and intern Japanese Canadians living on the West Coast of British Columbia. This cataclysmic event shaped Roy's formative years as an intellectual and as a writer. In the 1980s, as one of the spokespersons for the Japanese Canadian redress movement, he served on the Strategy Committee of the National Association of Japanese Canadians (NAJC), the organization that negotiated the historic redress settlement with the Canadian government on 22 September 1988. He has written numerous articles on redress as well as two books: with Cassandra Kobayashi, *Justice in Our Time: The Japanese Canadian Redress Movement*, a history of the NAJC's movement (NAJC/Talonbooks, 1991) and, more recently, *Redress: Inside the Japanese Canadian Call for Justice* (Raincoast, 2004), a work that blends archival sources, personal history, interviews, and critical commentary. Roy has also published four books of poetry, *Saving Face* (Turnstone, 1991), *Random Access File* (Red Deer Press, 1994), *Surrender* (Mercury, 2001), and *There* (New Star Books, 2006), as well as *Broken Entries* (Mercury, 1998), a collection of critical essays that examine race issues, writing, and subjectivity. *Surrender* was selected for the 2002 Governor General's Award for poetry. As an editor he has published work by bpNichol, George Bowering, and Roy K. Kiyooka. His most recent edited work is Kiyooka's *The Artist and the Moose: A Fable of Forget* (LineBooks, 2009). Three books are forthcoming: *Mannequin Rising* (New Star Books), a book of poems, *In Flux: Transnational Signs of Asian Canadian Writing* (NeWest Press), a collection of essays, and *Dolphins' SOS* (Tradewind Books), a children's story written in collaboration with his wife Slavia Miki. Roy received the Order of Canada in 2006 and the Order of British Columbia in 2009.

By Turns Poetic: Redress as Transformation

For Canadians of Japanese ancestry, the 22 September 1988 redress settlement with the federal government stood as the culmination of a difficult effort to resolve a complex of injustices endured in the 1940s—from mass uprooting to dispossession, internment, and, for many, the ignominy of deportation. That was the historic day when they received the long-awaited acknowledgement of the injustices, along with individual and community compensation, pardons for those wrongfully convicted, citizenship for those who had been deported as well as their children, and a public foundation to fight racism, eventually established as the Canadian Race Relations Foundation.

My account of this event in *Redress: Inside the Japanese Canadian Call for Justice* situated the redress movement in the multi-faceted interplay between the national politics of citizenship with its democratic values and the subjective spaces of memory and desire that constituted the history of Japanese Canadians (hereafter JCs), myself included, across several generations.[1] The heart-wrenching consequences of dispersal from our West Coast homes saturated the nooks and crannies of my childhood, feeding my imagination with stories of tearful separations and losses, not only of properties and belongings, but more deeply of dignity and well-being. Once we were branded "Enemy Alien" and reduced to nothing more than "of the Japanese race," a phrase devised by the government, we were transfigured as scapegoats who would bear the mark of the enemy.[2,3]

As far back as memory takes me, this mark was attached to the body, acting very much like a hovering shadow, *there* even when it was not apparent in consciousness. The shadow spread over the broader imagination of the events that dismantled the social, cultural, and economic fabric of ties *back* to the family homes in Haney, British Columbia, the small town in the lush, fruit-laden region of the Fraser Valley. In my young imagination, my family's expulsion from the West Coast meant that my own birth during their confinement in the site of relocation, Ste. Agathe, a small French-Canadian town not far from Winnipeg, must constitute a form of exile. Such a condition spawned an often-aching sense of absences—of a much richer and grounded home site *back there*, of closely knit community ties *back there*, and of a nurturing geography *back there*. Always *back there*. These absences were made tangible in memories of lost family photo albums, stored in a trunk with other memorabilia to be saved by neighbours, only to be sold off for a pittance at one of many government-sponsored public auctions. The few photos that were kept for the trip across country, as mementoes of what was left behind, became haunting icons of pre-internment life. It was the aura of estrangement from the past that shaped my childhood memory of the inner streets of Winnipeg where I grew up in the postwar years. Nowhere was this more palpable, at least to my young ears, than in one story, a bona fide ghost story, my father, Kazuo, told me many times.

Kazuo was born in BC in 1906 and grew up in *Nihon machi* (or "Japantown"), the area around Powell and Alexander Streets in Vancouver, where the majority of JCs in the city lived prior to the mass uprooting. One dark and stormy summer evening—yes, it had to be dark and stormy—a friend from the Fraser Valley, who couldn't return home, decided to stay at a Powell Street hotel. All the rooms were booked except for the one that was normally left empty. Rumours circulated in the community that it was haunted by a young woman murdered by her lover. Not superstitious at all, in fact, scoffing at the belief in ghosts, my father's friend rented the room. Well, not unexpectedly, since this was a ghost story, he was awakened in the middle of the night by moaning sounds. There in the smoked glass of the door appeared the figure of a woman with long black hair crying out to him for help. When the figure disappeared, he fled the hotel. The kicker, my father said, and this has always stuck with me, the ghost disappeared with the community when *Nihon machi* was dismantled in the mass uprooting in 1942. The story stuck with me so closely that my own version of it came to me in a poem, first written in the early 1970s. It invoked the figure of an old woman who used to wander the streets and back lanes of our central Winnipeg neighbourhood. She constantly talked to herself in Japanese, and in her rambling speech she was always hunting for signposts of her lost Vancouver community. Like the ghost in my father's story, she became a manifestation of the internal effects of internment. I had recently moved to Vancouver, and as I wandered the Powell Street area, as I often did at the time, she appeared in my imagination, for me a premonition of the redress movement on the horizon—a movement that, in many ways, was driven by the desire to mediate a past haunted by the unacknowledged traumas of internment.

It is not surprising that, at first, many JCs shied away from public meetings on redress. There was the anxiety of being visible, of being perceived as other, and even of a racist backlash. Redress awakened memories of a past that had not been put to rest. When their surfaces were rubbed, even in casual

Photo: National Archives of Canada C47398

conversations, individuals relived the scenes of uprooting, confinement, and suffering; once again unable to mediate the violations they had endured. They had learned that to be JC was to inhabit a consciousness that was divided by an internal contradiction: while "Canadian" signified the security of citizenship rights, national belonging, and democratic forms of governance, "Japanese" conjured the ghost of Enemy Alien, an identity that had condemned them to the dark underside of the nation—where they had been deprived of voice and the power to defend themselves.

Although government authorities, including the RCMP and the military, knew from evidence that the mass uprooting was not a necessary security measure, and that it reflected a capitulation to racist pressures in BC, decades had passed and nothing official had been done to acknowledge the injustices. Without such public recognition, JCs continued to bear the stigma of being identified as Enemy Alien. Having undergone the pressure to assimilate— to become the model minority—they still carried deep inside them the emotional and psychic haunting of internment. But how to move from here to there—from the condition of haunting to the House of Commons, the inner sanctum of the nation's power?

By using the *War Measures Act* to intern JCs, the government could argue as administrators and politicians did that it acted legally. Consequently, when the National Association of Japanese Canadians (NAJC) initiated redress as a political movement, they based their call for justice on the abuse of the *War Measures Act*. In other words, the government's policies may have been legal, but the effects of these policies—mass uprooting, dispossession, forced dispersal, and deportation—far exceeded the norms of fairness and due process under the law. The violation of citizenship rights on the basis of ascribed racial origin—being categorized as "of the Japanese race"—could not be defended as a necessary security measure.

Designing the call for redress would involve urgent questions of narrative, voice, and position, all the elements that required a careful attention to the language of redress. Shaping these elements took over two years, as the NAJC worked to bring together a fragmented group of JCs, who lacked knowledge of political movements and who had to struggle against the temptation to remain silent. But more, the role of "victim," often raised in the context of redress, especially by the national media, was rejected by many JCs. While they held the government accountable for their losses, they remained proud of the ways in which they managed to rebuild their lives and to maintain their loyalty to the Canadian nation. Their belief in democratic principles explains why the language of citizenship struck such a resonant chord for them, confirming as it did their efforts over many decades to be responsible Canadians. The abrogation of their rights, especially for the *Nisei* (second generation) in Canada, signified the ultimate insult to their faith in democracy. This attitude became a critical component of the case for redress presented in the NAJC's 1984 brief to the federal government. Instead of adopting the voice of victims who sought compensation for losses and damages (the language of law), the brief focused primarily on the democratic system itself. When the government wrongfully interned JCs, it argued, the principles of democratic governance were "betrayed" in its actions. *Democracy Betrayed: The Case for Redress*, the key document that propelled the NAJC's redress movement into the area of national politics, was released in Ottawa on 21 November 1984.[4]

The redress settlement may have been a political end to a long struggle for justice, but it was also the very medium through which a painful past could be transformed. Redress dominated my daily life for nearly a decade, drawing me into a relentless schedule of meetings, talks, lobbying sessions, and trips all over Canada. At times, the endless attention it required was all so overwhelming that the threat of pessimism and failure—of a collapse into cynicism—was never far away. But deeply immersed in the struggle, perhaps because of this, there were the more poetic moments—those astonishing moments when a turn would occur to reveal one of the signposts on what eventually became an unfolding path towards the settlement. My old friend, the poet bpNichol, who died suddenly and unexpectedly just days following the redress settlement, often talked about the need to "trust in the process" to get us through a creative negotiation with form. Maintaining a belief in redress called for this same trust in process and a respect for what it would conjure at the most unexpected occasions. I'll draw from three poetic moments of many; these are ones of extraordinary significance because they occurred during the summer of 1984, a period when the national redress movement took on a shape of its own.

One

The summer of 1984 was a volatile time for redress. An all-party government report on the effects of racism in Canada called *Equality Now!* had been issued with a recommendation in favour of a redress settlement,[5] but the Liberal government of Pierre Eliot Trudeau, and especially Trudeau himself, aggressively ruled out both an official acknowledgement of injustices and direct compensation. The most his government would offer was a statement of "regret" for what happened to JCs and a few million dollars to set up a vaguely described institute to commemorate their internment. At this same time, the talk of redress was creating waves within JC communities, and debates suddenly became strained in the face of Trudeau's rejection.

Photo: Probably Tak Toyota, National Archives of Canada C46355

Photo: Leonard Frank, Japanese Canadian National Museum, Vancouver

Those of us trying to mount a redress movement in Vancouver decided to hold a public event on the evening before the large Powell Street Festival in Vancouver, the annual JC celebration held in Oppenheimer Park, set in the heart of what was once *Nihon machi*. Because of the reluctance of many senior JCs to be visible in public events, we knew that it was important to feature prominent speakers. Luckily, three speakers with large public profiles quickly said yes: David Suzuki, CBC broadcaster and scientist, Joy Kogawa, author of *Obasan*,[6] and Ann Sunahara, author of *The Politics of Racism: The Uprooting of Japanese Canadians during the Second World War*.[7] The only voice missing, at least from our perspective, was that of Tom Shoyama, one of the most well-regarded Nisei in the community. Shoyama had been the editor of *The New Canadian*,[8] the only community newspaper allowed to publish during the internment. In the postwar years, Shoyama garnered a national reputation as an influential organizer with Tommy Douglas's CCF (Cooperative Commonwealth Federal) party in Saskatchewan, and when he moved into federal politics he rose to become the deputy minister of finance under Liberal MP John Turner. Rumours were that Shoyama wanted to distance himself from the redress issue and, even more critically, did not support individual compensation. He had not responded to our invitation to speak at the event.

I was in Ottawa, more specifically at the Ottawa airport, on my way back home after a redress meeting, and worrying because we had not heard from Shoyama. If only I could talk with him face to face, so I thought, I could convince him to attend. As a highly respected Nisei, there was no doubt in my mind that his appearance would encourage many of his generation to attend. I had my head down, jotting down some notes for the conference, but then I glanced up and across the large waiting area of the airport. There, seated in the distance was a slender built man with a gentle face who looked like a JC. Tom Shoyama, I thought, could it be him? Could it actually be the one person I wanted to speak to at this very moment? I walked over to him and asked, "Tom Shoyama?" He smiled and nodded yes. After introducing myself as a coordinator for the conference, he politely said no thanks to the invitation. As a last resort I proposed that we sit together for the short flight from Ottawa to Toronto, his destination, and that if he felt the same way when we landed, I would respect his decision. He agreed, and luckily the flight was not full so we were able to sit beside each other. By the time we landed, he agreed to be our keynote speaker—and then off he went for another meeting of the Macdonald Commission on the economy, of which he was a member. At the public event, which filled to capacity (and more) inside the old Japanese Language Hall on Alexander Street, Shoyama publicly came out in favour of redress.

Two

That same summer the national political world was rife with anticipation, as John Turner replaced Trudeau, and all of the federal parties began campaigning for the September election. The NAJC was preparing a redress brief to submit to the political party that formed the next government. I was part of the brief writing committee, and given my background in academic research, I was asked to visit the national archives in Ottawa to make sure that our references to historic documents were accurate.

On the plane to Ottawa, I was busily working my way through one of the numerous drafts, noting which documents had to be located in which of the enormous number of files on internment that were housed at the national archives. While doing so, I was drawn from time to time into a conversation with a passenger next to me. As he picked up bits and pieces of what I was planning to do in Ottawa, he became more and more curious about the notion of redress and the brief we intended to submit to the federal government. He queried me about the mass uprooting, the destruction of the West Coast communities, and the confiscation of properties and belongings. He had grown up in the Maritimes, he said, and had little knowledge of the internment, but he expressed enthusiasm for the current decision to redress that past. I was in the process of pondering, yet again, the power of one BC politician in the cabinet of the Liberal government of Mackenzie King. Ian Mackenzie, a Vancouver MP, was perhaps the most vocal anti-JC voice in politics at the time, and his animosity evoked fear and anxiety among all JCs. Mackenzie campaigned stridently to expel them from BC, and they knew that in Ottawa his influence, as chair of the cabinet committee deciding on what to do about their presence on the west coast, had led directly to their mass uprooting and dispossession. It was Mackenzie whose campaign slogan was "Not a single Japanese from the Rockies to the sea!"[9] We cited his slogan in our redress brief, one of the most memorable of racist statements that were etched in the memories of JCs. Landing time came, and as we said our goodbyes my fellow passenger said that he would be watching for news about the progress of the movement. When we shook hands, he said his name was Ian Mackenzie—and then, as quickly as a moment passing, he blended into the crowd of departing passengers.

Three

On the last day of the parliamentary session, just before the campaign period began, Opposition leader Brian Mulroney challenged Trudeau's dismissal of redress. His voice rising in signs of anger, Trudeau once again declared that his government was not accountable for the past injustices endured by JCs.

Photo: Japanese Canadian Cultural Centre, Toronto

It was then that Mulroney declared that a Conservative government would "compensate" JCs, a statement that would be used in the four years ahead during which the NAJC would lobby his government. No one then expected the powerful Liberal machinery under Trudeau's leadership to crumble, but crumble it did by the time that John Turner took over as leader. In his brief public statements on redress, Turner revealed some distancing from the inflexible stance of Trudeau, though he did not make any commitments towards redress.

Turner's popularity was so unstable that his Liberal team decided that he should not take the chance of losing in Ontario and, instead, should run in the safest Liberal riding in Vancouver, the Point Grey riding of Quadra. The NAJC had not been able get close to Turner, but I thought that if we could simply talk to him we could get him to say his Liberal government would reconsider the question of redress. This is as much as we could expect, given Trudeau's response on behalf of the Liberal government.

I was sitting in our kitchen in our West 15th residence wondering what kind of strategy might work when I glanced outside to see a large bus coming slowly down the street. No doubt about it, the logo on its side boldly announced that the Liberal campaign was in full throttle in our neighbourhood. I quickly called my wife, Slavia, and my two kids, Waylen and Elisse, and then, just adjacent to our house, there was the man himself, John Turner, stepping down from the bus. I grabbed my camera and we all ran outside.

Looking somewhat haggard and drained of energy, Turner still remained upbeat, acting the role of the consummate politician. I thanked him half-jokingly for taking the time to visit me to talk about redress, and he smiled back in good humour. Surprisingly he seemed familiar with my work on the issue. We would wish him well, I said, if he would promise to keep the issue open after the election. He nodded, acknowledging that the issue was important to him, which for me was a positive-enough reply that the NAJC could use to continue lobbying for him in Ottawa. Turner would be elected in Quadra, but his party would suffer a devastating blow in the elections, losing 107 seats—from 147 to 40—in the House of Commons to a triumphant Conservative party. In the years ahead, when he assumed the role of Opposition leader, to his credit Turner consistently maintained support for a negotiated settlement with the NAJC. We marked the auspicious moment the Prime Minister paid us a visit by having his aide take a family photo with him—and then, as quickly as he arrived, off he went down the street with his liberal entourage.

Departures as Arrivals: Four Photo Collages

Being haunted by a history of absences, if left unmediated, can become an arrested condition of consciousness. The past takes on an overwhelming power and places a barrier between the imagination and the immediacy of the present. In the process, the future loses its potential fecundity and comes to reproduce the effects of absence. Redress was played out in the arena of public opinion and political dynamics, but it was always more than the settlement achieved on 22 September 1988, as large as that event was for JCs and for Canadians who supported them. What I have called the poetic moments offered a transitional turn from a haunted past to a present with the potential to imagine a more generative future. It was as if the signposts of redress were evidence that much larger forces of justice were at work—that redress even confirmed a spiritual energy that enabled new creative forms to emerge. For me, so much of the haunted past that was part of my childhood was invoked in the photos—of the figures departing for an unknown future—that have appeared many times over in various accounts of the internment. These photos acted as touchstones for me during the redress movement. The haunting of dislocation is manifest in their faces, even as they look into the camera's eye and make the most out of what is clearly a catastrophic personal and collective moment. I choose four of these photos for transformation in the accompanying collages. In these visual images, which also incorporate current photos of local sites—once local to prewar JCs—I have sought to imagine the event of departures as arrivals on the shores of a post-redress phase of transformation. These are not shores where the difficulties of encountering our current commodity culture are erased but spaces in which its complex complicities are imagined beyond the reproduction of a framed history *back there*.

Notes

1 Miki, Roy (2004). *Redress: Inside the Japanese Canadian Call for Justice*. Vancouver, BC: Raincoast Books.

2 Wood, S.T. (1942, February 7). A Public Notice by the Commissioner of the Royal Canadian Mounted Police Addressed to Male Enemy Aliens. Retrieved 2 November 2010 from: http://www.najc.ca/thenandnow/experiencec_firstorder.php

3 St. Laurent, L.S. (1942, February 26). A public notice by the Minister of Justice addressed to all persons of Japanese racial origin. Retrieved 2 November 2010 from: http://www.najc.ca/thenandnow/experiencec_removal.php

4 National Association of Japanese Canadians (1984). *Democracy Betrayed: The Case for Redress*. A Submission to the Government of Canada on the Violation of Rights and Freedoms of Japanese Canadians during and after World War II. Winnipeg, MB: National Association of Japanese Canadians.

5 Special Committee on Visible Minorities in Canadian Society (1984). *Equality Now! Report of the Special Committee on Visible Minorities in Canadian Society*. Ottawa, ON: Queen's Printer. Bob Daudlin served as Committee Chair.

6 Kogawa, Joy (1981). *Obasan*. Toronto, ON: Penguin Canada.

7 Sunahara, A. Gomer (2000). *The Politics of Racism: The Uprooting of Japanese Canadians During the Second World War*. (2nd ed.). Ottawa, ON: Ann Gomer Sunahara. Retrieved 26 November 2010 from: http://www.japanesecanadianhistory.ca/index.html

8 *The New Canadian*, an English-only newspaper that was billed as the voice of the Nisei, began publishing in 1938 in Vancouver. Tom Shoyama took over as English editor from the original editor, Peter Higashi, in 1939.

9 Dyer, J. (1944, September 19). 'No Japs for B.C.' Mackenzie's pledge. *The Vancouver Sun*: 19.

Ravi de Costa and Tom Clark

Ravi de Costa is Assistant Professor in the Faculty of Environmental Studies at York University, Toronto. He is an interdisciplinary social scientist who researches the political cultures of settler societies, relationships between Indigenous and non-Indigenous peoples, and the politicization of Indigenous peoples in the global context. Ravi has written extensively about reconciliation in Australia and treaty-making in Canada, as well as publishing two books that examine the global movement of Indigenous peoples.

Tom Clark is a tenured senior lecturer in the School of Communication and the Arts at Victoria University, Melbourne. He writes and teaches across a range of fields in Cultural Studies, Literature, and Public Relations, combining a scholarly background in poetry and poetics with professional experience as a policy advisor and political speechwriter in government and the union movement in Australia. At the time of writing this chapter, Tom is also completing a book-length study of poetic qualities inherent in contemporary political speech.

Ravi and Tom have been creative collaborators since 1993, when they were undergraduate students together at the University of Sydney. This chapter's research interest in non-Aboriginal discourses of reconciliation arises from a collaborative research project that both authors have been conducting in Canada and Australia since 2008. The idea of a shared non-Indigenous stake in processes of reconciliation is problematic across all settler societies where national governments seek to revisit and retool fundamental aspects of the colonial past. Canada's Truth and Reconciliation Commission is an internationally significant case of that movement.

Exploring non-Aboriginal Attitudes towards Reconciliation in Canada: The Beginnings of Targeted Focus Group Research

Reconciliation in settler societies like Canada is an optimistic but vague aspiration, one that most broadly connotes improved relations between Aboriginal and non-Aboriginal people. The motivations of would-be reconcilers and opponents of reconciliation vary widely, as do the specifics of what they think they mean by the word—and so it has a diverse array of critics and supporters. However defined, reconciliation is also a leading element of the mandate of the Truth and Reconciliation Commission (TRC), one of the key institutions of the *Indian Residential Schools Settlement Agreement*. In its variety and complexity, it has become an integral part of the response to the long and brutal history of residential schooling in Canada.

Part of reconciliation's difficulty is its malleability, which appears to ignore or even to normalize numerous other injustices of colonization—indeed many suggest the very process of reconciliation implies the legitimation of Canadian colonization itself. That its main vehicle in this case, the TRC, is an agency partly beholden to the state means such criticisms must persist. While the churches have a special role in the residential schools history, discussing that has become politically contentious, including for the TRC's own staff. Revealingly, the TRC's founding mandate does not define or characterize the responsibilities of Canada's non-Aboriginal population.

Our approach is to consider reconciliation as national discourse. Indeed, the TRC is largely mandated as an exercise in discourse. Its methodology, starting with the June 2010 national event we attended in Winnipeg, prioritizes testimony—residential school Survivors "telling their stories." That means research into its processes is first and foremost a case study in applied communications. It is also a study in discourse control: instead of testimony being "given," which implies an agency of the Survivor, the TRC (effectively an arm of the state, although it would position itself differently) is engaged as a proactive witness of sorts, soliciting and co-opting the expertise of Witness–Survivors in such statement-recording, and putting in place all the mechanisms of support deemed necessary.[1]

What should and can non-Aboriginal people seek to do as the TRC undertakes its work of documenting the history of residential schools and being "witness" to its legacy? As two non-Aboriginal academics with familiarity of the Australian experience of reconciliation, we argue that this is something that requires greater attention.[2] Moreover, we argue that the nature of Canadian social diversity and change has not been attended to in discussions of reconciliation; an assumption of an undifferentiated category of "non-Aboriginal Canadians" is no more a useful way to proceed than is the persistent generalization of Aboriginal people in a range of cultural discourse and policy discussions. We are currently engaged in a project that we hope will last at least the duration of the TRC, and what we present here are some initial findings.

In seeking to understand non-Aboriginal diversity then, and what role it may have in shaping attitudes towards reconciliation, we do not seek to make some defined groups more or less responsible for reconciliation than others. Our firm view is that all "newcomers" need to understand not only that Canada is a nation-state built on the territories of existing communities largely without their consent, but also that the original expropriation must always mark our response. Nevertheless, we do seek to understand how attitudes toward reconciliation vary, according to such factors as location, language spoken, and familial experience in Canada.

Two interrelated challenges for our research are: (1) how to understand the meanings of reconciliation among non-Aboriginal people in Canada; and (2) how to reflect on the ideological commitments underlying those meanings. In particular, we are interested in "quotidian discourses" of reconciliation. By this we mean ideas about reconciliation among groups who do not identify themselves as particularly politicized or actively engaged in issues affecting Aboriginal people in Canada. That is a conscious choice: we think the reality for many non-Aboriginal people is that they have few opportunities to articulate their attitudes towards reconciliation or Aboriginal people in social contexts and, consequently, misinformation and prejudice inform those few occasions when such issues arise. In moving from an understanding and practice of reconciliation that is less vague and more effective, we believe we need to know more specifically the patterns of misunderstanding that prevail.

Moreover, we think that this non-engagement is a crucial obstacle to a substantive shift in relations, whether that means greater autonomy for Aboriginal people on their own territories, or greater access to the prosperity of and in non-Aboriginal society, or both. For example, in our research we ask whether non-Aboriginal people in Canada have regular interactions with Aboriginal people. Of those, how many are positive or even civil? If reconciliation is to be of concern to more than a social and political elite, it will need to be grounded in a better understanding of everyday life than it currently is.

Consequently, we are especially interested in the *ways* in which non-Aboriginal people talk about reconciliation in Canada in non-Aboriginal discourses. The central insight of critical discourse analysis is that language is an important indicator of people's understanding of, and endorsement of, prevailing power structures and of their ideologies.[3] This manifests in the (referential) themes people discuss in relation to reconciliation, of course, but it also plays out in the (textural) poetics of their discourse. As Klemperer wrote, reflecting in the aftermath of another genocide, "What a man says may be a pack of lies – but his true self is laid bare for all to see in the style of his utterances."[4] Obtaining a deeper understanding of non-Aboriginal attitudes towards reconciliation in a multicultural settler society such as Canada's requires us to augment the thematic analysis of public and private discourses with the analysis of their poetics.[5]

Methodology

Scholars have fruitfully used analyses of comparative literature, of mainstream media, and of public or institutional documents to set out important insights and offer critical frameworks for understanding dominant discourses, particularly those pertaining to questions of race and identity. In Canada, scholars have, for example, written about the valorization of Canadian citizenship,[6] or non-Aboriginal violence affecting Aboriginal people, particularly women.[7] In other settler societies we can draw out various ideas from research that studies settler identities and attitudes using interviews[8] or ethnography.[9] However, in this research we are seeking out everyday discourses, initially using a methodology of focus groups. Focus groups have been used in comparable research elsewhere,[10] and lend themselves to the identification and mapping of latent discourses that emerge in social contexts. So far, we have learned some preliminary things about non-Aboriginal discourses.

Our approach is to locate or solicit non-Aboriginal discourses about reconciliation and particularly about residential schools among those not engaged in activism, solidarity, or campaigning on any Aboriginal policy issue. We held a small series of focus groups among undergraduate students at York University in June of 2010. Students were recruited with a poster campaign and using student bulletin boards on campus, and participants were offered compensation for their attendance. We gave potential participants a short questionnaire to ascertain their existing levels of knowledge, and also to learn whether they, their parents, and their grandparents were born in Canada. We divided the respondents into three groups: those who had been born in Canada and whose parents and grandparents had all been born in Canada (category A); those who had been born outside Canada (category B); and a group comprising those born in Canada but for whom more than one parent/grandparent had been born outside the country (category C). Our goal in doing this was to explore any role that one's length of personal or familial experience with Canada might play in shaping everyday discussions.

In total, we recruited four focus groups and a total of 29 people arrived to participate, with each group having between five and nine participants. We had enough respondents to form one group for category A (hereafter FG1) and category C (FG2), and two groups for category B (FG3 and FG4). Each discussion lasted about one hour and fifteen minutes. We recorded these sessions and made transcripts of the recordings. Each focus group was facilitated using the same Discussion Guide, which covered the Indian residential school (IRS) system, the Truth and Reconciliation Commission, and the national apology to those affected by the IRS system. Using these as a lens, we explored the following general themes:

(1) Is there an obligation to learn about Aboriginality and what should that entail?

(2) How is Aboriginal history understood; for example, as genocide, as misfortune, as survival, or as progress?

(3) Is there acceptance of Aboriginal cultural difference as an enduring fact of Canadian life?

Findings

For the focus groups, we had significant difficulty in recruiting people in category A. By the time we had recruited barely enough people for a group in that category, we had enough for two full groups in category B. We do not draw elaborate conclusions from this: there could be multiple explanations to do with the method of recruitment, the campus, or the time of year.[11] However, we are interested in the broader issue of non-Aboriginal people's willingness to engage in subjects that may lead to uncomfortable or unsettling realizations. Indeed, for some recent writers, it is precisely the question of "decentring" or "unsettling" the settler within that is the key to reconciliation.[12] Low response rates and levels of participation, then, may be an indication of a deeper concern.

Indeed, category A was the most reticent of all four focus groups we conducted. They appeared and sounded uncomfortable when the discussion began, and particularly on questions of present responsibilities for the IRS system. In particular, we observed numerous instances of the "why weren't we told?" syndrome.[13] In the following exchange from FG1, there is an implication that this was a policy carried out without public knowledge and against Canadian values and expectations:

> LINDA: But also I think Aboriginal cultures have been and still are so isolated from mainstream Canada. Like, I didn't even know this was going on and I'm sure that there were a lot of people even over that same time period that didn't know it was happening. The government obviously didn't tell people, "Hey we're taking this culture and trying to eradicate them." Maybe people would have been more up in arms about it, had they known. I don't know.

> MICHAEL: Well, it was founded in 1870, like, back then it was easy for people to grab on to catchphrases, right, that were easy to print like, "Kill the Indian in the child," right, and it becomes something that can kind of continue, yeah, taking over 100 years to fix it.

Indeed that assumption, about the inherent goodness of dominant societies, is, we think, one of the key obstacles to deeper social transformation. It is made possible by recurrent errors about the most basic facts of Indian residential schools. Across all four focus groups, the levels of knowledge about Aboriginal issues were limited and often mistaken about fundamental details. Our expectations here were not high, but we were still struck by the extent of respondents' misconceptions, spanning both those more and less sympathetic to the goals of the TRC. Among those who were cynical about its aims, one participant in category A suggested that the apology was a response to blockades that were going on around the country, a view that was uncontested by others in the group. No one in any of our focus groups could confidently provide more than rudimentary information about what took place in residential schools or what responses there had been. What they declared usually restated the few facts we had shown in a video extract from the Prime Minister's apology speech to the Commons. This is not a surprising finding—indeed much of the discussion about reconciliation and the TRC has sought to "break the silence" about residential schools—but given that these are students currently receiving education in a Canadian university, it does reveal the magnitude of the challenge that the TRC has in educating Canadians, or in imagining that such education will help to effect reconciliation.

Several participants recollected material on the IRS system from their school experiences, but several observed a distance between the issue and themselves or peers. Janet's (FG2) comments were indicative:

> JANET: Well, how I feel about that, as Canadians who've been born here, who've grown up here or immigrated here or whatever, I feel like a lot of people are aware of these kinds of things in a basic understanding, but I feel that a lot of students feel very segregated from it. Do you know what I mean? We're not exposed to it a lot and we're not really aware that much of it. Even in the media, I feel like there's such a lack of awareness, um, I don't

> know—as a student here, I feel very, very separated from the issues that are going on. Do you know what I mean?

All groups thought more education is necessary, but there was less consensus on what education should comprise and who it should be for. Some felt that better education should be provided for Aboriginal people so that they could succeed in Canadian society. Most participants felt non-Aboriginal people should learn more about Aboriginal people and their history, but there was a division in some groups over whether that should encompass learning about Aboriginal culture and history in general, or simply the specific history of residential schools and its legacy. Some felt these issues were fundamentally intertwined, but others saw them as very distinct. Several participants felt that learning about the IRS system constituted their own personal responsibility, but most discussed the need for education without specifying who it was that should be educated.

A related topic that we sought to explore was the idea of interpersonal relations between Aboriginal and non-Aboriginal people. Our respondents reported very little personal contact with any Aboriginal people (only two made any reference to such contacts), and yet there was a universal agreement that more extensive personal connections would be important to improving relations. Of the two who discussed Aboriginal individuals whom they knew personally, one in category B reflected that her relationships with Aboriginal people had helped her overcome considerable prejudices. One in category A mentioned that he knew Aboriginal people but went on to characterize them as victims, hopelessly afflicted by a life of drugs and alcohol.

Perhaps the most striking finding in terms of the subject matter was the readiness of the groups in categories B and C to talk about race and racial discrimination, whereas category A did not raise this at all. We did not use any of these terms in the topics we posed but many participants in categories B and C were able to swiftly represent the IRS system as racist. In thinking about the government's response to the IRS system, Catherine (FG2) asked: "They've said this apology, but what have they done? Just in their actions, what have they shown? They still have their discrimination, their biases towards the First Nations people in Canada, and it's really shameful." Zach's (FG4) comments were among some of the most sustained remarks of this sort:

> ZACH: I'm not sure if we even have a full grasp for what they went through. Because technically the proper term for residential schools and all these people went through is social and cultural genocide. And that is a horrific thing to go through, regardless of on whatever stage. It's not as simple as, "You're assimilating them into our culture." We were stripping them of all

of their needs, made them naked in every society, and powerless, and then turned them into little Indian robots for Canadian kind of wellbeing or what's good for us.

In fact, several respondents in categories B and C saw the discrimination against Aboriginal people as part of a broader orientation in Canada affecting all minorities. Ehi (FG3), who identified himself as being from Nigeria, put it as follows:

> EHI: It's almost the same concept of trying to create the perfect, white model of society. So I say it's Canadians like the government itself has a big responsibility like, trying to merge the cultures together, because it's the second Canada is multicultural above, it's... there's a model of an ideal Canadian and Aboriginals don't fit into that. Most immigrants don't fit into that. They have to walk on the aspect of the old Canadian cultural system to like, incorporate all different cultures into, because Aboriginals have certain beliefs, Blacks have certain beliefs, Italians have certain beliefs, and you know, it's...they have to merge that into taking stock of each person's perspective.

As we have suggested above, in addition to surveying literal questions of topicality—of *what* people know and believe—we want to explore *how*: the terms in which respondents express their knowledge and beliefs. In part, this is because it helps us understand what respondents think they mean by the terms they use, the information they cite. An especially revealing case in point was the use of personal pronouns *we* and *they* and their various grammatical aspects (*us, our, ours, them, their,* and *theirs*). When discussing reconciliation in an Aboriginal context, all respondents in all focus groups articulated a *we* that included all non-Aboriginal Canadians and a *they* that specifically and exclusively indexed Aboriginal people in Canada. In the context of reconciliation between *us and them*, this categorization entailed that all of Canada's non-Aboriginal people had a shared stake in the process. The only moment this lexis slipped was when one of our category B groups interrogated it explicitly—but the conclusion they drew (unprompted by us) was to affirm the prevailing us/them dichotomy. These remarks from recently immigrated Canadians seem extremely pointed in the broader consideration of non-Aboriginal attitudes—in mentioning the topic explicitly, these respondents have posed the exception that proves the rule:

> CYNTHIA: It's interesting that we're talking about, "they, they" and you said Canada, and I'm always asking myself, so Canada: who? Who is Canada? Who represents it? And who is responsible to make that apology? And you also mentioned about the Chinese experience, and that goes with so many other cultures. I could talk about the Black experience, I could talk about the Jewish experience, so everybody has their own issue they're all waiting for some sort of um, compensation or something that the government recognizes, but who? Who are we holding accountable at the end of the day? We say we are Canadian, that's a wild question to ask.

MARIA: It's hard to point fingers at someone. There were so many people involved in the process, the whole residential school, like, some of the priests they were never caught in their whole lives, so I don't know where they are. [Group laughs] Actually, some people, I found out later from my professor that some Aboriginal peoples were courageous enough to file a lawsuit. So some of the police they did get the justice even though, uh, it was ten years later. Yeah, so it's kind of hard to point fingers. There are so many. A lot of people took part in the process and some of them never admitted they were wrong, so, um, yeah.

THELMA: It's just easier to point the finger at the government.

MARIA: Yeah it is!

THELMA: As she apologizes, it's like, "Okay, well, clearly they're taking the blame so we can point at them when there are pictures, but it should be all our problems, at the end of the day." If we're Canadians, we're a part of this society.

A second virtue of stylistic analysis is that it reveals the acts of affiliation and dissociation that respondents perform as they endeavour both to articulate and to develop their points of view. An ability to capture this process of discursive alignment as it unfolds is central to the genius of focus group methodology. As numerous communications theorists have argued, it is also central to the negotiated development and exchange of political identity.[14] That is to say, people who want to express similarity to others will attempt to emulate their style. Within the focus groups, we found many instances of formula-repetition that revealed deeper agendas of affiliation and contestation.

A small number of respondents used formulas to indicate that they subscribed to an ideology they suspected most of their colleagues did not share and they were unwilling to negotiate with. Note the putative completeness of these popular formulations; they constitute what Wetherell and Potter have termed "self-sufficient propositions"[15] in the rhetoric of race relations. In this example, also from category B, the phrase "rationality" has become axiomatic, its value and relevance beyond question:

FACILITATOR: Patric ... you sort of said you sound impolite if you do certain things, but what do you think is the source of that?

PATRIC: I think it's the moralistic approach to education as opposed to a rational perspective. Because the moralistic approach says, "These people were bad," or did the wrong, and then, "These people are good," or were the innocent victims, and therefore you get this entire perspective of good and evil. You get this biblical conception of what happened when, like I said, the rational perspective is usually in a medium. Because not everybody in Canada participated in taking land, in raping children and killing babies and doing all this stuff. It was specific government officials or laws or things which are no longer part of the constitution, and if there are remnants of it, they're being worked on. So, therefore, I'm thinking the rational perspective will always benefit more so. Removing the moralistic perspective, the emotional aspect, that way we can see things clearly.

Other respondents used formulas recognizable from Canada's broader public discourse. This was abundantly true of respondents in all our categories. Such usages indicate individual and group alignment in the terms of political formations defined in public discourse, outside the controlled space of the focus group. In other words, through such formulas as these, we can see focus group participants clearly conscious of a need to relate their "present moment" conversation within the group to ongoing conversations outside it. This example, from a category C respondent, shows that urge to relate and align her opinions clearly overriding her lack of confidence about listing the facts in detail:

> CATHERINE: What are they doing to help people—like all these cultures, all these communities? They still don't have clean drinking water, they don't have adequate healthcare, they don't want to give them, um, mouthwash or you know, hand sanitizer when there was that breakout of—not SARS, that bird flu, because they fear, the government feared that Indians would—First Nations people—would use it to get high.

Conclusion

Of course, participants also conspicuously reused formulas their colleagues had uttered within the group, quoting (and misquoting) one another frequently. Olga captures the complexity and agility of this discursive strategy as she tries to reconcile the pro-apology stance of one colleague (Zach) with another's (Patric's) view that it was "ridiculous:"

> OLGA: I agree with Zach. I'm also not from Canada and I never heard about anything like that before I came here. I never heard about this apology. I have heard about residential schools from my friend because she is Native. So, and like, I've been to powwows and stuff like that, and she told me about it, that's how I found out. And I do agree with what Patric said, I do think it's ridiculous because they're apologizing for it now but like they're not doing anything to improve their lives. Like, she just came back from a residence, and, 'cause she like she volunteered there for the summer, and she said that people literally have nothing to eat. But like you're apologizing for them right now but at the same time you're not doing anything to improve their lives, so it's like an empty "I'm sorry" kind of thing. Like back it up, show them that you care about them, show them that you're sorry. Same thing like right now Indian people they still have like trouble, they're still fighting for their lands because a lot of companies want their lands to build like factories and stuff and they want their lands to like, go hunting and stuff, and still they're fighting the government for their rights. I don't think it's right for you to come up and say it's better than nothing, I guess, to say that you're sorry, but I don't think that you should... I think actions speak louder than words.

There is no turn of rhetoric more slanted towards consensus than quoting your interlocutor's own rhetoric back at her or him, as analyses of "affiliation behaviour" in talkback radio have demonstrated particularly clearly.[16] Group-internal affiliation behaviours are critical to understanding formations of private opinion about public matters across a society as large and complex as a university undergraduate population, let alone Canada as a whole.

Recognizing the geographic diversity just mentioned, one of the main aims for our research is to administer a much wider series of focus groups, using our sub-categories of non-Aboriginal Canadians. We aim to do this in a range of locations around the country, to deepen our understanding of the everyday speech of non-Aboriginal people in its variation. It is too soon to draw firm conclusions about the discourses we have examined and the commitments underlying them. However, what we have found obliges us to wonder what the connections may be between, on the one hand, a sense of belonging to or membership in a country, and on the other, attitudes toward those who belong nowhere else. One's sense of belonging, of entitlement to speak of and for others, and comfort in talking about race and racism appear to be factors in how non-Aboriginal people think about Aboriginal people and their histories. We need a much better understanding of these dynamics.

Observing the emergence of political identities and opinions in a group context will be a key to understanding these complexities, possibly harnessing and transforming the non-Aboriginal collective stake in Canada's reconciliation process. We anticipate conducting this research in the next two to three years, reporting significant findings as we encounter them.

Notes

1 We are grateful to Ashok Mathur for bringing this angle to our attention.

2 See: de Costa, R. (2002). New Relationships, Old Certainties: Australia's Reconciliation and the Treaty-Process in British Columbia (Doctoral dissertation) (retrieved 5 November 2010 from: http://adt.lib.swin.edu.au/public/adt-VSWT20050627.092937/); de Costa, R. (2009, May 20–22). Truth and Reconciliation and the Politics of Community. The Politics of Community and Identity: Learning from One Another Conference, University of Ottawa, Ottawa, ON, Canada.

3 Fairclough, N. (1995). *Critical Discourse Analysis: Papers in the Critical Study of Language*. London, UK: Longman Group Ltd.

4 Klemperer, V. (2000:11). *The Language of the Third Reich, LTI: Lingua Tertii Imperii: a Philologist's Notebook* (Trans. M. Brady). London, UK: The Athlone Press. (Original work published 1947.)

5 Clark, T. (under review). Sorryness as public poetics: Rhetorical figuration and poetic formulas in the Australian and Canadian 2008 Parliamentary apology debates.

6 Thobani, S. (2007). *Exalted Subjects: Studies in the Making of Race and Nation in Canada*. Toronto, ON: University of Toronto Press.

7 Razack, S. (2002). *Race, Space, and the Law: Unmapping a White Settler Society*. Toronto, ON: Between the Lines.

8 Bell, A. (2009). Dilemmas of settler belonging: Roots, routes and redemption in New Zealand national identity claims. *Sociological Review* 57(1):145–162.

9 Hage, G. (1998). *White Nation: Fantasies of White Supremacy in a Multicultural Society*. New York, NY: Routledge.

10 See: Augoustinos, M., Tuffin, K., and Rapley, M. (1999). Genocide or a failure to gel? Racism, history and nationalism in Australian talk. *Discourse & Society* 10(3):351–378; Wetherell, M., and Potter, J. (1992). *Mapping the Language of Racism: Discourse and the Legitimation of Exploitation*. New York, NY: Columbia University Press.

11 Our category A was not defined in ethnic terms, however, those whose grandparents and parents and who themselves had been born in Canada did not include any non-white individuals. This is not surprising even in a small sample, given the discrimination in Canada's immigration system until the late 1960s.

12 See: Regan, P. (2011). *Unsettling the Settler Within: Indian Residential Schools, Truth Telling and Reconciliation in Canada*. Vancouver, BC: UBC Press; Bell, A. (2008). Recognition or ethics? De/centering and the legacy of settler colonialism. *Cultural Studies* 22(6):850–869.

13 The question, "why weren't we told?" served as the title of a book by one of Australia's highest profile historians on Aboriginal-settler relations in Australia. Reynolds, H. (2000). *Why Weren't We Told?* Sydney, Australia: Penguin.

14 See: Voloshinov, V.N. (1973). *Marxism and the Philosophy of Language* (Trans. L. Matejka and I.R. Titunik). New York, NY: Seminar Press. (Original work published 1929); Fairclough (1995); Wetherell and Potter (1992).

15 Wetherell and Potter (1992).

16 See: Fitzgerald, R., and Housley, W. (2009). Membership category work in policy debate. In R. Fitzgerald and W. Housley (eds.). *Media, Policy and Interaction*. Farnham, UK: Ashgate Publishing: 13–25; Crofts, S., and Turner, G. (2007). Jonestalk: The specificity of Alan Jones. *Media International Australia* (122):142–149; Ferencik, M. (2007). Exercising politeness: Membership categorisation in a radio phone-in programme. *Pragmatics* 17(3):351–370.

Mike DeGagné and Jonathan Dewar

Mike DeGagné is Executive Director of the Aboriginal Healing Foundation, a national Aboriginal organization dedicated to addressing the legacy of Canada's Indian residential school system. He has worked in the field of addiction and mental health for the past twenty-five years, first as a community worker on reserve in northern Ontario and later with the Addiction Research Foundation, the Canadian Centre on Substance Abuse, and the National Native Alcohol and Drug Abuse Program. Mike lectures nationally and internationally on issues of Aboriginal health, residential schools, reconciliation, and governance. He serves on a number of boards, including Champlain Local Health Integration Network. He is currently Chairman of the Child Welfare League of Canada and was past chairman of Ottawa's Queensway Carleton Hospital. His Ph.D. focuses on Aboriginal post-secondary education.

Jonathan Dewar has served as Director of Research at the Aboriginal Healing Foundation since 2007 and is a past director of the Métis Centre at the National Aboriginal Health Organization. He was the founding executive director of the Qaggiq Theatre Company in Iqaluit, Nunavut—a youth, culture, and social-issues-focused arts organization—and served in that capacity for four years. During that time he also worked with the Office of the Languages Commissioner of Nunavut and the Inter-governmental Affairs and Inuit Relations unit within Indian and Northern Affairs Canada, Nunavut Region. Jonathan has several years of First Nations-, Inuit-, and Métis-specific policy and research experience in a variety of areas in both government and non-government organizations, including the arts, health and wellness, language legislation and promotion, justice and crime prevention, social issues, land claims, and education. Jonathan self-identifies as a person of mixed heritage, descended from Huron–Wendat, Scottish, and French Canadian grandparents and is completing a doctorate in Canadian Studies, specializing in Aboriginal art and reconciliation.

Into the Ranks of Man: Vicious Modernism and the Politics of Reconciliation

As it became both popular and influential, the political idea of human rights acquired a particular historical trajectory. However, the official genealogy it has been given is extremely narrow. The story of its progressive development is often told ritualistically as a kind of ethnohistory. It forms part of a larger account: the story of the moral and legal ascent of Europe and its civilisational offshoots. Blood-saturated histories of colonisation and conquest are rarely allowed to disrupt that triumphalist tale.[1]

Redress, from this position, becomes a public responsibility that looks forward to a healing of the democratic system—and, by implication, of the nation. By situating violated "citizens" inside the nation, the brief portrayed Japanese Canadians not as "victims" but, more significantly, as the agents of change.[2]

The politics of identity… [in] the 1970s brought an unprecedented paradox into their lives… From being social pariahs in the 1940s, "Japanese Canadians" were now reborn as model "citizens," whose rapid upward social mobility in the aftermath of the mass uprooting demonstrated their loyalty to the nation.[3]

What does a critical post-colonial commentary on human rights look like? What does such a commentary in the colonial settler nation-state of Canada look like? And, indeed, what kind or kinds of humans are at its centre? This essay proposes that the dominant mode for thinking about human rights as a significant feature of contemporary life has now been popularly and even intellectually reproduced primarily as a consequence of the Second World War. Thus, the 1945 *Universal Declaration of Human Rights*[4] is widely understood to follow in the wake of the tragedies of war and ethnic cleansing in mid-twentieth century Europe. However, I want to propose that the context of nation-state apologies to the Indigenous people of Turtle Island (hereafter Canada) and the desire for reconciliation reference a much longer history of struggles for human rights that are simultaneously the foundation of the 1945 *Universal Declaration of Human Rights*[5] and the evidence of a vicious modernity that cemented European conceptions of Man as if it was indeed the only way to conceive of being human in the world. The impetus of my argument is to point to the ambiguity of the practice of apologies and its resultant politics of reconciliation. My claim is that reconciliation requires a wholesale rethinking of the contemporary stakes of human life for the last 500-plus years.

Susan Buck-Morss has written that the understanding of Western modernity is always problematically formulated if questions of transatlantic slavery are excluded from it.[6] One might amend her insights to add Indigenous colonization, attempted genocide, and, in some cases, genocide. Drawing on the case of Haiti, Buck-Morss demonstrates and argues that Western political philosophy failed to implicate slave labour in the colonies and indigenous colonization at the exact same time as the Enlightenment discourse of freedom as "the highest and universal political value"[7] was being produced by Enlightenment thinkers. She asked how such a blind spot was possible? And, further still, how is it that such a blind spot continues to be perpetuated today? What Buck-Morss's questions reveal is that the afterlife of European colonization has as its backbone or foundation the colonization of the Americas, with its near-genocide and genocide and its enslavement of Africans as both its material and intellectual inheritance. Buck-Morss's claims pose a significant problem for how the politics of reconciliation is understood and practised in late-modern Canada, which must be understood in light of its embedded history in the colonization of the Americas, European global expansion, and the ways in which the ideas of coloniality continue to shape its governing and ordering of geo-political space, people, and institutions.

To fully appreciate the problematics of Buck-Morss's insights I turn to the Caribbean philosopher, or rather philosopher of the Americas, Sylvia Wynter, to delineate the ways in which European inventions of Man ordered the world and set up the terms of being human for which nation-state apologies are a tactical acknowledgement of having done wrong and, at the same time, are premised upon the perpetuation of European genres of the human invented in their attempt to rule the globe from a perspective that is entirely within their conception of what the globe and being human means.[8] Wynter has consistently attempted to make sense of the invention of the Americas or the New World as a problematic of our contemporary global humanity. In an intellectual project that seeks to make sense of how a post-Columbus globe is re-shaped on the terms of shifting European consciousness, Wynter details a *religio–secular–politico–cultural* complex, crossing a range of intellectual fields, which articulates how the White, the Red, and the Black as types or genres come to be. She maps how Europe's ideas move from supernatural to religious to secular and how the secular comes to be constituted and lodged in discourses of the political and the cultural. Those discourses of the political and cultural also come to mark the governing logics of "races" and peoples, all of them fundamentally invented on Europe's terms and simultaneously in resistance to Europe's reign. These genres of Man's human others—in this case the Red and the Black—are the infra-humans of which contemporary apologies are meant to signal their pathway into the ranks of Man. Wynter argues that these categories or types of man were invented in the moment of a hybrid European colonial domination that produced "the indio/negro complex" which was later transformed in a *degodded* Europe to "the nigger/native complex."[9] Wynter suggests that such designations point to how Europe's conception of Man, which "overrepresents itself as if it were the human itself,"[10] is one of the most difficult material and conceptual political, cultural, and philosophical issues facing us today. The end of formal colonialism does not produce any relief from European dominance of what being human might mean and be. Wynter tests her claims in the region of the Caribbean, which has been also the site of Europe's laboratory for its encounters with its invented genres of Man's human others and, in particular, its encounters with the question of freedom and unfreedom as Buck-Morss so skillfully points out concerning Hegel and Haiti, the former having theorized his master/slave dialectic at exactly the same time that the Haitian revolution was headline news in Europe's papers and cafés.

If we take Wynter and Buck-Morss seriously, the question of what constitutes European modernity is a complicated story of genocide, slavery, ecocide, and, most strikingly, the production of a new world not just for those colonized and enslaved but for those engaged in the project of expansion as well. The New World moniker is not a sentimental or history-denying term, but it does reference the brutal realities of life in the Americas as the bedrock of European modernity and its satellite campuses like Canada. The Enlightenment's naming and ordering of peoples, places, and things has bequeathed to us those namings and orders as the very terms through which it might be challenged. The Haitian revolution of 1791 took up liberty as its central rallying cry from the same French Revolution that sought to crush it. In our time we have become Black and Aboriginal, among other names we have been forced to take on, and internalized them out of the very cartographies of Europe's global expansion since the fifteenth century. It is indeed these names that only partially make sense in the logics of, and appeals to, the invented genres of European Man that apologies are meant to assuage. The question we are often faced with is: how are we to make other conceptions of being human and of traversing the globe appear? What intellectual, political, and cultural—not to mention economical—space do different conceptions of human life have to offer our present globalized, networked humanity? In my view the politics of reconciliation throws these questions up without offering answers. The politics of reconciliation ask us to come into the apology as the people Europe invented, not as people we once were. And one cannot be romantic about a past, given that how history has intervened to be a part of the conversation often means one must in some way work with Europe's violently profound re-ordering of the globe and the peoples within. Thus, one is often left asking: what is being reconciled, with whom, and to what?

Reconciliation suggests a past action. It suggests that some wrongdoing has been done for which the possibility of forgiveness is an act of coming together again. Reconciliation suggests a significant rupture of some kind has occurred. Above I have suggested that European colonial expansion from the fifteenth century onwards produced a rupture in the Americas, which in part produced the settler colonial nation-state of Canada, which also produced new states of/for being indigenous peoples and belatedly African peoples. Those kinds of collective namings—Indigenous, African, Indian, Asian, and even European—are the cataloguing evidence of the historical rupture for which European Man comes to overrepresent itself as if it was indeed Man. As Paul Gilroy suggests, the "[b]lood–saturated histories of colonisation and conquest are rarely allowed to disrupt that triumphalist tale,"[11] and one that apologies and the politics of reconciliation attempt to make invisible in the contemporary moment. Thus reconciliation also suggests a certain kind of suturing is possible in the aftermath of the brutalities that makes it a necessary response in the first place. But what reconciliation does not appear to do is dismantle the institutional basis of the present arrangements of human life. Reconciliation does not ask us to rethink where we are; it asks us to accept the present as an accumulation of injuries for which apologies must suffice as the entry into the flawed ecocidal, genocidal, anti-human, late-modern world still premised on Europe's partial conception of the human as the only option for being human in this world. Reconciliation might provide us a view towards new and, or more, hopeful human relations, but it does not allow us to seriously grapple with the brutalities that have brought us together in these new geo-political zones and their multiple disadvantaged relations of Europe's invented Others. In short, reconciliation does not absolve histories and practices of brutality.

For the immigrant population coming out of the Caribbean who, under the rules of European modernity, had to make themselves "not native to the place we were in,"[12] and whose histories of enslavement and colonization entangle in complexly creative and maddening ways with Indigenous cultures of the Americas, the nation-state of Canada's and European imperial powers'—past and present—apologies and reconciliation mark the perversity and viciousness of modernity and its incomplete promise of human liberation.

For the former slave, indenture, and the hybrids of all sorts in the "archipelagoes" of poverty,[13] the struggle to be human is one conditioned by the terms upon which European discourses could both be internalized and turned upside down to produce them as subjects worthy of being considered Man, if only tangentially so. The struggle against Atlantic slavery, especially in imperial Britain, is now understood as the first actual global human rights struggle. The brutalities of African slavery and Indigenous resistance to life-altering colonial expansion are indeed the bedrock of what is now a neutered human rights discourse emptied out of ideas that sought to fundamentally and radically rethink what human life might mean.

It is my contention then that the politics of reconciliation only matter to the extent that such practices tell the alternate and much more disturbing story of global capitalism's apparent triumph and, concurrently, the attempts to resist it and undo its impacts in the past, present, and future. What is at stake is an exercise that tells the tale of the cost of European expansion as one which is bigger and more brutal than the myth of Europe's conception of the world being the only valid idea of human life and a brutal practice and logic that must continually repress ideas of living differently in many pre-contact cultures that remain with us still. I have written elsewhere that Black/African diaspora discourses, or the stories of those not fully human in Europe's terms, matter because such discourses are the B-side to the celebratory narratives of globalization (especially in the academy) now offered as the triumph of Europe's vision of a global humanity.[14] In this view, the brutality that narratives of the black diaspora offer temper and provide other indices of globalization's history and its impact, as well as its present so that modernity's vicious charms may be unmasked and its consequences laid bare. Black/African diaspora narratives then are about the historical unfolding of Europe's run at global domination, but they are also about the continuous refusal of that domination by various global forces since its inception. Significantly, Black/African diaspora narratives are also about the making of meaningful lives within the context of Euro–Western Enlightenment and modernity—both as products of it and crucially as re-signifiers, inventors, and originators of what can only be described as discrepant modernities for those who have borne the brunt of Europe's expansionist practices.[15] In essence, it might be argued that those produced in the crucible of the New World are truly *the* modern people—that would be *Natives/Negros*. What I am trying to stress is that the Atlantic region, with its history of territorial theft, transatlantic slavery, and genocide, is the *incubator* of a set of conditions that we have inherited as a global situation organized on the basis of Euro–Western traditions of thought and the human, and from which we must figure out how to extricate ourselves because it is only a partial story of human existence. A sober conversation about what that extrication means will account for political economy, cultural borrowing, sharing, mixing, and its outcomes and impacts—contradictory and otherwise—and our entangled histories of power, knowledge, and land. I am not sure that apologies and the language of reconciliation takes us there, but as a Western and modern subject I am also not prepared to throw it away just yet either. This is the ambivalence that I signalled above.

One of the central claims of European Enlightenment and modernity was to make a better human, but such desires were premised on making some not human; and then only admitting them into humanity, sometimes partially so, based solely on models from Europe's perspectives after significant and massive resistance to Europe's domination. Grappling with such a history would prove useful and powerful as a central aspect of the politics of reconciliation because it is in fact the various ways in which deployments of Western conceptions of the human function that continue to be the basis from which desires for reconciliation are meant to rescue us collectively. Reconciliation is conceived as a practice of forgetting when the violences unleashed by the need for reconciliation remain all around us still. In the case of the "new world" for Indigenous and Blacks, specifically, reconciliation can only be but a beginning towards a much more profound and challenging discussion and towards a potentially new institutionality of what it means to be human that rests upon the multiple perspectives of humanness in which European concepts are but one among many others. Reconciliation might then be partly understood as an element of the process of beginning to recognize the Americas as a zone of creolization where land, violence, and history conspire to produce new modes of being human. Reconciliation is but a beginning or opening; as yet unimagined transformation is the desired outcome.

Notes

1   Gilroy, Paul (2010:55). *Darker Than Blue: On The Moral Economies of Black Atlantic Culture*. Cambridge, MA: Belnap Press of Harvard University Press.

2   Miki, Roy (2004:234). *Redress: Inside The Japanese Canadian Call for Justice*. Vancouver, BC: Raincoast Books.

3   Miki (2004:310).

4   United Nations (1948). *Declaration of Human Rights*, G.A. res. 217A (III), U.N. Doc A/810 at 71. Retrieved 2 November 2010 from: http://www.un.org/en/documents/udhr/index.shtml

5   United Nations (1948).

6   Buck-Morss, Susan (2000). Hegel and Haiti. *Critical Inquiry* 26(4):821–865.

7   Buck-Morss (2000:821).

8   Wynter, Sylvia (2003). Unsettling the coloniality of being/power/truth/freedom: Towards the human, after man, its overrepresentation—An argument. *CR: The New Centennial Review* 3(3):257-337.

9   Wynter, Sylvia (1995). The Pope must have been drunk, the King of Castile a madman: Culture as actuality, and the Caribbean rethinking modernity. In A. Ruprecht and C. Taiana (eds.). *The Reordering of Culture: Latin America, The Caribbean and Canada, In the Hood*. Ottawa, ON: Carleton University Press: 17-41.

10 Wynter (2003:260).

11 Gilroy (2010:55).

12 Kincaid, Jamaica (1996:29). The flowers of empire (Significance of Botanical Gardens to One Woman). (Excerpt of speech by Jamaica Kincaid.) *Harper's Magazine* (April):28-31.

13 Wynter, Sylvia (1992). Rethinking 'aesthetics': Notes towards a deciphering practice. In M. Cham (ed.). *Ex-Iles: Essays on Caribbean Cinema*. Trenton, NJ: Africa World Press: 237-279.

14 Walcott, Rinaldo (2006). Salted cod… : Black Canada and diaspora sensibilities. In *Reading the Image: Poetics of the Black Diaspora*. Chatham, ON: Thames Art Gallery.

15 I am using the term "Euro-Western" to signal the ethno-centred organization of what we have come to call the West. It is a term meant not only to signal Europe but also those satellite settler colonies like the USA, Canada, Australia, and New Zealand who understand themselves to be Euro-Western in founding and organization. However, as much of my argument suggests or implies, the West itself is now so complicated that it would be a conceptual problem to take "new world" black people out of it. Thus, the term Euro-Western works to anchor the particular discourses that I am addressing here to a Europe, at a certain historical moment, understood itself as mono-ethnic insofar as its expansionist project was concerned.

Mitch Miyagawa

Mitch Miyagawa is a writer and filmmaker from Whitehorse, Yukon. He was born and raised in Edmonton, Alberta, and moved to the Yukon in 1998, where he lives with his wife and two sons. Mitch began his writing career in 2002 with the production of his first play, *The Plum Tree*. It was produced in six cities across Canada, including at the prestigious playRites Festival in Calgary, and was published in 2004 by Playwrights Canada Press. He was the playwright-in-residence at Nakai Theatre in Whitehorse, where he wrote *Carnaval*, produced by Nakai Theatre in 2007. In film, his documentary for the National Film Board, *Our Town Faro* (2004), won the Northern Sights Competition and was nominated for a Golden Sheaf at the Yorkton Short Film Festival. He co-produced *The Lottery Ticket* (2003), an award-winning short for BravoFACT, and *Artifacts* (2007), a short drama for Haeckel Hill Pictures. He co-wrote a feature film for Force Four Films called *The Asahi Baseball Story*. He is currently in post-production on a one-hour documentary on government apologies, commissioned by TVO for their point-of-view documentary program, *The View From Here*. As a freelancer, Mitch has written for several magazines, including *Geist*, *Up Here*, *North of Ordinary*, and *The Walrus*. He won honourable mentions at both the Western and National Magazine awards for his work. He is a graduate of the Masters of Fine Arts program in Creative Writing at the University of British Columbia.

A Sorry State

[*A version of this article was published in 2009 in* The Walrus *6(10):22–30.*]

The government of Canada gave my family our first apology, for the internment of Japanese Canadians during World War II, in 1988. I was seventeen, and I don't remember any of it. I had other things to worry about. My mom had just left my dad, Bob Miyagawa. She'd cried and said sorry as my brother and I helped her load her furniture into the back of a borrowed pickup. Her departure had been coming for a while. At my dad's retirement dinner the year before, his boss at the Alberta Forest Service had handed him a silver-plated pulaski, a stuffed Bertie the Fire Beaver, and a rocking chair. My mom, Carol—barely forty years old and chafing for new adventures—took one look at the rocking chair and knew the end was near.

Three months after she left, on September 22, Brian Mulroney rose to his feet in the House of Commons. The gallery was packed with Japanese Canadian seniors and community leaders, who stood as the prime minister began to speak. "The Government of Canada wrongfully incarcerated, seized the property, and disenfranchised thousands of citizens of Japanese ancestry," he intoned. "Apologies are the only way we can cleanse the past." When he finished, the gallery cheered, in a most un–Japanese Canadian defiance of parliamentary rules.

The clouds may have suddenly parted in Ottawa; the cherry blossoms in Vancouver may have spontaneously bloomed. I missed it all. It was graduation year. Every day after school, I worked at West Edmonton Mall, diving elbow deep in Quarterback Crunch ice cream so I could save up for a pool table. Weekends, I visited my mom at her new place, a small apartment within walking distance of the tracks by Stony Plain Road.

Up until then, and perhaps to this day, being half Japanese had just been something I used to make myself unique. A conversation starter. A line for picking up girls. The internment my dad and 22,000 others like him suffered was something to add to the story. It increased the inherited martyr value.

I didn't get many dates.

Four years earlier, when Brian Mulroney was leader of the Opposition, he'd asked Pierre Trudeau to apologize to Japanese Canadians. Exasperated, Trudeau shot back, "How many other historical wrongs would have to be righted?" It was Trudeau's last day in Parliament as prime minister. He finished his retort with righteous indignation: "I do not think it is the purpose of a government to right the past. I cannot rewrite history."

Trudeau must have known that the apology door, once opened, would never be closed. Mulroney might have known, too. Redress for Japanese Canadians was the beginning of our national experiment with institutional remorse—an experiment that has grown greatly over the past twenty years, intertwining itself with my family's story.

I like to look at the glass as half full: my parents' divorce was not so much a split as an expansion. They both remarried, so my kids now have more grandparents than they can count. And I've gained the most apologized-to family in the country—maybe the world.

I watched Stephen Harper's apology for Indian residential schools with my dad's wife, Etheline, on a hot night in the summer of 2008. Etheline was the third generation of her Cree family to attend an Indian mission school. She went to Gordon Residential School in Punnichy, Saskatchewan, for four years. Gordon was the last federally run residential school to be closed, shutting down in 1996 after over a century in operation.

When I talked to my mom in Calgary afterward, she casually mentioned that her second husband, Harvey's father, had paid the Chinese head tax as a child. Harper apologized to head tax payers and their families in 2006.

I was aware that my family had become a multi-culti case study, but when I realized the government had apologized to us three times it went from being a strange coincidence to a kind of joke. (*Q: How does a Canadian say hello? A: "I'm sorry."*) Soon, though, I started wondering what these apologies really meant, and whether they actually did any good. In seeking answers, I've mostly found more questions. I've become both a cynic and a believer. In other words, I'm more confused than ever before. I'm no apology expert or prophet. I'm so sorry. All I can offer is this: my apology story.

In the fall of 2008, I travelled from my home in Whitehorse to Vancouver. The National Association of Japanese Canadians had organized a celebration and conference on the twentieth anniversary of Redress. It rained as I walked to toward the Japanese Hall on Alexander Street in East Vancouver, in what was once the heart of the Japanese community.

In the distance, giant red quay cranes poked above the buildings along Hastings, plucking containers from cargo ships anchored in Burrard Inlet. The downpour soaked the broken folks lined up outside the Union Gospel Mission at Princess and Cordova, a few blocks from the hall. Some huddled under the old cherry trees in Oppenheimer Park, beside the ball field where the Asahi baseball team, the darlings of "Japantown," played before the war.

Inside the hall, a few hundred people milled about, drinking green tea and coffee served from big silver urns by bluevested volunteers. The participants on the first panel of the day, titled Never Too Late, took seats on the wide stage at the front. They represented the hyphenated and dual named of our country: a Japanese-, Chinese-, Indo-, Black, Aboriginal, and Ukrainian-Canadian rainbow behind two long fold-out tables. Their communities had all been interned, or excluded, or systematically mistreated. Apology receivers and apology seekers. A kick line of indignation, a gallery of the once wronged. (*A Japanese-, Chinese-, Indo-, Black, Aboriginal, and Ukrainian-Canadian all go into a bar. The bartender looks at them and says, "Is this some kind of joke?")*

In the fictional world of *Eating Crow*, a "novel of apology" by Jay Rayner, the hottest trend in international relations is something called "penitential engagement." To deal with the baggage from the wars, genocides, and persecutions of the past, the United Nations sets up an Office of Apology. The protagonist of the novel, Marc Basset, is hired as Chief Apologist, partly because of his tremendous ability to deliver heartfelt apologies, but also because of his "plausible apologibility." His ancestors captained slave ships, ran colonies, slaughtered natives, and waged dirty wars. Backed by a team of researchers and handlers, Basset circles the globe, delivering statements of remorse.

Penitential engagement is closer to reality than you'd think. The Japanese government has made at least forty "war apology statements" since 1950. All of Western Europe remembers German chancellor Willy Brandt's famous *Kniefall* in 1970, when he fell to his knees on the steps of the Warsaw Memorial, in silent anguish for the victims of the Warsaw Ghetto uprising. During the past twenty years, Italian prime minister Silvio Berlusconi has apologized for the colonial occupation of Libya, South African president Frederik W. de Klerk has apologized for apartheid, and the Queen has issued a Royal Proclamation of regret to the Acadians in the Maritimes and Louisiana. In 1998, the Australian government began its annual National Sorry Day for the "stolen generations" of aboriginal children. In 2005, the US Senate apologized for its failure to enact federal anti-lynching legislation. And both houses of Congress have now passed apologies for slavery.

At the 2001 UN World Conference against Racism, Racial Discrimination, Xenophobia and Related Intolerance, held in Durban, more than 100 countries called "on all those who have not yet contributed to restoring the dignity of the victims to find appropriate ways to do so and, to this end, appreciate those countries that have done so." Working toward this goal is the International Center for Transitional Justice in New York, which "assists countries pursuing accountability for past mass atrocity or human rights abuse." As if in response, jurisdictions across Australia, the United States, and Canada are passing apology acts designed to allow public officials to apologize without incurring legal liability.

Concerned about our precious self-image as a peacemaking, multicultural country, Canada has been making every effort to lead the sorry parade. In addition to the residential school and Chinese head tax apologies, the federal government has also now said sorry for the *Komagata Maru* incident, when a ship full of immigrants from India was turned away from Vancouver Harbour, and established a historical recognition program "to recognize and commemorate the historical experiences and contributions of ethno-cultural communities affected by wartime measures and immigration restrictions applied in Canada." And we became the first Western democracy to follow South Africa in establishing a truth and reconciliation commission, for the residential schools.

Not surprisingly, other groups have come knocking on Ottawa's door. Among them are Ukrainian Canadians, on behalf of those interned during World War I, and the residents of the bulldozed Africville community in Halifax, now a dog park. Some who have already received an apology clamour for more, or better. Harper's *Komagata Maru* apology was issued to the Indo-Canadian community outside Parliament. Now they want the same as every other group: an official, on-the-record statement.

I sat down on a plastic-backed chair in the deserted second row. Seconds later, an old *Nisei*, a second-generation Japanese Canadian named Jack Nagai, plunked down beside me. He sighed and lifted the glasses hanging around his neck to his face. "Gotta sit close for my hearing aid," he said, then looked at me and grinned. I pulled out a notebook, and he watched me out of the corner of his eye, fingering the pen in his breast pocket.

Black scuffs, I wrote. The pearly walls and floor of the Japanese Hall auditorium were marked and streaked. A fluorescent light fifteen metres above my head flickered and buzzed. The hall had a school gym wear and tear to it. Jack noticed my scribbling and jotted down something on the back of his program.

The brown spots on his bald head reminded me of my Uncle Jiro, who passed away suddenly in 2005 at the age of seventy-seven. As it turned out, Jack was from Lethbridge as well, and had known my uncle from the city's Buddhist Church. My Uncle Jiro, "Jerry" to his non-Japanese friends, had helped the blind to read, bowled every Sunday, and kept a meticulous journal of the prices he'd paid for groceries and the sorry state of his golf game. He'd been a bachelor, mateless and childless, like several others on my dad's side.

Those few of us in my family who now have kids have Caucasian spouses, so our strain is becoming less and less Asian. The Miyagawa name may disappear here with my two sons, and with the name would go a story seeded a hundred years ago.

My grandmother and grandfather farmed berries on three hectares of rocky slope in Mission, BC, starting in the 1920s. They were their own slave-drivers, labouring non-stop to clear the land and get the farm going. Grandmother produced the workforce, delivering a baby a year for a decade. My dad was near the end, the ninth child of ten. By 1941, the Japanese controlled the berry industry in BC. My grandparents' farm expanded and flourished.

Then came Pearl Harbor, war with Japan, and the dislocation of more than 20,000 Japanese Canadians from the West Coast. On a spring day in 1942, my dad and his family carried two bags each to the station and boarded a train bound for the sugar beet fields of southern Alberta. They never made it back to Mission. The Japanese Canadians weren't allowed to return to BC until four years after the war was over, so the family instead settled in Lethbridge. Dad moved away soon after he came of age, and ended up in Edmonton, where I was born.

For my dad, the apology was pointless. Like many others in the Japanese Canadian community, he had already turned the other cheek. *Shikata ga nai*, the saying goes—what's done is done.

I admire and marvel at his ability to let go of the past. He even calls his family's forced move across the Rockies a "great adventure." For a ten-year-old, it was a thrill to see the black smoke pouring from the train engine's stack as it approached the Mission station.

Mist softens a train platform in the Fraser Valley. Last night's rain drips from the eaves of the station, clinging to the long tips of cedar needles. All over the platform, families are huddled together by ramshackle pyramids of suitcases. Children squat around a puddle on the tracks, poking at a struggling beetle with a stick. A distant whistle; their mother yells at them in Japanese; they run back to stand beside her. Their father stands apart, lost in thought. He's trying to commit to memory the place where he'd buried his family's dishes the night before, in one of his berry fields a few kilometres away.

Clickety-clack. Clickety-clack. A screech of brakes, a sizzle of steam. The train pulls in, the doors open, each one sentinelled by a Mountie with arms crossed.

The families become mist, along with their suitcases and the Mounties. Everything disappears except the train. It's quiet. An old conductor in a blue cap sticks his head out the window. No need for tickets on this train, he says. Step right up. Welcome aboard the Apology Express.

The conference began, and Jack and I leaned forward to hear. The panellists took their turns bending into low mikes, paying homage to the hallowed ground zero of apologies. Chief Robert Joseph, a great bear of a man in a red fleece vest, hugged the podium and said, "The Japanese Canadian apology was a beacon." Everyone at the tables looked tiny, posed between the high black skirting framing the stage and the minuscule disco ball that hung above them.

The people telling the stories of their communities were the same ones who had put on their best shoes to walk the marbled floors of Parliament, who had filed briefs for lawsuits. They spoke in the abstract—reconciliation, compensation, acknowledgement—and kept up official outrage as they demanded recognition for their causes. "We have to remember, so it will never happen again" was the panel's common refrain. After an hour, Jack's eyes were closed, and he'd started to lean my way. I could hear soft snoring from the other side of the room, where a group of seniors slumped and tilted in their chairs.

This wasn't what I'd come to hear either. After studying and listening to official expressions of remorse to my family and others, after reading the best books on the subject (*The Age of Apology*; *I Was Wrong*; *On Apology*; *Mea Culpa*), I'd come to believe that government apologies were more about forgetting than remembering.

I righted Jack as best I could, and snuck out the back of the hall for some fresh air.

I've always imagined that my mom met Harvey Kwan in a room full of light bulbs. They both worked for the Energy Efficiency Branch of the provincial government. She wrote copy for newsletters; he did tech support. In my mind, Mom would watch the way Harvey methodically screwed the bulbs into the bare testing socket. She appreciated his size. Not quite five feet tall, my mom likes her husbands compact (though she did dally for a time with a rather tall embezzler from Texas). She was further attracted to Harvey's quiet voice, his shy smile as he explained wattages and life cycles. Perhaps they reached for the same compact fluorescent and felt a jolt as their fingers touched.

Mom and "Uncle Harv" were both laid off soon after they started dating, so they moved from Edmonton to Calgary, closer to their beloved Rockies, and became true weekend warriors, driving past the indifferent elk on Highway 1 to Canmore and Banff to hike and camp and ski. Mom was afraid of heights; Harv took her hand and led her to the mountaintops.

Harvey's father had sailed to Canada aboard the *Empress of Russia* in 1919, at the age of fourteen. He paid the $500 head tax, then rode the CPR with his father to the railroad town of Medicine Hat, on the hot, dry Alberta prairie. Around the time he became an adult, in 1923, the Canadian government passed a *Chinese Immigration Act*, which remained in force for twenty-five years. Under the act, no new Chinese immigrants could come to Canada, so a young bachelor like him could only have a long-distance family. He managed to sire three sons with his first wife in China during that time, but she never made it to Canada, dying overseas. He eventually took a second wife, Harvey's mom, who had to wait several years before she could enter the country. In the meantime, she lived unhappily with Harvey's father's mother, probably waiting on her like a servant.

And that's all Harvey knows. He doesn't know about his father's life, those twenty-five years away from his first wife and their children, then his second. He doesn't know his grandfather's name. He doesn't know what his grandfather did. He doesn't know where the man is buried. They never spoke of that time.

> Mr. Speaker, on behalf of all Canadians and the Government of Canada, we offer a full apology to Chinese Canadians for the head tax and express our deepest sorrow for the subsequent exclusion of Chinese immigrants... No country is perfect. Like all countries, Canada has made mistakes in its past, and we realize that. Canadians, however, are a good and just people, acting when we've committed wrong. And even though the head tax—a product of a profoundly different time—lies far in our past, we feel compelled to right this historic wrong for the simple reason that it is the decent thing to do, a characteristic to be found at the core of the Canadian soul.—*Stephen Harper, June 22, 2006*

Apology comes from the Greek *apo* and *logos* ("from speech"), and as every first-year philosophy student who reads Plato's *Apology* knows, it originally meant a defence of one's position. But somewhere along the line, it became a Janus word, adopting its opposite meaning as well. Rather than a justification of one's position or actions, it became an admission of harm done, an acceptance of responsibility. When Harper spoke on the head tax, you could see both faces of the word at work: *Those were different times. We're not like that now. We should, in fact, be proud of ourselves. Pat ourselves on the back. Reaffirm our goodness today by sacrificing the dead and gone.*

Rather than bringing the past to life, statements like these seem to break our link with history, separating us from who we were and promoting the notion of our moral advancement. They also whitewash the ways in which Canadians still benefit from that past, stripping the apologies of remorse. Rendering them meaningless. Forgettable.

I wasn't the only one taking a break from the conference. I followed a Japanese Canadian woman with short grey hair down the street to Oppenheimer Park, watching from a distance as she placed her hand, gently, on the trunk of one of the old cherry trees. I later learned that these were memorial trees, planted by Japanese Canadians thirty years ago. The City of Vancouver had been planning to chop them down as part of a recent redevelopment scheme, but the Japanese Canadian community rallied and saved them (though the old baseball diamond will still be plowed under).

I arrived back at the hall in time for lunch. Ahead of me in line was the author and scholar Roy Miki, one of the leading figures in the movement for Japanese Canadian redress and a member of the negotiating committee for the National Association of Japanese Canadians. Miki was an "internment baby," born in Manitoba in 1942, six months after his family was uprooted from their home in Haney, BC. He laughed when I told him about my family and, intrigued, pulled up a chair beside me for lunch. He had neat white hair, parted to one side, and wore blue-tinted glasses. We balanced bento boxes on our knees, and he told me something that astounded me: the negotiators hadn't wanted an apology very badly.

"We wanted to shine a light on the system—to show its inherent flaws," he said. "Our main concern wasn't the apology or the compensation. The real victim was democracy itself, not the people." What those pushing for redress wanted was an acknowledgment that democracy had broken down, and that people had benefited from the internment of Japanese Canadians. They wanted to change the system in order to protect people in the future.

Miki remained wary of government expressions of remorse, concerned that the emotional content of apologies—the focus on "healing"—distracted from the more important issue of justice. "Now the apology has become the central thing," he said. "It allows the government to be seen as the good guy.

But there's a power relationship in apologies that has to be questioned; the apologizer has more power than the apologized-to."

Mulroney, in his apology to Japanese Canadians, said the aim was "to put things right with the surviving members—with their children and ours, so that they can walk together in this country, burdened neither by the wrongs nor the grievances of previous generations." Both the victimizer and the victim are freed from their bonds. Japanese Canadian internment "went against the very nature of our country." With the apology, so the redemption narrative went, Mulroney was returning Canada to its natural, perfect state. Cue music. Roll credits. The lights come up, and all is right with the world again. I find the storyline hard to resist, especially when the main characters are long gone. But of course not all of these dramas took place once upon a time.

My dad met his second wife, Etheline Victoria Blind, at a south Edmonton bingo. Yes, he found a native bride at a bingo, in front of a glass concession case where deep-fried pieces of bannock known as "kill-me-quicks" glistened under neon light.

I was working for an environmental organization at the time. Like most Alberta non-profits, we depended on bingos and casinos as fundraisers. Dad was one of our A-list volunteers. He was retired, reliable, and always cheerful, if a bit hard of hearing. Etheline, on the other hand, was on the long-shot volunteer list. She was the mother of the high school friend of a colleague. I didn't know her, but I called her one night in desperation.

I don't remember seeing any sparks fly between Dad and Etheline. He was sixty-five at the time, and not seeking to kick at the embers of his love life. But Etheline invited him to play Scrabble with her, and so it began.

Dad and Etheline had a cantankerous sort of affair, from my point of view. They lived separately for many years—Dad in a condo on Rainbow Valley Road, Etheline in an aging split-level five minutes away—but moved gradually toward each other, in location and spirit, finally marrying a few days after Valentine's Day, eight years after they met. I flew down from Whitehorse with my son, just a year old then. He was the only person at the wedding wearing a suit, a one-piece suede tuxedo.

And so Etheline became my Indian stepmother.

Stephen Harper's apology to residential school survivors was a powerful political moment. You had to be moved by the sight of the oldest and youngest survivors, side by side on the floor of Parliament—one a 104-year-old woman, the other barely in her twenties. The speeches were superb, the optics perfect.

Yet personally, I felt tricked. Tricked because the apology distilled the entire complicated history of assimilation into a single policy, collapsing it like a black hole into a two-word "problem": residential schools. Here was the forgetful apology at its best. By saying sorry for the schools, we could forget about all the other ways the system had deprived—and continued to deprive— aboriginal people of their lives and land. The government had created the problem, sure, but had owned up to it, too, and was on its way to getting it under control, starting with the survivors' prescription for recovery. If they were abused, they merely had to itemize their pain in a thirty-page document, tally their compensation points, stand before an adjudicator to speak of their rape and loneliness, and receive their official payment. All taken care of.

And yet. And yet.

Etheline, I apologize. I knew you for ten years and never really knew where you came from. I'm educated, post-colonial, postmodern, mixed race, well travelled, curious, vaguely liberal, politically correct. "You're the most Canadian person I know," I've been told. And yet I never once asked you about your time in residential school. I never really related until that night, after we'd watched Harper's shining moment, that powerful ceremony—and I'd watched how it moved you, felt the hair on my arms rise and a shiver in my back when we talked late and you told me how your grandfather was taken from his family when he was four, the same age my oldest son is now; told me how he'd never known his parents, but relearned Cree ways from his adopted family and became a strong Cree man even after his own children were taken away; how he'd raised you when your mother couldn't; how you were in the mission school, too, for four years, and your grandfather wouldn't let them cut your braids, and you'd feel the cold brick walls with your hands, and the laundry ladies would only call you by your number, and you would stare out the window toward the dirt road that led away from the school and cry for your *Kokum* and *Meshom*. I never knew. Or if you told me, I only listened with half an ear. And I apologize again, for bringing it all up, for writing down your private pain. But I know we need to tell it again and again. It has to be there; it has to get into people's hearts.

And here I make an apology for the government apology. For whatever I feel about them, about how they can bury wrongs in the past instead of making sure the past is never forgotten, about how they can use emotion to evade responsibility, they have indeed changed my life. They've made me rethink what it means to be a citizen of this country. They've brought me closer to my family.

Near the end of the conference, the woman with short grey hair stood up and told a story. After World War II, when she was a schoolgirl, she'd one day refused to read out loud from a textbook with the word "Jap" in it. She was sent home, where she proudly told her father what she'd done. He slapped her across the face. The apology, she told everyone at the hall, had restored her dignity. The conference ended the next day, and I returned home with something to think about.

It's summer as I write, almost a year since the conference, and the apologies have kept coming. The state of California apologized for the persecution of Chinese immigrants last week. Thousands of former students of Indian day schools, feeling left out of the residential school apology, filed a statement of claim at the Manitoba legislature yesterday.

I'm sitting on the beach of Long Lake, just outside Whitehorse. Though it's hot outside, the water here always stays cold, because the summer's not long enough to heat it. Still, my two boys are hardy Yukoners, and they're running in and out of the water, up to their necks. I watch their little bodies twist and turn, then look at my own thirty-eight-year-old paunch and search the sky. What will we be apologizing for when my children are adults? Temporary foreign workers? The child welfare system?

Tomio bumps into Sam, knocking him to the ground. Sam cries. "Tomio," I tell my oldest, "say sorry to your brother." "Why?" he asks. "I didn't mean to do it."

"Say sorry anyway," I reply.

We say sorry when we are responsible and when we are not. We say sorry when we were present or when we were far away. We are ambiguous about what apologies mean in the smallest personal interactions. How can we expect our political apologies to be any less complicated?

A long time ago—or not so long ago, really, but within our nation's lifetime—another train hustled along these tracks: the Colonial Experiment. She was a beaut, shiny and tall. Ran all the way from Upper Canada; ended here in this lush Pacific rainforest. The Colonial Experiment was strictly one way, so it's up to the Apology Express to make the return trip.

Watch as we go by: a Doukhobor girl peeks out from under her house, her head scarf muddy. The police officers who took her sister and her friends away to the school in New Denver are gone and won't be back for another week. A Cree boy, hair freshly shorn into a brush cut, stares out the window of a residential school in the middle of the Saskatchewan grasslands, watching his parents' backs as they walk away. A Japanese fisherman hands over the keys to his new boat. A Ukrainian woman swats the mosquitoes away, bends to pick potatoes at Spirit Lake, and feels her baby dying inside her. A Chinese man living under a bridge thinks about his wife at home and wonders if he'll see her again.

But take heart: at every stop on the way back, someone important will say sorry for their lot. Just like the man in the top hat on my son's train engine TV show, he'll make it all better, no matter how much of a mess there's been.

All aboard. If you feel a little sick, it's just the motion of the cars. Close your eyes. Try not to forget.

Jen Budney and Jayce Salloum

Jen Budney is interested in epistemology, or the nature and scope and limitations of knowledge. Working as a curator allows her to explore this arena in collaboration with a wide variety of artists, writers, and other creative individuals and groups. Her study foci for several years, both professional and personal, include the relationships between land and language in Indigenous cultures worldwide, Buddhist theories of impermanence and no-self, the roles and practices of museums, and the function of monuments. In 2002, she completed a master's degree in anthropology, in which her research focused on racial attitudes and barriers to equity in the contemporary art world of Brazil—a subject inspired by her friend and long-time collaborator, the Brazilian artist Maria Thereza Alves. Jen has contributed essays to catalogues and journals including *NeoHoodoo: Art for a Forgotten Faith* (ed. Franklin Sirmans, Menil Collection, Houston, TX), *American West* (eds. Jimmie Durham and Richard W. Hill, Compton Verney, UK), *Parkett*, *Third Text*, *FUSE*, *Art AsiaPacific*, and the now defunct *World Art*. She lives with her husband, baby daughter, and two border collies in Saskatoon, Saskatchewan, where she works as a curator at the Mendel Art Gallery.

Jayce Salloum: "I have been producing art, collecting things, making things happen, and mixing it up for as long as I can remember. It was always part *art* and part *social facilitation*, or maybe that makes it all "art"; anyways, it was usually counter whatever the "culture" happened to *be* at the time and involved people from various parts of the "community" in liaison and/or at odds with each other. Lately, the work has involved production and facilitation in Lebanon, Berlin, New York, the former Yugoslavia, Kamloops, Cumberland House, Vancouver, Aotearoa/New Zealand, Afghanistan, and Australia. My practice exists within and between the personal, quotidian, local, and the transnational. In one sense it has always been about mediation—the gap between the experience and the accounting/telling/receiving of it—engaging in an intimate subjectivity and discursive challenge while critically asserting itself in the perception of social manifestations and political realities." Jayce has worked in installation, photography, drawing, performance, text, and video since 1979, as well as curating exhibitions, conducting workshops, and coordinating a vast array of cultural projects. He has exhibited pervasively at the widest range of local and international venues possible, from the smallest unnamed storefronts and community centres in his Downtown Eastside neighbourhood to institutions such as the Künstlerhaus Bethanien, Berlin; The Museum of Modern Art, New York; and the Musée du Louvre, Paris. Recently his work has been featured in *The Archive* (Whitechapel/MIT, 2006), *Projecting Migration: Transcultural Documentary Practice* (Wallflower, 2007), and *Practical Dreamers: Conversations with Movie Artists* (Coach House, 2008).

Engendering Audience Responsibility:
The work of Jayce Salloum "in affinity with"

Jayce Salloum is a Vancouver artist best known for photo-based and multimedia works that explore identity, migration, border changes, and territorial shifts in a transnational context. Media theorist Laura U. Marks once described his practice as one that "redefines citizenship, and artistic citizenship in particular,"[1] across the boundaries marked by exhibitions, funding, municipalities, regions, nations, and the international *nowhere* sphere of festivals and biennials. Marks's account stressed Salloum's sense of civic responsibility, wherein art—its making, curation, and dissemination— becomes one of many means of achieving social justice. A photo-based artist best known for his ongoing *untitled* videotapes series, Salloum has also always been engaged with collaborative art-making groups, such as *desmedia*, the Downtown Eastside media collective in Vancouver. While the participants in desmedia include several Aboriginal artists, since 2005 Salloum has been making videotapes and producing collaborative art-making workshops specifically with Aboriginal communities in Interior British Columbia and, most recently, northern Saskatchewan. And although the contents of both the videotapes and the workshops are of vital interest, it is the process of their production and reception that particularly interests me as being of critical relevance to the reconciliation movement in Canada. Unique to both Salloum's *untitled* videotapes and the products of his collaborative art-making workshops are the ways that these works demand that audiences become actively responsible for the co-production of meaning. This engendering of responsibility in the viewer is a step towards a new, or renewed, conception of citizenship that is essential to the reconciliation process.

What does it mean to be a citizen, let alone an *artistic* citizen, in Canada today? In Eurocentric modern sovereignties like Canada, citizenship has generally been framed in terms of political, civil, and social rights of which the former two constitute defences against abuses of power by the state, while the latter requires the active intervention of the state to equalize citizens' opportunities to the first two. The responsibilities of citizens *to each other* (not to the state) are typically underemphasized. Canada, as a so-called 'nation of immigrants,' is of course a colonized territory in which the descendants

BP's leaves, bingo card, west coast inspirations, Berge's colour zones, Oppenheimer Park riffs, Ricky's horns/antlers, Eagle Ed's ovoids/s/u forms filled in based on his specs, and many more.

Collaborative painting from the desmedia workshops (produced at the Carnegie Centre, Oppenheimer Park and other sites) as installed in Pigeon Park Savings, 92 E. Hastings St., Downtown Eastside, Vancouver (2004–2005) of settlers, immigrants, and Indigenous people share citizenship unequally. Citizenship can be passively enjoyed by those who benefit from the uneven distribution of resources and imbalanced access to political, civil, and social rights. Within this context, it is all too easy for members of the dominant class—which in Canada includes mainly the descendents of settlers and European immigrants—to become complacent or even defensive and protective. Essentially, the position enjoyed by the dominant, largely *white* community blinds it to its own power and privilege, so that this community's own culture becomes a self-invisible norm, and all other cultures and social positions come to be seen as *Other*.[2] The forms of individualism and myopia nurtured in this scenario interfere, in the extreme, with the formation of cross-cultural and cross-class alliances in the service of social justice. In the arts, this has meant a very long history of segregation, wherein the dominant cultural community has remained ignorant of the cultural productions, issues, and ideas of non-European immigrants and, even more so, of Aboriginal artists. Across the country, there are only a few models of creating interaction between Aboriginal and non-Aboriginal visual arts communities. (One of the oldest now is TRIBE: A Centre for the Evolving Aboriginal Media, Visual and Performing Arts Inc., based in Saskatoon, conceived by its co-founders in 1995 as a nomadic Aboriginal artist-run organization that would infiltrate mainstream spaces with the work of Aboriginal artists in order to ensure that audiences of Aboriginal art were diverse, and not only Aboriginal or, more precisely, to ensure that members of the dominant culture would engage with the issues and ideas of Aboriginal artists.)

In his work of the past decade, Salloum has been one of a small number of non-Aboriginal Canadian artists to overturn this standard by actively seeking partnerships and collaborations with First Nations individuals and communities in his work. As the grandchild of Lebanese immigrants, he heard stories of the racism experienced by his parents and had first-hand experience of the repressed violence and vagaries of assimilation. Since he began his career as a professional artist in the late 1970s, he has always taken as a primary focus issues of political, social, and cultural representation, with an emphasis in his videotapes, on representations of the transnational in the Middle East and the Western portrayal of Arabs and of Lebanon. But after decades of making work in and about the Middle East, Eastern Europe, the USA, and elsewhere he turned his attentions homeward in 2005—literally, to his hometown of Kelowna, British Columbia, when he was invited by the Alternator Centre for Contemporary Art to produce a videotape for the city's Centenary. Salloum chose as his subject the history and effects of the settlement of Kelowna by Europeans on the local Westbank First Nation.

Jayce Salloum, from *untitled part 1: everything and nothing*
videotape, 40:40, 1999 (2001)

Soha Bechara, former Lebanese secular resistance fighter, weaving between representation and subject, speaking closely of the distance of what was lost, what is left behind, and what remains.

JS: "Here, this is ... your home?"

SB: "My home. It's not easy to define home ... is it where one lives, the house that one was born and grew up in? As Lebanese, the war taught us—and because we changed homes so many times—that every house is a home. It is enough for me to stay a week somewhere to feel a sense of a belonging and a connection with that place. I feel the same thing regarding this room I am living in now.

"I also learned from the civil war that the moment after leaving my home, a place that was lost, destroyed by shelling ... to stop thinking about it. I should think of the future. If I only think and live in the past, I am bound to fail. One should think of what is to come.

"The past is a history, a lesson to learn from in order to proceed into the future. I do feel at home here. I have been here for two months now."

Jayce Salloum, from *untitled part 4: terra incognita* (2005)
videotape, 37:30

Wilfred (Grouse) Barnes retracing/pointing out the linguistic/territorial map of the N'syilxcen speakers, the Syilx (Okanagan) peoples of the valley—at the WFN Community Centre, Westbank, British Columbia: "N'syilxcen nation, see, this is the language we speak in our territory—N'syilxcen, not Okanagan, N'syilxcen, N'syilxcen Nation. So if you ask me where I come from, I'll say N'syilx."

Although this work, *untitled part 4: terra incognita* (2005), involves interviews with many members of the Westbank and Okanagan First Nations, who speak of such things as the community's memory of the creation of the reserve system, the legacy of residential schools, and the lack of access to sacred places located within city boundaries, it is not a documentary in the typical sense. Whereas documentaries create or impose frameworks for representing their subjects, inserting images and text in such a way that the documentary's position appears seamless, Salloum instead deliberately engenders, in this videotape as in others, what he refers to as "productive frustration" in the viewer. The usual subject of the gaze becomes the speaker, but unlike typical documentaries, Salloum's videotapes do not frame the speakers so much as dance with them, around them, and next to them. The presence of the camera operator is almost always perceptible by the way the image shakes or wobbles, or by the sound of Salloum's slightly muffled voice; there are no soundtracks insisting upon a certain mood or sense of drama. Instead, the wind whips voices from microphones, a telephone rings off screen, or there are other audible cues and interruptions alerting us to the contextual nature of the particular video clip; and often spoken words do not align themselves neatly to the images, such as when one speaker recounts the story of his younger brother's death from depression and substance use, but the screen shows only the shadow of a leafy tree blowing gently in the breeze.

In a country where opinions proliferate about the so-called Native situation, yet where few white people—particularly from the middle (and upper) class—have any real acquaintance with Aboriginal people or culture, Salloum's tactics challenge viewers to coordinate their own experiences and assumptions with the presented material to arrive at knowledge. In some cases the diverse realities represented in the videotapes and the prior experience and assumptions of the viewers may on occasion coincide or find agreement, but at other times they may collide or compete with each other, and sometimes the viewer will simply be faced with silence, such as a blackout in the image or an untranslated remark. Yet even these experiences produce a kind of knowledge for viewers, not just about the Westbank First Nation, the artist, or Interior BC, but also about systems of communication and representation, from language itself to tourism promotion to academia to prime-time TV. Viewers are forced to challenge their own preconceptions about what they think they know and what they are able to know (that is, not everything). This self-reflection is as essential and desired an outcome of Salloum's work as any information he may try to communicate or translate about an individual, thing, place, or situation. To put this in other words, *untitled part 4: terra incognita* resists equally: the anthropologist's desire

*Roxanne Lindley at the 3 x 3 metre fenced-in area, which is the only
sacred Syilx site protected by the city of Kelowna—at a cost to the WFN
(Westbank First Nation) of $25,000 ... stalling outright disappearance of "key
indicators"; uneasily, ancestors rest here. "We could never come here to
have a ceremony. We could never come here and acknowledge the spirit of
the land. This is a fishing area, this is a harvesting area, from Mission Creek
this way, you know ... and from Mission Creek this way, it didn't matter. The
whole integrity of the site has been destroyed."*

Jayce Salloum, from *untitled part 4: terra incognita* (2005)
videotape, 37:30

Leonard Raphael at his WFN house recounting residential school survival, confronting foreign brick walls, and meeting his siblings and other children there, the alienation and fear, the repercussions, and the doors and paths: "What had happened, I guess most of the time at nights, you'd recognize the children that missed their parents, or missed their sisters and brothers. They would be ... crying. You could hear that. You know the sound of when somebody's missing in a family; the family structure is breaking down. So I guess that would be some of the things that we would hear as we were growing up in the residential school.

The spiritual sense is the one that brought us back, will keep us going mainly because of the strength that has always been there. The belief in Mother Earth and what she's taught us in our lives. How to share and what it means to share these things that are so beautiful that she provides for us freely.

Having to realize that what was in our past was also ... like doorways, having to look at doorways, recognizing that there are teachings within each door that will reopen or close, whenever we allowed ourselves to grow up in that kind of environment ... it teaches us a lot about what is in front of us yet to come."

Jayce Salloum, from *untitled part 4: terra incognita* (2005)
videotape, 37:30

Elizabeth Lindley Charters, a Syilx elder, in her yard just up from the lake, pointing out how and where the reserve was marked out by runners and sliced off in three successive colonial dispossessions (1856–1861, 1877, and 1912–1914).

"...they picked this one guy and they told him, 'Okay, you go, go down Powers Creek, and then you got Powers Creek, you follow that water right up, right up to the top, follow that creek right up to the top, and then you go north ...' and then they mentioned a mountain, and then you come down to the ... you go by creeks, hey. And that is how big your reserve will be. This guy he went out, and ... he just ... this little area here, well other than a little bit more, that ... we did have all that taken from us anyhow, so what's the difference? We lost some lands, cut off here and there ... he did come ... there's a straightaway I know that ... parts of it ... that are cut off by Westbank ... we just made a little ... and he got back, you know, they ... they packed him up a lunch and said, 'Go, you go that way, you go that way.' Packed him up a few days of lunch, and he comes back when the sun is way down there just getting close to the top of them trees. He came back and the Elders, they said, 'Well, how come you're back?' 'Oh,' he says, 'If I went too far where you wanted me to go, way around...' he says, 'those poor white people would get tired if they have to go around.'"

Jayce Salloum, from *untitled part 4: terra incognita* (2005)
videotape, 37:30

to categorize, label, and consign; the liberal's desire to feel pity and also to be redeemed by the implication of a (different) culprit; the policeman's desire to locate and confine; and even the politician's desire to ignore and dismiss as the product of an artist with a fixed, biased position. In my view, this videotape offers a crucial lesson about how true reconciliation can take place: it is not enough to passively observe the process. Instead, all citizens must actively engage and participate.

Critics on the right have occasionally labelled Salloum's work as "ugly political propaganda,"[3] while some on the left have questioned his engagement with the stories of people who do not fit the artist's own identity profile, particularly his work with First Nations communities. The latter questioning acknowledges the colonial practice of cultural appropriation, but also disengages from active solidarity. In one interview for a large anthology on Canadian film and video makers, Salloum was asked: "Haven't we seen too many Native stories told by others?"[4] The artist replied: "There are many powerful Aboriginal filmmakers and video artists in Canada, such as Alanis Obomsawin, Zacharius Kunuk, Annie Fraziér Henry, Dana Claxton, Loretta Todd, Barb Cranmer, Cease Wyss, to name just a few. I'm not sure how many of them you've interviewed … For me it [is] not a question of speaking for others (appropriation) versus carving out a space for suppressed voices (emancipation)—it is much more complex than that. I speak in affinity with."[5] (In fact, none of the artists Salloum listed were interviewed.) The fact is, colonialism and the legacies of the residential school system are not an "Aboriginal issue," but an issue that impacts all Canadians, affecting us all, in wildly divergent ways: economically, socially, and psychologically. There is no healing unless we all are healed (and for some, it means being healed of racism and ignorance), and to achieve this we must know each other and work together for change.

Affinity and collaboration are guiding principles not only for Salloum's *untitled* videotape series but also for his collaborative art-making workshops, one of which, the Native Youth Art Workshop (NYAW) in Kamloops, BC, was designed to bring the voices of Aboriginal youth from Kamloops and surrounding regions to the wider Kamloops community. Salloum's project was funded by the Kamloops Art Gallery (KAG), and was co-facilitated by Meeka Morgan, a Secwepemc/Nuu-chah-nulth writer and performer, along with Victoria Morgan and Rob Hall. In a city where Aboriginal parents had recently protested the lack of First Nations cultural education in the city's public school system, the workshops, held monthly or bi-weekly at the KAG and at some reserves in the Thompson–Nicola Regional District, provided a regular outlet for a broad cross-section of Native youths (including First Nations, Métis, and Inuit, urban, "rez," traditional, or foster kids in white homes, ranging in age from

Shoshana Wilson sketched the main figures, about a month later her father Barry Wilson dropped in to help, as did (uncle) Henry Venn Robertson. Tara and many others contributed along the way. "This canvas represents first nations and culture, and the many traditions of first nations people around the province. The central whale represents the Wilson's family crest with the sun in the left hand corner that explains their family story. Everything in the whale represents the lifestyle on the coast. This canvas shouts native pride and identity."

Native Youth Art Workshops (NYAW), *whale/history/culture*
collaborative painting, 95" x 59"
Kamloops Art Gallery, 9/14/2008 - 10/2009

Nathan Lynn created the central theme/figures in this work, other participants worked on the peripheral figures/areas. "This piece represents the technologically influenced pull away from one's culture."

Native Youth Art Workshops (NYAW), *wireless*
collaborative painting, 95" x 59", Kamloops Art Gallery, 2/2009-9/2009

Image on following spread: *Workshops were designed in response to the interests of the participants, to focus on sharing their experiences, to articulate and express their concerns, and to gather work done with and accounts shared by local elders. The context of the projects is within the links that exist between community and individual or self, both inextricably connected.*

All the paintings were designed for the large gallery wall facing the street and public library, visible day and night. "Much of this canvas represents our families, community traditions, and how identity changes with the influence of other cultures and environments."

yellow/Bonaparte/Soo Cartoon (Jordan, Robert's central figures)

Native Youth Art Workshops (NYAW)
collaborative painting 95" x 59", Kamloops Art Gallery, 8/9/2007-12/2008

three to mid-twenties), along with one or two non-Native children, to share experiences, meet with contemporary First Nations artists, come in contact with Aboriginal art history, and express themselves collectively in paint and sound. Importantly, the workshops never focused on the participants' points of origin, except to acknowledge the different kinds of impacts of the residential school system on them and their families; rather, Salloum and Morgan, as facilitators, along with the participants, set themselves the task of identifying and exploring their divergent and shared histories, with the goal of painting their present conditions and mapping out a future together.

Like Salloum's videotapes, the paintings produced in NYAW contain equal mixes of beauty and pain, hope and violence, and voice and silence. More symbolic than narrative, the highly colourful works tend to be largely symbolic, with elements of graffiti and poetry. The multi-hued, at times child-like or crude, style of the NYAW works, speaks openly to Aboriginal and non-Aboriginal people alike. They don't *mean* anything, at least nothing that can be easily summarized; rather, they are expressive of a great deal of energy, shared conversations and points of reflection, and a common goal. At their first public display, during the opening of Salloum's touring retrospective at the KAG, the paintings were mounted in a long, windowed corridor, visible to passersby on the street, framed by the names (in vinyl lettering) of all the youths involved and of their ethnic origins, as they self-identified. While the majority of participants were Interior Salish, and identified simply as Secwepemc, a huge number claimed hybridized roots, from St'át'imc–Secwepemc to Ojibway–Gwichya Gwich'in–Cree to Gitxsan–Chinese and Blackfoot–Irish. More than particular stories that were embedded in the canvasses, the NYAW works and their installation spoke of the fact of sharing—the sharing of past, present, and future—even if the shared past and present has been ignored by the majority of non-Aboriginal people in Canada until recently, and even if we are still uncertain about our shared future. Confrontation is carried out in these works in subtle and sharp ways that keep spectators not only engaged, but also challenged, which is an integral part of the process of sense-making. The paintings, like the videotapes, and like all of Salloum's work, do not impose a sense of guilt but a sense of recognition that is a powerful tool in any process of reconciliation.

Channelle Edwards, Tara Wilson, Diana Charlie, Cheyenne Chanin, and Chaynoa Chanin working on the "whale" painting

Native Youth Art Workshops (NYAW), Kamloops Art Gallery studio, 3/14/2009

NYAW participants ranged from three-and-a-half to over 60 years old. At first we tried to define "youth" and thought to limit the age from 14 to 24, but soon many outside this age bracket started attending (youth started bringing their own kids and some older parents started hanging around and participating), so we opened it up to be inclusive of other family members and friends (Native and non-Native) participating within the Native youth-focused framework of the workshop. Work on the paintings involved discussion of images, negotiating space, continuity, and skill development. The participants' self-expressions and self-representations are at the heart of this project.

Native Youth Art Workshops (NYAW), Kamloops Art Gallery studio, [Sue Buis photograph], 6/6/2009

The focus of the project was on the development and production of large collaborative works that incorporated aspects of oral histories combined with the youths' experiences of living their own history within the context of the past they carry with them. Nathan is by the "wireless" canvas, Geo (George Ignace) is coming in to work on the music CD, and Henry Venn Robertson, Shoshana Wilson, and Barry Wilson, are working on the "whale" painting.

Notes

1 Marks, Laura U. (2003:18). Citizen Salloum. *FUSE magazine* 26(3):18.
2 For more on this subject see: Frankenberg, Ruth (ed.) (1997). *Displacing Whiteness: Essays in Social and Cultural Criticism*. Durham, NC: Duke University Press.
3 Dirlik, John (2007:27). Canadian museum decision, reversal angers both Arabs, Jews. *The Washington Report on Middle East Affairs* 21(1):27.
4 Hoolboom, M. (2008:201). *Jayce Salloum: From Lebanon to Kelowna*. In M. Hoolboom (ed.). *Practical Dreamers: Conversations with Movie Artists*. (1st ed.). Toronto, ON: Coach House Books: 185–202.
5 Hoolboom (2008:201).

Rita Shelton Deverell

Rita Shelton Deverell: More than 40 years as a broadcaster, television host, theatre artist, professor, and public speaker has taught me that there are questions which are important to audiences, yet remain un-answered by my usual biographical sketches. If these questions are stuck in the listeners' ears they can't hear what I'm saying. Since I don't want that to happen to you dear readers, I'm dealing with these Frequently Asked (in an embarrassed sort of way) Questions about Rita Shelton Deverell, B.A., Adelphi; MA, Columbia; Ed.D., OISE/University of Toronto; presently the 12th holder of Nancy's Chair in Women's Studies at Mount Saint Vincent University:

Q: Where are you from?

A: It turns out this really means "where were you born?" Answer: Houston Negro Hospital in 1945. For the record, I have been black and female ever since.

Q: Why did you come to Canada?

A: The answer, though I'd like it to be more dramatic, is that I married a fellow graduate student in New York, who was and still is Canadian.

Q: Did he stick around?

A: Yes, although I hasten to add that I'm not old enough to have been married 43 years. He is.

Q: Was emigrating a mistake?

A: At first I thought it might be. I immigrated in 1967, the year Canada gave up British titles. What rotten luck! Like any little girl who wished herself a princess and an actress, I wanted to be a "Dame." All is happiness, though, because I was made a Member of the Order of Canada in 2004.

Q: How do you stand our winters?

A: Personal temperature comfort is a matter of metabolism, not determined by birthplace. My elementary school teachers in the South always felt I was underdressed for winter. When I first lived in a colder climate, I felt instantly happier, more productive, and had a lively spring in my step. Everything else, dear readers, about the relationship of Aboriginal peoples to this immigrant, is in the essay that follows.

Slavery Endangers the Masters' Health But Please Don't Shoot the Messenger

Preface

I am an immigrant to Canada. What follows is a chronological account of my relationship as a settler to the Indigenous population. It is hoped that by leaving nothing out we can live together in the contemporary aspects of an ancient meeting of cultures.

1971–72

There are shadowy brown people creeping around the edge of what feels like a USA Wild West town square. In my mind's eye, it resembles 1940s Texas, where I grew up.

But focus. Get a grip, woman. This is not Texas. This is Canada, my new country, the 1970s. This is Thunder Bay, Ontario. I am still black; however, these brown people are not Afro-Canadians.

Regina is my final destination this first trip west from Toronto, and there I come to understand that these mysterious brown people are Aboriginal. The déjà vu feeling is correct though. Aboriginal persons are literally and figuratively on the margins. They are excluded from the center of society's hustle and bustle.

In those days I was an actress and thrilled beyond words to have been hired by Regina's professional theatre, The Globe. It was not easy for black and other visible minority actors working in *mainstream* theatre back then, and not much easier now. But that's another story for another article.

1971: only three years have passed since the assassination of Martin Luther King, Jr., and memories of the civil rights era are still fresh. Many Regina citizens still have vivid memories of news footage featuring police dogs, fire hoses, and angry mobs shaking their fists at little black girls. When Saskatchewanites mentally connect me with this racial trauma they've witnessed on television, they begin to chant with passion and compassion, "We are not racist" (in Canada). Quickly I discover that these same *not racist* people believe that Indians are all on welfare, are lazy and shiftless, are not proactive about their children's education, have messy family lives, and are drunks. I tell at least three individuals per day that these attitudes directed at an identifiable group constitute racism. They have become convinced that only if their negative feelings are directed at black people, of whom there are almost none in Regina, are they being racist. "Racism" and "Aboriginal people" are not yet terms that can be logically linked together for most folk. So I tell at least three people a day that I, a middle-class, well-educated, employed in professional theatre of all places black person, identify with the Aboriginal targets of racism. Never mind that I know next to nothing about the lives, issues, history, and concerns of these Plains peoples. It is a skin-deep, knee-jerk identification thing that has followed me for forty years.

Now to the actual work I am in Regina for: to perform for the Globe Theatre School Tour in over one hundred Saskatchewan communities from Thanksgiving to Labour Day. My inclusion makes the Globe cast multiracial. Our company carries three plays, one for kindergarten to grade three, another for grades four to six, and a high school anthology called *Shakespeare's Women*. When we get to our first small-town school that is near a First Nation community we all spot several rows of dark big guys and gals with baseball hats at the back of the gym. Who are they? Teachers tell us "the Natives may have to catch the bus early. Pay no attention when they walk out." Or, if "the Natives don't listen to your show, don't worry, the others will." This isn't quite good enough for actors as an explanation of how our art is being received. All high school audiences are tough. Go to a Stratford Festival "school matinee" if you don't believe me! And, as with any successful performance, when our shows work well it is because the audience finds something with which they can identify at a very deep level. Theatre people are artistically and ethically responsible for that kind of true communication, and when it is working, the audience will meet you halfway and you can commune.

Sometimes the communication was true and real. The big guys who were bused in from First Nations had tears in their eyes at Shakespeare's tales of betrayal, abandonment, jealousy, love, romance, hate, corrupt government, and witchcraft. Sometimes we blew it. There would be a near-riot of gum popping, snoring, catcalls, and spitballs. Five actors from Toronto learned a lot about what happened when you did not connect with an audience, across your differences, about what was most important to them. But we would sometimes get it right with those audiences. And there is no high like it.

1975–76

Broadcasting is now another of my occupations, obtained after another three-year stint in Toronto. I become an official messenger, a reporter, a presenter. I have the opportunity to do feature stories for *24 Hours*, the CBC TV supper-hour news show in Regina. True, this is the hind-end of the CBC system. We are so under-resourced that our Regina studio is in Moose Jaw, and *most days* I can get a crew. But I have been hired as a messenger. How am I going to use that power? In an early meeting with the news director I say: "Aboriginal people are 30 per cent of the population. You'd never know that from looking at our show. So I'd like to do stories with them, about their issues." The news director's response is pretty close to: "I'm not going to stop you, but I'm not going to help you. Those people are impossible. They are always late, or don't show up at all, pay them on Friday, they don't show on Monday, et cetera, et cetera. Good luck to you." The Aboriginal stories get on the air though. And I do learn a few basic lessons in "diversity journalism," which continue to come in handy and, I hope, deepen over the years.

Some of those lessons are:

- Women are excellent story contacts, experts, and spokespersons in Aboriginal communities, and most other communities as well.

- It takes time and patience to develop relationships, but these pay off for the media person. My crew and I went on night patrol with a Native women's organization, got an exclusive with the spokesman for the Warrior Society, got inside the economics of inner-city housing, and more.

- Being the messenger has its dangers. I was questioned by the police twice simply because of being seen with the interviewees in my stories. To this day I cannot say whether the police wanted information from me, which I was not going to give beyond what was on television and therefore readily available or whether I was being warned off the Aboriginal subject matter, contacts, issues, the messages.

- Finally, there is the dawning understanding of how I have come to be middle-class, well-educated, and working at my chosen professions in spite of having grown up black in the violently segregated and racist US South. Privileges and opportunity were mine for a number of reasons: my parents had been able to own land and houses from the beginning of their long marriage in 1940, as had their parents and grandparents. While by no means rich, they had steady employment, savings, insurance, were able to obtain mortgages, thought education was the most important thing in the world, and were able and willing to pay my tuition fees through graduate school. I, as an only girl child, had two ambitious, intelligent, politically astute parents deeply devoted to my development and their own advancement in the world. Canada was happy to welcome an immigrant in 1967 who brought all those assets into the country. I came to understand over time that these were all advantages that most, though not all, Aboriginal people who had been here since time immemorial, simply did not have.

With hindsight I also know that I did not know much then. There are Aboriginal realities that other Canadians, recent or long-term immigrants, have to work hard to discover. For example, during the Saskatchewan years I drove by the former residential school at Lebret many times. I did not know what it was, found out nothing about residential schools, nor were the schools mentioned in my stories. My contacts were not yet ready to reveal their experiences, and I didn't even know what questions to ask.

1985–89

Being a professor of Journalism, and then acting Director of the School of Journalism and Communications at the University of Regina, places me in an official capacity to train messengers. This is both rewarding and frustrating in terms of First Nations issues specifically.

At that time there was very little information, investigation, or even curiosity from the "white" students I was teaching. During my five-year tenure there was a grand total of two visible minority students: one was a Spanish speaker, a recent immigrant from South America; the other was a Muslim with a Pakistani background who had been in Saskatchewan since elementary school. Coexisting with the School of Journalism and Communications was the Indian Communications Arts (INCA) Program of the Saskatchewan Indian Federated College, later to become First Nations University. We could not establish a working relationship regardless of how potentially fruitful and necessary it appeared. The settler journalists certainly needed to learn from INCA students and faculty, and they in turn could have made use of our resources, human and material. So I am very pleased to look at the U of R and FNU websites in 2010 and see that there *is* a relationship, and that the settler journalism school knows that it is in Treaty 4 Territory. For me, twenty-five years ago though, this was a crisis in training messengers.

1990

Lurching to another more visible and famous crisis, a telephone call came out of the blue during Oka. Dorothy Christian, an Okanagan–Shuswap woman I had never met, phones me at Vision TV and asks if I would do the peaceful side of the Oka story.

Dorothy and a number of other women were planning to make a peace march to Oka and do peace ceremonies behind the barricades. Dorothy said she could not interest any mainstream media in this story and thought that perhaps the current affairs unit of Vision TV would be interested. Well we certainly were, all three of us, who produced a one-hour, weekly current affairs magazine show for a network that had little money. Thus began a working relationship with Dorothy Christian that lasted for ten years and a friendship that still continues. She had no formal media or journalism training, was slightly over forty, but was very willing to learn, deeply committed to telling several other sides of Aboriginal stories, committed to communicating with the settler and recent immigrant production team, and with our audiences. We were patient with Dorothy learning the tricks of the TV current affairs trade. She was even more patient with what we did not know about Aboriginal issues. Dorothy produced, directed, and wrote award-winning stories. She was on pundits' panels. She did phone-ins from various locations and was very active in our annual production team planning meetings.

There was a truckload of learnings that came from this experience:

- Peace stories are hard to do in media, but are important.

- We needed to introduce our multi-faith and multicultural audiences to a diversity of Aboriginal points of view, not just one POV.

- As long as we were willing to play ball there would be Aboriginal people ready to do the work of educating us and our audiences. They would also be ready to share respectfully in whatever expertise we had to offer.

1991–99

We learn that our annual production planning meetings are significant. Over the years we go from producing a weekly show to daily current affairs series, and frequently both at the same time. The teams, technical and editorial, usually consist of persons with the following faith and ethnic backgrounds: Muslim, Jewish, Hindu, Quaker, Roman Catholic and Protestant Christians, Humanist/Atheist, Buddhist, New Age, Aboriginal spirituality; recent or ancient ancestry in Chinese, Japanese, Pakistani, British Isles, West Indian, Swiss, American, prairie Mennonite, Atlantic and Pacific regions, Quebec, urban and rural cultures, all with diversity in class, ability, sexual orientation, and age.

We had to be able to explain our personal and professional assumptions to each other. We had to do this non-defensively, with humour, and with trust. These annual production planning meetings had a strong educational component. That was why we were getting together. First, over the days and seasons, everyone got to lead the team in meditation/worship/reflection/ their spirituality, or whatever you wish to call it. Second, everyone got to lead the team in their storytelling expertise. We had team members with dazzling picture sense, or brilliant writing skills, or wonderful approaches to editing, or riveting presentation techniques. We were sharing our strengths as workers, individuals, and cultures; and the production teams became stronger every year. We were award winning: Geminis, Women in Film and TV-Toronto, Canadian Council of Christians and Jews, Urban Alliance on Race Relations, et cetera. Our stories ranged from serious investigative journalism to profiles to multi-faith comedy.

1999

The first serious information comes into my head about residential schools, in the way that it has come to many non-Aboriginal Canadians, via Phil Fontaine.

On the tenth anniversary of Vision TV we decided to do ten programs on human rights topics in ten provinces and territories. Fontaine, then National Chief of the Assembly of First Nations, talked about the physical, sexual, and cultural abuses endured in residential schools. He said that such things had happened to him and that it was time he talked about it. There was tremendous power in the humility of Phil Fontaine's message at that time. He was willing to appear vulnerable and weak, a way of being strong for other Survivors. Now I knew a bit more, and residential schools stayed with me as a subject to be explored with the ROC—the rest of Canada.

2000

"The churches will be bankrupt!" by the residential schools settlements is the rumour that is flying through the corridors of Vision TV. Since churches are one of the many constituencies with whom we work, and we have always dealt with Aboriginal issues, and share some of our information programming with CBC Newsworld, I propose a co-production. The third partner is to be the just-launched APTN where a longtime colleague, Dan David, Mohawk from Kahnawake, is news director. The project is ambitious and fraught with editorial and technical pitfalls for all of us, but especially for APTN, which has been on the air about fourteen months. Finally, we have five hours on residential schools to be broadcast on all three networks. The host for newbie APTN is splendidly articulate Rick Harp. I am fronting for Vision TV, and veteran Anne Petrie is there for Newsworld. In addition, APTN and VTV are responsible for the documentary style "field pieces" that walk with real Survivors, Victims, and Players. Newsworld handles the studio segments in which early participants in the Aboriginal Healing Foundation examine the present and the future as well as the past.

Our programs are called *Canada's National Shame;* and we are tripping landmines. The churches are wary of the economics of apology. The government is not apologizing. Both parties finger point. Some Aboriginal people do not see why APTN should talk to Vision TV and CBC Newsworld. CBC seriously questions how the other two production partners can be *objective* about such an emotional subject.

We survived. We went to air. Everybody managed to tell the truth from where they stood. Working out those shows was a major exercise in cross-cultural communications and finding solutions. We have no regrets.

2002–05

After thirty-ish years in the TV trenches, I am invited to be Director of News and Current Affairs at APTN. The task is to mentor my Aboriginal successor and kick-start a daily news show. On editorial content I seldom try to convince my all-Aboriginal team that something is or is not a story. They know more about that than I do. My job is simply to clarify, to keep our writing and our focus sharp, and to build the kind of well-oiled machine that can reliably produce daily, fifty-two weeks of the year.

Part of my learning curve is to hear almost weekly about the fallout from residential schools on our live open-line show *Contact,* on APTN National News, and, naturally, on specials. The other big story is the Ipperwash Inquiry. We decide to broadcast three hours a week of the hearings. Mainstream media outlets are really not covering this Commission, created by the government of Ontario after ten years of pleas and threatened lawsuits from Sam George, brother of the murdered unarmed protestor Dudley. The lack of interest in the Ipperwash proceedings in Forest, Ontario, speaks volumes about a land claims story that takes seventy years to resolve. It is a story of the appropriation, misappropriation, exploitation, and reclaiming of land. It is a long story. The mainstream can only deal with sound bites.

In August 2005, near the end of my time at APTN, Hurricane Katrina makes a landfall on the Gulf Coast. For five days after, Canadian newspapers run front-page pictures of 100,000 trapped, poor black people. I know those people. But nobody is talking about the racism, classicism, and cronyism that trap those former slaves. I ask permission to write an opinion-editorial piece from my boss, APTN CEO Jean LaRose. He says, "go ahead." Mr. LaRose, Abenaki from Quebec, is disturbed by the news coverage too. And as an Aboriginal person he immediately sees that the same thing could and does happen in Canada. The news gets it right on the sixth day after the hurricane though; that is, they get the racism part right. They do not get that it could and does happen here.

I do not have to write that editorial right then. But three years later, I have worked up a head of steam about all the money, time, and tears Canadians are spending *down there* without looking in our own backyards.

2008

This year sees a play written and performed by me in Winnipeg named *Big Ease, Big Sleaze*. I do not think *Big Ease, Big Sleaze* is my finest dramatic hour; however, what I need to say is this: before Canadians attempt to achieve salvation by assisting people in far-flung lands, like the ninth ward of New Orleans after Katrina, let us recognize that we have tons of sins to deal with right here. We save ourselves by recognizing those sins and changing our relationship to Aboriginal people, beginning with being truthful. My central characters in *Big Ease, Big Sleaze*, both Canadians, are an older brown gentleman and a young white woman. They both realize they do not have to get on an airplane to attempt to right wrongs. The wrongs are at their doorsteps.

2006–09

More successful than *Big Ease, Big Sleaze*, I hope, is a TV docudrama, *Not a Drop*, first broadcast in 2009 on OMNI. By nature of service, mandate, and conditions of license, OMNI, a multilingual broadcaster, does not deal with Aboriginal languages and issues (APTN does that), or Francophone matters (Radio-Canada and TVA do that). OMNI is interested though in the story I want to tell about the relationship of recent or long-term immigrants to Aboriginal people. The story centers down on a fictionalized graduate school class in Diversity Journalism, based on real events. One of the students, Jeremy, who is black, stresses that he almost doesn't take the course because:

> Like from my own personal background I didn't think there was anything I could even learn about diversity, but when you showed us some of those other experiences of people who've been here for so long, but still feel disenfranchised, still feel isolated, it made me think to myself—like there's way more to cover out there than fatherless Jamaican families, not to put that down.[1]

While we were in pre-production for *Not a Drop* the Sunrise Propane explosion hit Toronto on 10 August 2008. This caused me to write an opinion-editorial piece in the *Toronto Sun* on the differences between Ontario's downtown capital city and the Walpole Island First Nation where the documentary portions were being shot:

> *Just how high and how fast can last Sunday morning's Sunrise Propane explosion make Queen's Park jump?*
>
> *If I were a gambling woman, I'd say the provincial government will close the loopholes around the Technical Standards and Safety Authority in three months…*

Now, here's another bet: Just how high and how fast can Queen's Park jump about some longer term chemical problems in the province?

I wager it'll take 50 years for politicians to vibrate and pontificate about Chemical Valley. The dice are loaded. I've won already, because it has taken them at least that long to date.

Who lives in Chemical Valley? The people of the Walpole Island First Nation, the Sarnia First Nation, and the small city of Sarnia. It's the area that produces approximately 40% of the oil, gas, and petrochemicals for Eastern Canada.

We're talking the southwestern part of the Queen's Park empire, on Lakes Huron, Michigan, and St. Clair, and the St. Clair River. It will take a lot longer, if ever, to decide what an acceptable level of risk is for those people. They are farther away from the centre of power, fewer in numbers, many of them Aboriginal, and it's a slow, cross-generational danger. More like a leak than an explosion.

Sunday's dangerous events happened to thousands at once. They're getting lots of justified media attention in the capital city. Toronto was also beyond lucky that only two people died.

How can that be compared to 50 years of gradual chemical spills, and possibly related gradual deaths, and non-births?...If the warning system works, at least people are told not to swim, not to drink the water, and not to eat the fish. Sometimes they're not warned in time though, and that makes the communities suspect that the high number of miscarriages, new diseases, birth defects, and fish with cancer has something to do with chemical spills...

Walpole Island can make its own laws, just like Queen's Park. It's on territory that was never ceded to the Crown. Trouble is, the laws can't stop spills from coming down the river to the First Nations, or into Sarnia and Wallaceburg.

What has been agreed upon by the government of Ontario and the Walpole Island First Nation is that their unceded territory is home to 50 endangered or at risk species. Maybe that's 51, if we add in human beings.

There is no universal agreement in Chemical Valley that gradual hazards to life are such a bad thing. The refineries are major employers of people in the cities and minor employers of First Nations citizens as well.

Therefore not everybody is calling for new legislation, instant investigation, and the closing of loopholes.

Not as many live within sudden death distance like we've just experienced in Toronto.

They just live in the shadow of slow, quiet, possibly fatal, health and environmental hazards.[2]

In *Not a Drop* the people of Walpole Island eloquently explain to the young journalists, and all the rest of us in the audience, the place of the land in their world view. And they give us a tour of the slice of creation for which they feel spiritually responsible.

2009–11

The Halifax mayor's apology to the people of Africville happens during the time I am privileged to live and work in the Atlantic region. The apology includes a commitment to a new church to be built on the site of the old one, and there is to be an interpretive centre that explains how the land of these black citizens came to be expropriated. Financial compensation goes to the black community, not to individuals.

True, the damage was done fifty years ago. A historic black community that had lived on the shores of the Bedford Basin for generations found their church bulldozed in the middle of the night, their possessions and themselves loaded onto garbage trucks and dumped into public housing in the inner city. Halifax needed to build a bridge where Africville's destroyed homes had been. I had produced a program for *CBC Access* about Africville thirty-three years previously and so thought the problem had been solved! It took a lot more than my one show for the land to be reclaimed.

Roberta Jamieson, distinguished head of the National Aboriginal Achievement Foundation, was a convocation speaker at Mount Saint Vincent University in the spring of 2010. Her honourary doctorate was presented at the ceremony for graduates in Education. Why? The administration hoped, and Ms. Jamieson agreed, that what was said to these people who were teachers and principals in Nova Scotia schools was terribly important. They were the people who would continue to put false histories or true communication about the Aboriginal past, present, and future into the classroom. They were important gatekeepers for positive self-images of young Native people and the esteem with which all ethnicities would hold each other. Jamieson said that the grads had a choice. They could build classrooms and worlds of inclusion or of exclusion. They had this power. The educators were the people who would tell the truth, or not, about the bulldozers, garbage trucks, airplanes, and other expropriation vehicles of history. We welcomed her message. Roberta Jamieson was very generous to give the graduates another chance to decide which path to take.

However, being the slave masters is very bad for the masters' health. It is our tradition in Canada to shoot the messenger who brings this news; we are killing our souls when we exclude. We have charged messengers with exaggeration, lying, inaccuracy, or simply misinterpreting the intentions of the masters forever. 1922 was the publication year of Dr. Peter Bryce's book about residential schools, *The Story of a National Crime*. Bryce, who had been suppressed by the Canadian governments who hired him, was talking about death rates of nearly 50 per cent in western Indian residential schools, and the denial of this evidence by the Canadian government and churches.[3]

We shot the messenger then. But the time has long since past when we can afford to silence the bad news about residential schools, about land, resources, or our lives with one another. The current Truth and

Reconciliation Commission is probably our last chance as societies to hear the messengers. The mental, physical, and spiritual health of those of us who are black (like me), brown, yellow, white—or red—depends on our speaking, walking, and living the truth.

Notes

1   Excerpted from the screenplay, *Not a Drop*. See: Deverell, Rita Shelton (Producer/Director/Writer) (2009). *Not a Drop* [Docudrama]. Toronto, ON: OMNI.

2   Deverell, Rita Shelton (2008, August 15). Toronto blast gets action, what about elsewhere? *The Toronto Sun*: 21.

3   Bryce, P.H. (1922). *The Story of a National Crime: An Appeal for Justice to the Indians of Canada, The Wards of the Nation: Our Allies in the Revolutionary War : Our Brothers-in-Arms in the Great War*. Ottawa, ON: James Hope & Sons, Limited. Retrieved 9 November 2010 from: http://www.archive.org/details/storyofnationalcoobrycuoft

George Elliott Clarke

George Elliott Clarke, O.C., O.N.S., PH.D., LLD (etc.): I was born in 1960. My identity was shaped most profoundly by my parents, then my cultures—African/American/Aboriginal, English, Christian (Baptist), Nova Scotian, working-class/middle-class, Canadian, Occidental, 'Leftist,' intellectual, artist. No wonder I'm such a mess of (I hope, productive) tensions! I resent white Nova Scotian racism, but I love my native province, which has been supportive of me quite absolutely. I love The Holy Bible and the African United Baptist Association of Nova Scotia, but I am, as one of my professors once said (though he was just guessing), "a sinful bastard." Damn! I pray that I have these slightly redeeming qualities: (1) an effort to be a decent father, (2) an attempt to be a true writer, and (3) an endeavour to be a scholar in service to my various communities. The latter, public 'works' have seen me work as a journalist, editor, parliamentary aide, legislative researcher, and professor, first at Duke University (1994–1999), and subsequently at the University of Toronto (with visiting stints elsewhere). I pioneered the study of African-Canadian literature, editing two anthologies, a special issue of a scholarly journal, and publishing *Odysseys Home: Mapping African-Canadian Literature* (University of Toronto Press, 2002). My imaginative works consist of poetry, a novel, a screenplay, four plays, and three opera libretti. My scholarship and my art have brought me many awards and rewards. I'm thankful for all, but I still feel I've got much left to do. Next up? An epic poem: *Canticles: Hymns of the African Baptists of Nova Scotia....*

"Indigenous Blacks": An Irreconcilable Identity?

Sentiment

In autumn 1978 I was eighteen, attending a 'Youth Multiculturalism Conference,' in Halifax, Nova Scotia, when I first heard the term *indigenous*, used to refer to the historical black—settler—population of Nova Scotia. If memory serves, it was my then-mentor, the brilliant actor, gifted poet and playwright, and polemical journalist Walter M. Borden, C.M., who employed the term to distinguish those of us of long residency in Nova Scotia, in Canada, from more recent black arrivals, most from the Caribbean and a smattering from the United States and from Africa. I probably first began to use the phrase myself then, for, as I was beginning to voyage beyond Nova Scotia, I began to encounter *brother and sister* blacks from other parts of the African Diaspora, who would wonder, like many white folks, just who the hell was I, anyway, and what strange black culture did I possess, when bagpipes could make me weep almost as sentimentally as any Motown hurtin' song. In identifying myself as an "indigenous Black Nova Scotian," I meant no disrespect to the *real* Indigenous people, the Mi'kmaq, nor was I out to erase their claim to original presence, to an absolute indigeneity. What I was trying to do—like Borden and Africadian activist Dr. Burnley "Rocky" Jones, O.N.S., LLD—was demarcate this small, forgotten band of African (more or less) Americans from other, *newer* Black Canadians because we were, in fact, different, despite our allegiance to the rhetoric of pan-Africanism.

Moreover, our difference was *native*. Unlike the newer African Canadians, we could not look back only one generation to some other native land where we were either the majority or could wield significant power. Nor could we appeal to any foreign embassy to intervene with the governments of Canada and Nova Scotia to address our concerns. We were not only renters in cities; we held land in impossible-to-farm districts, which were practically reserves, from which we filed mornings to work as cheap labour in white homes and in white-controlled cities and towns. (Note that some of those Caucasian settlements had explicit "sunset" laws, until the late 1960s, demanding that we clear our "Coloured" selves out of *their* areas by sundown.) In stark contrast to the first-generation West Indian immigrants especially, we were considerably indigent and proverbially illiterate, with few valued skills and little class mobility, except to jump on a train or bus and vamoose to Montreal, Toronto, Boston, or New York. Too, save for relatively isolated Preston and its environs, we were—are—visibly, multiply Coloured—especially in the Annapolis Valley, on the South Shore, in the Nor'east, and even in the Capital itself. Our 'blackness' is indelibly *Métis*[1]—brown, tan, copper, gold, yellow, indigo, ivory, blue, even white. No matter how much we align ourselves, culturally and politically, within the larger African Diaspora, and even with our *kissing cousins* in America, we were—and we remain—a community apart. Scholars even recognize the existence of African-Nova Scotian Vernacular English, a version of African-American Vernacular English that is as distinct as the variants spoken in Liberia and in Sierra Leone.

Because I felt—as a writer and a scholar—that "Black Nova Scotian" or "African-Nova Scotian" or even "indigenous black" did not and do not answer to our specificity as a broken-off branch of African America, landed and abandoned in coastal British North America, I invented the term *Africadian* to describe us, our *essence*, and our being and I dubbed our communities (*our land-base*) *Africadia*.[2] My 1991 coinages have not—yet— won wide adoption or circulation, perhaps because some think I am resituating Black Nova Scotians as "Black Acadians." No, there is no such intention in my neologisms. Frequently, I have pointed out that *"cadie"*—from which *Acadie/Acadia* may derive—is a *Mi'kmaw* suffix that means *abounding in*. If so, then *Africadia* means, literally, (a place) abounding in Africans. Far from articulating an inaccurate vision of African Nova Scotians as all being *Afro-Acadiens* (though some Africadians *are*, indeed, "Afro-Acadiens") I was and am, in my neologism, signalling our attachment to Mi'kmaw territory.

In her monograph, *African Nova Scotian-Mi'kmaw Relations*, Paula C. Madden charges that my espousal of "Africadian" identity is, although "an innocent notion," still "a statement of claim against the land and territory of Mi'kma'ki."[3] For Madden, then, ignorant and nearly insolent are Africadian complaints regarding the city-council-directed obliteration between 1964 and 1970 of Africville, a centenarian 'Coloured' district of Halifax: protests against its destruction, and calls for reparations and reconstruction, obscure, Madden posits, the primary claim of the Mi'kmaw to that land. In effect, ex-Africville residents are crying over lost land that was never truly theirs to lose. Madden also maintains that attempts to conjoin Africadian and Mi'kmaq struggles have seen the former overshadow the latter. Moreover, she suspects, Afro–Abo collaborations show awkwardness, as in the operation of the Indigenous Black and Mi'kmaq (IBM) Law Program at Halifax's Dalhousie University. Madden also charges that the phrase "indigenous black" flouts pan-African solidarity, separating newer immigrant blacks from those whose roots are not indigenous, merely deeper.

Madden's charges are significant, and I do feel compelled to reply, though my response may not succour either her or hardcore black nationalists or First Nations irredentists. Many Africadians—if not most—are Métis; that is to say, mixed with First Nations peoples, eminently—but not only—the Mi'kmaq. I owe thanks to Dorothy Mills–Proctor's novella-length memoir, *Born Again Indian: A Story of Self-Discovery of a Red-Black Woman and Her People*,[4] for my improved understanding of just how extensive black and Mi'kmaq unions have been, and the past, Herculean efforts that *black* and *red* couples made to hide this biracial and bicultural heritage from their children. According to Mills–Proctor's memoir, blended African and Aboriginal households would *pretend* that a child's light(er) complexion was due to a supposedly European or Caucasian ancestor.[5] The reason for this deception was the hope that Negrophobia and anti-Native prejudice could be mitigated if a child or children were passed off as *mulatto*, as opposed to *half-breed*.[6] How vast was this purposeful camouflage? It is impossible to know. But there are many Africadians with Aboriginal and/or Mi'kmaw ancestry who know nothing of their roots and who are a mystery both to themselves and to *pure-bred* Natives.[7] Indeed, many African-Nova Scotian communities and surnames are, simultaneously, essentially Métis and Mi'kmaq: see locales such as Three Mile Plains, Mount Denson, Truro, and Lequille, et cetera, or look up surnames like Croxen, Francis, Johnson, Robinson, States, et cetera. None of this information challenges Aboriginal primordiality in so-called Nova Scotia. However, the truth of black and Mi'kmaq *métissage* complicates Madden's too-easy and too-pat division between the two communities and also her too-simplistic notions regarding the political surrealism of Africadian land claims (i.e., primarily around Africville, but possibly extending to other historical, rural, 'black' communities) and the political realism of Africadian Pan-Africanism.

The uncomfortable fact (for some) is, African-heritage peoples and the First Nations are intertwined prodigiously in Nova Scotia, even if both entities are ignorant of this reality (and history), and they have much in common, beginning with DNA and extending to cultural assertion. In my own family—matrilineal Aboriginal and African—I see aunts, uncles, cousins, *et al.*, who can *pass*, not as white, but as Native. When I look at First Nations representatives, or meet *our* people in my travels, I see folks who resemble many Africadians. Yes, I do identify myself—and I'm usually so identified by others—as being black. Yet, I boast, around my ears, what older folks call "Micmac curls," and my handsome, gorgeous tint—I'll call it gold cinnamon—is common to those of us of some Aboriginal admixture. I take pride in uncles, aunts, and cousins who never gave up passed-down knowledge of forestry work, wilderness cultivation and survival, herbal medicine, and all the lore associated with these activities. When I consider my inherited, uncultivated, three-quarter-acre lot on Highway 1 in Three Mile Plains so utterly wild with spruce, pine, and crabapple trees, blackberry bushes, and anthills, I do feel—romantically—one with the land and my 'Native' *cultures*. When I consider the late and esteemed Africadian basket weaver, Edith Clayton, I wonder just how much of her craft was indebted to West Africa and how much to Mi'kma'ki. When I consider the late and heroic Mi'kmaq activist Donald Marshall, Jr. (1953–2009), once wrongfully convicted and jailed for murdering an Africadian teen (Mr. Sandy Seale [1953–1971]), a crime actually committed by a white derelict, I understand afresh just how similar have been Aboriginal and Africadian experiences of white racism in 'New Scotland.' When I read the late and gifted Mi'kmaq poet Rita Joe, P.C., C.M., LLD (1932–2007), I feel that I am reading a sister, with the only major distinction between us being her access to a truly Indigenous tongue, one remote to me. When I read the African–American cultural critic bell hooks (Gloria Watkins) and her essay, *Revolutionary Renegades: Native Americans, African Americans, and Black Indians*,[8] about the political bonds between African Americans and Native Americans, I feel that she could have—should have—added a paragraph on Africadia. Occasionally, mischievously, I almost feel moved to redefine "Africadian" as denoting a Métis who identifies with African-American culture. Then again, perhaps I should offer such a redefinition, given that many of us culturally black Africadians have also been accepted formally into the Eastern Woodlands Métis Nation Nova Scotia (EWMNNS), a fact that defines us legally as "Aboriginal" under section 35 of Canada's *Constitution Act 1982*. Yes, I use *us* deliberately here: I joined the EWMNNS in 2010. Why? So that my daughter (who also has some Native heritage on her Québécoise mother's side), if she so chooses, might explore this inheritance when she is older.

Argument

Too much of what I write above belongs to *sentiment*, abjectly and practically apolitically. So what if I am part-Aboriginal, or that Africadians are also often part-Mi'kmaq, part-Cree, part-Cherokee, et cetera? Big deal. More importantly, how much do I—or *you*—know about the wanton wrongs perpetrated against the First People of the Americas? Mills–Proctor's catalogue of these evils includes, "diseases, alcohol, residential schools, eugenics, Christianity (forced conversion), the treaty frauds, racism, constant abuses by the invaders who still act within a culture of occupation." She concludes with an awful prophecy: "The adverse effects brought to bear on the indigenous peoples by the Europeans, will mark the history of the Americas until the last days of the last days."[9] Nay, she is right. Open John S. Milloy's *"A National Crime": The Canadian Government and the Residential School System, 1879 to 1986*,[10] and read therein of the state-sponsored cultural genocide and physical assaults meted out to Aboriginal children and youth, for more than a century, to *begin* to appreciate just *one* example of national, organized, anti-Native terror. Milloy demands we remember "the terrible facts of the residential school system, along with its companion policies — community removal, the Indian Act, systemic discrimination in the justice system..."[11] and he need not stipulate the forbiddance of the electoral franchise until 1960, mandatory sexual sterilization, plus many other violations of elemental civil and *universal* human rights.

Yet, I could place Milloy's necessarily Gothic account of sinister priests and rapist teachers, Machiavellian bureaucrats and Orwellian bishops, beside an even more Sadean and sanguinary document; namely, Bartolomé de Las Casas's *The Devastation of the Indies: A Brief Account*,[12] which chronicles the multi-million-victim genocide, conducted by *Christian* Spanish and Portuguese conquistadors, pirates, and enslavers against Caribbean, Mexican, and South American Natives. In fact, it was to forestall the extinction of Aboriginal people in the southern Americas,[13] that Las Casas and others advocated the importation of African slaves—as a *humanitarian* relief (albeit misguided), in the early sixteenth century.

Thus, we need to recall, with Mills–Proctor, "the abuses [both] against black slaves and occupied First Peoples."[14] I do want to say with her, "I could no more separate their [twin] struggle[s] for freedom than I could remove the Indian DNA from my body."[15] This point is not rhetorical. In March 2004, Doudou Diène, Special Rapporteur on racism, racial discrimination, and xenophobia and related intolerance to the United Nations Commission on Human Rights, delivered a report declaring that Canada practises racism *in particular* against African-heritage and Aboriginal peoples. Whether anyone likes it or not, "The Red and the Black" is not just a title by French writer Stendhal; it is a *potential* alliance and, sporadically, an actual amalgamation. (For one thing, as there is a Ministry of Indian and Northern Affairs under the Government of Canada, so there is a Department of African–Nova Scotian Affairs under the Government of Nova Scotia.)

The great First Nations filmmaker, Alanis Obomsawin (with whom I have been privileged to enjoy several serious conversations), has commented on the pernicious "lack of education [in Canada] concerning the country's history"[16] and on her personal work "fighting for the inclusion of Aboriginal history in the educational system."[17] Here is where any effective African-Canadian and First Nations reconciliation must begin, with an acknowledgement of each other's historical repression, genealogical bonds (as Métis), and our mutual efforts, sometimes in coalitions (usually not even of convenience, but of *happenstance*), to insist on our rights and respect— *right* in the stony, white-supremacist face of the state.

Surely it is in our mutual interest to insist on First Nations land claim settlements and respect of treaty rights. It is also in our mutual interest to support reparations for the exploited labour of Africans. (Stolen First Nations resources and African slave labour together built up the wealth of modern Western Europe and the Americas, especially its northern reaches.) I do go further: I propose that one per cent of the property taxes paid by all Canadians, everywhere in the nation, should be dedicated to First Nations peoples, in perpetuity, to allow for their strengthening *and flourishing*. (Yes, money can't buy happiness, but it sure can improve living standards.)

Whether *indigenous black* is an appropriate term or not, I must let others decide. Yet, there are Black Indians or Red/Black people (to use Mills–Proctor's term), and there are many Africadians, such as myself, who may claim such a title. What I do know is: no African-Canadian community may properly thrive until we have understood and embraced the Indigenous People and their campaigns for justice, and that we champion these struggles as our very own.

Identity

Being *pur-sang* métis, my charisma's

Ambiguous—like dark wine that's *rosé*,

And my tongue sports obscene mutterings—

Cusses—squawks and squiggles, ripples and raps,

Clear and superficial as ink, trenchant

As prayer. The carnal, ungodly poet,

That's me—acid-bathed, not sugarcoated,

An monster ecstatic, a jabbering chimp....

Should I be as colourless—but bloody—as

Whitehall, The White House, Versailles, and La Tour

De Bélem, and other slave monuments?

I lark with crows, make Camelot a Hell.

I'm rooted in the Sargasso. My smile

Backstabs: I chuck Bibles at you like stones!

Notes

1   I appreciate that this word is political, and that its status is jealously guarded by the Métis National Council, who trust that the term denotes only the Red River Valley people and their historical presence. I do not contradict this view; however, I do wonder whether exclusivity may have the consequence of numbering only 'Caucasian' Métis, and not those of partly 'Negro' origin, that is to say, of perpetrating a kind of *apartheid*...

2   Clarke, George Elliott (ed.) (1991:9). *Fire on the Water: An Anthology of Black Nova Scotian Writing.* (Vol. 1). Lawrencetown Beach, NS: Pottersfield Press.

3   Madden, Paula C. (2009:100). *African Nova Scotian-Mi'kmaw Relations.* Halifax, NS: Fernwood Publishing.

4   Mills–Proctor, Dorothy (2010). Born Again Indian: A Story of Self-Discovery of a Red-Black Woman and Her People. *Kola* (22(1):44–137.

5   Mills–Proctor (2010:48).

6   Mills–Proctor (2010:47–48).

7   Mills–Proctor claims: "To be sure, there were black Indians in other parts of Canada but not as many as in Nova Scotia" (2010:49). She also insists, "Many Red-Black people are quantitatively more Indian than Black, [but] because of their African features it is difficult for them to broach the subject. It appears to be much easier to claim white blood than Indian blood" (2010:108).

8   hooks, bell [Gloria Watkins] (1992). Revolutionary renegades: Native Americans, African Americans, and Black Indians. In *Black Looks: Race and Representation.* Boston, MA: South End Press: 179–184.

9   Mills–Proctor (2010:69).

10 Milloy, John S. (2001). *"A National Crime": The Canadian Government and the Residential School System, 1879 to 1986.* Winnipeg, MB: The University of Manitoba Press.

11 Milloy (2001:305).

12 Las Casas, Bartolomé de (1974). *The Devastation of the Indies: A Brief Account.* (Trans. Briffault, Herma). New York, NY: Seabury Press. (Original work published 1552.)

13 Hugh Thomas cites, "the complete collapse of the population of the Caribbean," in Thomas, Hugh (1997:96). *The Slave Trade: The Story of the Atlantic Slave Trade: 1440–1870.* New York, NY: Simon and Schuster.

14 Mills–Proctor (2010:92).

15 Mills–Proctor (2010:92).

16 Obomsawin, Alanis (2002:88). Imaginative geographies. Interview with Monika Kin Gagnon. In Kin Gagnon, Monika and Richard Fung (eds.). *13 Conversations About Art and Cultural Race Politics.* Montréal, QC: Artextes Editions—Collection Prendre parole: 88–93.

17 Obomsawin, Alanis (2002:91).

Diyan Achjadi

Diyan Achjadi was born in Jakarta, Indonesia, to a West-Javanese father and an English-Canadian mother. She grew up moving between Jakarta, Hong Kong, London, and Washington DC, relocating every three years or so for her father's job. Her formative years were spent negotiating different educational, political, and cultural systems, leading to an ongoing interest in how our understanding of ideologies is influenced and informed by the visual popular culture that surrounds us. Diyan received a B.F.A. with a concentration in printmaking from the Cooper Union School of Art in New York in 1993, and an M.F.A. in Studio Arts/Print Media from Concordia University in Montreal in 2002. Her printed works have been exhibited widely throughout Canada and the US, in venues such as the Mendel Art Gallery (Saskatoon), the Ottawa Art Gallery, Centre A (Vancouver), Centre MAI (Montreal), Open Studio (Toronto), and AIR Gallery (New York). Her animations have been screened at festivals worldwide, such as the Images Festival (Toronto), Kinofilm Short Film Festival (Manchester), Interactions XVI (Sardinia), and Le Instants Video de Manosque (Manosque, France). Since 2005, Diyan has been teaching print media and visual arts at Emily Carr University in Vancouver.

Girl: An Aesthetic Amalgamation

> To recognise the injustices of colonisation as a history of the present is to rewrite history, and to reshape the ground on which we live, for we would recognise the ground itself as shaped by such histories. If the violence of what happened is recognised, as a violence that shapes the present, then the 'truths' of history are called into question. Recognition of injustice is not simply about others becoming visible (though this can be important). Recognition is also about claiming that an injustice did happen; the claim is a radical one in the face of the forgetting of such injustices. Healing does not cover over, but exposes the wound to others: *the recovery is a form of exposure.*
>
> — Sara Ahmed, *The Cultural Politics of Emotion*[1]

Vancouver, British Columbia. Unceded Coast Salish Territory. 2010
As I sit in my Main Street apartment, enjoying the rare West Coast sunshine, I wonder about these words above. What does it mean to be an immigrant to a country that still celebrates its colonial past and sweeps over its colonial present? What does it mean to immigrate to what is essentially an occupied territory? How am I complicit in the politics of this land?

I have lived here now for five years. First, as a Landed Immigrant—one granted permission to reside permanently in this country—and, more recently having taken the oath of citizenship, as a new Canadian. This city is now my home. Prior to my move here, I had only been to Vancouver once before, for a short work visit. While the landscape and the weather were completely alien to me, I felt an instant sense of familiarity here: the abundance and diversity of Asian foods, places, and peoples and which continue to comfort me during the moments of acute homesickness. When here, I am closer to Home, to where I was born, where my parents are. I look westward and imagine Jakarta at the other end of the Pacific Ocean, dense, loud, colourful. Yet, my history and connection to Canada goes back farther than this.

I grew up as the child of an English-Canadian mother and a West Javanese-Indonesian father. My parents met in Ottawa in the 1950s, where my father

Ready and Waiting (They're Coming!) (2007)
Inkjet on paper, 30" x 60"

was stationed in his first diplomatic post abroad, and my mother worked at the new Indonesian embassy as a local staff. They got married and then moved to Jakarta. My mother eventually became an Indonesian citizen, which, at the time, meant relinquishing rights to the country of her birth. "You are no longer considered a natural-born Canadian," states the official letter from the Canadian consul. My siblings and I grew up as Indonesian, our only connections to Canada being the stories of our mother's childhood in Quebec and Ontario, letters and occasional visits from our foreign grandmother, and speaking English as well as Indonesian at home. Canada became, to me, a kind of mythical land, exotic and strange.

Indonesia is a relatively new country, barely sixty-five years old. It is an archipelago of thousands of islands, with hundreds of ethnic groups and distinct languages. As a nation, it is a somewhat constructed entity, its borders and limits defined by the vestiges of the territorial boundaries of the Dutch occupation. Europeans first sailed to the Indonesian islands in the 1500s in search of spices, initially setting up trading posts that eventually expanded into full-fledged colonies.

My father is of a generation that experienced colonization first-hand, born in what was then known as the Dutch East Indies, he lived through the Japanese occupation during World War II and participated in the movements for Indonesian self-determination that were occurring then against both of these foreign governments. After independence was proclaimed in 1945, my father, then fifteen, joined the mobilized youths sent to villages and towns across the islands to inform people that they were now citizens of the Republic of Indonesia. My father, and my grandfather, did not cooperate with the Dutch; they spoke Indonesian as a matter of principle; they worked towards building the country.

Ottawa, Ontario. Around 1953

There is a small, square, blurry photograph of my father. There are three people in this picture: my father and another Indonesian man, both dressed in a suit and tie, and in between them an older Aboriginal woman in a beaded leather dress. My father is in his mid-twenties, dapper, and smiling. I ask him if he remembers what the photograph is from. He takes his glasses off and peers closely at this picture. "No. Oh, wait. I think we visited a reservation. Yes, that must be from the trip we took to the reservation."

My mother was born in Montreal to a British father and Anglo-Canadian mother. Her mother's family had been in Canada for generations, having landed in the New England colonies from England or Scotland sometime

Diyan Achjadi, *Ceremony* (2007)
Inkjet on paper, 30" x 60"

in the 1600s, moving north with the Loyalists when the movement for independence began in the States, staying true to the monarchy and ending up in Ottawa. At the age of nineteen or twenty, my mother found a job at the Indonesian embassy there, without even really knowing what or where Indonesia was; she just needed the work.

Not long after she met my father, they married, and she followed him on his assignments. They were first posted to Washington DC and lived in Virginia where, in 1957, their mixed marriage was technically illegal due to the anti-miscegenation laws. They were finally called back to Indonesia in 1958. Once there, my mother did not return to Canada for over twenty years.

As a child, I do not remember there being many "new Indonesians." My mother was the tall white woman who could sometimes be spotted in native dress—a batik skirt, a kebaya, hair in a soft bun—standing a foot over all the Malay women. Everyone recognized her; it was easy to find her. It was only when we were moved to England when I was seven that I realized that there were lots of women as tall as her, and only a few girls who looked like me.

Jakarta, Indonesia. 2009
I sit in a taxi with my mother, going from a garish, air-conditioned mall to her home in the suburbs. My mother says the address to the driver in Indonesian; he replies in English and comments on how good her Indonesian is. He asks her where she is from. She says, "I am from here. I have been here longer than you have been alive."

There is a single recurring character in my work, only known as "Girl." She is a golden-skinned, brown-haired child, always clad in a sweet dress and surrounded by a candy-coloured, disjointed, miniaturized landscape that teeters on the edge of destruction. In some of the pictures, Girl can be seen engaging in a series of synchronized group activities—marching, saluting, parading—performances meant to demonstrate the cohesion of a unit and the potential power inherent in a unified crowd. In others, Girl is seen in conflict with her double, engaging in an uneasy struggle for authority and control. It is unclear where Girl stands. She is both the perpetrator of the destruction that surrounds her and the victim of its circumstance.

Girl is ethnically unidentifiable, other than by the fact of what she is not: white. This characterization is crucial, as it indicates her position outside of the dominant pictorial discourses in North America. But more importantly than her non-whiteness is her unfixability; if we cannot place who or what she is exactly, she could then be any and all of us who have been positioned by our difference.

Diyan Achjadi, *Spar* (2010)
Inkjet on paper, 30" x 44"

Diyan Achjadi, *They See They Have Company* (2010)
Inkjet on paper, 30" x 44"

Diyan Achjadi, *In Celebration Of...* (2009)
Inkjet on paper, 30" x 60"

In these pictures, there is no Other. Everyone is the same: you see Girl over and over again, repeated, duplicated, and cloned. She/they wear seemingly identical dresses—with subtle variable markers: sleeves, socks, belts, hats, and other embellishments—suggesting where and how a particular Girl fits into this world's social structure.

These works are not autobiographical; I am not Girl. Rather, Girl is an amalgamation of stories, fears, and desires. She is not a blank screen—gendered and racialized as she is—but a screen nonetheless, open for projection. Girl functions as an avatar, both in the graphical sense of a drawing that is a stand-in for a real-life person in an imagined, constructed environment and as a "manifestation or presentation to the world as a ruling power or object of worship." She is there, conveniently able to step into any role; she is simultaneously aggressor, victim, and innocent bystander. Girl is always surrounded by the suggestion of violence and conflict, while often seeming quite separate from what is happening around her. Finally, Girl is always larger than her surroundings, a mary-jane-clad Godzilla in a pink and orange world, a monster of sorts, toying with the miniaturized landscape around her.

In making these pictures, I think of histories of nationalisms and by extension the role of militarism and violence in defining and maintaining the borders of nation-states. I think of the idea of a home or a homeland and how a place that one is deeply connected to may be steeped in conflicts that one must come to terms and reconcile with. I think of the ideologies—from the banal to the menacing—that one is inculcated to from an early age through the images and texts that circulate around us, reinforcing their supposed normality through their repetition.

In *Understanding Comics: The Invisible Art*, Scott McCloud describes how a simply drawn, iconic cartoon character functions as "an empty shell that we inhabit which enables us to travel to another realm. We don't just observe the cartoon, we become it."[2] Girl is simple enough that anyone can step in and inhabit her character, regardless of one's gender or origin. Through this identification, it is my hope that the viewers of these pictures begin to question their own relationship to the world around them, their place in that world, and their relationship to the spaces that they occupy. We are all, to varying degrees, complicit in the systems and environments that we live in, from the social to the political, to the material. Perhaps, it is through artistic inquiry and spectatorship that we can interrogate and begin to come to terms with these intertwined and complicated histories.

Notes

1   Ahmed, S. (2004:200). *The Cultural Politics of Emotion*. Edinburgh, UK: Edinburgh University Press.

2   McCloud, S. (1993:36) [capitalization and emphasis in original removed]. *Understanding Comics: the Invisible Art*. New York, NY: Harper Perennial.

Kirsten Emiko McAllister

Kirsten Emiko McAllister comes from a family that brings together two different political and social worlds. Her mother's family is Japanese Canadian, and her father is Scottish-German. She began exploring the wartime experiences of Japanese Canadians just after the National Association of Japanese Canadians negotiated a redress settlement with the Canadian government in 1988. In 1989 she ran the oral history project for the Japanese Canadian Citizens' Association (JCCA) of Vancouver, working closely with elders who brought to life worlds that no longer existed. The "return" to her mother's community was as much about her own need to explore her place in the province's terrain of memory as it was a matter of the community "re-claiming" her as a member of the postwar generation. Kirsten is currently Associate Professor at Simon Fraser University in the School of Communication. While there have been many important influences that have shaped her at an early age, including time she spent in the Philippines in the Canada World Youth Program learning about underdevelopment and colonialism, the wartime experiences of Japanese Canadians have had a strong, lasting effect. After completing her B.A. in Geography and her M.A. in Communication at SFU, she went to Ottawa for her Ph.D. at Carleton University. At Carleton her research focused on a memorial that Japanese Canadian elders built to mark the valley in where they were incarcerated during WWII with their history of injustice and their hopes for a future just society. She then travelled even further from the Pacific coast, across the Atlantic to England, to Lancaster University where she researched the photographs that Japanese Canadian internees took illicitly during the war, examining how they tried to instill meaning and a sense of future into the bleak spaces of incarceration. Kirsten eventually returned to the Pacific coast in 2003 where she currently lives and works.

Memoryscapes of Postwar British Columbia:
A Look of Recognition

Always (in the) Present[1]

November. It is now November. The coast will soon be in the damp cold clutch of winter with its dramatic storms and icy clear days of quiet contemplation. Though not yet evening, the city has been submerged in darkness. I am at my desk writing aimlessly, not certain of where the words are taking me. I head off on a long, slow jog along English Bay. The sea is an inky black with the lights of freighters stretching back towards Vancouver's shoreline like long gleaming tears.

Over the Burrard Street Bridge, a small arch into the sky, to Snauq, Kitsilano Reservation No. 6, and turning right onto a dimly lit street, I wonder where it will take me. As I approach the shore, rising above me I am astonished to see a totem pole. When I return home and after a flurry of research, I learn the pole was carved by Mungo Martin, a renowned carver and highly esteemed authority on his culture. Born around 1880, a member of the Kwakwaka'wakw in Fort Rupert, he held the high-ranking hereditary name, *Naka'pankam* (potlatch chief 'ten times over').[2]

The totem pole in Snauq is one of two identical poles that Mungo Martin was commissioned to carve for the centennial year of the colony of British Columbia in 1958. The other totem pole was shipped to England as a gift to her Majesty Queen Elizabeth II.[3]

It is hard not to see the 1958 centennial celebrations as gruesomely macabre, with the one hundred years of occupation more fitting to mourn than celebrate. But Mungo Martin made a powerful statement by making the official gift to mark the centennial, a totem pole. In his greetings to the Queen he spoke in Kwak'wala, the language of his people, and explained, "I designed this to show the family stories of my tribe, the ... [Kwakwaka'wakw]. This is the way we show our history. This pole will show the crests of ten tribes."[4] The act of sending the lineage of his people, a lineage with roots in the land that go back thousands of years, Martin Mungo can be seen as asserting the continuous presence of Aboriginal people on their territories and their right to self-rule. His assertion called on the Queen to remember the terms of the *Royal Proclamation of 1763* that cite the Crown's responsibility to ensure that the sovereign rights of Aboriginal people are respected. Thus Mungo Martin transformed the province's celebration of the

Crown colony's centennial into a political ceremony between two sovereigns: a Kwakwaka'wakw chief and the Queen of England.

> On that dark, cold November day, I stood before this chief's totem pole, uncertain of the proper decorum in its powerful presence. But then it was as if the totem took my gaze upwards... tilting the weight of my head back as I looked from Cedar Man and Halibut Man, to Sisuitl and Whale, and upwards. I felt my throat extending, opening the cavity of my chest wherein my heart lies, and bearing all that I am, there, before the ten Kwakwaka'wakw Tribes.[5] Their family crests ascended upwards, lifting my vision from what I just saw before me, upwards into the infinity of the night sky.

An Invitation

When I was invited to contribute to this volume I had understood it was because of my work on the damaging legacy of Japanese Canadian internment camps. My mother and her family, like thousands of other Japanese Canadians, were classified as enemy aliens by the Canadian government, who seized their homes and properties shortly after Japan bombed Pearl Harbour in 1941, and removed them from coastal British Columbia to internment camps in the interior of the province or to sugar beet farms in the prairies where entire families were forced to work as labourers. I have spent much of the last twenty years exploring the silences and absences as well as the creative and critical work of activists and artists trying to transform the destructive after-effects of Japanese Canadian internment.

It was not easy to accept the invitation to contribute to this volume. With great respect I look to the Aboriginal Healing Foundation and the profound work that has been done to address "the healing needs of Aboriginal People affected by the Legacy of Physical and Sexual Abuse in Residential Schools, including the intergenerational impacts."[6] In asking people like myself from non-Indigenous communities to step forward and make a contribution, I recognize that the Foundation has created a space to take part in the process of (re)conciliation so necessary for healing. I recognize that this process requires building new relationships and understandings. In the face of the continued occupation of the territories of Indigenous People and the devastation of ongoing colonial violence, the leadership you extend to us is humbling.

Here, I understand that stepping forward is necessary. Writing about our work in dialogue with the Foundation is one way to step forward. But to accept an invitation means one must offer something worthy of the honour of being invited. Yet, at the most fundamental level, I have little confidence in the very language, the very words and gestures, I rely on to communicate. Words place people in relation to one another. They carry histories; painful histories. Even if a writer is unconscious of that history as it lives on in her or his words, gestures and even "good" intentions, it is there, re-enacted with the enunciation of the words with all the assumptions, the ignorance, the injustice, and the plain stupidity. So I have been circling around the invitation for several months. It has not felt right to simply present the work I have done on Japanese Canadian internment camps. Like many other Japanese Canadians concerned with social justice, my work has been inspired and informed by the work of Indigenous leaders, Elders, scholars, and artists; it has also immersed me in the material and psychic devastation of the internment camps, tracing the damage as it has unravelled across generations, including through my own body and psyche. This memory work has focused on how this history has reached into the present and kept a suffocating hold over the community. As Japanese Canadian redress activists and scholars have made clear, Japanese Canadians were only one of many racialized groups the government aimed to remove from the Canadian territory.[7] Moreover, their persecution was part of a much larger colonial project whose prime target has been Aboriginal people. Eradicating people with world views that respect the land, sea, rivers, and life, in general, has been an essential step for colonial regimes driven by capitalism, which is a destructive system aimed at reducing all forms of life into exchangeable objects that can amass profit. This colonial history has shaped the realities for postwar British Columbia, marking anyone who is not recognized as some variation of an ideal British subject as a perpetual outsider who threatens the integrity of what is imagined to be this province's social body. Critical scholars and activists have been so focused on critiquing colonial occupation and persecution as well as the legislation that restricted, segregated, and physically removed people who were categorized as racially undesirable segments of the population; and it is only recent that researchers have begun to examine the nature of the relations between Indigenous people and racialized migrants.[8]

Thus, rather than presenting the work I have done with my mother's community, it seems that this relation needs to be addressed first, even if it requires much more ongoing research, thought, and, importantly, dialogue and exchange. To address this relation, it would be easy for me to simply revert to statements of political solidarity or remorseful guilt. While solidarity is obviously a requisite and an honest acknowledgement of the fact that Japanese Canadians have contributed to, and benefited from, building the infrastructure of the British colony is necessary, in themselves they are insufficient. Statements of solidarity and guilt are too easily turned into clichés that do not allow us to understand the intricacies of these relations, both in their insidious forms and the possibilities they hold to create something else. Moreover, these clichés can be used by activists and academics like me, as moral discourses to shame others and place us in a superior position. In terms of discourses of guilt, first, I turn to Elder Fred Kelly who makes clear that reconciliation requires: (a) honest acknowledgement of harm, (b) sincere regret, (c) readiness to apologize, (d) readiness to let go of anger and bitterness, (e) commitment not to repeat the injury, (f) sincere effort to redress past grievances, and (g) entering a new mutually enriching relationship.[9] Thus, if guilt is all that racialized settlers like me have to offer, this is very troubling since it is said that guilt is an aggressive emotion, a Christian one, I think, though I was not brought up with religion, so perhaps I am simplifying. Guilt is a way to punish oneself for something one feels wrong about doing. While it is necessary to regret the harm one has inflicted, it is something different to stay forever in a position fixated on one's guilt, especially in public forums, whereupon the invocation of guilt asks others to relate to us primarily in a relation of aggression, an aggression against oneself. This hardly seems like a good path forward.

The guilt-habit can also be a way to draw attention to oneself, away from the work that needs to be done. Forgoing the fixation on guilt does not preclude regretting the wrongness, the destructive impact, and what can be the sickness and pathology of our actions. But here the point is to move from what can paradoxically become a safe space of guilty confession as well as the moralizing and shaming of others to start trying to understand what are the necessary changes to transform how we live on this earth with all other beings.

I begin with an introduction of my family. Both sides of my family, the Nakashimas and the McAllister/McQuarries have lived in British Columbia for four generations. In many ways it has been their stories that have woven my family's memories into the land of your territories with a sense of wonder as well as respect and knowing that a life can easily be snatched away in a storm or at the wrong turn along a mountain ridge. The stories instruct the listeners that it is foolhardy to make assumptions about other people, especially those one meets in the remote corners of this province, as their wisdom is likely based on experiences that make listeners, like me, the ignorant ones.

My family has not lived in any particular place over the years, but there are places where different family members feel a particular kinship towards. These places hold a certain power over them. They can hold a sense of loss for what is no longer there and the people who have passed on. To return to these places is to honour the memories these places hold, whether a dilapidated, sagging house no longer inhabitable or a sandy bay pounded by the Pacific Ocean off the west coast of the Island. I don't think anyone feels as if they have rights to the land, even over the property where they live. This perhaps is because of my mother's family history of dispossession and displacement and because of my father's family's itinerant movements during the First and Second World Wars, whether from Nelson to the coast, within Victoria, or to Vancouver, as they debated and debauched as artists and anti-war activists over the years.

The Nakashimas and the McAllister/McQuarries were from two different worlds, though as a child I did not think much about this. In Vancouver we'd visit my favourite cousin, Dana. Her parents, my Uncle Joe and my Auntie Sheila, transformed their arts and crafts house into a vision of West Coast modernism with skylights and a studio space for Auntie Sheila, my father's sister, who was always in the grips of a creative project, exploring the coastal imagery, whether through silkscreens and oil painting or ceramics and sculpture. My Grandma Clare lived for a number of years on Galiano Island in a forest green house with an apple orchard. We spent a considerable amount of time with my mother's family in Vancouver, especially during Japanese New Year's and other holidays. My *Ojiisan*'s and *Obaasan*'s[10] household was the centre of the Nakashima family, and even as adults, my brothers and I continue to turn to my uncles for their advice and guidance. My *Ojiisan* was the central figure in the family, overseeing everyone's well-being; and when he passed on, my *Obaasan* became the matriarch. Like many *Issei*, while they did not want their daughter to marry a white man and warned my mother about "round-eyed" children, once my father proposed, he became part of the family, being called to Vancouver to deal with all manner of family crisis and conflict. Never that close to his own parents, he had a deep bond with my Ojiisan. The only time we have seen him cry was when my *Ojiisan* died.

In writing this piece, I have been taken back to many places in my past. I have tried to follow where my words have taken me and found myself trying to understand my presence here, in this land, as it is tied to multiple histories of displacement and dispossession. I explore how I have located myself or more precisely imagined myself here in the province's layered memoryscape, which includes the stories of my family and begins with a memory of a Mount Currie roadblock. The piece has allowed me to question the absences and explore the forces at play in this memoryscape, which locates me as a child growing up in British Columbia in the 1960s and 1970s. In writing this piece, I came to realize with terror—I cannot recall any Indigenous children from Nanaimo attending my schools, as I will recount below—where were the children my age?

Memoryscapes

I was a child when my family first took a trip to Lillooet in the early 1970s. Across the river from Lillooet is East Lillooet, a place that became familiar to me through the stories of my mother's family. East Lillooet sits high above the Fraser River on an arid alluvial terrace between two mighty mountain ranges. It was the location of one of many internment camps in the interior of British Columbia where the federal government held thousands of Japanese Canadians during the 1940s. These camps were part of a systematically deployed plan to remove all people of Japanese racial descent from British Columbia. This was one of many projects instigated by the Government of Canada to remove what it classified as racially undesirable sectors of the population inhabiting the territory it claimed to be under its jurisdiction.

East Lillooet is where my mother's family was incarcerated during the war. The summer we returned was hot and dry. The plan was to drive inland through the coastal mountain ranges from Pemberton to Mount Currie and then north along Anderson Lake to Lillooet. I have a vivid image of my father at the wheel with his battered canvas hat driving cautiously along the logging road that hugged the steep valley wall high above Anderson Lake. The truck was a four-wheel drive, pale yellow International Harvester Travelall. My father, with his puritanical Scottish inclinations, selected the bare-bones model, which was basically like a steel shell with thinly upholstered seats. Complaining was not tolerated. My brothers and I sat in obedient silence on the backseat with our husky–wolf dog, Kashtanka, who was shedding large white tufts of fur from her winter undercoat that settled like low-lying clouds over everything within her radius.

What I remember most is the roadblock at Mount Currie. The Lil'Wat man in charge of stopping cars approached us. My father started rolling down his window to greet him, but when the man saw my mother and us three sun-baked brown kids he simply waved us on. In my child's mind I remember that moment. It is imprinted into my memory. Amid the line of cars and trucks, the dust, the summer heat, the tension, and confusion I remember his look. He didn't come over to inspect us, ask for our identification, and then deliberate over whether we had permission to pass; rather, in one glance his look took us in and beckoned us through … into what I now know to be Lil'Wat territory.[11]

That moment has stayed with me over the years. As I explore what it was about this moment that left such an impression on me, I find myself trying to imagine myself back into this period of my life, into my child's world on Vancouver Island. We lived in the northern district of Nanaimo where swaths of old forest had been cut down for postwar housing, though in the 1960s and 1970s the cliffs above the sea and the slopes leading up to the ridges and bluffs were still carpeted with massive Douglas fir, wild honeysuckle vines, and emerald green mosses. My father insisted on using local flora in our garden, so he planted salal around our house that merrily grew into thickets entangled with wild rose that, over time, began to engulf the house and yard. Every now and then my mother would attempt to clear room for an ornamental plant, but the salal usually won. The oldest residents were three ancient cedars towering over our home like graceful giants. My father built our front deck around one of them. Every few years, as the cedar's girth would expand, he'd saw a few inches off the deck to give the cedar room to grow.

When I started school I was introduced to Nanaimo's other world. During elementary school there were very few children from non-white families, though I recall that there were a number of other families like ours, with parents who crossed the "racial lines." They were around my parents' age. Most had recently moved to Nanaimo to work as marine scientists, physicians, biologists, lawyers, professors, nurses, college teachers, surgeons, and technicians, making Nanaimo a post-colonial outpost of sorts for young professionals with cosmopolitan interests in jazz and modern art who would have been educated in the 1950s, the decade following the Second World War. There was also my friend, A.H. Her older brothers were successful commercial fishermen. She had a strong sense of pride in her Indigenous heritage. Her mother, I think, was from a Nation from the north end of the Island, as I remember her showing me the prestigious blankets that her mother had inherited. I also remember her telling me that the government did not recognize her mother's status because she had married her father, a white man, and thus lost her birthrights.

As a child I was too young to understand how bodies were mapped into the racialized terrain of the province. I had no language to articulate the disease and discomfort, the uneasy feelings and simmering resentment that could unpredictably erupt into hostility and violence. In my first school all I knew was that "jap, nip, chink, paki, injun" were ugly words with their shortened vermin-like syllables that had strange monstrous powers. It was as if whoever uttered those words transformed, nightmare-like, shaping their faces and tongues around vectors of hostile energy with the power to reduce you into something despicable and inhuman.[12] My mother proudly tells me that I punched a boy in the nose when he made racist slurs against one of my friends. When I was detained after school, my mother indignantly questioned why the teachers hadn't reprimanded the boy or met with his parents.

That was the only way I knew how to respond at the time—physically. I was overtaken with outrage. How dare this boy think of treating my friend like this. As I grew older I knew too well how the power of words could leave you helpless, stripping your power of speech. You couldn't reason, never mind argue, with your tormentors. Appeals to their compassion would be met with scorn and cackling laughter. Words would fall from your mouth as if mute, and in their hands, mutable. What you said, no matter how logical and factual, meant nothing. Your speech lost all power. Your tormentors did not regard you as another person, as another whose body and being mattered[13] and whose feelings and thoughts they felt compelled to consider.[14]

In grade five I transferred schools. At my new school I became conscious of the dynamics of racism in its subtle as well as its most blatant forms. The new school was in a neighbourhood that could have been straight out of a photo shoot from one of my mother's 1960s' *Sunset Magazine for Western Living*, but the residents in these modern dream homes, one has to remember, were not from a modern dream. Many residents living here would have thought nothing about the fact that the Snuneymuxw First Nation was restricted to six tiny reserves in the south section of the city, cut off from the wealth of their vast territories. Within their lifetimes, it had been less than one hundred years since "the British established the Colony of Vancouver Island, giving charge of land and settlement to the Hudson's Bay Company."[15] As Paul Tennant explains that before 1849, "nothing occurred that can reasonably be regarded as having affected aboriginal title in British Columbia... the few whites were everywhere vastly outnumbered, and the companies did not seek to intrude directly into the life or politics of the Indians. Control over Indian societies and Indian lands thus 'remained in Indian hands',"[16] until thousands of white men began flooding into their territories in search of gold. Such a radical change in the political social world of this region in less than one hundred years was forgotten, or more accurately, was never acknowledged by the influx of settlers who simply saw land and resources to be exploited followed by newer residents taking advantage of the opportunities in the province's postwar economy.

If the residents in these new suburban homes cascading down once-forested slopes were adults in the 1960s, they also would have lived through the 1930s' Depression and then the Second World War, either as children or as adults. They could have witnessed the RCMP rounding up Japanese Canadians living in Nanaimo and confiscating their properties during the 1940s when they were sent to internment camps. Some would have taken possession of their properties and moved into their homes. As they grew up, it would have been normal that Chinese Canadians and Indo-Canadians lived in areas segregated from the rest of Nanaimo's population with legal restrictions that made these groups undesirable "second-class citizens," without the right to vote until 1947[17] and with restrictive immigration laws, including a total ban on immigration for people from China and severely restricted terms of migration for South Asians that were not fully dismantled until the 1960s.[18]

Thus the adults of my childhood living in these modern suburbs designed with clean lines of the future all grew up in a highly segregated, racialized society. But then there were parents like my mother and father who brought together the segregated worlds. My parents' lives criss-crossed the racial lines of Nanaimo, not only among the other young professional couples of their generation. They were friends with the Wong family, the owners of the clothing store and tailor shop; the Yoshidas, the owners of the fusion Grotto Restaurant; and the Dubés, a physician and family from Trinidad. They also were in contact with the White family of the Snuneymuxw Nation after becoming involved with Tillicum Haus, as I'll explain below. But going back to Nanaimo, my mother decided to move me to the new school in grade five I suspect because the academic standards of the old school didn't meet her expectations. For me, it simply meant that I was cut off from my childhood friends. My parents had selected my first school precisely because there was a mixture of children from different backgrounds, whether from fishing families, the daughters of mill workers, lawyer's sons, or the children of lumber barons. It was a decision that reflected their era's progressive Co-operative Commonwealth Federation/New Democratic Party "equal rights" vision of society.

My first school is couched in mythic imagery. It was a small three-room school with split classes from grades one to six. It was a two-mile walk from our home, northward past Hammond Bay. During recess and lunch, in addition to seasonal games of marbles, skipping, and various ball games, we'd build forts on the edges of the surrounding forest and dam the countless streams criss-crossing the school property with huge muddy grass sods, creating minor floods throughout the grounds. But as I move into this memoryscape, other imagery comes into focus, just as intense, but clearly separated from the images of adventure. I recall being surrounded by large thuggish boys who would harass me, backing me into stinging nettles as they spit and swore, though amid the cloud of fear, I would also hear the voice of an older girl trying to reason with them: "she is just little, leave her alone... " It is incredible to think that these children were only ten to eleven years old and already with so much hatred and anger and so much compassion and courage. My older brothers went to this school as well, but I don't remember seeing them much. I don't even remember walking home with them. As adults, they don't discuss their elementary school years, though from what I can discern there was a lot of brutality.

For many children, as it was for me, the education system was a blunt introduction to the social hierarchies and values of British Columbian society; though as mentioned above, I didn't have the language to articulate the forces at play. Even the teachers from my first school would target children. Reflecting back, I now recognize that these children were usually from families on the economic margins. They were struggling with their studies and having difficulties socially integrating with the other students. The school system treated these children as mentally deficient or, in the lingo of the time, as "mentally retarded" and dealt with them by sending them to remedial classes. This gave license for the rest of the children to treat them as if they were abnormal. There are three students—two sisters and a brother—I remember clearly. The teachers treated them with particular scorn. They were newcomers. Their family rented a modest wooden cottage on Hammond Bay Road. The oldest sister had gleaming blonde hair and startling transparent sky blue eyes. And if I remember correctly, the complexion of her small brother was more like that of my brothers and me, if not darker. Crowds of wildly jeering children would surround them during recess and lunch. The teachers did nothing to intervene, even though these attacks took place not 15 metres from their staff room. It wasn't until the children's home burnt down that the teachers became sympathetic and organized everyone to bring donations. I can't remember if the cause of the fire was determined. The family left the area the next year.

"Race" was but one system of denigration in this mid-sized BC town. It never operated in isolation and it's important to note that it was not necessarily always a determining factor in our interactions. There were different power hierarchies, whether based on class position, your family's social status, and allegiances between families as well as between children whose older siblings were friends (or enemies) in the higher grades. For instance, the fact that my parents were professionals and that my mother did not hesitate to question the education system, and, if necessary, mobilize other concerned parents, I imagine meant that teachers in general were more cautious about how they treated me. In addition, my older brothers left a network of support in each school they attended. That said, in my second school I also learned how racism operated in a middle-class milieu. There were fewer fights and schoolyard attacks making it more difficult to identify the source of hostility and its insidious forms. These students were adept in racism. There was a group of boys from Nanaimo's established business class who began targeting me during recesses and lunch breaks in a coordinated pack, brushing by and uttering racist comments under their breaths. Yet equally skilled was a group of girls who stepped forward to report them to the teachers. The teachers in this school took swift action to change the culture of my class, setting up a series of group exercises devised to encourage each student to positively relate to one another. Perhaps this is why my mother sent me to the new school, though the aggression incited by racial difference is never a matter of two or three bad individuals. It's much more insidious, like a fine mesh of living nerves running through bodies and spaces, creating an emotional ecology of resentment, confusing desire, and compulsions that reach back into our colonial legacies and population control programs.[19]

As I try to locate my childhood experiences in relation to other racialized communities in Nanaimo I find absences. I know the town historically had generations of Chinese Canadians, Japanese Canadians, Sikh Canadians, and of course the founding people, the Snuneymuxw First Nation, as well as a number of African Canadians.[20] Local history books[21] make little mention of the fact that the government rounded up Japanese Canadians in Nanaimo and sent them to internment camps in 1942, but the books do recognize the other racialized communities, even if they normalize the fact they were confined to specific sites within the old town's geography. Chinese Canadians were hired as labourers in Nanaimo's coal-mining industry and were forced to move their residential and business district at least three times before it burnt down in 1960.[22] Less is written about the Indo-Canadian community; though a *gurdwara*[23] was built in the early 1920s that was open to all South Asians regardless of religion in the area, making it an important community venue in what was a hostile environment.[24] Like other racialized groups, though, it is important to remember that this community contributed to the colony's competitive resource extraction-based economy. Mayo Singh, for instance, who came to Vancouver Island in 1916, established a forest empire in Paldi and Cowichan Lake, later setting up a state-of-the-art mill in Nanaimo in 1958.[25] The Snuneymuxw First Nation, who had jurisdiction over the entire region before colonization, was restricted to six "reserves" south of the town centre. According to Tennant, James Douglas made fourteen land purchases from 1850 to 1854 on behalf of the Hudson's Bay Company (HBC), a number of which were from the Snuneymuxw, which Canadian courts subsequently claimed were treaties.[26] But Tennant points out that it is sometimes incorrectly assumed that Douglas purchased the land on which the Nations built their houses and garden plots and that he regarded all the other land as "'waste' land," not owned by anyone. In this line of logic, HBC then permitted the Nations to continue to live on the land it purchased. But as Tennant explains, Douglas's so-called treaties, in fact, show "unequivocal recognition of aboriginal title": they owned "the whole of the lands" they traditionally occupied.[27]

I've tried to recall students from all these communities. There were only a few Chinese Canadian students at my junior high school in Wellington, and even fewer Indo-Canadian students, probably since most lived in the Harewood area. Only after I left Nanaimo did I hear about the levels of racism and exclusion they had to endure. My mother was a member of a committee to revise the school board's policy on racism, and she heard many accounts about the entrenched racism, especially against Indo-Canadian students. I remember her recounting how one Indo-Canadian parent told her that she cried when she read that racism in schools was under study. This mother described how her children were victimized by students and teachers throughout their schooling in Nanaimo. Apparently, when a group of Indo-Canadian students at the senior high school took a proactive stance to raise awareness about racism, they received little support from the school's staff. Yet, despite the barriers, they went ahead and sponsored an Anti-Racism day and conducted role-playing exercises at different schools.

But, most fundamentally, I keep going back to my inability to recall Aboriginal students, other than A.H., especially at the senior high school. This is where students from across Nanaimo went for grades eleven and twelve. Surely there had to be some Snuneymuxw students. I was at this school only for grade eleven but can't think of anyone. Searching through the local history books, I came across a few lines that indicate that children from the Nation initially were sent to "Indian Day Schools" in the late 1800s in Nanaimo but then later were sent to the Kuper Island Residential School. My heart starts racing. In the schools I attended, where were the Aboriginal children my age? I start feverishly looking for more accounts about Kuper Island. I find references to this residential school scattered across publications like Mary-Ellen Kelm's *Colonizing Bodies* and Suzanne Fournier and Ernie Crey's *Stolen From Our Embrace,* and more recently there is Qwul'sih'yah'maht, Robina Anne Thomas's chapter, "Honouring Oral Traditions of My Ancestors."[28] This place, Kuper Island—as I piece together these publications as well as the film by Peter C. Campbell and Christine Welsh called "Kuper Island: Return to the Healing Circle" and the children's novel *No Time To Say Goodbye: Children's Stories of Kuper Island Residential School* by Sylvia Olsen, with Rita Morris and Ann Sam[29]—was a nightmare residential school, a reality ripped out of the most terrifyingly sick horror film. I read that it opened in 1890 and was operated by the Order of Mary Immaculate of the Roman Catholic Oblate missionaries,[30] and like other residential schools, the buildings and land and most of the funds required to operate the internment centre were provided by the federal government. As Kelm writes:

> These arrangements for running the residential schools were beneficial to both parties. For a limited cost, the department could boast that residential schools had spread across the country with the assistance of the churches. For their part, the Christian churches were aided in gaining access to a population of children to proselytize without the competing influences of either indigenous religion or rival denominations.[31]

The only way to get to the island was by boat. The island is across from Chemainus, north of Salt Spring Island and west of Galiano Island where, eerily, there were Japanese Canadian communities before the war. The children sent to the residential school on this island—an island probably much like the islands around Nanaimo where my brothers and I played as children—would have been trapped. There are accounts of children who courageously tried to escape the cruel predatory Catholic sisters and brothers. At night there were some who tried to cross the channel on logs even though the distance from Kuper Island to Chemainus is four nautical miles. In the winter month of January 1959, two sisters tried to escape. Their small drowned bodies were found in the following days.[32] Cold and fatigued, they must have slipped off their log into the water's depths. When I was growing up in Nanaimo, I ask again, where were the Aboriginal children my age … where were they? I panic and start looking for dates. When did the Kuper Island Residential School close down? Was every child from Nanaimo sent to Kuper Island? I finally email the editors of this volume and ask if anyone at the Aboriginal Healing Foundation might have information about the dates for Kuper Island. If this was the reality for the Snuneymuxw children and their Nation throughout the first half of the century, was this horrific nightmare reality happening while I was a child, safely tucked in bed at home in Nanaimo?

Why didn't I know about the existence of Kuper Island Residential School? How could this be? I ask my parents. They did not know about Kuper Island either. How could this be? The Foundation sends back some information from the BC Archives and the National Archives.[33] I start an online search. Most of the documents have restricted access and are not online. In the British Columbia Archives you can access the online lists of the records (not their contents) made by the Oblates of Mary Immaculate: there are daily journals, punishment books, and agricultural work record books. As I search more broadly for clues about key dates, I am shocked at the volume of records on governing every aspect of the education and health of Aboriginal people. It feels uncomfortable to look through these records, even if they are just inventories of the actual documents. Given the highly painful nature of these records for individuals, families, and communities, researchers need to ask themselves what is the purpose of their research, what level of detail is appropriate, and what might be of social impact on families and communities. I search for dates, but not descriptions of what happened at Kuper Island. The Survivors, their families, and their communities will decide what is made public and how it is made public, as some have done so already in publications and other forums. As someone who grew up in Nanaimo, I am looking for the children of my generation. I find out that Kuper Island was closed down in 1975. The operation of the school reverted to the government in 1961. I cannot determine the date when children from Nanaimo stopped being sent to Kuper Island, though one of my mother's friends taught in one of Nanaimo's elementary schools attended by Aboriginal children sometime in the 1970s; but this does not mean that children were not still being sent to Kuper Island. While there are no residential schools in operation today, shockingly, there is legislation that still exists with "provisions which give the Minister the authority to establish and operate Indian Residential Schools and allow for the forcible removal of children from their homes ... [And while Section 119] has not been used in years [it still] ... allows for the appointment of truant officers who may take a First Nations child into custody and 'convey the child to school using as much force as the circumstances require.'"[34]

Again I ask: where were the children? Where were the teenagers of my generation in Nanaimo? In the film *Kuper Island*, Survivors gather in a healing circle and share photographs of those who have not survived. Some photos look like they could have been right out of my high school yearbook with the shag haircuts and feathered bangs. Some smile shyly and others look you in the eye with the seeming confidence of youth. All this is gone now. I finally ask one of my older brothers if he remembers any Aboriginal students. No, he does not. How can it be that this reality was not even on the edges of my consciousness while living in the same town, in the same place, but so removed from it? I only have questions now, no understanding...

A Gesture

Given all of this, what did it mean when the Lil'Wat man swept us up in his look and beckoned us through the roadblock? Why has this moment stayed with me? There was no ambivalence, no uncertainty, he simply gestured us through.

I also remember my mother turning to my father and, with a few words, she broke the magic ... "maybe he thought I was Aboriginal?" I felt a pang of anxiety. Had he mis-recognized us? Had he beckoned us through, thinking we were other than who we were? In a world where I was acutely aware of how my body was out of place, causing anxiety and, at times, hostility, I knew about mis-recognition. This was a world where there were few places to be at home, except perhaps in the dream of my parents in the rebellious love of their youth when not much more than a decade after the war they decided to marry. I knew mis-recognition. There's that unnerving moment when whoever so warmly welcomed you registers that you are in fact not what they thought you were and, instead, unknown and alien. The realization spreads over their faces and bodies like an icy shock. You've deceived them, even though this wasn't your intent. You want to apologize, but when it is your body, a body that is ambiguous that can slip across borders and is never really at home except in spaces between, what are you to do?

Yet if I recall my mother's words, "maybe he thought I was Aboriginal?" the way she spoke suggested a sense of familiarity. She did not have my anxiety about mis-recognition. It was as if she was familiar with the gesture, this protective gesture of being invited into Indigenous space. There was an echo of youthful wonder, not quite sure of all the reasons for being granted this privilege, yet feeling that glow of specialness a child feels when she or he is included.

It is now coming back to me; when I was a child my mother enrolled me in a beading class at what is now known as the Tillicum Lelum Aboriginal Friendship Centre. The class was in the south end of Nanaimo, a long distance from our home on Horswell Bluff. Recently, I asked her why she decided to enroll me in this class. She said she was on the centre's board in the 1960s, and my father was involved too. Tillicum Haus,[35] the centre, offered a community space and support services for Indigenous youth who came to Nanaimo from northern communities to attend high school. Families in Nanaimo billeted them. My mother said that the United Church was initially involved. Apparently there was a radical young priest who initiated the centre, though I am not sure in what capacity or if at all. Our family did not go to church nor practise any form of organized religion. And while I seem to recall my father's deeply ingrained dislike for churches,[36] my parents cannot remember now how they became involved. According to my mother, most of the people on the board were Indigenous, status and non-status. The Friendship Centre arranged socials, like dances (and this is where board members like my dad were asked to be chaperones), and cultural and heritage programs for the youth.

The beading class was one of many cultural programs at the centre. It was significant that my mother turned to Snuneymuxw First Nation for what they could teach her daughter in what was a racially divided white working class town during the 1960s. It was a small act, but for me, one I remember. The other girls in the class were much more advanced than me, but the women running the class patiently taught me how to bead daisy chains and other wondrous creations.

I think about this Nation and their generosity and openness to my mother and her small daughter.[37] I think of the First Nations and other acts of generosity and profound care, even to us who have been occupying their land. There are stories about the time when the Canadian government began rounding up Japanese Canadians in 1942 and sending them to camps. There were Nations who had close relations with Japanese Canadians living in their region, and these Nations offered them shelter, not just temporary shelter, but they invited them to become one of their people, which meant the RCMP could not take them away. I wonder how the First Nations would have viewed my mother and her generation, interned on their territories. My mother was interned on the territory of the St'át'imc Nation. How would have the St'át'imc Nation viewed her and the other Japanese Canadian children—all those small children—incarcerated on their land by the federal government? And then after all restrictions on the movement of Japanese Canadians were lifted in 1949,[38] like many other restless young *Nisei*, my mother was eager to leave the confines of the isolated settlement where her family ended up.[39] Her teachers, especially Mr. Berry, the principal and teacher of English 11 and 12 in Lillooet, encouraged her to work hard and win the school's entrance scholarship for UBC. Imagine this teacher championing a Japanese Canadian student in this small rural town. Her father did not believe it was appropriate for a girl to attend university. If she was to pursue further education, it would be secretary school, like her older sister who had already travelled alone to Vancouver. It was only when a respected *Issei* woman stepped forward and gave my *Ojiisan* firm counsel on the importance of education that he finally conceded and permitted my mother to leave for Vancouver to attend UBC.

And thus she moved to Coast Salish Territory. My mother says she can't recall meeting many Indigenous people in Vancouver. There was Gloria Cranmer who was also a student at UBC. She was the daughter of a powerful Alert Bay chief. My mother describes Gloria Cranmer as having a glamorous movie star-like presence. After finishing her degree in Anthropology she returned to Alert Bay to establish the now famous U'mista Cultural Society. My mother also recently recalled another First Nations student in the law program. When she worked as a student at the provincial health laboratory, which was across from the courthouse, she remembers him coming up to introduce himself. My mother noted that he became the first Indigenous judge in British Columbia. I think this must be the Honourable Alfred J. Scow, who was born 10 April 1927 at Alert Bay, the first child of Chief William and Alice Scow of the Kwicksutaineuk Nation.[40] While my mother did not necessarily have a political conscience at the time, it is significant that these students made a point of introducing themselves, suggesting their political awareness and perhaps also their recognition of the dispossession and displacement my mother and other *Nisei* students had experienced.

In the 1950s, how would the Coast Salish have seen my mother and the other 18- and 19-year-olds travelling alone back to Vancouver, where many lived as children before the government stripped their citizenship rights and sold off their families' personal belongings, homes, boats, and businesses to strangers? Young *Nisei* like my mother were coming back to a city whose residents had stood by and watched it all, some who now were in possession of what they had been forced to leave behind with the Custodian of Enemy Alien Property.[41]

Some *Nisei* have told me that as children in the internment camps they were strangely sheltered from the wartime realities that the adults struggled with to survive. It was only as they left the isolated camps as young adults, keen to pursue training and employment, when they directly had to face the hostility now laced with the guilt of postwar populations. My mother does not see this as part of her experience, though she talks about the way Jewish students looked out for her and included her in their circles of friends, including her dear friend Bianca, a beatnik from the United States.

I wonder if many *Nisei* would be able to return the Indigenous look of recognition—to acknowledge what Indigenous people saw in them, as if it was something Japanese Canadians themselves have been unable to fully face: the reduction of their parents, their brothers and sisters, their teachers, elders, and themselves to "nips" and "japs." Viewed as such the Canadian government would thus ignore their appeals to uphold democratic principles and respect their rights as fellow human beings—all this remains too difficult to bear. Today, those in my community still painfully bear the burden of blame for what happened to them, and they continue to yearn for acceptance from the system that had been only able to see them as "japs" and "orientals." This makes it very difficult for them to see how their realities are mirrored in the government's persecution of Indigenous Peoples, even if the persecution and dispossession of Indigenous Peoples are unfathomably more extensive.

A Look of Recognition

At the roadblock, was the Lil'Wat man's look of recognition really mis-recognition? Given what Indigenous children and youth were undergoing in the hands of the government and churches, perhaps he saw something he recognized. It was not whether this family was Japanese Canadian or Indigenous, but something else. A legacy of dispossession? A generation who had no certain place in postwar society and whose losses, humilities, and devastation had yet to play out across future generations? Even though what Japanese Canadians underwent was neither of the scale nor the level of the ongoing devastation that Indigenous people face; nevertheless, we received the Lil'Wat man's look of recognition, which also, profoundly, was a gesture of inclusion.

It is true that he could have mistaken us for an Indigenous family. I can never know what he saw. For me, his gesture comes as a gift with all the questions and possibilities it holds. There was something profound in his gesture that, over the years, I have seen echoed in other looks. The look of recognition differs from a look of pity, empathy, or sympathy. To pity, empathize, or sympathize you must be able to acknowledge the fact that certain actions have taken place that have made another suffer. But, all define the feelings of the person who acknowledges the suffering and loss of others, whether feelings of indignation, sorrow, or contempt. To pity is to have "feelings of sorrow aroused by a person's distress or suffering"; whereas to be sorry involves "grief or sadness for loss of good or occurrence of evil." To pity entails "regrettableness" and feeling "sorry for them." It separates the person from the object of their pity, who embodies loss of goodness or evil, which I describe below more generally in terms of a deficit. At worst, pity can involve "contemptuousness."[42]

Empathy involves "the power of projecting one's personality into (and so fully comprehending) the object of contemplation." Projecting one's personality into another person as the method to comprehend this person means using your own personality as the primary model for all others, obliterating the uniqueness of experience and perspective that constitutes the difference of the other. This form of empathy, which involves projecting yourself "into" the other differs from what Jill Bennett calls "self-reflexive *empathy*" or what Dominick LaCapra calls "*empathetic unsettlement*," where you feel for another but are aware of the distinction between your perceptions and the experience of the other person,[43] although these forms of empathy still remain very complex processes fraught with power relations as well as the danger of being engulfed in another's psychological landscape. Forms of empathy where the other is viewed as "an object of contemplation," reduce the other person into an object that belongs to your mind. As such, this form of empathy can be said to consume an *other* to cannibalistically incorporate them into your *self*.

Sympathy is different insofar as it entails "being simultaneously affected with the same feelings as another ... [the] tendency to share, or state of sharing another person's or thing's emotion or sensation or condition ... [the] mental participation *with* another in his trouble or *with* another's troubles ... compassion (*for*) ... in agreement (*with*) in opinion or desire." In this definition, supposedly because you share another's emotion, sensation, or condition you can "mentally participate" *with* their troubles, which contrasts empathy where you project yourself into others. Yet at the same time, to be able to "have" sympathy for another suggests a degree of distance. You must be "mentally" removed enough from their conditions to be in a position where you can *give* sympathy. This means there is a distinction between your state and the state of the sufferer, who might be, for example, overwhelmed by their emotion or condition. Thus the sympathizer positions her or himself as having, to some degree, overcome the pain, humiliation, degradation, or deprivation of the sufferer.

The Lil'Wat man gave us neither a look of pity, empathy, or sympathy. Each of these looks see the other in terms of an injury or loss. A look of recognition entails another type of relation. It starts with an understanding that the very possibility of one's existence in this world is fundamentally interconnected with all other beings. If you regard all to be interconnected, then this also means that the well-being of all is interconnected, and thus you are aware of the rippling consequences of your actions in the intricate interconnected networks of the whole. Here it is not a matter of seeing others as simply the same as you as if there is no difference and distinction between being/beings in the world. To be interconnected already means each has their own ways of being/coming in the world with their own particular paths and struggles, none better or worse than any other. A look of recognition comes with no assumptions and no prescriptions about an other's heritage or historical legacy, which each person navigates in their own way. This is what the look of recognition grants, an openness to an *other* way of being.

Yet if all is interconnected in a world where there is loss, injury, violation, and destruction, how do we relate to those who bear so much more of the suffering? This is something my father taught me: one does not relate to others just in terms of their injuries. One does not reduce them to what the individual who pities, empathizes, or sympathizes views as their deficit. You respect their dignity; you respect their person.

Yet coming from a community with a history of persecution, I've seen how people suffering can, in turn, incur more injury, whether psychical or physical. They can construct elaborate realities that justify their destructive chaos, servile relations, suffocating control, or toxic states of anger. Anyone who questions or, even worse, refuses to comply with the terms of their reality, can cause rage. Thus in this struggle with my historical legacy, I am coming to slowly realize that the concern for the well-being of another means recognizing not just the other but also one's self in this suffering with all that it entails. It requires neither romanticizing nor demonizing the sufferer or, for that matter, one's own suffering. There can be a confused sense of being somehow responsible for taking care or supporting the "victims" of chaos and a guilt for removing yourself from what is in fact a prescribed role. But if you view those who suffer and yourself not just in terms of injuries, then there is also a recognition of that person's capacity to be, your own capacity to be in relation to others that is interconnected to others and to be in the world in a way that can transform. Otherwise, to see others/yourself comparatively in terms of a deficit means failing to see them/yourself and what they/you are and can be. It lets them/you and you fall into the abyss of expanding destructive circles. There can thus be a compulsion to distance oneself from the suffer/suffering-self, as one fears being engulfed.

Yet there is another way. A gesture offers an opening—open to people to come forward if they so wish. The gesture in itself is one that is necessarily grounded in the place one stands. This takes fortitude and strength and clarity. The Lil'Wat man welcomes; it is he who is in a position to invite others into his territory. Accepting the invitation to go forward entails recognition of his place, there in his territory, and here on this earth. A gesture of welcome is not an act that forces another to respond. It is not a means to control. It does not impose a relation between yourself and the other person. It recognizes the other's capacity to act, to decide, and to determine if and how they respond. What it does require is that they recognize your presence in your own right, distinct from theirs, just as the Lil'Wat man standing there in his territory. In such an opening, what is offered is a place of acceptance— not blind acceptance and supplication but a place for an other—that entails mutual regard and respect. This is an acceptance that comprehends there are losses and suffering, and that person has had to find a way to live with their legacy, whether they are in struggle or at peace. There have been those who have granted me this acceptance. There is no claim to authoritatively know me. And again, here it does not reduce a person to any injuries they might have had … nor importantly does it result in becoming pulled into what can be the smoke and mirrors of a troubled psychological landscape. I find it hard myself, to be, and hard to be roaming this landscape.

What is entailed in this look of recognition? What did the Lil'Wat man grant in his invitation? He might have seen dispossession and displacement but he did not reduce us to that. The Lil'Wat man has shown me there is much to learn. I can just say I am only beginning to see all that is involved in understanding my dislocation in relation to my presence here on this land through the many stories and, most significantly, the absences in my memoryscape.

A Return

I end with a more recent memory of the 2010 Women's Memorial March for Missing and Murdered Women in the Downtown Eastside on the 14th of February.[44] Women and men, we filled the streets: Gore, Hastings, and back down past Oppenheimer Park. Outside the temporal flows of the city, we walked to another rhythm, the drummers and singers honouring the sites of loss and mourning. As we walked, a new space was created through our warm, moving bodies and the wafting trails of smudge. The march ended at the Japanese Language School. Before they were interned in 1942, my mother, along with other Japanese Canadian children living in the Powell Street area, once filled the halls of this school learning about their culture, their language, and their history. On that cold, bright sunny day in Vancouver, the halls were filled again with generations, but now of many Nations of children, adults, Elders, as well as members of different communities gathering to commemorate the daughters, mothers, sisters, friends, and loved ones taken from this world, where we live today, as part of the continuing legacy of colonialism in Canada. This was a moving memorial, making a powerful statement in the present. In the Japanese Hall, now it was Aboriginal people who welcomed all with bannock, chili, and stories; it was they who created time, which on this day was the time of memorialization to remember those lost to us, but through this march, still and always present.

Notes

1   I'd like to thank and acknowledge the support and feedback of Ashok Mathur, the lead editor of this volume, who gave advice and encouragement over the months it took me to write this piece. My parents, Rosalie Chitose McAllister and Carey Douglas McAllister, patiently read through earlier drafts and provided details and accounts about my family's history and my childhood years in Nanaimo. Dorothy Christian offered critical insights, especially regarding the political and philosophical statements derived from Mungo Martin's work. As well, Dorothy Christian introduced me to the complexity and importance of working in what she refers to as "the cultural interface" between Indigenous and non-Indigenous peoples. Here I'd like to acknowledge what I learned from working with Dorothy Christian while she was in the graduate program at SFU. See Dorothy Christian (2010) "A Cinema of Sovereignty": Working in the Cultural Interface to Create a Model for Fourth World Film Pre-production and Aesthetics." Unpublished M.A. thesis, School of Communication, Simon Fraser University, Vancouver, BC. I would like to thank and acknowledge the systematic and detailed feedback and corrections provided by Flora Kallies, Senior Research Officer, and Jane Hubbard, Research Officer, from the Aboriginal Healing Foundation. I also want to thank and acknowledge Jonathan Dewar, Director of Research, and Wayne Spear, Director of Communications, at the Aboriginal Healing Foundation for kindly providing information about the Kuper Island Residential School. And finally I must thank the Aboriginal Healing Foundation for inviting me to contribute to this volume. While I have received support from these learned and experienced people, all lapses and oversights are entirely mine and mine alone.

2   He was also an esteemed painter, singer, songwriter, and teacher and had eight heredity names in addition to *Naka'pankam*. See: Nuytten, Phil (1982:107). *The Totem Carvers: Charlie James, Ellen Neel, Mungo Martin*. Vancouver, BC: Panorama Publications. For an account of his life and achievements with recollections by people who knew him and quotes by Martin himself, see: Nuytten (1982) as well as The B.C. Indian Arts Society (1982). *Mungo Martin: Man of Two Cultures*. Sidney, BC: Gray's Publishing Limited.

3   B.C. Indian Arts Society (1982:21); Nuytten (1982:104).

4   Nuytten (1982:104). Phil Nuytten describes how Mungo Martin concluded the ceremony by giving the Lt. Governor-General a Kwakwaka'wakw name, *Giutlas*. This name was held by Martin's great-grandmother's father, and Nuytten explains that the name means "Everyone is always going in the same direction." In addition, Nuytten notes the name *Giutlas* is similar in sound and meaning to a shortened version of Helen Hunt's name, his adopted daughter and assistant and translator in ceremonies. See Nuytten (1982:105) and Helen Hunt in B.C. Indian Arts Society (1982:33-35). It would seem that by (re)naming the Queen's representative, Martin Mungo incorporated him into an Indigenous system of jurisprudence, giving him a role equivalent to that of Helen Hunt who, as a chosen intermediary, communicated his statements on his behalf to other sovereigns and those outside his realm.

5   Retrieved from the U'Mista Cultural Society website: http://www.umista.org/kwakwakawakw/index.php

6   Aboriginal Healing Foundation (1998:1). *Funding Agreement: Aboriginal Healing Foundation and Her Majesty the Queen in Right of Canada, as represented by the Minister of Indian Affairs and Northern Development*. Ottawa, ON: Aboriginal Healing Foundation.

7   Adachi, K. (1991). *The Enemy That Never Was*. Toronto, ON: McClelland and Stewart Ltd.; Miki, R. and C. Kobayashi (1991). *Justice in Our Time: The Japanese Canadian Redress Settlement*. Vancouver, BC: Talonbooks and National Association of Japanese Canadians; and Sunahara, A. Gomer (1981). *The Politics of Racism: The Uprooting of Japanese Canadians During the Second World War*. Toronto, ON: James Lorimer and Company.

8   Academics and writers Rita Wong and Mona Oikawa are currently working on projects
    funded by the Social Sciences and Humanities Council of Research to explore these
    relations. Publications on earlier relations include: Haig-Brown, Celia and David A.
    Nock (2006). *With Good Intentions: Euro-Canadian and Aboriginal Relations in Canada.*
    Vancouver, BC: UBC Press; Perry, Adele (2001). *On the Edge of Empire: Gender, Race, and
    the Making of British Columbia, 1849–1871.* Toronto, ON: University of Toronto Press.

9   Kelly, Fred (2008:22). Confession of a born again pagan. In Marlene Brant Castellano,
    Linda Archibald, and Mike DeGagné (eds.). *From Truth to Reconciliation: Transforming
    the Legacy of Residential Schools.* Ottawa, ON: Aboriginal Healing Foundation: 11–40.

10 We referred to our grandfather as *Ojiisan* and our grandmother as *Obaasan*.

11 Lil'Wat people set up the roadblock in July 1990 on Duffy Lake Road (Lillooet Lake
    Road) and in February 1991 on the Ure Creek logging road.

12 As a university student I remember when I first read the work of Frantz Fanon. See
    Fanon, F. (1967). *Black Skin, White Masks.* (Trans. C.L. Markmann). (Original work
    published 1952). New York, NY: Grove Press. I was amazed at finding a writer who
    captured what I have experienced so precisely. As a young man in his early twenties,
    Frantz Fanon wrote about how others perceived him and other black men from former
    French colonies, examining the patronizing, condescending, and dehumanizing
    manner in which white men and women regarded them through not just what was
    said but also how they would viscerally react to the very presence of their bodies or
    respond to their eloquence or knowledge about French philosophers. See his essays:
    "The Negro and Language" and "The Fact of Blackness" in his book, *Black Skin, White
    Masks* (1967).

13 This became more clearly articulated for me through discussions that took place in my
    graduate 2010 seminar on memory and political violence. Graduate students included:
    Vincent Andrisani, Julia Aoki, Ayumi Mathur, Azin Mirsayah, Nawal Motut, Cynthia
    Oka, Olga Orda, Megan Robertson, Jennifer Schine, Elizabeth Schulze, Milan Singh,
    and Itrath Syed.

14 Many have written about the power of looking. How you look at someone
    situates them in relation to you. See: Berger, John (1972). *Ways of Seeing.* London;
    Harmondsworth, UK: British Broadcasting Corporation and Penguin Books Limited.
    It can be a relation of respect or care, but it can also position the other as inhuman.
    Vivian Sobchack, for instance, refers to Audre Lorde's autobiographical account
    of sitting on a bus when she was a small child. She notices a white woman in a fur
    hat looking down in her direction with disgust. As Sobchack recounts, seeing the
    woman's look of disgust, Audre wonders what it is that is so repulsive and worries
    that there is something disgusting like a roach on her seat beside her and pulls her
    snowsuit closer, away from whatever is so disgusting. But then she realizes that the
    woman is in fact looking at her with repugnance. As Lorde recalls, "I don't like to
    remember the cancellation and hatred, heavy as my wished-for death, seen in the
    eyes of so many white people from the time I could see." In Lorde in Sobchack, Vivien
    (2004:197). *Carnal Thoughts: Embodiment and Moving Image Culture.* Berkeley and Los
    Angeles, CA: University of California Press. Sobchack describes this look in terms of
    a "perceptual pathology of an other," which is a cultural disease deeply embedded in
    our society. As a look that "eviscerated" Audre as a small black girl, it takes "away the
    certainty of the body... [and gives] one grounds to doubt one's body, perhaps indeed to
    lose one's entire body in total doubt" (Sobchack, 2004:197).

15 Tennant, P. (1990:17). *Aboriginal Peoples and Politics: The Indian Land Question in
    British Columbia, 1849–1989.* Vancouver, BC: UBC Press.

16 Tennant (1990).

17 *Canadian Citizenship Act,* S.C. 1946, c.15 (the "1947 Act").

18 Thobani, Sunera (2007:97). *Exalted Subjects: Studies in the Making of Race and Nation in
    Canada.* Toronto, ON: University of Toronto Press.

19 McLaren, Angus (1990). *Our Own Master Race: Eugenics in Canada, 1885–1945*. Toronto, ON: McClelland and Stewart; Stoler, Anne Laura (1995). *Race and the Education of Desire: Foucault's History of Sexuality and the Colonial Order of Things*. Durham, NC: Duke University Press; Eng, David L. (2001). *Racial Castration: Managing Masculinity in Asian America*. Durham, NC: Duke University Press.

20 Retrieved from the Nanaimo African Heritage Society website: http://www. nanaimoafricanheritagesociety.com/site/index.php/nahs-library/1-honoring-pioneers/1-starks-monument.html

21 Peterson, Jan (2003). *Hub City: Nanaimo: 1886–1920*. Nanoose Bay, BC: Heritage House Publishing; Peterson, Jan (2006). *Harbour City: Nanaimo in Transition, 1920–1967*. Nanoose Bay, BC: Heritage House Publishing. Also see: Chong, Denise (1994). *The Concubine's Children: A Portrait of Family Divided*. New York, NY: Viking.

22 Retrieved from the Nanaimo Chinatowns Project website: http://chinatown.mala.bc.ca/introduction.asp

23 A *gurdwara* is a Sikh temple.

24 Thobani (2007:314, note 115).

25 Peterson (2005:19).

26 Peterson (2006:19).

27 Peterson (2006:20).

28 Kelm, Mary-Ellen (1998). *Colonizing Bodies: Aboriginal Health and Healing in British Columbia 1900–50*. Vancouver, BC: UBC Press; Fournier, Suzanne and Ernie Crey (1997). *Stolen From Our Embrace: The Abduction of First Nations Children and the Restoration of Aboriginal Communities*. Vancouver, BC: Douglas and McIntyre; Thomas, Qwul'sih'yah'maht, R. (2005). Honouring the Oral Traditions of My Ancestors through Storytelling. In L. Brown and S. Strega (eds.). *Research as Resistance: Critical, Indigenous, and Anti-oppressive Approaches*. Toronto, ON: Canadian Scholars' Press Inc.: 237–254.

29 Campbell, P.C. and C. Welsh (1997). Kuper Island: Return to the Healing Circle [Film/DVD]. Victoria, BC: Gumboot Productions. (Available from Moving Images Distribution, Vancouver, BC); Olsen, Sylvia with Rita Morris and Ann Sam (2001). *No Time To Say Goodbye: Children's Stories of Kuper Island Residential School*. Victoria, BC: Sono Nis Press.

30 MS-1267 Finding Aid: volume list for the Kuper Island Indian Industrial School, British Columbia Archives.

31 Kelm (1998:60).

32 Milloy, John S. (1999:317). *A National Crime: The Canadian Government and the Residential School System, 1879 to 1986*. Winnipeg, MB: University of Manitoba Press; Miller, J. R. (1996:286). *Shingwauk's Vision: A History of Native Residential Schools*. Toronto, ON: University of Toronto Press.

33 Jonathan Dewar sent me this information researched by Wayne Spear of the Aboriginal Healing Foundation in an email dated 29 October 2010.

34 Indian and Northern Affairs (no date). Update to the *Indian Act* (retrieved 11 January 2011 from: http://www.ainc-inac.gc.ca/ai/mr/nr/m-a2010/23370bg-eng.asp). The *Indian Act* still contains the provisions that past Ministers have used to forcibly remove Aboriginal children from their homes, which can still be used to this day.

35 Retrieved from the Tillicum Lelum Aboriginal Friendship Centre website: http://www.tillicumlelum.ca/

36 Despite his repulsion for "church," my father does remind me that he taught a Sunday school class at the United Church where he took children on field trips to the seashore to explore tide pools with stories pulled from novels and scientific analyses of the composition of everyday objects.

37 As we were growing up, my father's work as an oceanographer for the federal fisheries meant he met and worked with representatives of various First Nations. While these

events took place twenty-five or more years ago, and he has told me his memory of names may not be accurate, the events, the testimonies, and magnificent rebuttals and political brilliance and knowledge of the Indigenous representatives remain vivid in his mind. His accounts of these events left strong impressions on me even before the era of "identity politics" in the late 1980s. With his family's socialist roots, despite being employed by the federal government, he has always been cynically critical of government and corporations. His stories about the hearings and negotiations instilled in me a sense of awed respect as he recounted the political intelligence and strategy, the oratory, and rhetorical power of their leaders as well as their tolerance for him as a federal fisheries employee and kindness towards him as a person.

38 I feel I should say something to give some context for her return to Vancouver, back to that traumatic site where so many Japanese Canadians lived up until 1942 when Prime Minister MacKenzie King enacted the *War Measures Act* to classify them as enemy aliens who were threats to national security. After the war, for many Japanese Canadians, it was not possible to return to Vancouver. Some, like my mother's family, managed to evade the orders to leave British Columbia in 1945. Several years after the restrictions on their movement back to British Columbia were lifted, some families had managed to save enough to send their older children to the coast where they could find work and enroll in training and education programs in an attempt to start integrating into the vastly changed postwar economy. These young people also laid the grounds for their parents and younger siblings to return to Vancouver and re-establish themselves back on the coast. So, like other young Nisei, my mother and also my aunt, though the family makes few references to her in this period, travelled to the coast.

39 They were in a "self-support" camp, which meant they leased the land where they were interned from a local landowner, Mr. Palmer. They also paid for all the costs of their internment using their savings and funds from enterprises they managed to run, like the farming collective set up by internees. This was different than the government-support camps where the Department of Labour leased the land and ran the camps, making it straightforward for the administrators to terminate the leases, dismantle the shacks, and arrange for the transportation to remove Japanese Canadians from these camps in 1945.

40 Retrieved from the University of British Columbia Faculty of Law website: http://www.law.ubc.ca/alumni/profiles/alumni/scow.html

41 See Order-in-Council 1665 (1942, March 4), whereby the property and belongings of Japanese Canadians are entrusted to the Custodian of Enemy Property as a protective measure; Order-in-Council 5523, whereby the Director of Soldier Settlement can lease or purchase farms owned by Japanese Canadians; and Order-in-Council 469 gives the Custodian of Enemy Alien property the right to dispose of Japanese Canadian properties without their consent.

42 The definitions for pity, empathy, and sympathy are from *The Concise Oxford Dictionary* (6th ed.). (1976). Oxford, UK: Oxford University Press. [Emphasis in original].

43 Bennett, Jill (2006:8). *Empathetic Vision: Affect, Trauma, and Contemporary Art*. Palo Alto, CA: Stanford University Press.

44 The first march was held in 1991.

Georges Erasmus, President

The Aboriginal Healing Foundation

Georges Erasmus is a Dene from Yellowknife, NWT. He is a former President of the Indian Brotherhood of Northwest Territories/Dene Nation and the Denendeh Development Corporation, a former National Chief of the Assembly of First Nations, former Co-Chair of the Royal Commission on Aboriginal Peoples, and currently is the President of the Aboriginal Healing Foundation and Chief Negotiator for the Dehcho First Nations.

Georges has received multiple honours and awards, among them an Aboriginal Achievement Award for Public Service, and the Order of Canada (Member, 1987, and Officer, 1999). He has been awarded an honourary Degree of Doctorate of Laws from Queen's University (1989), University of Toronto (1992), University of Winnipeg (1992), York University (1992), University of British Columbia (1993), Dalhousie University (1997), University of Alberta (1997), University of Western Ontario (2006), and the University of Dundee (2007).

Publications include *Drumbeat: Anger and Renewal in Indian Country* (Summer Hill Publishers, 1990) and *Dialogue on Democracy: The LaFontaine-Baldwin Lectures, 2000–2005* (Penguin, 2006).

Conclusion: The Way Forward

It is not without irony that we contemplate the title of this volume's and the series' proverbial final word as a "conclusion." Even pairing that matter-of-fact title with a subtitle such as "the way forward" results in at least two meanings, and hopefully many more. The first, reflected at the outset of this volume by Georges Erasmus, is the fact that the Aboriginal Healing Foundation (AHF) is winding down toward its end date of 31 March 2012, when its mandate under the *Indian Residential Schools Settlement Agreement* comes to an end. This wind-down is a formal, necessary, and responsible process wherein the AHF Board of Directors and staff work to ensure that the AHF meets these final obligations with the same high level of professionalism and accountability as all other operational responsibilities since 1998.

The second meaning is found in the deliberate juxtaposition of a sense of finality and forward movement. It is an acknowledgement that the Aboriginal Healing Foundation was but one part of the larger healing movement(s), spanning decades and truly with no end in sight. The latter is not said to strike a note of pessimism; rather, it is a simple, frank statement of fact. We, and others over the years, have reported that there is still much work to do. But there has always been hopefulness.

There were many contributing factors to the various successes within the movements of which the AHF was a part—along with many contributors. We certainly took note of that in the days and weeks following the release of *Budget 2010*, on 4 March 2010, when the Government of Canada confirmed that there would be no additional funds allocated to the AHF to address the recommendation within the Indian and Northern Affairs Canada report *Evaluation of Community-Based Healing Initiatives Supported Through the Aboriginal Healing Foundation*, which called for the "Government of Canada [to] consider continued support for the Aboriginal Healing Foundation, at least until the Settlement Agreement compensation processes and commemorative initiatives are completed."[1] We took note of the vocal support the AHF received as the emergency debate in the House of Commons post-Budget on 30 March 2010 and its aftermath played out. This was followed in June 2010 by the *Study and Recommendations of the Standing Committee on Aboriginal Affairs and Northern Development Concerning the Aboriginal Healing Foundation*, which reiterated on 17 June 2010 the recommendation to extend funding to the AHF for program funding set to lapse 31 March 2010 for three additional years.

But it was not to be.

There was an air of finality to the government's response to that report, despite continued vocal support from the many parties engaged in efforts to address the legacy of residential schools. Regardless, the Aboriginal Healing Foundation turned to the business at hand. This included the completion of activities within our communications and research capacities and a concerted focus on that portion of our mission to "provide resources which will promote reconciliation and encourage and support Aboriginal people and their communities in building and reinforcing sustainable healing processes that address the legacy of physical, sexual, mental, cultural, and spiritual abuses in the residential school system, including intergenerational impacts."[2]

This third and final volume in the *Truth and Reconciliation* series speaks to that commitment. It, like the first two volumes, is in no way a final word or *conclusion*. Its strength and promise lies in the wisdom and experience of the contributors. We were honoured to feature these perspectives in all three volumes in the hopes that discussion and dialogue—a key feature of this third volume—would engender more discussion and dialogue that would, in turn, "help create, reinforce and sustain conditions conducive to healing, reconciliation, and self-determination."[3]

We are confident that these efforts, as the efforts that came before and continue to inspire us, will be of use to grassroots initiatives and formal processes, including, of course, the Truth and Reconciliation Commission (TRC). As with the first volume that was positioned as an opportunity for a variety of voices to speak into the unknown to a yet-to-be constituted TRC and the second volume that followed the Prime Minister's apology on 11 June 2008, this volume presents challenges and opportunities. It is not our intent with this closing section to reiterate those ideas and perspectives. However, if there is one message to highlight it is the fact that several of the pieces featured within are themselves evidence that people—individuals and collectives—are already *doing* as well as talking. What is clear is that there is a current of dialogue and action across cultures, something the TRC and its many partners can, will, and must tap into.

As the Aboriginal Healing Foundation prepares to sunset, there remain many horizons ahead of us and the soil is rich and fertile because many have worked